ANSELM STUDIES

Anselm Studies
An Occasional Journal

I

KRAUS INTERNATIONAL PUBLICATIONS
Millwood, New York • London, England • Schaan, Liechtenstein
A Division of Kraus-Thomson Organization Limited
1983

Contents

Contents

Note

Anselm Studies is an international journal, launched in connection with the Third Anselm Conference which was held under the auspices of the International Anselm Committee at Canterbury, 2-5 July 1979.

The journal will carry both a selection of conference papers from this and future International Anselm Conferences, and articles submitted directly to the editors. Contributions may be in English, French, German or Italian and may be concerned with any aspect of Anselm's life and work, whether philosophy, religion, theology or history, or with his influence throughout the centuries.

All correspondence on editorial matters and articles for consideration should be addressed to the Secretary of the International Anselm Committee:

Dr Helmut Kohlenberger
Michael-Pacher-Strasse 8
D-8228 Freilassing
Federal Republic of Germany

Abbreviations

Certain works which have been frequently referred to throughout the volume have been abbreviated:

Ans.Op.Om.   *S. Anselmi Cantuariensis Archiepiscopi, Opera Omnia*, edited by Fransiscus Salesius Schmitt, 6 vols. (Rome and Edinburgh, 1938-61).

Mem.Ans.   *Memorials of St Anselm*, edited by R.W. Southern and F.S. Schmitt, Auctores Britannici Medii Aevi, 1 (London, 1969).

PG   J.P. Migne, *Patrologiae Cursus Completus, Series Graeca*, 162 vols. (Paris, 1857-1912).

PL   J.P. Migne, *Patrologiae Cursus Completus, Series Latina*, 221 vols. (Paris, 1844-64).

Anselm of Bec and Canterbury
The Third International Anselm Conference:
Address given at the Conference Service
4 July 1979
Michael Ramsey

We commemorate today the greatest of the Archbishops of Canterbury, Anselm of Bec. He served God as a monk, as a man of contemplation who led many and still leads many in the way of prayer, as a loving pastor, as a profound thinker, and as a courageous statesman. To excel in two or three of these roles is not indeed rare in the story of Christianity. But we see Anselm using all five talents to the full, and it is remembered not only that all these talents were his but that these aspects has an inner unity and were all of one piece. Anselm was all of one piece. The monastic life, the praying, the reasoning, the caring for people, the statesman's judgement and courage, all had a single root, and the separation of them would have been for Anselm impossible and without meaning.

All of one piece. The monk in Anselm was uncompromising. To pray, and to remain in one place and to pray there: that was Anselm the monk. 'Let a monk', he says, 'rejoice in finding himself where he can remain for the rest of his life'. Yet the singleness of his quest never isolated him from people, from the world. To the selflessness of the quest for God there belongs the selflessness of human caring and compassion, sometimes with severity and always with love and wisdom. Not as one alone, but as one whose life is shared, can Anselm say:

> God of truth,
> I ask that I may receive
> So that my joy may be full.
> Let my mind search it out,
> Let my heart love it
> Let my mouth speak it
> Let my soul hunger for it
> My flesh thirst for it
> My whole entire being desire it
> Until I enter the joy of the Lord
> Who is God, one and triune, blessed for ever.

Every human faculty is drawn into this quest for God: praying, caring, and reasoning as well. Reason is the free action of the mind in its integrity, and reason is no less a part of the adoration of God. Here again, reasoning Man has his fellow men, and reasoning includes his dialogue: the exchange of mind with mind and person with person. So the theologian cannot help being the pastor as well, for it takes a person to learn the truth and to share it with others.

So the vast range of Anselm — student, monk, abbot, bishop, statesman — has at its root a single principle: the monk's quest for God. But what of the statesman? What of the conflicts with a Rufus and a Henry? Here, surely you say, is another life, another world, another talent, as when today sometimes an academic is persuaded to leave his study and teaching for the strange world of church leadership. No. Strangely different as is the tale of Anselm the statesman from the tale of Anselm the monk of Bec, there is, yet, at the heart of his statecraft, the singleness of purpose of one who, when faced with the claims which invade the rights of God, said firmly, 'No, no, no, and yet again no, no, no'.

Looking at the subsequent centuries it has indeed been possible to admire Anselm greatly, and yet to feel the limitations of his impact on, and his meaning for, the present day. It is not difficult to point to the elements of datedness in some of his writing, for instance the *Cur Deus homo*, though the discussion of Anselm's theology has sometimes suffered from being studied in isolation, rather that in the context of the man and his spirituality. As to statesmanship, the difference between the times and the tasks of Anselm and those of our own day is enormous. In his world, for all its confusion, the issues before the Christian statesman were fairly simple. Today, the complexities of the political, social and moral scene are vaster by far, as are the issues which Christianity has to face. Nor is it so clear that the Benedictine way, as Anselm knew it, has a timeless universality, for some kind of cultural tinge colours most spiritual movements. Yet, how great are the themes of Anselm which stand and speak now to our contemporary needs.

One is his fearless integrity in the use of reason. In a modern way, some words of F.J.A. Hort express this: 'Truth of revelation remains inert until it has been appropriated by a human working of recognition which it is hard to distinguish from that of discovery'. If Anselm would not quite have said that, here are other words of Hort which may be nearer to Anselm: 'The truth of God revealed in Christ calls not for the separate exercise of a unique facility but for the response of every power by which we can read ourselves and hold converse with whatever is not ourselves'. Hort might be describing Anselm himself when he says in the same Hulsean Lecture, 'A life devoted to truth is a life of vanities abased and ambitions forsworn'. Both for Anselm and for Hort, the reason which thinks about God is a part of the self which seeks God in adoration.

Next to integrity, Anselm shows how theology and pastoral care belong together. Nothing is more sad in our contemporary theological scene in England than the frequent separation of academic theology from spirituality and pastoral responsibility. Nothing could sadden Anselm more than this trend, and it not a trend which characterised the great names of English divinity through successive epochs. It is not just a question of drawing together those who are called academics and those who are called pastors or churchmen. Anselm shows that the question is about the nature of theology itself. Theology is not only the study of theologians, but the knowledge of God in all that bears upon that knowledge and all that shares it with human beings. The nature of theology itself shows that the theologian is one with the man of prayer and the pastor of souls.

But the contemporary message of Anselm is a message not only for the schools but for everyone. It is Anselm himself who speaks by being who he is: Man in the presence of God and Man linked with his fellows. Man in the presence of God: Anselm's devotions tell of this, and the more widely they can be known the better. Man linked with his fellows: the letters tell of this, and the more their spirit is known and spread the better. If contemplation is recovering its place in the Christian life, and I believe it is, nothing can help us more than Anselm's own approach.

> Come now little man,
> Turn aside a while from your daily tasks,
> Escape for a moment from the tumult of your thoughts,
> Put aside your weighty cares
> Let your distractions wait,
> Free yourself awhile for God,
> Rest awhile in him.
> Enter the inner chamber of your soul,
> Shut out everything except God
> And that which can help you in seeking him
> And when you have shut the door, seek him.
> Now, my whole heart, say to God
> I seek your face,
> Lord, it is your face I seek.

Close the door. It is from this that many shrink — closing the door. But closing the door in contemplation comes with opening the heart in compassion.

It is the man Anselm who speaks. We see him as the eager student; the surrendered monk; the living body; the friend and counsellor; the serious thinker; in his coming to England; through his courageous 'No, no, no'; in exile; and in his victory for the Church. By his victory, Anselm ensured that Christianity in England continued to be part of the larger church-life of Christianity in Europe. We see him also as he comes to die: 'Lord Father, we understand you are to leave the world for your Lord's Easter court', they say to him on Palm Sunday. He replies, 'If his will be so I will gladly obey his will. But if he will rather that I should remain among you, at least till I have solved a question I am turning in my mind, I shall receive it, for I know not who will find it after I have

gone'. Comparisons have been made with the story of Richard
Hooker's dying: 'He did not beg a long life for any other reason but
to live to finish his three remaining books of polity and then, "Lord
let thy servant depart in peace"'. He died 'meditating the order and
number of the angels, their blessed obedience and order, without
which peace could not be in heaven and O that it might be so on
earth'. Anselm and Hooker, here indeed are men of unity, and today
the growing friendship of Bec and Canterbury is the promise of a
more wonderful unity still to be recovered. Anselm shows the unity
of the little and the great, the dying creature and the infinite
creator for, indeed, the glory of God is a living Man and the life of
Man is the vision of God.

I
Anselm in the World

Anselm at Canterbury

R.W. Southern

I

It has never been doubted that Anselm's period of office as Archbishop had important consequences for the later history of the
Church in England. But agreement on this point has not made it
easier to agree on his personal importance or outlook as an ecclesiastical statesman. At one time it was taken for granted that he
was, in contrast to Lanfranc, a Hildebrandine reformer. More
recently, there has been a tendency to look on him as a statesman
in the same tradition as Lanfranc, especially in his insistence on the
rights of Canterbury and in the skill which (as can be argued) he
displayed in safeguarding these rights. This line of argument has led
to an increasing tendency to insist on his political and practical
abilities — a tendency amply illustrated at the recent Anselmian
Conference at Canterbury, not least in the eloquent address of
Archbishop Ramsey, who hailed his predecessor as the greatest archbishop of them all. Probably no one would dissent from the judgement that, as a theologian and philosopher, and as a saint and
teacher of the spiritual life, he was the greatest of the archbishops
of Canterbury. But the claim that he was also an effective man of
action, who directed the Church in England along lines which he had
planned in advance, raises a number of problems which are not
easily resolved. In the first place, it suggests that he was a man of
all-round ability, who could turn from prayer to abstract thought,
and from abstractions to practical affairs with equal or almost
equal effectiveness. It also suggests that he had some kind of plan
for the reorganization and reform of the Church which he carried
through consistently and skilfully in the face of great difficulties. I
have doubts on both these points.

I do not think that he was in the least degree an all-rounder in
the ordinary sense of that word. He was not one of these robust
and varied characters whose purposes and actions are enriched and
stimulated by a diversity of unforeseen challenges: the 'masterly
administration of the unforeseen' was not something on which he
would have prided himself, or for which he was endowed by nature.
He was a man with a passion for God and for nothing else. The
richness and variety of human life meant nothing to him, or nothing
good. Many of his sayings show that the renunciation of the world
was his permanent, practical and unshakeable aim. Not only was he
himself incapable of acting from worldly considerations, but he

could not understand that men with their eyes open would prefer the world to the things which lead to eternal salvation. He was indifferent to the possessions that most men hold dear. Peace of mind, quietness for meditation, the acts of renunciation and alms-giving, and the daily routine of monastic observance were the only things of the world which he valued, and it was with reluctance that he turned his mind to other subjects. Consequently, he loathed business. It was a distraction from his proper task of worshipping and leading people to God and one from which he shrank with physical distaste. He went to sleep when he should have been con-ferring, planning, arranging and preparing to meet new problems. He was widely believed to prefer exile to his task of administering an ecclesiastical province, and there was some ground for this belief. He left the routine business of his Church to an able, but not specially qualified, man of business who, after a military career, had become a monk at Bec and came with him to Canterbury. Anselm himself used to say that he had never been so happy as when he was Prior of Bec: prior, not even abbot, responsible for the inner life and discipline of the community, not its temporal well-being or public affairs. This was a just assessment of his essential qualities: all his best thoughts were provoked by a small society of like-minded monks.

All this does not mean that he was ineffective in action. On the contrary, the mystery of his motives gave his actions an unexpected source of strength: it made them inscrutable and unpredictable to his enemies, because they did not understand the source from which they flowed. Indeed, their source is not easy to understand, and I believe that we are just as apt to misunderstand him as his contemporaries were, though in different ways. *They* were apt to think that he must have cherished secret ambitions in becoming archbishop, but that he was too mild and lamb-like for effective action. *We* are apt to think that, since he was a serious and holy man, he must have had plans for changing the Church, and that he must have pursued these plans throughout his years as archbishop. That he planned, whether as archbishop or abbot or prior, to change the individuals committed to his charge by example, teaching, admonishing, advising and, when necessary, threatening cannot be doubted. But his aims beyond this remain mysterious, and it is the purpose of the following pages to examine them.

II

The problems which surround Anselm's years and activities as arch-bishop may be divided into two main groups: those connected with the period between his election in March 1093 and his enthronement at Canterbury in September 1093; and those connected with his actions as archbishop from 1093 to 1109. We may take them in turn.

His election

The main problem here is why he consented to his promotion to the archbishopric. As Abbot of Bec he had been very reluctant to countenance the removal of monks from his monastery to bishoprics, or even to abbacies, elsewhere. Ambition, the desire for a change of life, and instability were all abhorrent to him; and, while admonishing others, he had used phrases which encouraged all his monks to believe that he himself would never leave them. When he did so, they were dumbfounded, and a wave of varying incredulity and indignation swept through the community. The evidence for this can be found in an unparalleled succession of letters, all testifying to the wounds and unhappiness of this time. Anselm certainly did not seek the archbishopric, and he did not think himself well-qualified for it; he accepted under protest, hoping that something would prevent it. But he accepted it nevertheless, and a surprising number of his most intimate friends doubted his motives.

No one is likely now to share their doubts, but it may continue to seem strange that the grounds of his own objections never included those which are now most conspicuous — namely, the irregularities of his election. He was not elected by the monks or by any properly constituted ecclesiastical body, but bluntly nominated by the King, who signified his wish in the old-established manner by giving him his pastoral staff. Anselm never denied this, and never semed to think that it required excuse. But it was an example of lay nomination and investiture of the kind that the Hildebrandine reformers were most determined to put an end to. At the time, Anselm clearly did not know about the decree of the Roman Council of 1078 forbidding and excommunicating those who took part in this kind of procedure. No one can blame him for this; but he does not seem to have been very active in discovering papal legislation on this or any other subject. A papal legate came to England in 1095 (of whom, more later) — a man deeply critical of Anselm: did he not tell him of the decree? In the same year, the Council at Clermont repeated the decree: Anselm had a representative at the Council. Yet he continued to consecrate bishops nominated and invested by the King as late as June 1096, and he disclaimed all knowledge of papal legislation on the subject until 1099.

Moreover, the King from whom he received the archbishopric had been, in the eyes of the papal legate at least, a schismatic. In 1093, when he gave Anselm the archbishopric, he had still not recognized Urban II as Pope five years after his election. And Anselm, who had himself recognized Urban while he was Abbot of Bec, allowed the King to dawdle for another two years in making up his mind between pope and anti-pope. No sense of urgency here.

Here then we have a complex bundle of problems. Was Anselm weak, or inactive, or indifferent, or simply perplexed? The scope of

these questions will become clearer when we turn to the second
stage of his career as archbishop.

The period from 1093 to 1109
We start with the visit of the papal legate in 1095. His arrival
signified the King's decision, at last and taking his own time, to
recognize Urban II as Pope, and he brought the pallium from Rome
which at last conferred on Anselm the fullness of archiepiscopal
power. In conformity with the papal policy of using legates as a
main instrument in ruling the Church, the Cardinal-Bishop of Albano
hoped to be more than a mere messenger. He asked Anselm to sum-
mon a Council which would meet in his presence and, naturally,
under his presidency. The need was obvious and, in the eyes of anyone committed to the papal government of the Church, the request
was reasonable. Anselm refused. He explained that it would be useless to hold a Council without the King's consent. The legate then
asked Anselm to meet him to discuss the affairs of the Church.
Again, Anselm refused. He explained that the King had committed
to him the defence of the south coast against invasion, and he
could not leave his post. Why was Anselm so unco-operative; so
tender about the King, so hard to the legate; so concerned with
immediate secular issues, so unconcerned about the ideal?

We go on five years to 1100. Anselm had returned to England
after his first exile. In Rome, he had at last heard the papal decree
against lay investiture. He had been present and had assented to it.
On his return to England, he observed it scrupulously. So far as he
was concerned, he would in future have nothing to do with bishops
who received investiture from the King: he would not consecrate
them or associate with them. But it is noticeable that he never
defended the decree as a matter of principle. Towards the theory of
church government, of papal authority, of the separation of lay and
ecclesiastical functions which lay behind the investiture decrees, he
showed complete indifference. The decree bound him personally,
absolutely; but he would do whatever he could to help the King to
get a relaxation of it in his favour if the Pope would grant it. He
showed himself neither for it, nor against it. In making the rule,
the Pope had acted within his rights; but, it was not a matter of
necessary justice and righteousness. To the whole matter of
principle Anselm remained indifferent.

Then, in the next year, there arose again the question of a
papal legate in England. In 1101, the Pope appointed the Archbishop
of Vienne as his legate in England. He arrived, and Anselm refused
to receive him. He wrote to the Pope asserting, on the basis of the
unwritten testimony of the 'men of this kingdom', that the legatine
authority had belonged to the Church of Canterbury from ancient
times: this position, he said, was necessary for the well-being of the
Roman and English Churches alike, and any other arrangement would
be full of difficulty, and 'indeed impossible'. Here, therefore,

Anselm expressed his opposition to the long-term strategy of the Hildebrandine popes in terms of striking vigour.

Precisely the same thing happened over the question of Canterbury's primacy. Once more it was part of the papal strategy to cut down the local primacies of such churches as Hamburg, Lyons and Canterbury over wide areas of their respective countries. These over-mighty subjects were to be replaced by bishops and archbishops under the direct jurisdiction of Rome, or by legates or primates temporarily appointed at the Pope's discretion. Anselm, even more truculently than Lanfranc, stood out against the diminution of the status of Canterbury. In one of his last letters to the Pope he wrote that he 'could on no account remain in England' if this position was weakened: in a word, he proposed to use against the Pope the same weapon of exile that he had used, or suffered, in opposing the King.

Here then, in the second set of problems raised by Anselm's action as archbishop, we are faced with the same fundamental question: what were Anselm's principles as archbishop? It is very clear that he did not share the outlook of the Hildebrandine reformers. The grand and comprehensive vision of the universal papal government of the Church through legates, councils, courts, juridictional processes and papal bureaucracy — a vision that was to captivate the brightest minds of Europe for nearly two hundred years and leave an indelible mark on all institutions of government — was not shared by Anselm. And this is strange, when we consider the strong sense of universal order in all his theological works, and also the use in his political letters of phrases, so characteristic of his theology, expressing his detestation of divisions and departures from the ideal order of things. In politics, as in theology, Anselm was an extremist, not a compromiser; but his extremism was not associated with papalism. He was always more concerned with the rights and duties of men on the spot, of kings, bishops, archbishops and local religious communities in moulding the framework of life, than with the advocacy of papal government.

Despite this, he was clearly not a moderate, strong-minded, statesmanlike man of action like Lanfranc pursuing a consistent policy of local archiepiscopal hegemony. One of the reasons for distinguishing him sharply from Lanfranc is that he took none of the steps which were necessary for carrying out a determined policy of local government. The key to any such policy was a close study of canon law. Lanfranc had known this, and one of his first actions as archbishop had been to introduce in England a compilation of canon law, which soon became widely distributed throughout England. Anselm must have known this collection. He should surely have studied it — or, better still, some more recent collection. There is no sign that he ever did so. His letters after 1093 contain not a single quotation from canon law. Nor do they show any other sign

of the study of canon law; but many signs of the lack of such
study. It is true that in 1093, in the months immediately after his
election, he quoted two passages from Lanfranc's canonical
collection in letters to the Bishop of Paris and a member of his
chapter. We shall return to these letters later, for they teach us a
good deal about Anselm's view of the proper government of the
Church; but for the present, it is enough to remark that the
quotations from canon law are clearly an afterthought, inserted to
convince a hostile bishop over whom he had no authority; and it is
highly likely that they were provided by Gilbert Crispin, the Abbot
of Westminster, with whom Anselm was probably staying when he
wrote the letters.[1]

Quite apart from the absence of quotations from canon law, it
is significant that Anselm never uses the key words of contemporary
ecclesiastical controversy in their controversial sense. *Sacerdotium*,
for him, is always an office which a man exercises as a priest; it is
never a general description of an organized interest or power in the
Church. Similarly, when he uses the word *regnum*, he is always
referring to a definite kingdom of England or France, or a more
often of heaven; he never uses it as the concept of lay power in
contrast to the *sacerdotium*. Similarly, the laity, for Anselm, are
never conceptualized as a class of people who may lay uncon-
secrated hands on forbidden sacred things; they are only men or
women. And so, through the whole range of his vocabulary, Anselm
shows his predilection for concrete and individualized concepts
rather than for polemical generalizations. After his first exile, he
was obliged to use the word *investitura* in the sense in which it was
used in contemporary polemics, but he had never used it before, and
only seldom afterwards. In contemporary terms, therefore, he
appears profoundly unpolitical.

So what are we to say of him as archbishop? Were his principles too deep for political expression? Did he simply react to
situations as they arose, showing always a preference for things
near at hand, and especially for the Church of Canterbury? How
can the various threads in his thought and actions be brought together to form a single whole? It seems scarcely likely that a man
whose strongest impulses were for order and lucidity, and whose
intellectual habits were hostile to confusion and loose ends, should
not in his practical life have been guided by some vision of an ideal
whole. To get any further, we must go back to the moment of his
election, and ask what stock of experience he brought with him to
his new position.

III

In 1093, Anselm was sixty years old. He had been a monk for
thirty-three years, and his becoming a monk in 1060 had been a
real act of conversion. Of his life before this date, we have only a

few fragmentary recollections: his love for his mother whom he lost
in his youth; his early longing for some eternal beauty and happiness
which he failed to find; his hostility to his father and his flight
from home; and, if his meditation is to be trusted, a loss of vir-
ginity deeply embedded in his consciousness. Lanfranc was the
instrument of his conversion to a monastic life; but his removal to
Caen in 1063 separated them, and Anselm's intellectual gifts, as
well as the intensity of his personality quickly distinguished the
outlook of the two men. Monastic conversion meant for Anselm a
systematic and total rejection of the world and the flesh, and an
unremitting search for the reality which lies beyond the senses and
is attainable only by rigorous mental and spiritual discipline. By
about the age of forty, after some twelve years of this discipline,
his character, aims and ideas had been fully formed. There is no
sign that he changed in any important way after he first began to
write for a wider public in about 1075, and except in a few small
details, he never changed anything he had written.

His general view of Man's state, and the steps which were
needed to remedy its deep abasement, were formidably stern. The
texts, to which he most readily referred for guiding others into the
paths he had himself followed, were these: 'Many are called but few
are chosen' (to which he would add, 'How few we cannot tell; so
you are not safe unless you belong not only to the few, but to that
part of the few — the saints — whose salvation is assured'); 'he that
despiseth small things shall fall little by little'; 'keep thy heart with
all diligence' (to which he would add, 'let your mind never relax its
vigilance nor your heart'); 'No man having put his hand to the
plough, and looking back, is fit for the kingdom of God'; 'obey them
that have the rule over you, and submit to them'. All these texts,
and the way in which he developed their message, required scrup-
ulous, unremitting watchfulness and obedience, and threatened damnation to backsliders.

These are the grim foundations on which his life was built. But
everywhere, tied in with them, often in the same documents and in
consecutive phrases, there is a surprising alleviation. When every
worldly pleasure has been renounced, when Man appears before God
as a delinquent servant who has lost all claim to his Lord's good-
will, there remains one pleasure which belongs to this world, the
pleasure of friendship. And this is expressed in terms of the
warmest and most abundant affection:

> Whatever I feel about you is sweet and pleasant to my
> heart; whatever I desire for you is the best that my mind
> can think. What I have seen of you I love, as you well
> know; what I hear of you I desire, as God well knows.
> Wherever you go, my love follows you; and wherever you
> remain, my desire embraces you.

Phrases like these abound in Anselm's letters, and in the stern context in which they appear, they require an explanation. An easy explanation might be that, like many men who have given their lives to the service of God, Anselm still retained a soft centre of sentimentality, of frustrated sexuality, in which he relaxed the tensions of a harsh and austere self-denial. This would not be very extraordinary or blameworthy: it might even be a saving human grace in an over-strained personality. But there are a number of reasons for rejecting this explanation in Anselm's case. For one thing, he wrote words of comparable warmth to people, both men and women, whom he had never seen. Moreover, he chose his words carefully, and his words of friendship display a formulaic repetitiveness which is characteristic of his style: once he had found a phrase, or even a sequence of sentences, which accurately expressed what he wanted to say, he would repeat them on different occasions, simply because they could not be improved. They were not struck off in the heat of the moment in response to a passing mood. Like everything else that he wrote, they are carefully considered, and their intensity is directly related to a theological plan. The warmest expressions are reserved for those whose intentions are fixed upon a life of religious dedication. As men or women recede from this position through lukewarmness or indecision, and still further through dissatisfaction or disobedience, the superlatives cease and the words of love and longing give place to cooler words of formal respect; and finally, when the person addressed has been disobedient and rebellious, the cooler words give place to admonition or plain rebuke. Anselm knows nothing of friendship outside an association of obedience and dedication to the love of God.

This is a fact of the greatest importance for understanding Anselm's view of all human relationships, and even for understanding his politics. For Anselm, human friendship arises entirely from a communion of wills in the service of God, and the supreme expression of this communion is the monastic community. These communities, and these alone, are associations of those who have irrevocably sealed their intention of resigning themselves and everything they possess into God's hands. The importance Anselm attached to this irreversible commitment can be illustrated from many of his letters, but nowhere more dramatically than in his contrast between the man who gives the produce of his orchard year by year to his Lord, and the man who gives up his orchard and all its produce once and for all. In effect, they both give up all they possess, but the first makes a conditional surrender renewable year by year, while the second makes a complete surrender. The second alone is perfect; it is also a perfect symbol of the monastic life, and the necessary condition for entry into the closest circle of Anselm's friends.[2]

There is no reason to think that Anselm would have shrunk from the conclusion that if everyone became a monk or a nun, the history of mankind would soon end: after all, it would end as soon as the perfect number of the elect was completed, neither sooner nor later, and the sooner the better. Meanwhile, there was but a thin stream of salvation issuing from the mass of humanity.

Naturally, he recognized that the world would not in the foreseeable future be composed solely of religious communities, and his friendship extended — though in diminishing degrees of warmth — to those outside. There were people in the world who, without taking monastic vows, dedicated themselves to the secular equivalent of these vows, which may be expressed as justice, almsgiving and self-denial. These were the virtues which Anselm, enlarging on their biblical sanctions, urged on those whose duties tied them to the world. But he also urged that this secular service, faithfully accomplished, should be completed by assuming the monastic garments and vows in the last hours of life.[3] This, of course, does not imply that he approved the common practice of covering a life of violence with a monastic habit at the end: it only implies that he saw the monastic habit as a final fulfilment of a long-cherished purpose.

To be joined together in the self-abandonment of the monastic life, whether in present reality or intention, was the condition of admission to the inner circle of Anselm's friends. The love which bound them together was a reflection of the love which identified their wills with that of God. For those outside this circle, he could feel sorrow, anxiety, pity, pastoral concern; he could (and did) explain in the most forceful terms what lay before them; he could encourage them to enter; but he could do no more — they could not be his friends. Despite the emotional terms in which his friendship was expressed, it was a relationship not of feeling but of will. For those whose wills are divided from his, there was no basis for friendship.

If we now apply this model of circles of friendship to human society in general, it may seem to imply a very contracted view of political life. The only aim in human life for which Anselm seems to have had any deep and lasting sympathy was the aim of binding together and enlarging the dedicated groups of men and women — either in monasteries, or associated in some way with a monastic intention. Yet, limiting though this aim is in one sense, it also allows a large degree of tolerance for the institutional forms of secular life, if only because their importance is relatively small. All human institutions, so far as they do not oppose the formation of the dedicated groups of God's people, are tolerable; and no institutions, apart from those which by their existence and example hold up a model of the Kingdom of God on earth, can do much to forward the work of increasing this Kingdom. Consequently, Anselm looked benignly on all existing institutions which had a tendency to extend the monastic life and to increase the number of monastic communities. All associations and authorities which enlarged the area of peace, justice and charity partook in some degree of the monastic purpose. Anselm had no quarrel with any of them — least of all with kings, who had traditionally been the greatest patrons of monasteries. For Anselm, the model of all authority was the paternal authority of the abbot in his monastery: advising, commanding, informing, and labouring for the good of all members of the community. His ideal of authority was expressed in the opening words of the Benedictine Rule:

> Listen, my son, to the commands of the master, and open the ears of your heart to receive the counsel of your loving father, so that by the labour of obedience you may return to Him from whom you have departed by the sloth of dis- obedience.

These words, 'I command and counsel', are frequently associated in Anselm's letters. The advice was paternal, the authority absolute, provided that the advice was rooted in the source which the Rule summarised: the Bible. He had lived with this combination of authority and paternal care for thirty-three years as a monk. He never abandoned it. Even as archbishop, he never gave up his right to advise and command the monks of Bec. It was his for ever, and he exercised this right quite openly in the choice of his successor. As archbishop, the paternal authority which he had exercised as abbot was extended to a much wider circle — to the monastic community at Christ Church, to all people in his diocese, to his province and to the wider area of his primatial position, to the King, bishops, religious communities, and those who sought his aid or needed his admonition. He did not need to read books of canon law to discover the nature of this paternal authority or how to exercise it: he had it already completely formed in his mind by he Rule of St Benedict. And, in so far as he needed more, he had the words of his consecration as bishop, of his enthronement as arch- bishop and the words which had been used, and which later he him- self used, in the coronation of the king to guide him.

    Whether as a monk, prior, abbot or archbishop, he had a number of authorities above him in their different spheres. Most important, there was the King of England and the Pope. In becoming arch- bishop, he exchanged the authority of the Duke of Normandy for that of the King. To both of them, he was prepared to allow a greater scope than the new generation of ecclesiastical statesmen thought acceptable. As to his relationship with the Pope, this significantly changed on his becoming archbishop: as prior or abbot, he had had a number of superiors — his old Abbot Herlwin, his old master Lanfranc, his diocesan Bishop of Evreux, and the Archbishop of Rouen. All of them stood between him and the Pope. But now the Pope alone was his ecclesiastical superior; and it is to be remarked that the only treatises which he submitted for the Pope's approval were those which he wrote as archbishop. His only earlier act of comparable submission as a writer had been to Lanfranc his master.

IV

How did he approach this new complexity of relationships; what guides did he have? We have already noticed that he did not instinctively turn to collections of canon law. There were, I think, two reasons for this. The first was that collections of canon law texts are necessarily collections of derivative sources, secondary authorities for the manner in which the Christian life was to be lived. In all his thoughts, it was Anselm's universal practice to go to the original source from which secondary authorities, however eminent, drew their doctrine. The second reason was that he belonged to a generation which drew its inspiration from Scripture, supported by symbols, ceremonies and sacraments, rather than by legal texts, courts, judicial processes and administrative procedures. No doubt, the contrast between these two main frameworks of Christian life is rather blurred in practice; but it is a real one, nonetheless, and the balance was rapidly swinging from one to the other in Anselm's lifetime. Anselm did not swing with the world. Consequently, the sources of inspiration which dominated his life and activity as archbishop were the words of the Bible, supported by those of the liturgy and the Rule of St Benedict which provided the most reliable summaries of the Bible.

The liturgical rituals which defined Anselm's duties and powers as archbishop were those of episcopal consecration and enthronement and the receiving of the pallium. Those which defined his relations with others were those for the coronation of king and queen; consecration and profession of bishops and archbishops; and the benediction of abbots. All of these have something to tell us about Anselm's view of his responsibilities and position in society. The precise forms of these rituals were subject to many changes as the texts passed from see to see and from occupant to occupant, but we know enough about the Canterbury formularies to be sure of the main outline of the doctrines they contained. It is virtually certain, for instance, that the rite by which Anselm himself was consecrated referred to him as having been 'elected by the King with the consent of clergy and people'. This in itself solves the problem of his acquiescence in the form of his election, however ill it may have been looked upon by the more theoretically motivated among his contemporaries: the manner of Anselm's nomination exactly conformed to the requirements of the liturgy. In the absence of any

scriptural prohibition, I doubt whether Anselm would have thought
any higher sanction necessary or admissible.

Again, it is almost certain that the ritual of his consecration
would have contained a promise of fidelity, perhaps even of obedience, to the Church of Canterbury; and it is quite certain that it
would have required a declaration that the single author of the Old
and New Testaments was God himself. He would also have promised
to follow the path of Scripture and the traditions of the orthodox
Fathers and the decretal constitutions of the apostolic see in
interpreting ecclesiastical rules, and to correct with modesty those
who refused to follow this path. We wholly mistake the liturgical
spirit of Anselm's generation if we think that these words were
taken in any other than their full and literal sense. They were not
'ritual statements' in the sense in which this phrase is commonly
used to indicate that they sit rather loosely on practical life, and
need interpretation in the light of general theory and actual
circumstances. This attitude belongs to a later, though only slightly
later, generation than that of Anselm. Unless I am mistaken, for
Anselm and those of *his* generation, ritual statements were defin-
itive in a way that more general theories could never be. Certainly
he felt no need, as one of his immediate successors did, to make
the slight alteration which transferred to the clergy and people the
responsibility for his election, and reduced the role of the king to
that of giving his consent. As soon as we allow ourselves to take
seriously the binding force of liturgical words in providing a rule of
conduct, many of the problems of Anselm's conduct as archbishop,
and especially those relating to his indifference to more recent
theories of church government, simply disappear. The words which
he used in crowning the King gave ample authority for his respect
for royal rights. He had prayed God to enable the King to nourish
and teach the Church; he had asked God to give the King the gifts
he had given to Moses, Gideon, Samuel, David and Solomon; he had
asked Christ, the mediator between God and Man, to confirm the
King as mediator between clergy and people. In a word, he had
most distinctly acknowledged the King as his partner in the rule of
the Church. He had, with all his filial respect for the Pope and
with all his obedience to apostolic constitutions, used no words of
comparable distinctness or binding force about the Pope. Equally,
despite all his deference towards the Church of Rome, his binding
words of obligation to the Church of Canterbury were far stronger
and could more easily be assimilated to his experience of pastoral
care. If he believed too easily what the monks of Canterbury told
him about the ancient constitution of the Church in England, he had
in a sense promised to do just this. I say 'in a sense', partly
because we do not know the exact words he had used, but even
more because he was bound by an authority even stronger than the
words of the liturgy or the Rule of St Benedict or any code of
canon law. His ultimate authority was the Bible.

At first sight it might seem that we will look in vain in his writings for any proof that this was his ultimate authority. It is well known that, as a general rule, Anselm did not quote authorities. Certainly, in his theological works, he never quoted authorities to support his arguments, and for this he was reproved by Lanfranc. Equally, in his political letters or his letters of spiritual counsel, he seldom quoted authorities as proof-texts to support or establish a position, or to reinforce his advice or commands. Having said this, however, we must at once make two further remarks. The first is that, though there are very few direct quotations in Anselm's writings, apart from those I shall mention presently, there are very many echoes of the Bible, the Rule of St Benedict, the liturgy, St Augustine, and Boethius. The second is that, in contrast to Anselm's general rule, there are, in fact, many direct and acknowledged quotations from one single work — the Bible. It is the only work which he quotes frequently and explicitly. Moreover, he quotes it, not as most of his contemporaries did to support or illustrate his argument, but as the starting point of his arguments. Even the argument of the *Proslogion*, which comes most immediately from his own meditation, is a meditation on biblical texts: 'enter into thine inner chamber'; 'shut the door'; 'the fool hath said in his heart, "there is no God"'.

We come here to the source of Anselm's thought and view of the world. It was his fixed and universal principle to go to the fountain-head for all his arguments and rules of life. The Bible was the source beyond which it was impossible to go for all rules of life and conduct: in the memorable phrase of his consecration, 'God was its only author'. Therefore he quoted it frequently, and from nearly all its parts, in all his writings.

In saying this, we must be careful to avoid any of the modern connotations of such a statement. Anselm did not quote the Bible in any spirit of protest against the Pope, or the Fathers, or the body of canon law. He quoted the Bible, not because he had arrived at conclusions which differed from those of its interpreters, whether Pope, Fathers or Councils, but because he preferred the water at its source to that in the channels which flowed from it, even though it was the same water both at the source and in its later channels. Anselm had no quarrel with the authority of the Pope, and certainly none with the Rule of St Benedict to which he had taken a vow of perpetual obedience. But they both derived their authority from their conformity to the word of Christ which was expressed most fully in the Bible.

There is an important testimony to this conviction in the letters which I have already mentioned which contain as an afterthought the quotation from canon law. The most important of these letters is to the precentor of the cathedral of Paris who had recently become a monk.[3] Anselm expressed his joy at the precentor's con-

version; and then his fear that the new monk would give way to his
bishop's demand that he should return to his duties in the cathedral.
Anselm wrote to warn him against this temptation of the devil, and
warned him that his bishop's authority would not save his soul from
the judgement pronounced by Christ against those who, having put
their hand to the plough, looked back: 'in those words', he wrote,
'Christ calls you to complete what you have begun'. And then he
added:

> Just as bishops preserve their authority so long as they
> agree with Christ, so they themselves destroy their authority
> when they disagree with Christ. Every bishop who has the
> voice of Christ, is Christ, and 'the sheep hear him, for they
> know his voice'. Read in the Gospel the words which come
> after this: 'The sheep do not follow him whose voice they
> do not know'.[4]

It follows from this that no bishop (and, by implication, no pope) is
to be obeyed who does not speak with the voice of Christ.

We may notice here the very personal and individual way in
which Anselm treats his biblical text in bringing it to bear on the
subject of his letters. He does not use it in the common way
against those who had become bishops contrary to canon law, and
had thus not entered the sheepfold by the prescribed door. He uses
it against a fully authorized bishop who did not speak with the
voice of Christ. Not speaking with the voice of Christ, here, meant
causing someone who had put his hand to the monastic plough to
look back to the world. The fact that he also spoke against canon
law was a welcome aid, but it was not the essential point, as
Anselm's attitude to nuns who had worn the veil without taking
monastic vows shows. The essential test was conformity to the word
of Christ in the Bible, and Anselm declared that *all* bishops were
subject to this test. Does this 'all' also include the Pope? He
nowhere suggests that it does not. Would it include even the Rule
of St Benedict? For Anselm, the Rule never deviated from the
voice of Christ: nevertheless it stood or fell by fidelity to its
source.

Here then, at last, we have the reason why Anselm never
quoted canon law or even the Rule to support an argument or
enforce a command. It was because he quoted the higher source
from which they derived their authority. In everything that he said
or did he went back to this source. He accepted everything in the
existing order of the Church and lay society which did not contradict the voice of Christ in the Bible, and he scrutinized with an
open mind the changes which others made in this order. He was
prepared to allow kings a much greater share in the affairs of the
Church, in the appointment, investiture and homage of bishops, in
the choice between rival popes, and in the calling of Church

Councils, than the Hildebrandine reformers of his day allowed. This laxity, as the reformers would have called it, was for Anselm a concentration on essentials. What mattered for him was not the form but the reality: not how the choice was made, but whether it was the right one. Sin was making the wrong choice; error was reaching the wrong conclusion. The difference between sin and error, on the one hand, and righteousness and truth on the other, lay not in the methods by which a choice between them was made but in the final decision itself. The same criterion applied to the decisions of bishops and popes, as to those of kings and princes: if they spoke with the voice of Christ, they were to be obeyed; if they went against the voice of Christ, their authority vanished. The manner in which their authority was to be put aside depended on circumstances. Twice in reality and a third time in intention, exile and renunciation seemed to Anselm the appropriate way of disallowing the errors of two kings and of a pope in matters which fell within his own personal responsibility. He may almost be said to have invented exile as a spiritual weapon: it was his main political invention.

All this gave his political actions the appearance of fluidity and lack of principle. But if in some ways he was more flexible than Lanfranc, in other ways he was more rigid — in insisting, for instance, that someone who had once worn the veil could not draw back without grievous sin, and that married clergy should at once leave their wives. If the voice of Christ called for this renunciation, the timing of it no longer lay in the hands either of the person concerned or of the archbishop. It had passed beyond earthly authority into a higher realm of righteousness.

It is right, therefore, to say that Anselm had no theory of politics and no plan for ecclesiastical reorganization. This is because there was no middle distance in Anselm's thought: he dealt either with eternals or with immediate things and people. Politics, the art of the middle distance, is concerned with directing groups, organizations, and people *en masse*. These were not Anselm's concerns. He was concerned only with right and wrong choices, with the individuals who made them and the ends to which they were directed. He had a deep respect for order as an ideal and as a present reality, but he placed no strong reliance on legal texts, which always deal in derivative generalizations. He belonged to no party, for parties always deal in means rather than ends. If he was prepared to believe too readily what his monks at Canterbury told him about ancient rights, or about ancient relics and venerable sanctities, his agile mind easily saw how these rights or these devotions could fit into a universal order. He did not pore over texts to test the truth or falsity of these claims, but with a trusting heart accepted what he was told and what he found around him, so long as it did not contradict the voice of Christ in the Bible. In the same spirit and to the same extent, he accepted papal legislation and monastic customs, even when they seemed fairly pointless: so long as they kept within their appointed bounds and encouraged no weakening of the dedicated will, he obeyed and counselled obedience in others. The deeper we go, the more clearly we can see why he acted as he did, and why his actions follow none of the formulas of the day, but only what he had come to recognize as the voice of Christ, as it sounded in his deeply pondered and strictly disciplined spiritual life.

NOTES

1. For the evidence see R.W. Southern, 'St Anselm and Gilbert Crispin, Abbot of Westminster', *Mediaeval and Renaissance Studies*, 3 (1954), 90-1.

2. See *De humanis moribus*, 84, in *Mem.Ans.*, pp.73-4.

3. See *Epistola* 325, *Ans.Op.Om.*, V, 256-7.

4. See *Epistola* 162, *Ans.Op.Om.*, IV, 35.

From Bec to Canterbury:
Anselm and Monastic Privilege

Marjorie Chibnall

'Brother Anselm, by profession and at heart a monk of Bec, by God's direction called archbishop of Canterbury';[1] in these words, addressed to the community of his abbey shortly after his election, Anselm summed up the obligations of monastic duty and obedience that remained the guiding principles of his actions as he made the difficult transition, in middle life, from abbot to archbishop and primate, from Normandy to England, from Bec to Canterbury. During his years at Bec the abbeys of Normandy reached a satisfactory, though precarious, *modus vivendi* both with their Duke, William the Conqueror, and with their diocesan bishops. Monastic exemption, though limited in almost every case to restricted archidiaconal rights, might be protected in the ducal court whether the deed defining it came from duke, bishop, or pope. The privilege of free election might concede a great deal to ducal nomination when that nomination followed consultation with spokesmen of the monastery and respected spiritual leaders, and took account of the character of the 'elected' nominee. A recognition of the distinction between spiritual and temporal authority, reached (as we shall see) in the early years of Duke William's rule, allowed the problem of lay investiture to lie dormant, and obscured the fact that the use of a pastoral staff to invest an abbot with his temporalities was a potentially dangerous confusion of symbols. Changes that would in any case have led to crisis or further compromise were just beginning when Anselm left Normandy; they were accelerated during his years as Archbishop.

A refinement of canon law and theological definition was already, by 1093, causing trouble with some bishops over the question of the profession of obedience due from a newly elected abbot. The prolonged visit of Urban II to France made appeal to the pope speedier and more attractive at a time when canon law was, in any case, strengthening the hierarchy; the canons of the Council of Clermont, including one that forbade homage by ecclesiastics, were promulgated almost immediately in the Synod of Rouen, in November 1095.[2] Within a few years, Ivo of Chartres, who had previously regarded the Norman procedure as acceptable, recognized the confusion of thought involved and changed his mind. Again, a growing activity in every sphere of government made the more precise definition of exemption essential to any abbey that cherished its privileges. To this must be added the change in personalities after the death of the Conqueror: Robert Curthose was too weak and ineffective, and William Rufus was too obstinate and inconsistent, to pursue their father's aims efficiently, while both were handicapped at first by the separation of England from Normandy. Anselm's reluctance to be forced into the archbishopric would have arisen naturally from his understanding of human nature, even if his heart had not been in Bec. When he had accepted it, as a duty, he faced the new problems squarely, in the light of his past experience. The consistency with which he maintained his principles in new and taxing situations is impressive. His attitude to monastic privilege is only one theme of several that might be chosen to illustrate the way in which he approached his work as archbishop, but it is a central one.

Anselm's work as abbot had frequently taken him to court, and had familiarized him with the practical side of an abbey's business. He recognized that one duty of any prelate, whether abbot or bishop, was to hand on his charge undiminished. He had been present, along with numerous other abbots and bishops, at the funeral of William the Conqueror, and had witnessed the dramatic and successful claim of Ascelin, son of Arthur, to be compensated for the loss of his patrimony — the land on which the church was built — in which the Conqueror was about to be buried.[3] Patrimonial rights, respected by laymen, were even more cherished by monasteries, who held that their endowments were the patrimony of the saint or saints they served, to be preserved in perpetuity. Even if Anselm had not absorbed this attitude from the aristocratic society in which he had been brought up, he would soon have learnt it among the lords and churchmen of Normandy.[4] One of his first tasks on becoming abbot was to visit the properties of his abbey in England, partly to encourage new gifts and secure old ones, in order to support a monastery that, though highly respected, was still too poor to provide adequately for the growing numbers of monks.[5]

In compiling his letter collection, Anselm had little interest in preserving any early records of his involvement in secular administration, but his name in the witness lists of charters sometimes indicates his movements and the kind of business transacted in his presence and with his participation. He was one of the abbots who confirmed the foundation charter of Lessay,[6] and one of the early charters of donation to the Abbey of Troarn.[7] When the monks of Lonley and Saint-Florent-près-Saumur, both claiming the Church of Saint-Gervais, Briouze, as a gift of William of Briouze, brought their case to the Conqueror's court at Caen, Anselm was one of the group of prelates to whom the case was referred; they decided that the monks of Lonley had no case, because they failed to fulfil the conditions laid down in William of Briouze's charter of donation.[8]

All this was routine business; his presence as a witness of a charter of King Philip of France to the Church of Saint-Quentin of Beauvais is more remarkable, particularly as it was issued in 1079 at Gerberoy, during the siege.[9] We know that Bec had close ties with the Church of Beauvais: the canonist, Ivo, who was Abbot of Saint-Quentin before he became Bishop of Chartres, had been a pupil of Lanfranc and became one of Anselm's friends, and there were others such as Ernulf, monk of Saint-Symphorien and later Prior of Christ Church, Canterbury, who belonged to the Bec-Beauvais-Canterbury circle.[10] Whether Anselm had broken journey on his way to Beauvais, or found himself at Gerberoy attempting to reconcile William the Conqueror with his rebel son, Robert Curthose (who, with assistance from the King of France, was holding out in the castle) he was the only Norman prelate present on this occasion.

Another more unusual case which he witnessed was one involving the jurisdiction of the Abbey of Saint-Wandrille in four parishes, where the Archbishop of Rouen challenged their claims.[11] The case arose because a monk of the abbey, through ignorance, converted an ordeal iron to other uses, and when the Archbishop was requested to bless a new iron he questioned the right of the abbey to hold the ordeal. Apart from the right to an ordeal iron, the privileges claimed by Saint-Wandrille were of the limited kind enjoyed by a number of Norman abbeys at the time, consisting of exemption from specified episcopal 'customs' in the parishes most closely subject to the abbey. Mont-Saint-Michel had put the case for such exemption most strongly, since weather, as well as war, sometimes cut off the Mount from the mainland and prevented monks and parishioners from attending ecclesiastical courts. In 1061, the Bishop of Avranches made the Abbot of Mont-Saint-Michel his archdeacon for the Mount, reserving to himself the administration of the ordeal and certain other cases.[12] The grant of archidiaconal rights by the diocesan bishop became the normal pattern of monastic exemption during the next thirty years, though the bishops struggled to retain the ordeal, and the Council of Lillebonne in 1080 recognized that, as a rule, it should be administered by the bishop at the cathedral church.[13] There is no list of the abbots present at Lillebonne, but the summons was general and the occasion an important one. Since Anselm was in Normandy engaged on business at the time, his presence at Lillebonne may be confidently assumed.[14] He was certainly familiar with the extent of monastic privilege possible, and may have noted in the Saint-Wandrille case that the privilege of holding the ordeal locally might still be granted with the consent of duke and bishop.

When Anselm sought privileges of jurisdiction for his own abbey, he secured the widest possible grant of archidiaconal privileges, comprising both freedom from exactions, jurisdiction over the parish of Bec, and some concessions even in cases involving the ordeal.[15] The privileges were granted between 1091 and 1093 in a charter issued by William, Archbishop of Rouen, which reserved to the Archbishop only matters requiring the power of orders and the administration of the ordeal, though in some cases the iron might be brought to Bec and the case settled there in the Archbishop's presence. He did not ask for wider privileges of exemption. The one point deserving special notice in Anselm's action on behalf of his own abbey is that he first approached Pope Urban II with a request, and only turned to the Archbishop after he had failed to obtain a papal privilege. Application to Rome was not unprecedented: indeed, Lanfranc had obtained a papal privilege to secure the limited exemption of Saint-Étienne de Caen when he was Abbot of the house.[16] But it was still unusual in Normandy.

It is important to bear in mind the limited nature of the exemptions sought and obtained by Norman abbeys in this period, since, apart from the few surviving authentic charters, the principal sources for the history of monastic jurisdiction and exemption come from a later period. They consist of forged charters, or interpolations in genuine charters, and treatises, such as the *De libertate Beccensis monasterii*,[17] written by an anonymous monk of Bec in the second quarter of the twelfth century, when conditions had changed and sweeping claims might be read into the actions of bishops and abbots of an earlier generation. In such matters Anselm worked within a well-defined custom, and was unlikely to face serious problems after he found himself an archbishop, except in so far as English custom was different, or his authority was complicated by his tenuously defined rights as primate. But there was another side to monastic privilege where the issues were very much more complex; where even though a *modus vivendi* had been reached in Normandy it was a precarious one; and where a number of abbeys were already coming into conflict with their bishops, and were shortly to find themselves in difficulties with their duke. This was the matter of free election, investiture, and the nature of the profession of obedience made by an abbot to his diocesan. Since the profession to the bishop was complicated by the nature of the profession any monk made when he renounced the world, Anselm was deeply and personally involved, and was prepared to tender advice even before he was drawn unwillingly into the conflict over investiture and homage.

To understand his position we must look carefully at the arrangements established in Normandy early in the reign of Duke William. The work of Jean Yver and Olivier Guillot has shown that a distinction between the grant of temporalities by the duke and the bestowal of spiritual power by the bishop (between *exterius* and *interius*) was made at an exceptionally early date in Normandy, probably shortly after the promulgation of early reforming decrees in the Synods of Tours and Lisieux in 1054.[18] Since the duke might confer the temporalities by handing over a pastoral staff, and this single act also confirmed an 'election' that might in practice have been acceptance of the ducal nominee, the practice involved a confusion of symbol and function that was fraught with difficulties as canon lawyers refined and clarified their concepts. Yet even so-learned a canonist as Ivo of Chartres could write as late as 1097, in his famous letter to Hugh of Lyons, 'What does it matter whether the grant is made by hand, or gesture, or tongue, or staff? since kings do not intend to confer anything spiritual, but only either to assent to the choice of the petitioners, or to grant to the elect temporal goods which the churches hold by the generosity of kings'.[19] When such a man as Ivo, who on one occasion at least resolved a legal question that Anselm had failed to clarify,[20] could be satisfied with so equivocal a practical solution, it is small wonder that Anselm, whose grasp of legal concepts was often confused by his insistence on moral issues, accepted the existing situation without demur. The change came for Ivo under papal pressure between 1097 and 1101, when he recognized that kings should have no part in episcopal elections,[21] as did Anselm, at the same time and for the same reason. Before that date, and as long as he was in Normandy, the real problem that exercised his mind was the nature of the profession made by an abbot to his bishop.

When Arnulf was elected Abbot of Troarn in 1088, he either anticipated or received demands from Odo, Bishop of Bayeux, which made him consult Anselm before being blessed by his bishop. Anselm's reply was misinterpreted by R.N. Sauvage in his history of the abbey, and consequently its significance has often been over-looked.[22] Certainly Anselm stressed a monk's duty to obey all his superiors, including his diocesan bishop; but he also emphasized that the profession made by a novice when he entered his monastery lasted for life, and that to repeat it was superfluous. He was, therefore, in favour of a simple promise of obedience, but opposed to a written profession; he did not simply advise the abbot-elect to comply with his bishop's demands.

Anselm's views, so positively expressed, may have been responsible for the resistance of other Norman abbots to similar episcopal demands at this time. The monks of Saint-Evroult were at loggerheads with the Bishop of Lisieux for over ten years. Serlo of Orgéres, elected in 1089, administered the abbey for two years without ever being blessed, because he refused to give a written profession of obedience. After Serlo's election as Bishop of Séez, his successor at Saint-Evroult, Roger of Le Sap, remained unblessed for ten years. Anselm was certainly present in the abbey at the time of Roger's election, as was Serlo, and both must have been involved in discussion about the legal and moral issues.[23] The next Norman abbey known to have had trouble with its diocesan was Bec-Helloiun itself — the dispute began over the admission of Anselm's successor, William of Beaumont, and continued with every vacancy for the next forty years. Throughout this period the actions and reasoning of the monks continued to follow Anselmian traditions. New abbots willingly promised obedience, but not one would yield an inch on the matter of the profession. Their resistance was reinforced by the development of a theory of the nature of the profession, which, for a short time, had an important place in their monastic spirituality.

The events are chronicled in the treatise, *De libertate*, and in the series of lives of the abbots.[24] In 1093, after some delay during which Anselm was consulted, the Archbishop of Rouen unwillingly waived his demand for a written profession, and blessed William of Beaumont as Abbot of Bec through the intervention of Robert Curthose, Duke of Normandy. Robert respected Anselm, though he had angrily criticized his election as Archbishop (only to admit, later, that he had spoken in haste and in error); the words attributed to him when he was asked to confirm the election of William of Beaumont, are '*Per mirablia Dei*, we must do as my lord Anselm commands', and, when he was told of the demand for a profession, 'In no way do I wish the abbot of Bec to make this profession'. By the time Boso became Abbot in 1124, Anselm was dead, but the tradition was established. Once again, when the Archbishop of Rouen demanded a profession of obedience, the lay ruler of Normandy, King Henry I, was persuaded to intervene. If the details given in the *De libertate* are accurate, he agreed not to exact homage from Boso, and commanded the Archbishop of Rouen not to demand a profession. When the Archbishop suggested that, although the King might do as he wished in matters concerning him, the Archbishop ought to be free to decide affairs that were properly his, the King replied, 'I have told you once, and, by Christ's death, I tell you again, that the abbot of Bec shall neither do homage to me nor make a profession to you'. When the time for the ceremony of benediction came, the King sent to the Archbishop ordering him to bless the Abbot without demanding a profession, adding, 'He will do this if he wishes to remain in my favour'. The Archbishop, according to the writer of the *De libertate*, like a prudent man, obeyed the royal behest. But the author of the *Vita Bosonis* adds details which indicate intervention from another quarter. The cardinal legate, John of Crema, was in Rouen at the time and attended the ceremony. When the Archbishop asked Boso the customary question, 'Do you wish to be obedient to this church, and to me and my legitimate successors?', and Boso replied, 'Volo', all the Archbishop's clergy began to clamour for him to say, 'Profiteor'. Boso again repeated, 'Volo'; the clergy pressed for 'Profiteor'. A third time Boso said, 'Volo, et ex corde volo'. At this the legate intervened, saying, 'Don't you hear what he says? What more do you want?' whereat the ceremony proceeded. It is a reminder that the time was coming when such things would be decided by popes, not lay monarchs.

On the issue involved, Paschal II had already given at least one ruling some twenty years earlier in a case involving the Abbot-Elect of Marmoutier and the Archbishop of Tours.[25] The elect, William, had refused to give a written profession, and the Archbishop had withheld his blessing, The monks took their case to Rome, and won: Paschal II gave as his reason that a monk was not obliged to repeat the profession he had made on his entry into the cloister and, on being questioned further, added that he meant this as a general ruling, not a special privilege for Marmoutier. The Pope may have expressed an opinion prevalent in the *Curia*; but it is worth noting that Anselm had recently been in Rome.

The theory behind this resistance to a second profession was being quietly developed at Bec during the years of active dispute, and has been briefly studied by Dom Leclercq in an illuminating essay.[26] The central theme was that the monastic profession was a second baptism — a sacrament. A sermon attributed to Lanfranc hinted at this by saying that many came to the cloister because they feared damnation through their failure to fulfil the promises made at their baptism. Anselm was less explicit, but he stressed the need for obedience and the duty of a monk to give his whole life to God, as a man might give not merely the fruits of a tree, but the whole tree; and in his letter to Arnulf of Troarn he stated unequivocally that a second profession was unnecessary, 'If a monk has once written out and read his profession, and has never renounced it, for anyone to require another from him is devoid of meaning' ('frustra aliquis ab eo aliam exigit'). Anselm's friend and fellow monk, Gilbert Crispin, took the question one step further, by maintaining that the profession was a second baptism: a baptism of penitence. The doctrine was refined and developed by a number of writers of the school of Bec; among them, Boso, Hamelin of St Albans (a pupil of Lanfranc) and the anonymous monk who wrote the *De libertate Beccensis monasterii*.

Among the works of the Anonymous of Bec were two treatises, *De professionibus monachorum* and *De professionibus abbatum*, in which he explicitly linked the nature of the professions of monks and abbots.[27] By this time the simple rules guiding the admission of a novice in early Benedictine monasteries had gradually given way to a liturgical ceremony. Recorded in the pontificals that became more and more numerous towards the end of the tenth century, these ceremonies varied from place to place; but all tended to approximate the ceremony of admitting a novice to that of blessing an abbot. As with the development of ceremonies of investiture, a practice was growing up that might establish precedents dangerous to a half-defined theory. The Anonymous of Bec, true to the tradition of thought in his monastery, placed great emphasis on the significance of the ritual, and assimilated the monastic profession to the sacrament of baptism. In his interpretation, the examination (*scrutinium*) of the novice on his readiness to assume the duties of monastic life and obey his superiors was an essential preliminary to the ceremony. At Bec, the *scrutinium* took place in a meeting of the chapter, before the Mass.[28] The questions requiring obedience followed the same pattern as those put to a newly elected abbot about to be blessed. The first anonymous treatise did not mention the *subscriptio* (the signature of the promise), and evidently attached no importance to it. The second treatise was particularly concerned with the profession of obedience made by an abbot to his diocesan during the ceremony of benediction. The demand for a written profession of obedience was regarded as either dangerous or useless: dangerous, if the intention was to make it a pretext for oppression; useless, if there was no wish to oppress, since it carried no greater obligation than the abbot had already undertaken when he became a monk and promised obedience to his superiors. All this, though more elaborate and highly developed, is in line with Anselm's thought, and shows how discussion and teaching on the subject might have been shaping while he was still at Bec. It was not the line of thought that prevailed in the end, but it serves to relate his principles to the practice of his day, and explains his approach to the problems of monastic obedience and exemption when he came to Canterbury and saw them from the other side, as Archbishop.

A small number of English abbeys had already put forward claims to special privileges of some kind. Archidiaconal rights had been granted in various places — for instance, at Worcester,[29] where the monks had probably exercised rights over the city churches since before the Conquest. Bury had no difficulty in substantiating similar claims in Lanfranc's time. These caused no real problems: they were familiar in Normandy, and acceptable. But more extensive claims were beginning to be foward and these were gradually established during the first century of Norman rule. The task of charting their progress is made particularly difficult by the existence of several groups of forged charters and bulls of uncertain date. Unfortunately, monastic historians of the twelfth century readily took these forgeries, with all the precocious clarity of their claims, at their face value, and their assumptions have been accepted by a number of modern historians of the early Norman Church. The Battle Abbey forgeries are relatively uncomplicated; they undoubtedly belong to the post-Anselmian period. But the Canterbury and St Augustine's forgeries are far more difficult to date. Though the 'Canterbury forgeries', concerned as they were with the question of the primacy, are outside the scope of the present discussion, the forger made use of the St Augustine's documents, and these were concerned with monastic exemption. If the Canterbury forgeries are early, part of the St Augustine's series must be earlier still.

Willhelm Levison, who subjected the St Augustine's charters to a penetrating analysis,[30] wrote before a case had been made for a possible twelfth-century date for the Canterbury forgeries,[31] and may have gone too far in postulating a date of about 1070 for all of them. In particular, there is, as far as I can see, nothing in the famous *bulla plumbea*, attributed to Augustine himself,[32] that would force us to place it earlier than the twelfth century. But Levison produced convincing proof that a number of the forgeries were known to Goscelin of Saint-Bertin, who wrote a history of the *Translation of St Augustine* in St Augustine's abbey and dedicated it to Archbishop Anselm.[33] This does not, of course, necessarily mean that Anselm himself had seen the forgeries, but any early documents are important in indicating the claims that were the main concern of the monks at that time.

Apart from the issue of free election, which was bound up with the question of royal authority in the Church, but might have involved the Archbishop if the King had relied on his counsel in approving or appointing prelates, the real bone of contention was the place of the diocesan in the ceremony of blessing a new abbot. At a slightly later date, an exempt abbot would claim three things: that he might be exempt from the profession of obedience, have the privilege of being blessed in his own abbey church, and freely choose the consecrating prelate.[34] These claims are not, at first, coherently voiced or consistently demanded, but some abbeys were groping towards them, and precedents — both favourable and unfavourable — were beginning to be established. In England, the position of the Archbishop of Canterbury was strengthened by his claims to primacy, and Lanfranc's decisive actions had begun to make themselves felt. He was not always autocratic, but Eadmer's summing up is a fair one: Lanfranc, said Eadmer, changed many English customs, 'often with good reason, but sometimes simply by the imposition of his own authority'.[35]

Lanfranc's influence was decisive in restoring and enforcing the written profession of obedience. Written episcopal professions had existed in England from the late eighth century onwards — they are the earliest in the Western Church — but they had been allowed to lapse in the tenth and early eleventh centuries.[36] Lanfranc revived them, and began to require them from some new abbots; indeed Scolland of Mont-Saint-Michel, who became Abbot of St Augustine's, Canterbury, in the very year of Lanfranc's appointment as Archbishop, made a written profession of obedience to the Church of Canterbury, apparently without resistance. There was more trouble over the appointment of the next abbot, Guy, another Norman; but the riots that broke out were due to opposition by the monks and citizens of Canterbury to the choice, and Guy himself made a written profession of obedience when he was blessed in 1087.[37] Lanfranc appears to have felt none of the scruples about demanding such a profession from a professed monk which were beginning to trouble Anselm at the time. He was more concerned with authority: the authority of the primate, and its relationship with that of the king. In the protracted and important case of Bury St Edmunds, Lanfranc was willing to concede Bury's claims to exemption from the diocesan, taking it to mean direct dependence on the primate; and his experience in Normandy led him to look to the King's court and the King's charter, rather than to a papal bull, for the effective enforcement of that exemption.

The Bury case, which is both early and well-documented, is important in the history of exemption. It arose from the attempt of the East Anglian Bishop, Arfast, to annex Bury as his cathedral monastery.[38] When, in 1070, Arfast attempted to transfer his see from Thetford to Bury St Edmunds, the case went to Rome, because papal permission was necesary for the transfer of a see. The monks secured a bull from Alexander II taking the abbey under papal protection and freeing it from the jurisdiction of the bishop, but upholding that of the primate.[39] In spite of this, Arfast's molestation continued for another decade; finally, in 1081, after two informal and one formal hearing, Abbot Baldwin of Bury secured a royal judgement exempting the abbey from the bishop's control. During the hearing, Arfast failed to produce either documents or witnesses in support of his claim. Herman the archdeacon, the Bury chronicler who has left the fullest account of the case, asserted that through the intervention of St Edmund he stammered in his speech, and so demonstrated the irregularity of his claim. Abbot Baldwin, on the other hand, was prepared to produce both earlier charters (though not one of them, as F.E. Harmer has demonstrated, is above suspicion of forgery),[40] and an argument drawn from the evidence of past history. The abbot, it was claimed, had exercised his authority freely for fifty-one years, as was proved by the fact that abbots had been blessed by any bishops they chose: Uvo by the Bishop of London, Leofstan by the Bishop of Winchester, and Baldwin by the Archbishop of Canterbury.

This interpretation is characteristic of exemption claims made in England and Normandy for the next half-century; similar statements occur in forged charters such as those of Battle Abbey or St Augustine's, Canterbury, and in treatises like the *De libertate Beccensis monasterii*. In this way, a somewhat looser diocesan structure, in which hierarchical control was much less formal than later, was cited in support of claims to exemption by individual churches. In the early and mid-eleventh century, if the diocesan was not available, another bishop might act in his place and with his approval. Orderic Vitalis summed up these earlier informal relations when he wrote of the dedication of a chapel in the diocese of Évreux by Hugh, Bishop of Lisieux, about 1059, 'No one need be surprised to hear of the bishop of Lisieux dedicating a church in the diocese of Évreux', and added that three bishops, Hugh of Lisieux, William of Évreux and Ivo of Séez 'were remarkable in Normandy for their religious zeal and perfect agreement; so great was their mutual affection that any one of them might perform any religious function in his neighbour's diocese, as time and circumstance required, without any envy or litigation, as he would in his own'.[41] But this was not the way in which the Abbot of Bury interpreted the apparent freedom of choice of his predecessors; to him, legal precedents acceptable to the judges had been established in a legal hearing in the King's court. It was this judgement, and a royal charter of very doubtful authenticity recording it, which came to be regarded by all parties for several decades as the basis of Bury's exemption. The papal bull was not cited, and may have been regarded as irrelevant: Lanfranc was even charged by Eadmer with confiscating it for a time when it came into his hands. Lanfranc himself, the monks of Bury, and even a Norwich writer favourable to the Bishop,[42] saw the guarantee of exemption in the judgement of 1081 and the possibly spurious royal charter, not in the papal bull. In this, no doubt, they were accepting the realities of the situation; even when in Anselm's time, Bishop Herbert Losinga attempted to revive the claims of his see at the papal court while he was in Rome on other business, nothing came of it.

Anselm was no stranger to England at the time of his election. He had crossed the Channel several times on the business of his abbey, and had stayed at Christ Church, Canterbury, where he had been received into the fraternity of the monks.[43] He had many friends among the Norman prelates in England, notably the monks of Bec, Gundulf, Bishop of Rochester, and Gilbert Crispin, Abbot of Westminster. He must have been familiar with Lanfranc's views on the primacy; but he had greater sympathy with English customs[44] — such as their ways of venerating their saints — and a subtler appreciation of certain moral issues. As in Normandy, he stressed the importance of obedience in a monk, even when he became Abbot; like Lanfranc, he thought of an abbot with any measure of exemption from his diocesan as being immediately subject to his primate. He turned to the Pope when no other authority seemed adequate or appropriate, but he expected some cases involving monastic exemption to end in the King's court, and he needed the King's co-operation in governing the Church of Canterbury.

Claims to exemption were voiced by three abbeys in particular during his primacy: Battle, Bury St Edmunds, and St Augustine's, Canterbury. Battle's claim was a relatively simple one; the monks asked to have their abbot blessed in their own abbey church by their diocesan, the Bishop of Chichester. The new Abbot, Henry, a former Prior of Christ Church, had been elected on the advice of Anselm, and Anselm had little difficulty in persuading him that he should obey his bishop, and allow the ceremony to take place at Chichester. The monks of Battle never forgave Henry for this concession but, in fact, the precedent did them no harm, and by the mid-twelfth century they had secured more extensive rights of exemption with the aid of forged charters and royal support.[45]

Bury's problems were of a different order; the abbey had already secured exemption from its diocesan, and the monks owed obedience directly to Anselm as primate. Its difficulties arose from a protracted vacancy after the death of Abbot Baldwin at Christmas 1097. The abbey remained vacant for the last two years of Rufus's reign, and when, on his accession, Henry I finally filled it, his choice fell unfortunately on an illegitimate son of Hugh, Earl of Chester. Robert, a monk of Saint-Evroult, was barely more than a boy and manifestly unsuited by character to rule an abbey. Anselm, from the moment he returned from exile, resisted the appointment on the grounds both of uncanonical procedure and the moral character of the intruded abbot.[46] He wrote, as was his custom in any case involving a monk, to Robert's abbot, urging him to exert his authority and recall the erring monk to Saint-Evroult: 'a monk', he declared, 'by his profession, but not in his life'. Getting no response, he urged the Bishop of Lisieux and the Archbishop of Rouen to bring pressure to bear on the abbot, who then insisted that Robert had, in fact, been professed at Saint-Sever, and was not under his authority. Persuasion failed, but Robert was one of the prelates deposed from office at the Council of London in 1102, with the backing of the King. His successor, Robert II, previously Prior of Westminster and a man acceptable to Anselm, was elected in 1102; but, owing to difficulties with the King arising from the questions of investiture and homage, and Anselm's second exile, he was not finally blessed by Anselm until August 1107, just a month before he died. No successor was elected until 1114, some five years after Anselm's own death. Most of Anselm's letters to the monks and Prior of Bury were letters of consolation, encouraging them in their many difficulties, and urging them to do nothing in any way contrary to the Rule of St Benedict, or without the advice of those to whom they should look for guidance in matters of spiritual authority.[47] But it did fall to him to bless Robert as Abbot, and the form in which he did so is of considerable interest.

The sources are not entirely explicit about the ceremony. Eadmer simply recorded that in 1107, Anselm blessed Robert, a monk of Westminster, as Abbot of Bury St Edmunds, and that the ceremony was performed at Canterbury.[48] The monk historian of the abbey who, towards the middle of the twelfth century, inserted marginal annals into a manuscript of Florence of Worcester's chronicle, went into greater detail. Robert, he said, was elected by the brethren and blessed by Anselm at the command of King Henry, in the presence of Ralph, Bishop of Durham, and Helgot, Abbot of Saint-Ouen, and others; and the monks established that the abbot should be blessed without making any profession to the metropolitan or any English bishop, on the grounds that no such profession had been made by any of his three predecessors.[49] It is apparently this entry that persuaded David Knowles into making his cautious statement that Anselm 'consecrated abbot Robert in 1107 without (if we may trust the chronicler) exacting any oath of obedience'.[50] This is not, however, quite what the chronicler says, and he makes himself clear in his account of the benediction of Abbot Alebold in 1114: 'He was blessed by Ralph, archbishop of Canterbury . . . without making any written profession, in accordance with the rule justly established by the monks ('iuxta rationem legitime a monachis confirmatam') in the presence of Archbishop Anselm, when Dom Robert, Alebold's predecessor, was blessed as Abbot.'[51] Whereas it seems unlikely that Anselm would have been prepared to dispense with a simple oath of obedience, all the evidence indicates that he remained as opposed to the practice of requiring a written profession of obedience as he had ever been in Normandy.

If the monks of Bury were at this time prepared to accept some measure of primatial authority in return for support in their troubles, such a solution could not last, and was later to be rejected. It was already proving unacceptable to another house with claims to exemption. Situated in the Archbishop's diocese, just outside his cathedral city, and boasting the first Archbishop of Canterbury as its founder, St Augustine's, Canterbury, shared in the honour of the Archbishop as primate; but successive abbots could secure the exemption they regarded as essential to their dignity only by establishing direct dependence on the papal see, since their diocesan himself, in his various capacities, occupied all the intermediate ranks of the hierarchy. Lanfranc had required written professions of obedience from the two abbots appointed in his time;[52] and the second of these, Guy, died in the year of Anselm's election as Archbishop. Already bearing the scars of the bitter struggle that had followed Guy's intrusion into the community, when many of the monks were banished to other English monasteries and twenty-four monks drafted in from Christ Church to replace them, the abbey now had to endure royal extortion during a long vacancy.[53] Sources disagree on the date of election of the new Abbot, Hugh, who is described by Eadmer as a monk of Bec not yet in holy orders, and by Thorne, writing long afterwards, as a novice at St Augustine's and an ex-knight.[54] If Thorne and Elmham are correct, he owed his appointment to William Rufus in 1099, when Anselm was in exile. His consecration was, in any case, delayed until after 1107, while Henry I and Anselm were slowly moving towards an agreement on election and homage.

At some time during the years 1070 to 1107, the monks, smarting under a sense of many grievances, began to produce a series of forged charters and bulls claiming to date from the first centuries of the abbey's history, and granting various privileges of exemption from secular and ecclesiastical authority. For some of the work they employed Guerno, a monk of Saint-Médard of Soissons, who confessed on his death-bed that he had forged deeds for several monasteries, including St Augustine's and Saint-Ouen, though the exact date and extent of his activities in Canterbury are not known.[55] Four of the forged bulls are mentioned in the abbey's first genuine papal privilege, a bull issued by Calixtus II in 1120.[56] If Levison's argument for a late eleventh-century date for most of the deeds is accepted — and the evidence is, in the main compelling — then their contents can be taken as a measure of the privileges to which the monks attached most importance in Anselm's time. All contain vaguely worded grants of 'liberty' and freedom from subjection to any external authority. On specific matters, seven assert the abbey's claim to the burials of kings and archbishops, which had long been ignored, but was therefore defended all the more vigorously, and was the claim most widely publicized. 'The monks of St Augustine's', wrote William of Malmesbury, 'who clung obstinately to an ancient custom, used to snatch the bodies of dead archbishops by violent means'.[57] Free election, about which feelings ran high after the troubles between 1089 and 1091, is promised in five privileges. A claim that the abbot had the right to be blessed in St Augustine's abbey occurs in only three; and this is the one question on which there was a clash with Anselm. It came towards the end of his pontificate, and very nearly led to deadlock.

Anselm was deeply concerned to end a vacancy that had effectively lasted for over fourteen years and was causing temporal and spiritual disorder. A delay of some months was necessary while the abbot-elect was ordained deacon and then priest; then Anselm proposed to bless him at Christmas 1107, in the cathedral church at Canterbury. The monks of St Augustine's immediately objected that this was contrary to their privileges, and that all new abbots should be blessed in their own abbey. According to Eadmer, Anselm stood firm; the monks appealed to the King, and though he and his nobles dismissed their 'privileges' as invalid or unauthentic, they persuaded him to direct Anselm to bless the abbot in the Church of St Augustine, on the grounds of ancient custom. This Anselm would not do, saying:

> If the king asked me for love of him to bless Hugh as abbot in his own church, perchance I might do so, on the grounds that my predecessors have enjoyed the right of performing their episcopal duties wherever they wished in England. But since he says that I should do this because it is customary, I reply that there is no such custom . . . I should thereby be made subject to him who ought in all things to be canonically subject to me and to my church. For the Archbishop of Canterbury is primate of all England, Scotland, Ireland, and the islands round about, and does not leave his own seat out of respect for any person, save only for the King and Queen. If the King wishes me to show the same honour to the Abbot of St Augustine's as to himself, he is making the Abbot his equal in the kingdom.[58]

Anselm added that this would disturb the right order of things, and be a disparagement to the rights of prelates and magnates throughout the realm.[59] A similar argument enabled him to refuse to bless the Abbot in the King's own chapel: he was accustomed, he insisted, to say Mass in the royal chapel only for the Coronation of the King. He agreed instead to perform the ceremony in the chapel of the Bishop of Rochester's manor of Lambeth, where he was staying at the time, and there, on 27 February 1108, Hugh was finally blessed as Abbot of St Augustine's, and promised obedience to the Archbishop. Those who were present complained that the ceremony would have been more dignified, and more conducive to the Abbot's honour if it had been performed in the cathedral church at Canterbury; but at least the vacancy was over, and Anselm had upheld the primatial rights of Canterbury.

If the forgeries were already in existence, can he, on the evidence, be charged with casuistry, with turning a blind eye to privileges that purported to rest on papal grants? He could turn a blind eye on occasion, as when he left England in 1103 without opening a papal letter he feared might force him into a whole series of of excommunications if he were to open it before leaving the country.[60] Yet he had suffered years of exile rather than disobey a mandate of the reigning pope; why, if the forged bulls of Boniface IV and John XII were in existence and known to him, did he disregard them? The answer may be that, whether or not he knew about them, both his experience in Normandy and the traditions of Lanfranc encouraged him to look to the King or his Duke for a decision on the validity of legal claims, even claims to ecclesiastical privileges. The monks had taken their case to the King's court; and the court had come to a decision on the grounds of customary right, not on the evidence of any documents that might have been produced. Anselm was content to accept the court's right to make a judgement, though he was ready to persuade the King that he was mistaken on the point of custom, and mistaken in a way derogatory to his royal dignity.[61] This is less casuistry than the willingness of a man who always insisted on a supreme duty to God to recognize that, in some matters at least, Ceasar was entitled to his due. And it is always possible that, as Margaret Gibson has recently suggested, the forgeries of both Christ Church and St Augustine's were directed by the communities of monks against each other, and were intended to bolster the prestige of each house, rather than to be used against any archbishop.[62]

There is a further question arising out of the St Augustine's dispute: in the matter of the profession, did Anselm, as archbishop and primate, claim more than had seemed just to Anselm as abbot? Eadmer says that he received the customary profession, by which Hugh promised to be obedient to the Church of Canterbury and its archbishops.[63] The word he used is 'promised', not 'professed'; and this should almost certainly be interpreted as a spoken promise of obedience, the kind of promise that Anselm expected every abbot to make to his superior, rather than a written profession. Anselm seems on this occasion to have acted as he had done when blessing the abbot-elect of Bury. Certainly no written abbatial profession has survived from his archiepiscopate, although there are two for St Augustine's from the time of Lanfranc. Such records were cherished by subsequent archbishops; it is more likely that none was exacted than that any were lost. We have to wait until the time of Gervase of Canterbury for a positive assertion that Hugh gave a written profession,[64] and Gervase, writing at a time when these had become normal as a sign of obedience, projected the custom he knew into an earlier period. By then, the form of profession had become clarified in canon law, so that the danger of seeing it as a repetition of the abbot's monastic vows was eliminated — it was simply a normal part of his act of submission to his diocesan.

Throughout the twelfth century, the written profession of obedience by non-exempt abbots advanced side by side with the written charter of privilege for exempt houses, as the ecclesiastical hierarchy was strengthened and direct dependence on the pope became necessary to ensure freedom from lesser authorities. The last two or three decades of the eleventh century and the first half of the twelfth were the years when innovatory demands for written professions and traditional demands for obedience were both countered by the production of forged privileges. Tentative and not wholly successful attempts at forgery in the earlier years were succeeded by a crescendo of activity towards 1120 and 1130, when appeals to the papal court, whether it was in France or in Italy, became more frequent, and interpolated or forged bulls and charters were reinforced by historical accounts designed to show that custom was on the side of the claimants.[65] Increasingly, from the third decade of the twelfth century, genuine new grants of exemption became more frequent, and compromises were worked out. Anselm was active in the earlier period of change and legal uncertainty; his answers to the problems confronting him were often individual, sometimes to be reversed or amended later, but always, where moral and spiritual principles were involved, wholly consistent.

Anselm, monk and philosopher though he was, was no recluse. 'He understood human nature', wrote William of Malmesbury, 'as we can see from his writings';[66] the theologian who wrote of the fall of man was well qualified to understand individual, fallen men. Even when similar rights and customs existed in England and Normandy, individuals were different; they had to be handled differently by various modes of persuasion, and Anselm could be very persuasive — as the arguments by which he won Henry I to his side in the case of St Augustine's showed. Often he had to face new situations after he came to Canterbury. On the question of free election, investiture he came to Canterbury. On the question of free election, investiture and homage, the growth and definition of canon law and his own increased awareness of it after his first exile forced him to adopt a more intransigent attitude to the secular ruler in England than had ever been necessary when he was an abbot in Normandy. On narrower issues he, like Lanfranc, found some differences in custom. There seems to have been a stronger and older tradition of recourse to Rome in pre-Conquest England than in Normandy: this reinforced some local customs, but was counterbalanced by the added strength of the Archbishop's claims as primate. In enforcing these claims, Lanfranc had been prepared to override local customs; Anselm, firmly convinced of his duty to defend the rights no less than the property of his see,[67] was nevertheless more ready to look sympathetically at English traditions, and always preferred persuasion to force. He followed Lanfranc in regarding an abbey's exemption from any part of the authority of its diocesan as implying direct subjection to the primate. But, on a matter of such importance to him as the exaction of a written profession from an abbot-elect, which he thought to be either harmful or unnecessary, he abandoned Lanfranc's innovation altogether.

Sensitive to changing issues, and to the vagaries of individual men, he never wavered on the principles that were central to his moral code: the necessity for obedience, and the inviolability of the monastic profession. These show through all his actions — on these no compromise was possible. 'If my life and monastic profession do not convince you of the falsity of the charge', he wrote in answer to some who accused him of scheming for the archbishopric, 'I do not know what will'.[68] The same answer might still be given to any present-day writer tempted to revive the charge. In his treatment of monastic exemption no less than in his approach to the wider problems of election and investiture and the complex relations of Church and State, Anselm, Archbishop and primate of Canterbury, remained steadfastly and simply, to the end of his life, 'by profession and at heart a monk of Bec'.

NOTES

I would like to thank Sir Richard Southern who read this paper and made a number of helpful suggestions.

1. 'Frater Anselmus, professione et corde monachus Beccensis Dei dispositione vocatus archiepiscopus Dorobernensis.' *Ans.Op.Om.*, IV, 61-2 (*Epistola* 178).

2. *The Ecclesiastical History of Orderic Vitalis*, edited by Marjorie Chibnall, 6 vols. (Oxford, 1969-80), V, 18-24.

3. *Orderic Vitalis*, IV, 106; William of Malmesbury, *De Gestis Regum Anglorum*, edited by W. Stubbs, Rolls Series, 90, 2 vols. (London, 1887-9), II, 337.

4. cf. *Ans.Op.Om.*, IV, 57-60 (*Epistola* 176) for his defence of the rights of the Church of Canterbury.

5. Marjorie Chibnall, 'The relations of Saint Anselm with the English dependencies of the Abbey of Bec: 1079-1093', *Spicilegium Beccense*, 1 (1959), 521-2.

6. *Regesta Regum Anglo-Normannorum*, I, edited by H.W.C. Davis (Oxford, 1913), no. 124. The date was 14 July 1080 at Caen.

7. R.N. Sauvage, *L'Abbaye de Saint-Martin de Troarn*, Mémoires de la Société des antiquaires de Normandie, 4ᵉ série, 4 (Caen, 1911), 352-3.

8. On 7 January 1080. See *Calendar of Documents preserved in France*, edited by J.H. Round (London, 1899), pp. 397-8; M.P. Marchegay, *Chartes normandes de l'abbaye de Saint-Florent-près-Samur*, Mémoires de la Société des antiquaires de Normandie, 3ᵉ série, 10 (Paris, 1880), 681-5; Davis, *Regesta*, no. 120.

9. Davis, *Regesta*, no. 115a; M. Prou, *Recueil des actes de Philippe Iᵉʳ, roi de France* (Paris, 1908), p. 242.

10. See M. Gibson, *Lanfranc of Bec* (Oxford, 1978), pp. 36-7; D. Lohrmann, *Papsturkunden in Frankreich*, n.F., 7, Nördliche Ile-de-France und Vermandois (Gottingen, 1976), p. 42.

11. Davis, *Regesta*, no. 146a; F. Lot, *Etudes critiques sur l'abbaye de Saint-Wandrille*, Bibliothèque de l'Ecole des hautes études, sciences historiques et philologiques, 204 (Paris, 1913), pp. 87-90 (no. 39).

12. J.F. Lemarignier, *Etudes sur les privilèges d'exemption et de juridiction ecclésiastique des abbayes normandes*, Archives de la France monastique, 44 (Paris, 1937), p. 159 (note 91); C.H. Haskins, *Norman Institutions*, Harvard Historical Studies, 24 (Cambridge, Mass., 1925), pp. 34-5.

13. Chibnall, *Orderic Vitalis*, III, 34.

14. cf. Davis, *Regesta*, no. 124.

15. A.A. Porée, *Histoire de l'abbaye du Bec* (Evreux, 1901), pp. 321-2; Denis de Sainte-Marthe, *Gallia Christiana*, XI, Instrumenta, col. 17.

16. P. Jaffé, *Regesta Pontificum Romanorum*, second edition, edited by G. Wattenbach, S. Loewenfeld, F. Kaltenbrunner, P. Ewald (Leipzig, 1885-8), no. 4644; cf. Gibson, *Lanfranc*, p. 109.

17. See *Annales Ordinis Sancti Benedicti*, edited by J. Mabillon, 6 vols. (Paris, 1739-45), V, Appendix, 601-5.

18. See J. Yver, 'Autour de l'absence d'avouerie en Normandie', *Bulletin de la Société des antiquaires de Normandie*, 57 (1965 for 1963-4), 189-283: O. Guillot, *Le Comte d'Anjou et son entourage au XIe siècle*, 2 vols. (Paris, 1972), especially I, 185-7.

19. Yves de Chartres, *Correspondance*, edited by J. Leclercq, I (Paris, 1949), 246-8 (*Epistola* 60).

20. See R.W. Southern, *Saint Anselm and his Biographer* (Cambridge, 1963), pp. 125-7.

21. Guillot, *Comte d'Anjou*, I, 186, n. 231, citing Yves de Chartres (*Epistola* 102), 'non enim licet regibus . . . electionibus episcoporum se immiscere vel aliqua eas ratione impedire'; cf. Robert L. Benson, *The Bishop-Elect* (Princeton, 1968), pp. 38-40.

22. *Ans.Op.Om.*, III, 263-4 (*Epistola* 123); Sauvage, *L'Abbaye de Saint-Martin*, p. 77, n. 4.

23. Chibnall, *Orderic Vitalis*, V, 260-2.

24. *De libertate Beccensis monasterii*, in Mabillon, *Annales OSB*, V, 602-5; *Vita Willelmi*, PL 150.713-23; *Vita Bosonis*, PL 150.723-32; *Vita Theobaldi*, PL 150.734.

25. *Histoire littéraire de la France* (Paris, 1733-1949), XII, 341-2.

26. J. Leclercq, 'Une doctrine de la vie monastique dans l'école du Bec', *Spicilegium Beccense*, 1 (1959), 477-88.

27. These are contained in the Bibliothèque Nationale, MS lat. 2342, described by A. Wilmart, 'Les ouvrages d'un moine du Bec', *Revue bénédictine*, 44 (1932), 21-46.

28. *Consuetudines Beccenses*, edited by M.P. Dickson, Corpus consuetudinum monasticarum, 4 (Siegburg, 1967), p. 180.

29. *The Cartulary of Worcester Cathedral Priory*, edited by R.R. Darlington, Pipe Roll Society, new series, 38 (London, 1968), p. 32.

30. W. Levison, *England and the Continent in the Eighth Century* (Oxford, 1946), Appendix 1, pp. 174-233.

31. R.W. Southern, 'The Canterbury forgeries', *English Historical Review*, 73 (1958), 47-62, has put the case for a possible later date.

32. P.H. Sawyer, *Anglo-Saxon Charters* (London, 1968), no. 1244.

33. *Goscelini Cantuariensis monachi historia translationis S. Augustini, PL* 155.14-15 (dedicatory letter).

34. See David Knowles, 'The growth of exemption', *Downside Review*, new series, 31 (1932), 201-31, 396-436.

35. *The Life of St Anselm, Archbishop of Canterbury, by Eadmer*, edited by R.W. Southern (London, 1962), p. 51.

36. Michael Richter, *Canterbury Professions*, Canterbury and York Society, 67 (Torquay, 1973), pp. xl, xlvii-lxxvi.

37. See 'Acta Lanfranci' in *Two Saxon Chronicles Parallel*, edited by Charles Plummer, 2 vols. (Oxford, 1892, 1899), I, 287-92.

38. The case is described by Knowles, 'Exemption', pp. 210-11; 'Hermanni archidiaconi liber de miraculis sancti Eadmundi', in *Memorials of St Edmund's Abbey*, edited by Thomas Arnold, 3 vols., Rolls Series, 96 (London, 1890-6), I, 60-7.

39. Jaffé, *Regesta Pontificum*, no. 4962.

40. F.E. Harmer, *Anglo-Saxon Writs* (Manchester, 1952), pp. 141-5.

41. Chibnall, *Orderic Vitalis*, II, 78.

42. V.H. Galbraith, 'The East Anglian see and the Abbey of Bury St Edmund's', *English Historical Review*, 40 (1925), 222-8.

43. Eadmer, *Life of Anselm*, p. 50.

44. Ibid., pp. 51-4; cf. also Anselm's letter to Wulfstan, Bishop of Worcester, seeking advice on the right of the Archbishop to dedicate churches in his own manors situated in other dioceses, *Ans.Op.Om.*, IV, 51-2, (*Epistola* 170). Lanfranc, however, was not wholly insensitive to local customs; see Gibson, *Lanfranc*, pp. 170-4.

45. Knowles, 'Exemption', pp. 222-4; *The Chronicle of Battle Abbey*, edited by Eleanor Searle, Oxford Medieval Texts (Oxford, 1980), pp. 100-3, 146-59; cf. *The 'Acta' of the Bishops of Chichester, 1075-1207*, edited by H. Mayr-Hartung, Canterbury and York Society, 56 (Torquay, 1964), charter no. 6.

46. J. Laporte, 'St Anselme et l'ordre monastique', *Spicilegium Beccense*, 1 (1959), 473-4; *Ans.Op.Om.*, IV, 162-3, 181, 186 (*Epistolae* 251-2, 266-7, 269, 271); Arnold, *Memorials of St Edmund's Abbey*, I, 353.

47. *Ans.Op.Om*, IV, 163-4, 182 (*Epistolae* 252, 267).

48. Eadmer, *Historia Novorum in Anglia*, edited by Martin Rule, Rolls Series, 81 (London, 1884), p. 188.

49. Arnold, *Memorials of St Edmund's Abbey*, I, 356.

50. Knowles, 'Exemption', p. 212.

51. Arnold, *Memorials of St Edmund's Abbey*, I, 356.

52. C.E. Woodruff, 'Some early professions of canonical obedience to the see of Canterbury by heads of religious houses', *Archaeologia Cantiana*, 37 (1925), 60-1, prints the two professions, but wrongly suggests that they were probably made during the vacancies at Canterbury.

53. 'Acta Lanfranci', pp. 290-2.

54. Eadmer, *Historia Novorum*, p. 188; Knowles, 'Exemption', pp. 405-6. Eadmer is most likely to have been correct.

55. Levison, *England and the Continent*; see *Literae Cantuarienses*, edited by J.B. Sheppard, 3 vols., Rolls Series, 84 (London, 1887-9), III, 364-8, for the letters describing how the monks had employed Guerno to forge privileges. Guerno died between 1119 and 1131.

56. W. Holtzmann, *Papsturkunden in England*, 1 (Berlin, 1930), pp. 231-3, no. 10.

57. William of Malmesbury, *De Gestis Pontificum Anglorum*, edited by N.E.S.A. Hamilton, Rolls Series, 52 (London, 1870), p. 15.

58. Eadmer, *Historia Novorum*, pp. 188-9; for Anselm's unwillingness to diminish the King's honour, cf. a simile in his *De moribus*, *Mem.Ans.*, p. 41.

59. Whilst there is no reason to doubt the truth of the facts Eadmer records, some of the arguments he attributes to Anselm seem to be rather a general defence of the primacy as Eadmer himself interpreted it than an accurate report of his words on this occasion. But the insistence that right order must be maintained is certainly characteristic of Anselm's own thought.

60. Eadmer, *Historia Novorum*, p. 149; his motives are discussed in Southern, *Anselm*, pp. 171-2.

61. Eadmer's statement about the action brought by the monks, 'omissis privilegiis suis, quae nulla vel non rata a rege et principibus comprobata sunt et damnata', is far from clear: he seems to imply that they did not produce any written privileges either because they had none or because those they possessed had already been found invalid. He may have been expressing the contempt of the Canterbury monks for the forged privileges of St Augustine's rather than recording what actually happened when the case was heard. If, in fact, the King disregarded any alleged papal documents that were produced and gave a judgement on the basis of oral testimony, he acted much as William I had done when he set aside the papal letter produced by the monks of Bury and confirmed their limited exemption by a judgement of his own.

62. Gibson, *Lanfranc*, pp. 235-7.

63. Eadmer, *Historia Novorum*, p. 190.

64. Gervase of Canterbury, *Opera historica*, edited by William Stubbs, 2 vols., Rolls Series, 73 (London, 1879-80), I, 72, 163-5.

65. cf. Lemarignier, *Les Privilèges d'exemption*, pp. 212-15. The monks of Saint-Evroult seem also to have tampered with their charters of privilege at this time (Chibnall, *Orderic Vitalis*, I, 68-75).

66. William of Malmesbury, *De Gestis Pontificum*, p. 122.

67. cf. the views expressed in his letters, especially *Epistola* 176 (*Ans.Op.Om.*, IV, 57-60).

68. *Ans.Op.Om*, IV, 18 (*Epistola* 156): "Quamvis sint quidam, ut audio – qui autem sint, deus scit – , qui aut fingunt malitia aut suspicantur errore aut coguntur dicere indiscreto dolore, quod magis trahar ad archiepiscopatum vitiosa cupiditate, quam cogar religiosa necessitate. Quibus nescio quomodo possim persuadere quae sit in hac re conscientia mea, si illis non satisfacit vita et conversatio mea'. It is possible that Robert Curthose was responsible for some false rumours about Anselm's motives; Anselm said later that Robert had apologized to him for having believed or said anything unjust about him, 'amore meo et dolore de amissione mea cogente, ob meam ad archiepiscopatum electionem'. *Ans.Op.Om.*, IV, 37 (*Epistola* 164).

The Posthumous Anselm

C. Holdsworth

Most of the surviving evidence about the activity of Anselm after his death is well-known. It makes a slim collection. Eadmer, in his *Life of St Anselm* and in the accompanying book of *Miracles*, mentions fewer episodes than can be numbered on one person's fingers and toes, and when John of Salisbury rewrote his work in connection with Becket's attempt to have Anselm canonized, he could only add one more incident, bringing the total to seventeen. Besides these episodes, there is evidence of reverence offered at the Archbishop's tomb in the time of King Stephen; the certain existence under his successor of a gild in the saint's honour at Canterbury; and the less certain, but fairly conclusive, evidence that Anselm's remains were translated sometime between 1163 and 1170.[1]

This essay does not present a large body of hitherto unnoticed evidence: rather, it discusses two small pieces and takes another look at some parts of the old, well-known material for, to some degree, they seem to contain an explanation for the paucity of the whole corpus. But first must come the two small additions to the evidence: a reference and a story, which I shall take in reverse chronological order.

At Christ Church, probably during the time of Archbishop Theobald, an anonymous member of the community wrote the life of the first great Norman Archbishop, Lanfranc. Traditionally, this work was attributed to Milo Crispin, and recently Margaret Gibson has established that it was written between c. 1140 and 1156. Now the author of the *Vita Lanfranci* refers to Anselm at one point, carefully calling him 'beatus'.[2] This backs up nicely the implication of Stephen's grant of land for the purpose of maintaining a light before the *capsa* containing Anselm's remains.[3]

Some time between 1132 and 1136 — that is to say almost a generation earlier — Osbert of Clare in writing to Archbishop Anselm's nephew (Anselm, Abbot of Bury St Edmunds) told him of a recent happening concerning his uncle.[4] He wrote at Easter time, the season in which the Archbishop had died, and the story seemed to him a suitable present for his correspondent, a kind of medieval Easter egg, perhaps. Recently, Osbert wrote, Roger de Somery had died and had been buried by his widow and son at a monastery dedicated to the Virgin standing near the river Severn. The dead man's possessions had to be divided so that a third could be given to the monastery to assist the salvation of the dead man's soul. Among these was a goblet which the widow claimed to have been Anselm's and upon which she had set her heart. Her desire for it was so great that she said she would give a hundred shillings, or more, for it, should it not fall within her allotted portion. One of the bystanders remarked that her devotion to the Archbishop should be rewarded and so, in fact, after invocations had been made to him, she was. The lady finally received the goblet which she kissed and kept as a precious relic of the Man of God.

The actors and the scene can be identified. Roger de Somery died in 1132 and two years earlier had paid money to have land in Kent which his mother-in-law held there. His burial place must have been Tewkesbury, and Roger the Prior, one of the observers of the happy lottery, became Abbot there in 1137.[5] How the goblet had come into Roger de Somery's hands we do not know — I have failed to find him among the obvious sources — and it is idle to speculate about whether the goblet was the very one which Lanfranc had given to the Archbishop and later wanted returning.[5] It may, however, be worth recalling that Tewkesbury was a place which did have some links with Anselm's circle. Gerald of Avranches, who first settled the monks from Cranborne in Dorset at their new site by the Severn, had been clerk to Hugh, Earl of Chester, one of Anselm's powerful lay friends. And, when Gerald died, it was at Rochester with Ralph d'Escures, another person who was close to the great Archbishop.[7] The story, then, casts a small beam of light upon that circle of people who had come into contact with Anselm and retained reverence and affection for him. But what became of the goblet?

This question leads us into that difficult area of relic lists and, as far as I can tell, no pieces of Anselm or of things associated with him occur in any of them. Both the goblet, and his belt, which Eadmer tells us was in his keeping and performed some miraculous cures, appear to vanish without trace.[8] Furthermore, it is particularly striking to find no mention of Anselm in a small collection of relics given by Nicholas, Prior of St Gregory's, Canterbury, to Waltham Abbey some time between 1241 and 1252, although it contained pieces connected with other great Canterbury saints, from Mildred, Dunstan and Alphege to Thomas Becket.[9] Our new scraps of evidence, therefore, reinforce the impression that Anselm fizzled out as a wonder-working saint very rapidly. Why was this?

Sir Richard Southern, to whom all students of Anselm are so indebted, has suggested that he was overshadowed — almost hopelessly upstaged — by Becket, which left little need for another lesser cult.[10] This certainly seems true, as does his suggestion that we might have a different impression of Anselm if one of his more credulous followers like Baldwin or Alexander, had written the *Life* which was widely circulated. Eadmer saw 'at once too much and too little' as he puts it, but amongst his observations there appears to be the basis for a sufficient explanation of the failure of Anselm's posthumous career.[11]

In the first place, Eadmer makes clear on more than one occasion that Anselm either did not wish to attempt to cure someone, or that, when he was asked to try, he did not wish the result to be considered as a miracle.[12] Admittedly, the holy man as a reluctant healer can be a *topos*, but in Anselm's case it may mean more than this and might have restricted the likelihood that posthumous cures would be ascribed to his influence. Secondly, it is surely no coincidence that a large proportion of the so-called 'miracles' are, in fact, visions. These may be 'unremarkable' as Southern has said but, nonetheless, they indicate another aspect of the saint which almost disqualified him from a career as a 'miracle-worker', but fitted him for a different role.[13]

Two of the posthumous visions are said to have been seen by an old servant of the Archbishop's, to whom the dead saint appeared.[14] When he was asked, 'Where you dwell, how you live and what you do', Anselm replied, 'Ibi vivo, ubi video, laetor, perfungor', ('There I live, where I see, rejoice and enjoy'). In this simple way, the servant had understood something about Anselm's mind and teaching which was profound and touching: that the knowledge Man could have of God here on earth was intellectually satisfying. Eadmer tells us that Anselm had visions twice as a mature person: once when he was puzzling over how the prophets could 'see both the past and the future as if they were present and set them forth beyond doubt in speech or writing', and once while turning over the arguments for his *Proslogion*.[15] In this latter case, we are told that 'the grace of God illumined his heart, the whole matter became clear to his mind, and a great joy and exultation filled his inmost being'.[16] The vision language here serves as a metaphor 'to convey intellectual clarification' and it is not, I suggest, stretching the evidence to see an echo of this in the vision seen by the servant.[17] He, like many others, had doubtless heard the Archbishop recall his own vision as a child when he had seen God on a mountain near his home, and had drawn comfort from the story that there was a light which could enlighten the mind and warm the heart.[18]

Anselm did not live on as a great 'wonder-worker', or a heroic Man of God. As a philosopher, he had few followers until the fourteenth century, but he did live on as someone who could convey the Gospel in concrete similes and could guide those who tried to pray. Few may have prayed to him or thought to visit his shrine, but his 'joyous meditations', as Alexander Neckham referred to them, have reached many readers who have found in them the same quality which persuaded William of Malmesbury in his day to call Anselm 'Lux Anglie'.[19]

NOTES

1. R.W. Southern, *Saint Anselm and his Biographer* (Cambridge, 1963), pp. 337-41.

2. *Vita Lanfranci, PL* 150.58; for its date, see Margaret Gibson, *Lanfranc of Bec* (Oxford, 1978), p. 196.

3. *Regesta Rerum Anglo-Normannorum*, III, edited by H.A. Cronne and R.H.C. Davies (Oxford, 1968), p. 56.

4. *The Letters of Osbert of Clare*, edited by E.W. Williamson (Oxford, 1929), no. 8, pp. 68-72, 201-3, for the editor's notes upon which the following paragraph is based.

5. *The Heads of Religious Houses: England and Wales, 940-1216*, edited by David Knowles, C.N.L. Brooke and Vera London (Cambridge, 1972), p. 73.

6. *Ans.Op.Om.*, I, 17-19, (*Epistola* 1).

7. See Knowles, *Heads*, p. 73; and *The Ecclesiastical History of Orderic Vitalis*, edited by Marjorie Chibnall, 6 vols. (Oxford, 1969-80), III, 217.

8. *The Life of St Anselm, Archbishop of Canterbury, by Eadmer*, edited by R.W. Southern (London, 1962), pp. 158-60, 163-6.

9. British Library, MS Harley 3776, f. 34rb.

10. Southern, *Anselm*, pp. 340-1.

11. Ibid., pp. 329-33. The phrase quoted occurs on p. 331.

12. Eadmer, *Life of Anselm*, pp. 117-19, 120-1.

13. Southern, *Anselm*, p. 318. Six of the sixteen separate incidents in the *Miracles* are visions.

14. Eadmer, *Life of Anselm*, pp. 162-3.

15. Ibid., pp. 12-13, 29-31.

16. Ibid., p 30.

17. Carolly Erikson, *The Medieval Vision* (New York, 1976), pp. 42-3.

18. Eadmer, *Life of Anselm*, pp. 4-5.

19. Alexander Neckham, *Super Cantica Canticorum*, Book VI, Chapter 13, British Library, MS Royal 4 D XI, f. 181b. After he has recommended the fruitful meditations of Augustine, and the sweetest meditations of Gregory, Neckham continues, 'Relege iocundissimas Anselmi Cantuariensis meditationes in quibus tam flores quam fructus suavitatis legere poteris, velut in orto quodam deliciarum constitutus'; William of Malmesbury, *De Gestis Regum Anglorum*, edited by William Stubbs, Rolls Series, 90, 2 vols. (London, 1887-9), I, 376.

II
The *Proslogion* Argument

Anselm and Aristotle's First Law of Modality

Charles Hartshorne

In a formalization of the ontological argument (hereafter OA) which I published in 1962, the assertion of the existence of God (call this assertion P) is shown to follow from two extra-logical premises.[1] The formal validity of the reasoning has been acknowledged by several logicians. The remaining questions concern the philosophical or theological meaning of this validity. The point I wish to make in this essay is that, although OA is not by itself a sufficient reason for believing P (since one of the premises — P is logically possible, i.e., involves no contradiction or absurdity — can be questioned), the argument is nevertheless a sufficient reason for disbelieving the widely held doctrine that the theistic question is empirical or such that observational evidence is the test of the true answer. On the contrary, observation can test only contingent propositions, and what Anselm discovered was that the assertion — deity exists — is either necessarily true or necessarily false. It follows that all legitimate arguments for (or against) the divine existence must be as *a priori* as OA. I have tried elsewhere to show how several such arguments can be stated.[2] Belief in God need not depend for its rationality either on OA alone or on empirical reasoning. It can be supported by rational non-empirical arguments other than OA.

If an *a priori* argument is to convince, two conditions must be met: the deductions from the premises must be supported by accepted rules of formal logic (such as those of Lewis's S5), and the premises themselves must be supported by what is well called 'informal logic'. The first or formal kind of support depends on relations between logical constants; the second on relations of extra-logical terms, such as those used in the definition of 'God'. Both kinds of relations are logical in the broad sense, that is, dependent only on the meanings of words.

Here is an outline of OA (omitting some deductive steps), as put in a modern notation by Hubbeling.[3]

'P' for 'Deity Exists' (assumes a definition of Deity)
'M' for 'Logically Possible' (German, *möglich*)
$\Rightarrow$ for 'Strict Implication' as in Lewis's system S5

Extra-logical premises (supported by informal logic)

(1) P $\Rightarrow$ LP (Anselm's Principle) God could not exist contingently
(2) MP God's existence is logically possible, coherently conceivable
∴P

The atheist must reject at least one of these two assumptions. If he rejects (2), then he admits that the question is non-empirical. Atheism of this kind is really positivism, the denial that theism makes sense.

The informal logic supporting Anselm's Principle was in part stated by Aristotle: 'With eternal things, to be possible and to be are the same'.[4] God is defined in terms that exclude genesis and destruction; moreover, it is coming to be that explains contingency. What caused the coming to be of this or that individual or species might not have caused it. The assumption here, which Aristotle wisely made, was that becoming is not subject to wholly sufficient but only to necessary conditions. This allows for the genuine freedom in the present, settling what antecedently was unsettled, choosing *this* when one could, granted the prior conditions, including one's own past actions and character, have chosen *that* instead. But a being by definition always existent and incapable of coming to be (whether by virtue of some cause or otherwise) cannot be supposed contingent on any such ground. On what other ground, then?

Opponents of Anselm ignore the incongruity of a possibly non-existent being which yet might exist eternally. Suppose it did, what would explain its existing? Obviously nothing; simply it would exist. Suppose it did not, what would make its existence possible? Possibility of existence is potentiality, and potentiality is a character of becoming, its aspect of futurity. Past events simply did happen as they did, but future events . . . there are none — the future, so long as it is future, does not consist of fully definite events. It is partly indeterminate, a mixture of chance and necessity, or of degrees of probability. Thus, as Aristotle and Peirce, two great logicians and speculative philosophers, have said, our eventually *somehow* dying is (conditionally) necessary (granted that we exist as animals), but just when, where, and how we die is contingent.

One way to see that 'eternal' implies 'necessary' is to ask how something's eternity could be known. One cannot wait forever to see whether the thing always continues to be. Even God could not do this. The idea of a timeless survey of all time contradicts the distinctiveness of 'time' or 'becoming' as compared to 'space' or 'being'. As Bergson said, it 'spatializes time' and insofar fails to talk sense. One can see this spatialization quite plainly in the Thomistic discussion of this topic. To see that something is eternal is to see that it *could not not be*, that there can be no conditions for its existing.

Why is contingency (possible P and possible not P) ordinarily valid of existential statements? Answer: ordinary conceptions show the contingency of their being instantiated in several ways, not all of which are stated by Anselm. The thing specified:

a)   can be conceived to come into existence as a result of prior conditions capable of other results instead;

b) requires a specific combination of elements capable of existing in other combinations instead;
c) requires a definite finite value or magnitude of one or more variables capable of other values instead;
d) occupies a place or places other things could universally occupy instead;
e) cannot be identified by a merely abstract description free from empirical reference. Thus human being is not merely 'rational animal' but rather such an animal that has evolved on planet earth (also even 'animal' is not free from necessary empirical reference).

None of the above intelligible marks of contingency applies to either classical or process-theological definitions of God.

Actual alternatives to contingent things are never mere nothings but always positive possibilities excluding the thing in question. Contingent things are competitive. Always something else will exist instead if the thing does not. If this competitive theory of contingency has been refuted, I know not by whom. And who has shown that the divine existence must be competitive in this sense?

Universal empricism is a dubious doctrine anyway. What experience could show that there was no experience, or that there was not a more or less ordered world, or that there had been no past by which the experience was influenced, or that there will be no future which that experience will influence? Yet it is true, though observationally unfalsifiable in principle, that there are experiences; that there is a world, some world or other; that there has been a past and will be a future. These are existential statements we can only verbally deny and by implication must in many ways affirm; but no experience could 'count against them'. Unqualified empiricism is untenable.

Anselm's weakness was in his definition of God as an unsurpassable maximum, incapable of increase. The process-theological definition is that God is unsurpassable by another, which opens the way for divine self-surpassing as new creatures come into existence and enrich the content of the divine awareness. Anselm's Principle still applies, but not the absurdity which John Findlay was the first to detect as the essential fallacy in Anselm's procedure. This was the glaring fallacious inference of a *concrete* or logically strong conclusion from a plainly *abstract* or logically weak definition. The formula, 'Such that nothing great can be conceived' is utterly abstract, yet the conclusion is supposed to be a reality unsurpassingly rich — if not concrete then super-concrete. I call this 'Findlay's Paradox'. What is overlooked is that the divine reality must have two aspects: the one definable in purely abstract and *a priori* terms, for example, cognitive infallibility; the other definable only in empirical and concrete terms, for example, infallibly knowing Jimmy Carter — if, or since, Jimmy Carter exists. Knowledge of the concrete presupposes the concrete and hence shares in the latter's contingency. Denials of this clear logical truth darken counsel.

Process theology, but not classical theology, can admit a real distinction between God's abstract and necessary properties and his concrete and contingent ones: for it admits an eminent form of 'becoming' and contingency in God. It thus can escape Findlay's Paradox. What is deduced from the definition of God is only the divine existence. It is not the full concrete actuality of God. And the divine existence is the abstraction 'divinity' as *somehow* concretized or instantiated in *some* suitable actual form. The full divine actuality is in the *how* of the actualization.

Bare existence is abstract even with ordinary individuals. Thus, as soon as I was born and given a name, Charles Hartshorne existed, but he lacked most of the specific characteristics which now qualify me. Existence and actuality are not the same, the latter being *how* a certain already-identified individuality is in contingent fact instantiated. In all this I assume (with Aristotle, Peirce, and most people) the incorrectness of Leibniz's notion that simply being oneself implicates one's entire career. Even the divine identity is abstract — indeed, uniquely so — and allows infinitely ample, open alternatives in the concrete instantiations. The necessity is not in the particular instantiations; simply, there must be some.

Some of the points made can be diagrammed as follows:

From Language to Reality

Transitions: 1   2   3

         Def   ?   CS $\triangleq$ Ex $<$ Act

'Def'	for definition or verbal explication of a term, e.g., 'God'.
'CS'	for consistent significance, essence, or concept expressed by the Def.
'Ex'	for existence, or the being somehow actualized of CS.
'Act'	for the concrete how or in what of the actualization.

Transition 1 is often problematic (e.g., class of all classes, greatest number, greatest being) as to the consistency of the Def.

Transition 2 is ordinarily contingent, non-deductive, requiring further evidence beyond the CS. In the divine case, however, transition 2 is deductive, an equivalence, and the concept (if it be really consistent) must be actualized (otherwise it could not be actualized). This is Anselm's Principle.

Transition 3 is never deductive. This is the limited element of truth in Kant (also Aristotle's and Gassendi's) 'existence is not a predicate' and could not be guaranteed by a concept.

Neither Anselm nor his critics properly distinguished mere existence from full actuality. The dichotomy essence-existence is misleading. Existence is a mere function of essence and actuality; and only the last is fully concrete.

It is not 'existence' that must be undeducible from an 'essence', it is 'actuality'. And the contingency of the latter applies even to God. Not to see this was the primary oversight of Anselm. To remedy it, the very definition of God must be revised. It must allow divine increase, divine self-surpassing, but exclude God's being surpassed *by another*. Anselm unwittingly discovered the necessary falsity of the kind of theism which he sought to support. But he also discovered the necessary falsity of universal empiricism. This double discovery was made, like many discoveries, somewhat in spite of, or partly unwittingly by, the discoverer. As Frank Knight, the economist, used to say, 'Of course great men have influence on history; but it is never the influence they want to have'.

To see how the foregoing analysis applies to Anselm, one must read far more of his text than *Proslogion*, 2, the most usually cited passage. If Anselm had contented himself with that short section, he would scarcely have deserved our attention. But in *Proslogion*, 3, he takes an essential step into the heart of the problem. We can, he says, conceive God as such that the divine non-existence cannot be conceived. This is the idea of logically necessary existence ('logically', here, in the broader or informal sense). God's existence is not just one more instance of existence, but a uniquely excellent manner of existing, existing without possibility of failing to do so, absolute security of existence, existence nothing else could possibly have caused or prevented, unconditioned existence and, therefore, existence not open to empirical tests. For, if there could be an experience showing the divine non-existence, then it would not be unconditioned existence that one was talking about, but existence on condition that no such experience was genuinely conceivable or possible. I submit that the only way a sceptic can combat Anselm here is by challenging the statement, '*We can conceive*' a being whose non-existence cannot be conceived. Hume and Kant deny that such a being can be conceived. We can verbally affirm it, but so can we affirm 'number such that no number could be greater'. The question is, does the description make consistent sense? Here Anselm is incautious and partly begs the question.

If unconditioned or non-contingent existence can be conceived, God must be conceived in its terms; for such existence is superior to conditioned, contingent existence. To be worthy of worship is to exist in the uniquely excellent way that Anselm is characterizing. On this ground Anselm is impregnable.

That Anselm agrees with Aristotle's First Law of Modality is made quite clear in *Responsio* 1 to Gaunilo.

> For that than which a greater is inconceivable cannot be conceived except as without a beginning. But whatever can be conceived to exist, and does not exist, can be conceived to exist through a beginning. Hence what can be conceived to exist, but does not exist, is not a being than which a greater cannot be conceived. Therefore, if such a being can be conceived to exist, necessarily it does exist.[5]

In other words, only the temporal (what can be conceived to exist through a beginning) is contingent, and only the eternal (what cannot be conceived to exist through a beginning) is necessary.

It also seems manifest to Anselm that to have always existed (without a beginning) is better than to exist through a beginning. Hence it is absurd to think of the being worthy of worship as conceivably existing through a beginning. It follows that it is equally absurd to think of God as possibly existing and possibly not existing. The alternative to theism is positivism, or as Charlesworth has it, *a priori* (not empirical) atheism, the denial of consistent meaning for the idea of God.

A vulnerable point in Anselm is the following, in *Responsio* 8.

> For . . . who . . . , supposing that there is some good which has a beginning and an end, does not conceive that a good is much better, which, if it begins, does not cease to be? And that, as the second good is better than the first, so that good which has neither beginning nor end, though it is ever passing from the past through the present to the future, is better than the second. And that far better than this is a being — whether any being of such a nature exists or not — which in no wise requires change or motion, nor is compelled to undergo change or motion?[6]

Now, I say that the last step in this hierarchy is a non-sequitur, a baseless assertion. To have existed always and without possibility of ceasing to exist is indeed better than to exist only since a certain time, or with possibility of ceasing to exist. Primordial and everlasting existence is infinitely *more* than existence for a finite time only. Here the contrast is positive, one of addition not subtraction. But the denial of change is negative, a subtraction, for all Anselm has shown. His unstated assumption is, of course, that change simply as such means loss or privation. Exactly this is the point at issue between philosophers of 'being' and philosophers of 'becoming'. The former view 'becoming' as a deficient form of 'being', 'being' minus something. A process philosopher thinks that 'being' is an abstraction, that concrete actuality is, in principle, 'process' or 'becoming'.

Bergson's cumulative-creative view of 'becoming', or Whitehead's 'creative synthesis' of previous actualites, implies that change in principle is addition, not subtraction; gain and not loss. 'Being' is either the reality of the past actualities, 'prehended' in the new actualities (including God as actual) and so 'objectively immortal', or it is an empty abstraction, what all past and possible future actualities have in common, a least common denominator. On this issue Anselm merely begs the question.

Let us now return for a look at the argument of *Proslogion*, 2. 'Being' or existence in the mind only, as a merely intended object, is held to be less than existence outside the mind or in actuality. What then is the *more* which actuality adds to merely conceived existence? For, of course, there is such a *more*, or conceived dollars would be as good as real ones. Most philosophers have been weak in answering this question. My answer to it is that only the actual is concrete, fully definite, and particularized: the merely possible or conceivable is an outline, an abstraction, lacking in the unambiguous particularity of the actual. Possible individuals are not really individual; possible particulars are not really particular. They are outlines only.

The 'essence' of God, as something identified by a verbal form-ula or definition, is a uniquely indefinite outline. Thus, 'God is all-knowing'. Does it follow that God knows you or me? Only if you or I exist does God know us as existents, and we might not have exist-ed and once did not. The attribute of omniscience cannot by itself imply a particular item in the world as something God knows. If it did imply this, then our existence, for example, would be as necessary as God's. To 'God, the all-knowing, exists', 'you and I exist' must be added if 'God knows you and me' is to follow.

Is Anselm justified in deducing God's existence from his unsur-passable excellence and the principle that the actually existing is more and better than the merely conceived? Certainly if what we worship is a merely conceived, not existing deity we are deceived in our worship. But that is what the agnostic or atheist suspects. So it is hard indeed to see that *Proslogion*, 2 offers much of an argument. *Proslogion*, 3 and *Reply* 1 (to Gaunilo), especially together with Aristotle's modal law, give the unbeliever at least much more food for thought. Above all they give philosophers and theologians generally reason to distrust merely empirical approaches to the theistic question. The essential form of that question is not, 'Does God exist?', but 'Can God be conceived' — not indeed in the full concrete richness of the divine life, for that, by definition, transcends human understanding, as Anselm partly though not adequately sees, but in abstract essence? If the answer is yes, then it is illogical to add, 'but perhaps God does not exist'. For the essence excludes that possibility. If the answer is no, then of course God does not and could not possibly exist. And no amount of observation can decide the issue. Only self-understanding, conceptual philosophical enquiry, or faith can decide it. Science as such, and merely empirical common sense, cannot do so.[7]

NOTES

1. Charles Hartshorne, *The Logic of Perfection and Other Essays in Neo-Classical Metaphysics* (La Salle, Illinois, 1962), pp. 50-7.

2. Charles Hartshorne, *Creative Synthesis and Philosophic Method* (La Salle, Illinois, 1970), Chapter 14.

3. H.G. Hubbeling, *Language, Logic and Criterion* (Amsterdam-Assen, 1971).

4. In a book not yet published, *Insights and Oversights of the Great Philosophers*, I explain several principles which I call Aristotle's Laws of Modality. The non-contingency of the eternal is one of these. Between Aristotle and Peirce, the theory of ontological modality was in a sadly confused state. It was not Kant who cleared up the confusion, nor was it Quine or Carnap – or even C.I. Lewis. Peirce rightly related his views on this topic to Aristotle. The greatness of both thinkers in logic, and in the philosophical problems most clearly related to logic, was particularly evident in their discussions of modal concepts. But most medieval Aristotelians, for reasons not hard to explain, largely missed the point. It was Peirce (in his theory of time and of Firstness, Secondness, and Thirdness) who took up the trail so long-neglected. Arthur Prior has formalized what he calls the 'Peircean' view of the relations of truth to time. (See A. Prior, *Past, Present, and Future* (Oxford, 1967), pp. 130-6, especially p. 136. But logicians are still largely under the spell of the classical theological view of timeless truth which is formally analogous to and deducible from timeless omniscience.

5. *Proslogium, Monologium; An Appendix on Behalf of the Fool, by Gaunilon; and Cur Deus Homo*, translated from the Latin by S.N. Deane (Chicago, 1903). *Ans.Op.Om.*, I, 137-8.

6. Ibid. (*Ans.Op.Om.*, I, 130-2.)

7. On the technical problems of formal logic involved in my version and general conception of the OA, see George L. Goodwin, *The Ontological Argument of Charles Hartshorne* (Missoula, Montana, 1978). Goodwin's discussion takes recent work on possible worlds and Quine's criticisms of modal logic into account. It also deals with John Hick's objection that OA uses 'necessary' ambiguously.

Cela dont plus grand ne puisse être pensé

Michel Corbin

L'argumentation improprement dite 'ontologique' repose sur le Nom qu'Anselme de Cantorbéry reconnaît s'être offert à lui alors qu'il désespérait de trouver une quelconque issue au conflit de ses pensées: 'in ipso cogitationum conflictu sic se obtulit quod desperaveram'.[1] Ce Nom contient une telle force de signification, répond-il à Gaunilon, que toute la démonstration qui le suit en découle par nécessité:

> Tantam vim hujus prolationis in se continet significatio ut hoc ipsum quod dicitur, ex necessitate eo ipso quod intelligitur vel cogitatur, et revera probetur existere.[2]

> La signification de cette expression contient en elle une telle force que Cela même qui est dit, par cela même qui est reconnu ou pensé, est prouvé par nécessité exister vraiment.

Le Nom est énoncé pour la première fois à la deuxième phrase du chapitre 2 du *Proslogion*: 'credimus te esse aliquid quo nihil majus cogitari possit',[3] que nous proposons de traduire en langue française par: 'nous croyons que Tu es *Cela dont plus grand ne puisse être pensé*'.

Quelle est cette mystérieuse force de signification? Que dit exactement le Nom en tant que donné à Dieu dans la prière que lui adresse la foi? Comment signifie-t-il, fait-il signe vers Dieu, comment appartient-il à Dieu pour que son audition et sa reconnaissance entraînent nécessairement la reconnaissance que Dieu est, et vraiment? La réponse habituelle a souvent consisté à faire du Nom un concept de Dieu, Le signifiant de manière *ontique*. On lit par exemple, dans un des résumés que donne Thomas d'Aquin de l'argumentation:

> Intellecto quid significet hoc nomen Deus, statim habetur quod Deus est. Significatur enim hoc nomine *id quo majus significari non potest*: majus autem est quod est in re et in intellectu, quam quod est in intellectu tantum: unde cum, intellecto hoc nomine Deus, statim sit in intellectu, sequitur etiam quod sit in re.[4]

> Une fois reconnu ce que signifie ce nom: Dieu, aussitôt on tient que Dieu est. Il est signifié en effet par ce nom: Cela dont plus grand ne peut être signifié. Comme ce qui est dans la chose et dans l'intelligence est plus grand que ce

qui est seulement dans l'intelligence, une fois reconnu ce
nom: Dieu, celui-ci est aussitôt dans l'intelligence, et par
suite dans la chose.

Selon ce type de lecture, la démonstration anselmienne s'accomplit
ou bien sous mode *analytique* – *essentia involvit existentiam* – ou
bien sous mode *synthétique*, passage du concept à l'existence qu'une
part de la tradition philosophique estime invalide.

Il est cependant une autre interprétation à laquelle est attaché
le nom de Karl Barth:

> Ce que la formule dit de son objet, c'est seulement une
> chose négative: on ne peut concevoir quelque chose de plus
> grand; on ne peut rien concevoir qui le dépasse ou puisse le
> surpasser, sous quelque rapport que ce soit . . . *C'est un
> concept de contenu purement noétique* qu'Anselme présente
> ici comme concept de Dieu. Il ne dit pas que Dieu est, ni
> ce que Dieu est, mais – sous la forme d'une interdiction
> perçue par l'homme – *qui* il est. C'est une 'définition
> purement conceptuelle'. Elle ne contient aucune indication
> relative à l'existence et à l'essence de l'objet désigné. On
> ne peut donc en déduire rien de semblable.[5]

Le Nom signifie, pour le théologien réformé, de manière *noétique*,
hors de toute alternative entre démarches analytique et synthétique.
Il parle comme l'interdiction biblique de faire une image du Dieu
Vivant: 'Tu n'auras pas d'autres dieux devant ma face. Tu ne te
feras aucune image sculptée, rien qui ressemble à ce qui est dans
les cieux, là-haut, ou sur la terre, ici-bas, ou dans les eaux, au-
dessous de la terre'.[6] Interdiction des images, et des idoles, le Nom
fonde ainsi un raisonnement par l'absurde qui permet à la foi de
reconnaître ce qu'elle connaît déjà en excluant l'idolâtrie de qui
pense ou imagine plus grand que Dieu. L'idolâtrie, sous la lumière
du Nom, se révèle intérieurement contradictoire; le Nom porte la
Parole qui démasque et pardonne le péché de l'homme.

Le Nom signifie-t-il de manière *ontique* ou *noétique*, conduit-il à
une argumentation *philosophique* ou *théologique*? Une première
constatation autorise une option préalable en faveur de la seconde
hypothèse: Anselme, dans sa réponse à la critique de Gaunilon,
reproche à ce dernier d'avoir déformé son écrit en remplaçant le
Nom par sa transcription ontique, *majus omnibus*:

> Saepe repetis me dicere, quia quod est majus omnibus est in
> intellectu, et si est in intellectu, est et in re; aliter enim
> omnibus majus non esset omnibus majus. Nusquam in omnibus
> dictis meis invenitur talis probatio. Non enim idem valet
> quod dicitur majus omnibus et quo majus cogitari nequit ad
> probandum quia est in re quod dicitur.[7]

Tu répètes souvent que j'ai dit: ce qui est plus grand que
tout est dans l'intelligence; s'il est dans l'intelligence, il est

aussi dans la chose; autrement ce qui est plus grand que tout ne serait pas plus grand que tout. Jamais, dans ce que j'ai dit, ne se trouve une telle preuve. Car il n'est pas équivalent de dire: ce qui est plus grand que tout et Cela dont plus grand ne puisse être pensé, pour prouver que ce qui est dit est dans la chose.

Gaunilon, qui entend sous le Nom un concept disant Dieu en référence à l'ensemble des étants, ne prête point attention à la lettre du Nom, impossible pourtant à confondre avec d'autres. Le Nom est *une proposition relative* dont les cinq éléments sont parfaitement reconnaissables: 1° un comparatif: *majus*; 2° une négation: *nihil* (parfois intégrée au verbe); 3° une référence à la faculté de penser de l'homme: *cogitari*; 4° le subjonctif du verbe signifiant le pouvoir qu'a l'homme de penser: *possit*; 5° une inversion formelle, en tant que le sujet de la relative n'est pas *aliquid* (ou *id*) mais *nihil majus*, qui renvoie à l'ensemble des étants réels ou possibles que l'homme peut penser. Un seul élément se rencontre dans *majus omnibus*, qui ajoute la référence à l'ensemble des étants réels; deux sont absents de la transcription que le chapitre 15 fait du Nom: 'majus quam cogitari possit',[8] à savoir la négation et l'inversion. Bref, si Anselme n'a pas choisi ses mots au hasard et s'il s'agit du Nom cherché avec angoisse, la signification de celui-ci ne peut pas être *ontique*, mais seulement *noétique*. L'inversion formelle et la référence à la pensée de l'homme manifestent que le Nom parle de Dieu en parlant de l'homme, désigne Dieu en signifiant à l'homme une interdiction.

II

Il se pourrait que les vocables choisis par Karl Barth pour préciser la signification du Nom soient assez impropres et que cette impropriété ait contribué au rejet presque unanime de son interprétation. Parler de concepts *ontique* et *noétique* présuppose en effet, à titre de précompréhension, le couple du sujet connaissant et de l'objet connu qui structure la *représentation* de l'étant et exerce sa domination dans la philosophie et la science de l'Occident. C'est définir la vérité comme *adaequatio rei et intellectus* d'une manière qui ne concorde pas avec le dire anselmien. Si donc les résumés de Gaunilon, Thomas d'Aquin et autres, pèchent par la modification qu'ils apportent au Nom, cette lecture pèche aussi par imprécision linguistique. Comment définir le Nom de manière 'purement noétique' et ajouter: 'il ne dit pas *que* Dieu est ni *ce que* Dieu est, mais . . . *qui* il est'? S'il en est ainsi, le débat, un instant tranché, est rouvert ou plutôt prolongé. Le résultat précédent demeure, mais sans les mots qui l'exprimaient et qui doivent être remplacés avec autant de neutralité que possible pour ne pas imposer au texte une grille herméneutique qui lui soit extérieure.

Nous proposons le couple: *direct/indirect* et recueillons l'analyse linguistique du Nom en cette proposition: *le Nom signifie de manière indirecte,* non pas directe, *le Dieu auquel Anselme s'adresse dans sa prière.* Le Nom *désigne* vraiment Dieu, sans quoi il ne serait pas un nom de la foi et ne permettrait aucune prière, mais, en raison de l'inversion formelle qui met la faculté de penser de l'homme à la place du sujet de la proposition relative, cette désignation ne s'accomplit pas sous mode direct. La signification, mode selon lequel s'opère la désignation, implique l'homme capable de penser et le monde des étants dans lequel il pense; elle commande si bien à cette pensée d'adopter une certaine attitude en face de Celui qui est désigné, que le Nom désigne en signifiant indirectement, en faisant signe vers l'homme.

Par cette modification, nous ne renions pas la lecture de Karl Barth, mais nous nous situons dans sa dynamique et son prolongement. Avec une exigence de plus grande fidélité à la lettre d'Anselme et une conscience aigue de l'ignorance où nous sommes encore du mode indirect de la signification, nous acceptons un chemin pour lequel nous n'avons aucune garantie. Aboutira-t-il à éclairer de manière satisfaisante un texte si âprement discuté? Sera-t-il fécond pour la recherche théologique d'aujourd'hui? Comment peut-il être parcouru? A ces interrogations, nous pouvons seulement proposer une constatation aussi simple que plus haut: après les chapitres 2 à 4 habituellement seuls à être pris en compte, le *Proslogion* comporte deux autres chapitres qui font fonctionner le Nom de manière aussi significative. Ce sont le chapitre 15, qui opère le passage du Nom au nom qui confesse l'incompréhensibilité divine:

> Ergo, Domine, non solum es quo majus cogitari nequit, sed es *quiddam majus quam cogitari possit.*[9]

> Seigneur, Tu n'es pas seulement Cela dont plus grand ne puisse être pensé, Tu es encore Cela qui est plus grand qu'on ne peut pas penser.

et le chapitre 5 qui ouvre la considération de l'essence divine:

> Quid igitur es, Domine Deus, quo nil majus valet cogitari? Sed quid es nisi id quod *summum omnium* solum existens per seipsum, omnia alia fecit de nihilo? Quidquid enim hoc non est, minus est quam cogitari possit. Sed hoc de te cogitari non potest. Quod ergo bonum deest summo bono, per quod est omne bonum? Tu es itaque justus, verax, beatus, et quidquid melius est esse quam non esse; melius namque est esse justum quam non-justum, beatum quam non-beatum.[10]

> Qu'es Tu donc, Seigneur Dieu, dont on ne sache penser plus grand? Qu'es-Tu sinon Celui qui, suréminent à tout, seul existant par soi-même, a fait toutes les autres choses de

rien? Tout ce qui n'est pas cela est moins qu'on ne peut penser, et l'on ne peut pas le penser de Toi. Quel bien manque au bien suréminent par quoi est tout bien? Tu es donc juste, véridique, heureux et tout ce qu'il est meilleur d'être que de ne pas être: en effet il est meilleur d'être juste que non-juste, heureux que non-heureux.

Ces quelques lignes, énigmatiques à force de concision, font jouer l'un sur l'autre le Nom et un autre nom: *summum omnium*, proche de: *majus omnibus* par quoi Gaunilon remplace le Nom. Elles sont en fait le résumé et l'approfondissement d'un chapitre très difficile du *Monologion*, le chapitre 15,[11] qui ainsi prépare, depuis plus longtemps qu'Anselme le dit, l'apparition du Nom. Est-il possible d'espérer que la lecture de ce texte peu connu donne accès au mode indirect de signifier du Nom, en offre la genèse? Un premier signe d'espoir est fourni par le Prologue du *Proslogion*: Anselme s'est mis en recherche d'un nom qui puisse servir d'argument unique parce qu'il était insatisfait du *Monologion*, terminé depuis seulement un an ou deux.[12] Un autre réside dans l'équivalence que le premier chapitre de cette oeuvre de jeunesse pose entre *summum omnium* et un autre nom qui contient déjà quatre des cinq éléments du Nom:[13] 'id enim summum est, quod sic supereminet aliis ut nec par habeat nec praestantius'.[13]

III

Le texte en question appartient à un ensemble de chapitres (13 à 28) qui se situe, dans l'ordre de la lecture, après deux autres ensembles: les chapitres 1 à 5 qui établissent la 'triple' preuve de l'existence de Dieu, objet de l'insatisfaction ultérieure d'Anselme, et les chapitres 6 à 12 qui déploient le rapport de création et mènent à la découverte d'une altérité intérieure à la *summa essentia*, Dieu n'étant jamais nommé, en cette méditation, que sous des vocables abstraits: *summa natura, summum bonum, summus spiritus*. Le deuxième ensemble n'intervient pas pour la compréhension du chapitre 15, car Anselme déclare devoir interrompre l'examen de la Parole intime de Dieu pour chercher quelques propriétés de l'essence suréminente — 'ejusdem summae essentiae proprietates aliquas studiose investigandas existimo'.[14] Ainsi le chapitre où nous espérons assister à la naissance du Nom est-il défini comme une recherche sur les *propriétés* ou *perfections* de Dieu, et placé, quant à sa problématique, en suite immédiate des cinq chapitres dont la complexité motive la naissance du Proslogion: 'considerans illud esse multorum concatenatione contextum argumentorum'.[15]

La triple voie proposée vers Dieu est d'autant plus importante à rappeler que le Prieur du Bec la résume dans sa réponse à Gaunilon. Le moine de Marmoustier ayant argumenté à partir d'une prétendue inintelligibilité du Nom, Anselme lui montre qu'il existe une base à partir de laquelle le Nom peut prendre sens: 'est unde possit conjici quo majus cogitari nequeat'.[16] Le verbe utilisé — *conjici* d'où vient le français: conjecture — suggère l'image du lancer, du jeter, comme s'il s'agissait d'un saut vers le haut, d'une ascension aux risques et périls de l'homme:

> Quoniam namque omne *minus* bonum in tantum est simile *majori* bono inquantum est bonum: patet cuilibet rationabili menti, quia de bonis minoribus ad majora conscendendo ex iis quibus aliquid majus cogitari potest, multum possumus conjicere illud quo nihil potest majus cogitari.

> Tout bien moindre étant semblable au bien plus grand en tant qu'il est un bien, il est clair, pour n'importe quel esprit raisonnable, qu'en *remontant* des biens moindres aux plus grands, il est possible, à partir des biens dont plus grand peut être pensé, de conjecturer Cela dont plus grand ne puisse être pensé.[17]

Ce passage reste énigme et objet de controverse si l'on ne remarque pas qu'il ne parle pas comme la quatrième voie de Thomas d'Aquin et ne s'inquiète que du *pur* mouvement d'ascension. Il s'éclaire à partir du chemin de naissance du Nom comme l'indicateur de ce chemin et donne l'*allure* générale de la triple voie: une remontée des étants qui peuvent être dits bons à Cela d'où provient cette bonté ontologique.

Parcourons ces premiers chapitres: il y a triple voie parce que les trois argumentations fournies aux chapitres 1, 3 et 4 sont de fait les trois aspects complémentaires d'un unique chemin qu'Anselme estime très évident et annonce en ces termes:

> Cum omnes frui solis iis appetant quae bona putant: in promptu est, ut aliquando mentis oculum convertat ad investigandum illud, unde sunt bona ea ipsa, quae non appetit nisi quia judicat esse bona, ut deinde ratione ducente et illo prosequente ad ea quae irrationabiliter ignorat, rationabiliter proficiat.[18]

> Puisque tous désirent ardemment jouir de cela seul qu'ils réputent bon, il est manifeste que (l'homme) tourne parfois l'oeil de son esprit pour chercher la trace de Cela d'où sont bonnes ces choses elles-mêmes qu'il ne désire qu'à moins de les juger bonnes; et qu'ensuite, conduit par la raison et précédé par Celui-là, il progresse rationnellement vers ce qu'il ignorait irrationellement.

En cette unique phrase se dit l'originalité du moine: le désir de Dieu qui unifie, dans le mode de vie du cloître, tous les aspects de l'existence humaine, l'impossibilité de disjoindre connaissance théologique et sagesse mystique. Beaucoup plus tard, dans le *Cur Deus homo*, Anselme explicitera magistralement cette ordination de la raison au discernement et du jugement au désir ou amour de Dieu:

> Ad hoc itaque factam esse rationalem naturam certum est, ut summum bonum super omnia amaret et eligeret, non propter aliud sed propter ipsum.[19]

> Il est certain que la nature rationnelle est faite *vers* cela: aimer et choisir par-dessus toutes choses le bien suréminent, non point pour autre chose, mais pour lui-même.

La remontée est alors le chemin que parcourt le désir, la sortie hors de toutes les choses ou étants, désirables pour autre chose, vers cette Chose qui seule est désirable pour elle-même. Tendre à aimer Dieu pour Dieu parce que Dieu est Dieu!

L'articulation du désir du Désirable se déploie sous la forme de raisonnements par l'absurde, par exclusion des hypothèses contraires à la foi. Nous lisons à l'endroit qui sert de clef pour l'ensemble:

> Cum tam innumerabilia bona sint, quorum tam multam diversitatem et sensibus corporeis experimur et ratione mentis discernimus: *estne credendum* esse unum aliquid, per quod unum sint bona quaecumque bona sunt, an sunt bona alia per aliud?[20]

> Puisque tant de bonnes et innombrables choses sont, dont nous éprouvons par les sens corporels et discernons par la raison de notre esprit la si nombreuse diversité, ne faut-il pas croire qu'est *un quelque chose*, par quoi sont bonnes toutes les choses qui sont bonnes, OU sont-elles bonnes, l'une par ceci, l'autre par cela?

Tout est joué sur cette alternative: si l'homme désire quelque chose, c'est que d'abord il juge cette chose bonne et désirable; s'il la qualifie de bonne, il la compare nécessairement à d'autres qui sont plus, moins ou également bonnes; s'il compare, il pose les choses dans *une communauté diversifiée*, qui résulte de la qualification: plus ou moins ou également bon. Que signifie ce phénomène de langage, d'où provient-il? Est-il à lui-même sa raison? Mais, s'il se pose par lui-même, une contradiction intolérable suit: si une chose, qui est *cette* chose en tant qu'elle se distingue de cette *autre* chose, était la source de sa propre bonté, et pareillement l'autre chose, ces deux 'bontés' se distingueraient comme les deux choses et n'auraient jamais cette commune mesure qui permet de parler de bonté pour les deux. L'existence d'une mesure commune et diversifiée renvoie, par exclusion de l'irréelle possibilité pour les choses de se donner leur propre bonté, à l'article de foi en Dieu créateur. Car tout bien vient de Lui et la communauté d'attribution découle de la libre communication qu'Il fait de sa propre bonté. Il est la source unique dont il est trop peu de dire qu'elle est par soi — Anselme rejettera l'anthropomorphisme de la *causa sui*; Il est le bien suréminent, *Bien au-delà de tout bien* qui ne possède ni égal ni supérieur.

Il faudrait lire les deux autres aspects de la démarche, sans doute l'oeuvre entière, pour entendre correctement ce passage, mise en correspondance du phénomène d'attribution à la confession que Dieu est. Qu'il suffise ici de noter que le chapitre 3 (2° aspect) reprend le raisonnement sous l'angle de ce qui est *commun* (idem in diversis) dans l'attribution et le chapitre 4 (3° aspect) sous l'angle de ce qui est divers et hiérarchisé (idem *in diversis*): Cela d'où proviennent toutes choses bonnes est nécessairement un et la pluralité ordonnée des choses bonnes implique un quelque chose qui soit *summum, maximum* et *optimum*. Qu'il suffise aussi de prêter attention à la manière dont Dieu est nommé au terme de cette triple voie:

> Quare est quaedam natura vel substantia vel essentia, quae per se est bona et magna, et per se est hoc quod est, et per quam est, quidquid vere aut bonum aut magnum aut aliquid est, et quae est summum bonum, summum magnum, summum ens sive subsistens, id est summum omnium quae sunt.[21]

> Il est une certaine nature ou substance ou essence, qui est par soi bonne et grande, qui est par soi ce qu'elle est, et par laquelle est tout ce qui est vraiment bon ou grand ou quelque chose. Elle est le bien suréminent, le grand suréminent, l'étant ou le subsistant suréminent, c'est-à-dire le suréminent à toutes choses qui sont.

Summum bonum: l'expression est composée de deux mots qui sont autant de moments nécessaires de cette nomination. En cette vie, l'homme ne peut voir Dieu que 'par miroir et en énigme':[22] s'il nomme en tant qu'il connaît et connaît en tant qu'il accomplit le mouvement de remontée et désir, ce mouvement *adhère* si bien au nom qu'il donne à Celui qu'il désire par-delà toutes choses qu'aucune image et aucun concept *uniques* ne sont possibles. Le dire est nécessairement diffracté en une dualité qui rappelle que la marche suppose toujours deux pas. Nous appelons moment d'*affirmation* le mode du mouvement qu'implique *bonum*, moment de *négation par transcendance* celui qu'explicite *summum*, plus exactement *summum omnium quae sunt*. Nous lisons, au chapitre 15, la mise en place réciproque de ces deux moments.

IV

Il n'est pas immédiatement équivalent de chercher, dans le texte, l'élucidation du mouvement dessiné par les deux moments d'affirmation et de négation par transcendance, le *recueil* de la triple voie en tant que mouvement, et de le situer, selon le dire d'Anselme, comme l'examen des *propriétés* de l'essence divine. Le mot 'propriété', visant cela dont il est question, invite à prendre les noms qui désignent ces propriétés dans une signification *directe*; le vocable 'recueil', en revanche, attire l'attention sur la signification *indirecte* des noms qui désignent Dieu en ses propriétés. D'un côté le regard s'exerce dans la direction du mouvement, VERS cela où il conduit; de l'autre le regard réfléchit sur le mouvement en tant que tel: nous nommons Dieu et Lui attribuons certaines propriétés ou perfections dans une nomination ou attribution qui est *nôtre*, chemin que *nous-même* parcourons. Déjà cette distance entre l'*actus exercitus* et l'*actus signatus* est une indication précieuse, car elle rejoint la question posée devant le Nom et le chapitre 5 du *Proslogion* où le Nom, à signification indirecte, fait reconnaître *summum omnium* et les autres perfections, dont la signification est directe.

Voyons comment le Prieur du Bec formule son interrogation: 'quid possit aut non possit dici de illa (summa essentia) substantialiter'. Ce titre est un peu éclairé par les premières phrases:

> Iam non immertio valde moveor quam studiose possum inquirere, quid omnium quae de aliquo dici possunt, huic tam admirabili naturae queat convenire substantialiter. Quamquam enim mirer, si possit in nominibus vel verbis quae aptamus rebus factis de nihilo reperiri, quod digne dicatur de creatrice universorum substantia: tentandum tamen est, ad quid hanc indagationem ratio perducet.[23]

> Me voici maintenant mû avec force, non sans raison, à chercher aussi studieusement que possible, parmi tout ce qu'il est possible de dire de quelque chose, ce qui peut convenir substantiellement à une si admirable nature. Je m'étonnerais en effet qu'il pût se trouver, parmi les noms ou verbes que nous adaptons aux choses faites de rien, quelque chose qui se dise dignement de la substance créatrice de l'univers; néanmoins il me faut essayer de voir vers quoi la raison conduira cette recherche.

La question suppose ce que les deux chapitres précédents ont rappelé de la triple voie: la création comme *alliance* de Dieu et de son oeuvre: 'eadem (summa essentia) est, quae in omnibus est et per omnia, et ex qua et per quam et in qua omnia'.[24] Etant accordé,[25] que Dieu porte et domine, enclôt et pénètre tous les étants, qui inversement renvoient à leur Créateur comme à Celui dont ils ne peuvent s'absenter, les noms et perfections attribués à Dieu ne peuvent appartenir qu'à l'ensemble des noms et perfections que l'homme attribue à telles ou telles choses 'faites de rien'. Ce *transfert*, ou *métaphore* si l'on préfère, est-il *possible*? Déjà naît l'idée de possibilité qui appartient au Nom et le distingue des autres, mais de quelle possibilité s'agit-il? Anselme se demande-t-il si un langage *sur* Dieu est possible? Nullement, car pareille question implique la volonté de remonter en-deçà de la Révélation et de cette alliance de création qui précède radicalement toute interrogation de l'homme. Certes il est concevable, à l'intérieur de la foi qui accueille l'alliance, de chercher ce que signifie cette possibilité donnée à l'homme et à quelle indentité inouïe de Dieu et de sa Révélation elle renvoie. Pareille identité, non dialectique, correspond au refus de toute séparation entre *Deus absconditus* et *Deus revelatus*, explicite la manière dont l'Eglise a, dès les premiers siècles, rejeté toute forme de modalisme. Mais Anselme ne questionne pas ainsi, du moins immédiatement; il relie simplement la notion de possibilité à une distinction classique depuis Augustin, celle des noms *substantiels* et des noms *relatifs*.

Qu'appelle-t-il substance et relation? Il ne veut pas, précisons-le, déduire a priori les diverses classes de noms divins, mais seulement classer ces noms qu'emploient les saintes Ecritures et la liturgie de l'Eglise. Car il n'est pas équivalent de nommer Dieu 'saint' ou 'Seigneur'. Le premier nom ne dit rien d'un quelconque rapport de Dieu à nous, la sainteté Le définissant en lui-même, tandis que le second implique un tel rapport. Il n'y a pas plus de Seigneur sans serviteur que de serviteur sans Seigneur. Substance et relation appartiennent à la table des catégories d'Aristote, comme la première et la dernière des dix modes du *dire* attribuant un prédicat à un sujet. Dans le cas des 'choses faites de rien', ces modes de la parole, ou prédicaments, renvoient de manière adéquate, aux modes d'**être** des choses, la diffraction *noétique* de la parole humaine répondant alors à la diffraction *ontique* des étants créés. S'il s'agit de Dieu, en qui n'existe pas cette faille intérieure qui définit la créature, semblable correspondance, adéquate, n'est plus possible. Peut-il y avoir cependant passage, même inadéquat, entre le *est* noétique de nos paroles sur et à Dieu et le *est* ontique de son être même? Anselme s'en étonne d'une manière que ne respecte pas cette position du problème comme chemin du noétique à l'ontique. Il dit: peut-il se trouver, parmi les noms que nous transférons à Dieu, certains qui Le désignent vraiment dans sa substance, abstraction faite de toute relation aux créatures? Il y a passage du noétique à l'ontique puisque la parole humaine entend désigner Dieu tel qu'Il est, mais ce passage est entendu comme une sortie hors de la relation vers la substance, possibilité d'absoudre Dieu de la relation en une parole qui implique toujours cette relation.

Lorsque nous nommons Dieu saint, juste, véridique, nous employons des mots qui, comme tels, n'impliquent pas une relation de Dieu à nous, mais, dans le même temps, impliquons, par le fait que *nous-mêmes* parlons, cette communication de la sainteté, justice et vérité de Dieu par laquelle nous sommes et dont nous avons quelque expérience. Nommerions-nous Dieu bon s'Il ne l'était pour nous? Rejoindrions-nous *Dieu* communiqué s'Il n'était pas Dieu *communiqué?* Notre chemin vers Dieu *adhère* à notre nomination de Dieu, nous parlons de et à Lui en effectuant un saut de désir sur le tremplin des étants: ce saut outrepasse-t-il la communication de Dieu qui le rend possible pour se diriger vers Dieu *même* qui se communique; outrepasse-t-il ce que nous connaissons de Dieu, et le chemin que nous faisons, pour en absoudre Dieu; outrepasse-t-il cette sphère du même, où l'homme se retrouve en retrouvant ses images, pour reconnaître l'altérité autrement qu'autre de Dieu en tant que Dieu? Peut-il y avoir des noms substantiels — absolus, absouts de la relation — et pas seulement des noms relatifs? Dans la mesure où l'interrogation sur la possibilité suppose la Révélation de Dieu comme le terrain de fait sur lequel elle est possible, ces questions reviennent à considérer l'*outrepassement* qui constitue l'originalité du *Proslogion.* Reste à montrer que l'équivalence est conforme aux textes.

V

Le corps du chapitre 15 est marqué par une constante oscillation du regard, indice d'une recherche qui n'a pas tout à fait abouti. Tantôt Anselme interroge sur le statut des noms relatifs, tantôt il revient sur le problème des noms substantiels, ouvre des pistes et aperçus qu'il ne développe pas. L'important, malgré tout, est qu'après la formulation de la question, il se penche sur les relatifs, précisément sur l'expression *summum omnium* qu'il identifie à *majus omnibus.* Première affirmation donc: *majus omnibus* dont la signification est *directe,* ne désigne pas la substance de Dieu parce que nom relatif:

> De relativis quidem nulli dubium, quia nullum eorum substantiale est illi de quo relative dicitur. Quare si quid de summa natura dicitur relative, non est ejus significativum substantiae. Unde hoc ipsum quod summa omnium sive major omnibus quae ab illa facta sunt, seu aliud aliquid similiter relative dici potest: manifestum est quoniam non ejus naturalem designat essentiam.[26]

Sans aucun doute, ce qui se dit de quelque chose relativement à autre chose n'est pas substantiel à ce dont il est dit relativement. C'est pourquoi si quelque chose est dit de la nature suréminente relativement à autre chose, il n'est pas significatif de sa substance. Aussi que l'on dise cette nature suréminente à ou plus grande que toutes les choses faites par elle, il est manifeste que cela ne désigne pas son essence naturelle.

Remarquons bien que les deux noms autour desquels nous questionnons, le Nom et celui que Gaunilon emploie à tort, sont tous les deux des relatifs. Le premier fait référence à la faculté humaine de penser, le second à l'ensemble des étants *réels*. En distinguant leurs significations comme *indirecte* et *directe,* nous posons ce couple à l'intérieur d'une nomination relative qui, par essence, est indirecte tandis que la nomination substantielle est directe. Sous cet angle, le Nom a une signification *doublement* indirecte, mais la nuance est de peu de poids puisque nous cherchons ce que veulent dire les modes direct et indirect quand ils distinguent les deux noms en cause; ce qu'ils veulent dire, vers quoi ils conduisent. Remarquons encore qu'Anselme ne choisit pas n'importe quel relatif mais justement *summum* qui exprime le moment de négation par transcendance.

Les phrases suivantes concernent le mouvement intérieur de *summum* entendu comme comparatif: *majus.* Elles déploient un admirable raisonnement, propre à convaincre de sottise quiconque estime la question des relatifs règlée dès qu'ils sont reconnus ne pas désigner l'essence:

> Si nulla earum rerum umquam esset, quarum relatione summa et major dicitur, ipsa nec summa nec major intelligeretur: nec tamen idcirco minus bona esset aut essentialis suae magnitudinis in aliquo detrimentum pateretur. Quod ex eo manifeste cognoscitur, quoniam ipsa quidquid boni vel magni est, non est per aliud quam per seipsam. Si igitur *summa* natura sic potest intelligi *non summa,* ut tamen nequaquam sit major aut minor quam cum intelligitur summa omnium: manifestum est quia 'summum' non simpliciter significat illam essentiam quae omnimodo major et melior est quam quidquid non est quod ipsa.[27]

> S'il n'était aucune de ces choses faites par elle, en relation auxquelles elle est dite suréminente et plus grande, elle ne serait pas reconnue suréminente et plus grande; cependant elle n'en serait pas moins bonne, ni n'en souffrirait aucun détriment en sa grandeur essentielle. Cela se reconnaît manifestement du fait qu'elle n'est pas par autre chose que par elle-même ce qu'elle est de bien ou de grand. Si donc la nature suréminente peut être ainsi reconnue non-suréminente, sans qu'elle soit plus grande ou moindre que lorsqu'elle est reconnue suréminente à toutes choses, il est manifeste que 'suréminent' ne signifie pas, simplement parlant, cette essence qui est de toute manière plus grande et meilleure que tout ce qui n'est pas ce qu'elle est.

Si n'était aucune créature! Les créatures qui présentement sont ne peuvent pas ne pas être *reconnues étant*; cependant, par cet étonnant privilège qu'a l'homme de penser et de réfléchir sur sa pensée, elles peuvent être *pensées n'étant pas.* L'hypothèse de ce non-être est possible, que le chapitre 3 du *Proslogion* interdira dès qu'il s'agit de Dieu.[28] Nul ne peut penser − *cogitare* − qu'Il n'est pas mais tout homme peut penser le temps où il n'était pas, et le fait nécessairement dès qu'il évoque la jeunesse de ses propres parents ou imagine la vie des temps passés. L'abstraction qui permet la pensée et donne naissance aux concepts et noms est la possibilité de s'abstraire soi-même, de se mettre hors jeu en se dirigeant vers les choses.

Où conduit l'hypothèse irréelle de l'inexistence des étants? A l'absence d'un des deux termes nécessaires pour qu'il y ait la relation d'ordre: 'plus grand que', à la négation de l'attribution de cette relation à Dieu. Il est plus grand que tous les étants et peut être pensé non-plus grand! Cette pensée qu'Anselme appelle encore, et à tort, reconnaissance (*intelligere*) n'entraîne pourtant ni augmentation ni diminution dans l'être de Dieu. Dieu est Dieu, sans jamais faire nombre avec son oeuvre, hors de l'ensemble des étants, par-delà le tout. Dans la langue du *Monologion*, pareille confession de la totale gratuité de Dieu dans l'oeuvre de son alliance s'exprime par l'utilisation de l'autre nom découvert au terme de la triple voie: Dieu est en même temps *bonum summum* et *bonum per se*, les deux notions d'origine et de transcendance allant de pair comme les deux formes complémentaires du moment de négation par transcendance. Si Dieu est *par soi*, si ces deux mots ont la fonction négative d'écarter que Dieu soit *par autre chose*, la présence ou l'absence des étants n'entraînent aucun changement de son être. Il est qui et ce qu'Il est[29] indépendamment et antérieurement à tout; Il est aussi bien suréminent que non-suréminent. Bref, l'équivalence du nom et de sa négation prouve nécessairement le caractère non-substantiel du nom.

Il y a plus. Le nom *summum*, dans son équivalence à *majus*, n'est pas n'importe quel relatif puisqu'il porte la négation par transcendance. Dire que Dieu est plus grand que *tout* est L'exclure de l'ensemble des étants (négation) non à cause d'un défaut mais d'un surexcès d'être (transcendance). Aussi, comme *summum* et *per se* sont indissociables, le mouvement qui mène à l'indifférence de *summum* et *non summum* peut être entendu comme un redoublement de la négation. Négation et négation de la négation s'égalisent. N'est-ce point cela que nous cherchions en demandant s'il est possible d'outrepasser la relation impliquée par toute nomination de Dieu, de passer outre dans la relation même? L'auto-négation de la négation n'est-elle pas l'auto-outrepassement de la relation? Une chose est étrange: aussitôt après avoir conclu que *summum* ne désigne pas l'essence divine, Anselme ajoute que celle-ci est de

toute manière plus grande que tout. Comment entendre cette
nécessité d'un nom qui ne désigne pas vraiment Dieu? Risquons
cette interprétation: ce relatif est nécessaire et nie, exactement
comme *per se*,[30] sa propre position, ou objectivation en Dieu. Il en
est comme pour l'expression scripturaire: 'Notre Père qui es aux
cieux' où le ciel n'est pas la demeure de Dieu, au sens physique et
local, mais l'indication *symbolique* d'un mouvement à effectuer
VERS Lui. Le *pur* mouvement VERS exclut si bien toute localisation
que l'Ecriture l'exprime parfois sous une forme *redoublée*: 'Gloire à
Dieu *au plus haut des cieux*'.[31] Or pareil redoublement linguistique
correspond très précisément à la lettre de *summum* qui est, en
langue latine, le *super*-latif de *super*.

Cette constatation ruine-t-elle l'équivalence posée entre
summum et *majus*? Comme *majus* est un *simple* comparatif, la
différence des vocables est patente. Pourtant *majus*, relation
d'ordre, n'est jamais employé seul; Anselme écrit: *majus omnibus*,
expression composée qui est vraiment équivalente à *summum
omnium quae sunt*. Aussitôt, en effet, que nous disons Dieu plus
grand que tout, posant dans l'exériorité du mot prononcé ou écrit le
moment de négation, nous situons Dieu dans le tout des étants hors
et au-delà duquel Il est. Parce qu'il n'est point de concept sans
image, nous faisons nécessairement de la négation par transcendance
une affirmation, ou position appartenant à cela qui doit être nié.
Denys le remarquait:

> Toute affirmation reste en-deçà de la Cause unique et
> parfaite de toutes choses; toute négation demeure en-deçà
> de la transcendance de Celui qui est, simplement, dépouillé
> de tout et qui se situe au-delà de tout.[32]

Autrement dit, le propre de la négation, négation par transcendance
et non simple négation logique, est d'être négation DE, de s'exercer
sur toute affirmation, y compris elle-même en tant que nous ne
pouvons jamais *exprimer* la pure fonction négative autrement que
sous mode d'affirmation. Dès que nous disons Dieu plus grand que
tout, la dynamique inclue dans 'plus grand' nous impose de nier
cette localisation de 'plus grand' qui fait de Dieu un étant dans le
tout des étants, l'Etre suprême. Ainsi s'articulent, semble-t-il les
deux moments d'affirmation et de négation, ainsi se découvre la
signification du huitième paragraphe de la Réponse à Gaunilon où
s'exposait le mouvement donnant sens au Nom. Nous appelons
moment de *suréminence* l'intelligence de cette articulation ou,
identiquement, de cette pure fonction de mouvement que possède la
négation par transcendance s'exerçant sur toute *affirmation*. Nous
notons également que cette intelligence n'est pas inscrite *comme
telle* dans la lettre de *majus omnibus*. Elle l'est en *summum*, à
condition de lui garder son redoublement et de le traduire par suréminent, non par suprême, mais cette condition indique que ce nom

revient toujours, par une sorte de pesanteur, à son équivalence avec *majus.* Le moment de la suréminence, n'ayant pas d'autre contenu qu'*herméneutique*, ne peut s'exprimer en un seul vocable ou *une seule* relation d'ordre. Le simple comparatif ne suffit pas.

VI

Apparemment le mouvement d'auto-négation et outrepassement de la négation par transcendance, parallèle, que celle-ci soit exprimée par *summum* (chapitre 15) ou par *per se* (chapitre 6), demeure sans suite immédiate. Une transition confuse dit:

> Quidquid est praeter relativa, aut tale est, ut ipsum omnino melius sit quam non-ipsum, aut tale ut non-ipsum in aliquo melius sit quam ipsum. 'Ipsum' autem et 'non-ipsum' non aliud hic intelligo quam verum, non-verum; corpus, non-corpus; et his similia.[33]

> Tous les attributs autres que relatifs sont tels que l'attribut X est en tout point meilleur que l'attribut non-X, ou que sur certain point non-X est meilleur que X. Par X et non-X, je n'entends rien autre que vrai et non-vrai, corps et non-corps, et autres choses semblables.

Bien que ces phrases se retrouvent presque telles quelles au chapitre 5 du *Proslogion*, point de départ possible pour l'examen de la signification doublement indirecte du Nom, l'énigme reste grande. Pourquoi ce langage si formel, cette utilisation de la relation d'ordre entre un attribut X et sa négation? En quels cas la relation joue-t-elle comme priorité de l'affirmation sur la négation, en quels cas s'établit-elle en sens contraire? Mais il suffit de lire:

> Melius quidem est *omnino* aliquid quam non-ipsum, ut sapiens quam non-ipsum sapiens, id est: melius est sapiens quam non-sapiens . . . Melius autem est *in aliquo* non-ipsum quam ipsum, ut non-aurum quam aurum. Nam melius est homini esse non-aurum quam aurum, quamvis forsitan alicui melius esset aurum esse quam non-aurum, ut plumbum.[34]

> En vérité quelque chose est en tout point meilleur que non-quelque chose: sage que non-sage, car le sage est meilleur que le non-sage . . . Meilleur est sur certain point non-X que X: le non-or que l'or. En effet il est meilleur pour l'homme d'être non-or qu'or, bien que peut-être pour certaine chose comme le plomb, ce soit meilleur d'être or que non-or.

Les exemples sont clairs: dans le premier cas, il s'agit des *perfections* sous forme adjectivée, lesquelles sont de toute manière meilleures que leurs contraires; dans le second se discerne la hiérarchie des étants, ou des *degrés d'être*: en tant qu'il n'est pas le degré inférieur, il est en un certain sens possible de parcourir l'échelle, le degré supérieur est meilleur. Plus profonde que cette distinction est cependant la relation d'ordre — *majus* — étudiée cette fois dans son *fonctionnement* concret sur les perfections et degrés d'être trouvés dans l'ensemble des étants. Là est sans doute le secret du texte. Anselme, qui recherche ce qu'il est possible de *transférer* des étants créés à Dieu créateur, s'est arrêté, sans conclure, sur l'étonnante équivalence, dès qu'il s'agit de Dieu, entre *summum* et *non-summum*. Un nom égal à sa négation, X égal à non-X: comment situer cette équation sans correspondant dans l'ordre des étants? comment entendre qu'un relatif soit en même temps nécessaire et nié, qu'il *se* pose et *se* nie?

> Patet ex eo quod summa natura sic intelligi potest non-summa, ut nec summum omnino melius sit quam non-summum, nec non-summum alicui melius quam summum: multa relativa esse, quae nequaquam hac contineantur divisione.[35]

> Il appert de ce que la nature suréminente puisse être reconnue non-suréminente de telle sorte que ni le suréminent soit en tout point meilleur que le non-suréminent, ni le non-suréminent sur certain point meilleur que le suréminent, qu'il existe beaucoup de relatifs qui ne sont jamais contenus dans la division précédente.

Où situer le 'cas' unique que nous avons interprété, en anticipant, comme mouvement d'outrepassement et de redoublement de la négation par transcendance?

En ce point précis surgit le trait génial qui engendre le chapitre 5 du *Proslogion* et porte, plus réellement que les influences littéraires, l'acte de naissance du Nom. Après une phrase embarrassée et un rappel, Anselme conclut sans préparation aucune:

> Sicut nefas est putare quod substantia supremae naturae sit aliquid, *quo melius sit aliquomodo non ipsum*, sic necesse est ut sit quidquid omnino melius est quam non-ipsum. Illa enim sola est *qua penitus nihil est melius*, et quae melior est omnibus quae non sunt quod ipsa est.[36]

> De même qu'il est impie de penser que la substance de la nature suprême soit un X dont le non-X lui soit parfois meilleur, de même il est nécessaire qu'elle soit tout X en tout point meilleur que non-X. Elle est la seule en regard de laquelle absolument rien n'est meilleur, elle est meilleure que toutes les choses qui ne sont pas ce qu'elle est.

A la différence près de la référence au *pouvoir* de penser, les deux phrases soulignées comportent le comparatif, la négation, l'inversion

et le subjonctif qui distinguent le Nom de tous les autres noms
voisins. Mieux, l'ordre des formulations inversés (en ce sens indirect)
et direct est exactement celui du chapitre 5 du *Proslogion* où le
Nom vient en premier, qui permet de *reconnaître* les divers noms
directs qui disent Dieu créateur, juste, heureux . . . Reconnaître ce
qui était déjà connu, c'est ainsi que Karl Barth caractérise
l'intelligence de la foi selon S. Anselme, c'est aussi donner au Nom
qui permet cette reconnaissance *une fonction herméneutique*: opérer
le mouvement de la connaissance à la reconnaissance. Ce n'était pas
pour rien qu'Anselme avait développé les deux possibilités de
fonctionnement de la relation d'ordre: entendre l'équivalence entre
summum et *non-summum* comme mouvement d'outrepassement et de
redoublement négatif est comprendre ce moment de suréminence
comme la fonction herméneutique qui règle le singulier mouvement
d'outrepassement de soi que le désir accomplit lorsqu'il se porte
VERS Dieu, désirable pour lui-même et non pour autre chose. Le
relatif *summum* est reconnu opérateur du mouvement, cela qui permet de faire un *tri* entre les divers attributs possibles pour Dieu,
d'écarter les uns et rejeter les autres:

> Non est igitur corpus vel aliquid eorum, quae corporei sensus
> discernunt. Quippe his omnibus melius est aliquid, quod non
> est quod ipsa sunt. Mens enim rationalis, quae nullo corporeo
> sensu quid vel qualis vel quanta sit percipitur: quanto minor
> esset, si esset aliquid eorum quae corporeis sensibus
> subjacent, tanto major est quam quodlibet eorum.[37]

> C'est pourquoi elle n'est ni un corps ni rien de ce que les
> sens corporels discernent. Car pour toutes ces choses il y a
> meilleur, à savoir ce qui n'est pas ce qu'elles sont, l'esprit
> raisonnable qui n'est perçu par aucun sens corporel ni dans
> sa quiddité, ni dans sa qualité, ni dans sa quantité, et qui
> serait d'autant moindre s'il était de ces choses qui tombent
> sous les sens corporels, qu'il est plus grand que n'importe
> laquelle.

Qu'est cette première conclusion sinon l'interdiction d'attribuer et
de transférer à Dieu des noms qui supposeraient quelque chose de
plus grand que lui? Interdiction des idoles, de confondre Dieu Vivant
avec quoi que ce soit de créé, de penser plus grand: le Nom est là
dans sa signification *indirecte, herméneutique*. Il n'est pas dégagé
comme tel mais implicite, non pas *désigné* mais *exercé* à la manière
de *Proslogion*, chapitre 5. Une chose est certaine: c'est ainsi, et non
autrement, qu'Anselme donne réponse, dans sa seconde conclusion, à
la question qu'il posait:

> Quare necesse est eam esse viventem, sapientem, potentem
> et omnipotentem, veram, justam, beatam, aeternam et quid-
> quid similiter absolute melius est quam non-ipsum. Quid ergo

quaeratur amplius quid summa illa sit natura, si manifestum
est quid omnium sit aut quid non sit?[38]

Ainsi est-elle nécessairement vivante, sage, puissante et
toute-puissante, vraie, juste, heureuse, éternelle et tout X
qui est, semblablement et absolument meilleur que non-X.
Que chercher alors de plus au sujet de ce qu'est la nature
suréminente, si ce qu'elle est ou n'est pas par rapport à
tout est manifeste?

Il faut attendre les chapitres suivants, 16 et 17, pour reconnaître
que l'ensemble de ces attributs ne désigne pas la qualité ou la
quantité, mais la quiddité de Dieu, ce qu'Il est vraiment et sub-
stantiellement. Ce résultat n'est pas acquis par la recherche de
quelque adéquation entre ces noms et le sujet dont ils sont
prédiqués mais par le déploiement et l'explicitation de la fonction
herméneutique de *summum*. Comment une nomination substantielle
est-elle possible au sens, défini plus haut, selon lequel la possibilité
se montre dans le parcours du mouvement? Parce que le redoublement et outrepassement de *summum* constitue une opération qui
s'exerce sur les noms affirmatifs possibles. En se niant et
outrepassant, *summum* fait sortir Dieu de toute relation à nous,
enracine, en les outrepassant VERS Dieu, tous les noms positifs sur
sa *simplicité* qui se communique en suscitant ce mouvement VERS.
Dieu est au-delà de tout au-delà, cela signifie: Lui seul est bon,
juste, vrai, lumière sans aucun mélange de ténèbres,[39] Oui sans
nulle repentance, par-delà tout oui et tout non d'homme.[40] Le
relatif *summum*, expression de la négation par transcendance,
s'efface ainsi devant l'affirmation qui désigne et signifie Dieu
directement, sans qu'il soit possible de l'omettre avant chacun des
noms substantiels. Dieu n'est pas bon sans plus, Il est *suréminement*
bon et *suréminente* bonté. 'Nul n'est bon que Dieu *seul*'.[41] Bref, il
n'est point de parole sur et à Dieu qui ne comporte deux moments:
la négation qui s'exerce sur l'affirmation et n'a d'autre fonction
qu'*herméneutique* et *indirecte*, l'affirmation devant laquelle s'efface
la négation en s'outrepassant et outrepassant toute affirmation
humaine, image et concept, VERS Celui qui est simplement, 'au-delà
de toute position, soit affirmative, soit négative'.[42]

Comment ne pas conclure, provisoirement, à la justesse du
chemin proposé dans cette étude? En conduisant sa question selon le
couple substance/relation, Anselme a clairement articulé le rapport
entre 'perfections' et 'noms', significations directe et indirecte. Ce
faisant, il a réellement déployé le mouvement de désir qui s'exerce
dans la triple voie VERS Dieu comme un mouvement supposant un
contenu — les noms substantiels et positifs — et une pure *forme*
réglant la signification de ces noms. Cette pure forme du
mouvement, son vecteur en quelque sorte, réside dans *summum*
d'abord identifié à *majus*. Et dire *summum* comme le vecteur

recueillant en lui-même tout l'élan du désir est identiquement formuler le Nom, ou du moins quatre de ses éléments, parmi lesquels *l'inversion formelle*. Il manque la référence à la pensée de l'homme, mais la présence de *l'inversion*, sans autre réalité linguistique que syntaxique, est présence de l'essentiel. La signification, indirecte, *herméneutique*, permet le tri des noms possibles en plaçant l'homme sous l'interdiction des idoles (dont on peut penser plus grand), en lui interdisant d'enfouir son désir en quoi que ce soit de créé.

VII

La présente étude serait achevée si le chemin parcouru n'entraînait trois questions, décisives pour la *vraie* intelligence du *Proslogion* et inquiètes de leur unité profonde. Pour Anselme, il est impossible de parler de et à Dieu sans que le mouvement de désir, qui met l'homme en chemin au-delà de tout étant, *n'adhère* à la parole qu'il articule sur et à Dieu. Cette adhérence du chemin au terme, de la relation à la substance, du mode d'accès à la Chose, tient au moment de négation par transcendance qui fait du chemin un outre-passement de soi VERS la suréminente simplicité de Dieu. *Summum* renvoie, par l'outrepassement de tout contenu représentatif, les noms substantiels à Dieu qui suscite ce mouvement; *summum* est la forme qui s'exerce sur le contenu et ainsi *recueille*, comme son vecteur et sa pure fonction herméneutique, le chemin de l'homme VERS Dieu. Or, dire un tel recueil, expliciter *summum* comme le redoublement négatif qui interdit toute confusion de Dieu Vivant avec quelque étant que ce soit, est quitter l'équivalence de *summum* et de *majus*, que Gaunilon considère aller de soi. Dégager le recueil est changer *summum* en une propostion complexe qui est déjà le Nom, son ébauche établie en règle herméneutique, première par rapport à *majus omnibus*:

> Illa enim sola est qua penitus nihil est melius, et quae melior est omnibus quae non sunt quod ipsa est.[43]

> Elle est la seule en regard de laquelle absolument rien n'est meilleur, elle est meilleure que toutes les choses qui ne sont pas ce qu'elle est.

Pourquoi la rupture de l'équivalence est-elle cette priorité du Nom, de son inversion formelle sur sa transcription directe? Pourquoi l'inversion qui porte la fonction herméneutique et la signification doublement indirecte précède-t-elle un nom à signification directe, simplement indirecte parce que relative à l'ensemble des étants? S'il y a *saut* entre les problématiques du *Monologion* et du *Proslogion*, si la découverte du chapitre 15 de la première oeuvre est embryon-naire parce qu'elle ne se constitue pas en principe architectonique de discours, pourquoi le saut que représente le Nom par rapport à *majus omnibus* implique-t-il la priorité noétique du Nom, seul capable de faire reconnaître et l'être et l'essence de Dieu?

A cette première interrogation s'ajoute une deuxième. Que l'expression *summum omnium quae sunt* devienne le Nom en recueillant le redoublement et outrepassement de la négation, que ce recueil fasse du moment de suréminence une compréhension herméneutique, cela explique la suffisance du Nom qui s'est offert, l'ayant prévenue, à la recherche angoissée d'Anselme:

> Coepi mecum quaerere, si forte posset inveniri *unum argumentum,* quod nullo alio ad se probandum quam se solo indigeret, et solum ad astruendum, quia Deus vere est, et quia est summum bonum nullo alio indigens et quo omnia indigent ut sint et bene sint, et quaecumque de divina credimus substantia, sufficeret.[44]

> J'ai commencé, en discutant avec moi-même, à rechercher s'il ne pouvait par hasard se trouver un argument unique, qui n'eût besoin de rien autre que soi pour se prouver et suffirait pour montrer que Dieu est, qu'Il est le bien suréminent n'ayant besoin de rien dont toutes les autres choses ont besoin pour être, et être bien, et aussi tout ce que nous croyons de la substance divine.

La prétention paraît exorbitante, si démesurée que la tradition d'interprétation anselmienne n'a guère noté que le Nom y est doté de l'auto-suffisance de Dieu. Il se pose et prouve lui-même, pose et prouve 'tout ce que nous croyons de la substance divine'! Comment peut-il en être ainsi? Certes nous savons que le Nom contient le mouvement de l'homme vers Dieu, redoublement négatif et outre-passement dits sous la forme inversée de l'impossibilité de penser plus grand. Redoubler la négation est outrepasser toute affirmation, y compris la position de la négation sous le mode immédiat du 'plus grand' localisé, c'est-à-dire refuser l'idole qui place Dieu dans le tout des étants. Nous en déduisons que la forme d'argumentation par l'absurde, qui permet de reconnaître ce qui est déjà connu par la foi, est présente dans le Nom comme la nécessité d'exclure plus grand que Dieu: que l'argumentation est réellement *analytique,* non point au sens 'ontologique' qui appelle un passage du concept à l'existence, mais en tant que l'égalisation entre le principe et la forme de l'argumentation fait de celle-ci le déploiement de la *vis significationis* du Nom, le dégagement du pur mouvement vers l'Autre, autrement qu'autre, hors du péché d'idolâtrie. L'idolâtrie est volonté de saisir, de figer l'affirmation et de localiser la négation. Nous comprenons et cependant ne voyons pas comment s'articule la suffisance du Nom comme suffisance de Dieu lui-même.

Troisième et dernière question qui succède logiquement à la précédente: si le Nom permet de *reconnaître,* en excluant toute tentation de la créature de se placer au-dessus de Dieu et de penser plus grand que Lui, ce que la foi *connaît* déjà, quel est le lien nécessaire entre l'acte de foi présupposé et l'argumentation en tant que passage de la connaissance à la reconnaissance? Ici réside l'insuffisance de la lecture barthienne. Commentant la finale du chapitre 2 du *Proslogion*, le théologien réformé écrit:

> Là où le nom de Dieu est annoncé, compris et entendu, là Dieu existe dans l'intelligence de celui qui entend; mais précisément à cause de cela, il n'existe pas seulement dans l'intelligence de celui qui entend, parce qu'un Dieu qui n'existerait que de cette façon se trouverait dans une contradiction intolérable avec son propre nom révélé et cru, parce qu'il serait appelé 'Dieu' et ne le serait pas . . . *Ce qui a été démontré, c'est seulement la négation.* La proposition positive relative à l'existence authentique, non seulement intramentale mais aussi extramentale de Dieu . . . ne découle pas de la preuve, n'en est pas déduite en aucune façon; elle n'est démontrée par la preuve que dans la mesure où la proposition opposée, relative à l'existence purement intramentale de Dieu, est démontrée absurde.[45]

Cette extériorité de la preuve et de la foi est confirmée par l'interprétation ultérieure de la dernière phrase du chapitre 4:

> La vérité a parlé, non point l'homme voulant croire. L'homme pourrait toujours ne pas vouloir croire. L'homme pourrait toujours être un insensé. Nous l'avons entendu: s'il ne l'est pas, c'est par l'effet de la grâce. Mais même s'il l'était: 'si je ne voulais pas croire que tu existes', la vérité a parlé; irréfutable, inoubliable; de sorte qu'il est interdit à l'homme — et, de ce fait, impossible — de ne pas la reconnaître.[46]

S'il y a suffisance du Nom, pareille juxtaposition est impossible, qui renouvelle, sans la résoudre, l'éternelle discussion sur le rationalisme ou le fidéisme d'Anselme. Puisque cette discussion n'a plus cours dès qu'est perçue la correspondance entre le Nom et la forme d'argumentation par l'absurde, comment cette correspondance est-elle liée à l'impossibilité de disjoindre acte de foi et démarche de raison? Comment le passage de la connaissance à la reconnaissance, exclusion de l'idolâtrie, appartient-il nécessairement à la foi?

Ces trois questions, disions-nous, sont en quête de leur unité. Leur solution ne se déduit pas logiquement mais s'impose, à qui voit par les yeux de la foi, comme cela qui attirait et appelait, depuis le commencement, la recherche. En effet, si nous lisons ce que dit l'Ecriture de la Parole de Dieu:

> Vivante est la parole de Dieu, efficace et plus incisive qu'aucun glaive à deux tranchants, elle pénètre jusqu'au

point de division de l'âme et de l'esprit, des articulations et
des moelles, elle peut juger les sentiments et les pensées du
coeur;[47]

Si nous nous rappelons que la Parole coïncide avec Jésus de Nazareth, que cette coïncidence éclate dans l'événement de Pâques où
rayonne la victoire du Crucifié, il est clair que le Oui de Dieu aux
hommes, Oui par-delà toute alternance de oui et de non, se communique comme la condamnation de toute idolâtrie ou violence
homicide. La Croix de Jésus où luit l'Amour qui va 'jusqu'au bout'[48]
— 'Nul n'a plus grand amour que de donner sa vie pour ses amis'[49]
— manifeste la vanité et le vide des idoles qui écrasent l'homme.
Elle sauve en condamnant:

> Il a supprimé notre dette en la clouant à la croix. Il a
> dépouillé les Principautés et les Puissances et les a données
> en spectacle à la face du monde, en les traînant dans son
> cortège triomphal.[50]

Et un mot, elle est, en tant que croix glorieuse *de* Jésus, Cela dont
plus grand ne puisse être pensé:

> L'homme qui, dans la foi, saisit pour ce qu'elle est l'oeuvre
> révélatrice de Dieu dans le Christ, doit être capable de voir
> ici quelque chose *quo majus cogitari nequit*, la manifestation
> d'un amour divin absolu, laissant évidemment en arrière tout
> ce que l'homme peut inventer de plus sublime comme révé-
> lation . . . La figure que Dieu propose, ce jeu entre sa
> propre liberté et la liberté de sa créature . . . a en elle-
> même l'évidence d'un *summum*. Non, il n'est pas possible de
> concevoir une chose plus grande. Elle est pourtant compré-
> hensible . . . Mais ce qui est ainsi représenté est reconnu
> indépassable, 'incompréhensible' et se trouve être — en
> corrigeant la première formule — *quiddam majus quam
> cogitari possit*.[51]

Sous cette lumière, que nul ne peut se donner, les trois difficultés
reçoivent leur point de convergence. Non pas une solution logique
qui supprimerait l'étonnement et la louange, mais cela qui outre-
passe toute démarche logique, l'attirant plus loin qu'elle-même, et
qui, donnant lumière, appelle la quête, toujours neuve, de la foi. Si
vraiment, le Nom *renvoie* au mystère pascal de Jésus, parle de
Jésus parce qu'il parle de Dieu en parlant de l'homme, le rejet de
l'idolâtrie n'est plus extérieur à la foi, le Nom possède vraiment la
suffisance de Dieu et la priorité du Nom sur ses transcriptions
directes — *majus omnibus* aussi bien que *quiddam majus quam
cogitari possit* — devient l'écoute du Prologue de Jean: 'Dieu,
personne ne l'a jamais vu, le Fils unique qui est, tourné vers le sein
du Père, lui, l'a fait connaître'.[52] Le dernier verbe — *exègèsato* —
nomme ici la fonction *herméneutique* du chemin de Jésus pour toute
connaissance de Dieu. Et de l'homme!

En mettant une majuscule, en appelant 'Nom au-dessus de tout nom'[53] la proposition qui sert d'*unum argumentum* au *Proslogion,* en donnant ce Nom à Jésus, Christ et Fils de Dieu, nous allons au-delà de la lettre d'Anselme et commençons de penser l'impensé christologique de son oeuvre. De plus, bien que le chemin proposé contienne ce débordement, nous ouvrons la possibilité de mettre en place, de manière unitaire, certains éléments du *Proslogion* que la tradition de lecture a laissés dans l'ombre. Pourquoi les nombreuses prières font-elles tant d'allusions au péché? Pourquoi Anselme interroge-t-il sur la concordance des attributs de justice et de miséricorde, dont l'unité sera l'objet central du *Cur Deus homo?* Pourquoi accorde-t-il de l'importance au déploiement de la simplicité divine en multiplicité d'attributs? Pourquoi enfin n'addresse-t-il sa prière qu'à Dieu Père, non à la Trinité comme l'exigerait la doctrine, classique, du *Monologion?* Ces questions sont intelligibles dans la perspective d'un passage du *Proslogion* au *Cur Deus homo,* d'un déplacement constant vers le mystère de Jésus-Christ. Elles désignent un travail que l'auteur de ces pages espère, Dieu aidant, mener à bonne fin. Car il se pourrait qu'en attribuant le Nom à Jésus, nous recevions un moyen technique de renouveler le langage christologique de l'Eglise en faisant l'économie du vocabulaire 'piégé' des deux natures. Jésus de Nazareth est le vrai Fils de Dieu en tant qu'il est, nous le croyons, *id quo nihil majus cogitari possit.*

NOTES

1. *Proslogion,* Prooemium, *Ans.Op.Om.,* I, 93.

2. *Responsio,* 10, *Ans.Op.Om.,* I, 138-9.

3. *Proslogion,* 2, *Ans.Op.Om.,* I, 101.

4. Thomas d'Aquin, *Summa Theologica,* Ia, q.2, a.1, obj. 2.

5. Karl Barth, *La Preuve de l'existence de Dieu,* traduit de l'allemand (Neuchâtel, 1958), pp. 66-7.

6. Exode 20:3-4.

7. *Responsio,* 5, *Ans.Op.Om.,* I, 134.

8. *Proslogion,* 15, *Ans.Op.Om.,* I, 112.

9. Ibid.

10. *Proslogion,* 5, *Ans.Op.Om.,* I, 104.

11. *Proslogion,* 15, *Ans.Op.Om.,* I, 112.

12. *Proslogion,* Prooemium, *Ans.Op.Om.,* I, 93-4.

13. *Monologion*, 1, *Ans.Op.Om.*, I, 15.

14. *Monologion*, 12, *Ans.Op.Om.*, I, 26.

15. *Proslogion*, Prooemium, *Ans.Op.Om.*, I, 93.

16. *Responsio*, 8, *Ans.Op.Om.*, I, 137.

17. Ibid.

18. *Monologion*, 1, *Ans.Op.Om.*, I, 13-14.

19. *Cur Deus homo*, 2, 1, *Ans.Op.Om.*, II, 97.

20. *Monologion*, 1, *Ans.Op.Om.*, I, 14,

21. *Monologion*, 4, *Ans.Op.Om.*, 17-18.

22. I Corinthiens 13:12.

23. *Monologion*, 15, *Ans.Op.Om.*, I, 28.

24. *Monologion*, 14, *Ans.Op.Om.*, I, 27.

25. cf. Romains 11:36.

26. *Monologion*, 15, *Ans.Op.Om.*, I, 29.

27. Ibid.

28. cf. *Responsio*, 4, *Ans.Op.Om.*, I, 133-4.

29. Exode 3:14.

30. Voir *Monologion*, 6, *Ans.Op.Om.*, I, 18-20.

31. Luc 2:14.

32. Denys, *Théologie mystique*, 5, PG 3.1048B.

33. *Monologion*, 15, *Ans.Op.Om.*, I, 28.

34. Ibid., 28-9.

35. Ibid., 29.

36. Ibid.

37. Ibid.

38. Ibid.

39. I Jean 1:5.

40. II Corinthiens 1:20.

41. Luc 18:19.

42. Denys, *Théologie mystique*, 1.2, PG 3.1000B.

43. *Monologion*, 15, *Ans.Op.Om.*, I, 29.

44. *Proslogion*, Prooemium, *Ans.Op.Om.*, I, 93.

45. Barth, *La Preuve de l'existence de Dieu*, pp. 116-17.

46. Ibid., pp. 156-7.

47. Hébreux 4:12.

48. Jean 13:2.

49. Jean 5:13.

50. Colossiens 2:15.

51. Hans Urs von Balthasar, *La Foi du Christ* (Paris, 1968), pp. 106-7.

52. Jean 1:18.

53. Philippiens 2:9.

Inintelligible et impensable
(Anselme, *Liber Apologeticus*, IV)

Joseph Moreau

Dans son *Liber pro Insipiente*, écrit en réplique au *Proslogion* d'Anselme, Gaunilon prend la défense de l'Insensé, celui qui, selon l'Ecriture, a dit en son coeur: *Non est Deus*; mais il ne se rallie pas pour autant à sa thèse; il le défend seulement contre le reproche qui lui est fait par Anselme de ne pouvoir penser réellement ce qu'il dit.[1] Gaunilon n'en convient pas moins avec Anselme, non seulement que Dieu existe, mais que son existence est incluse dans sa définition, qu'il existe nécessairement.[2] Que reproche-t-il donc à Anselme? D'avoir voulu dans le *Proslogion* prouver l'existence de Dieu par un *raccourci*,[3] a partir d'une notion sommaire et confuse, celle du *quo majus cogitari nequit*. La preuve cherchée, estime Gaunilon, ne peut être obtenue qu'à partir d'une définition méthodiquement élaborée, conçue selon la vérité de la chose (*rei veritate*, . . . *secundum rem veram*);[4] à l'expression QMCN ne correspond pour lui qu'une signification confuse dans la pensée (*in cogitatione*), mais non un concept défini dans l'entendement (*in intellectu*).[5]

A cela Anselme réplique que l'expression QMCN est une véritable définition de Dieu, à laquelle correspond dans l'entendement un concept parfaitement déterminé, attendu qu'on déduit logiquement l'existence de Dieu (son existence nécessaire) et ses attributs infinis (immensité, éternité).[6] On peut toutefois observer que de tels prédicats transcendent toute détermination objective, qu'ils dépassent tout objet de représentation, et que le concept du QMCN n'est pas constitué de déterminations incluses dans l'*objet* pensé, mais qu'il implique une référence à l'activité du *sujet* pensant, à son pouvoir de penser: c'est le concept d'un object tel qu'un plus grand que lui (*quo majus*) ne peut (*nequit*) être pensé (*cogitari*). Il faut donc convenir que la notion du QMCN, si elle n'est pas, comme l'estime Gaunilon, confuse, n'équivaut pas cependant à une définition strictement objective, d'où les propriétés de l'objet se déduiraient analytiquement. La négation de ces prédicats transcendants (existence nécessaire, immensité, éternité) ne contredit pas aux déterminations objectives d'un concept, mais à l'exigence d'infini incluse dans sa visée; elle n'est pas une contradiction dans les termes, la ruine d'une définition posée, mais le refus d'une requête essentielle de la pensée; elle est en ce sens radicalement *impensable*. C'est ce qu'on peut exprimer en disant que le raisonnement d'Anselme dépasse la logique, entendue comme *analytique*; il relève de la *dialectique*, si par dialectique on entend, avec Kant, un usage transcendant de la logique, dans lequel celle-ci n'est pas seulement un *canon* pour l'entendement, une règle du jugement, mais un *organon* de la connaissance, un moyen d'étendre la connaissance, par l'usage du pur raisonnement, au-delà des déterminations objectives opérées par l'entendement dans le champ des phénomènes.[7]

C'est contre cet usage dialectique du raisonnement que s'insurge Gaunilon. Pour prouver l'existence de Dieu, pour établir que sa négation est fausse, il faut montrer qu'elle contredit une définition vraie, et qu'elle est par conséquent inintelligible, inconcevable pour l'entendement. Si au critère de l'*intelligible*, qui s'explique par l'analytique, on substitue le critère dialectique de l'*impensable*, son usage se révèle ambigu et conduit à la confusion. Appliquons, par exemple, ce critère au cas de ma propre existence: 'Penser que je ne suis pas, dans le temps que je sais très certainement que je suis, cela m'est-il possible? Si cela m'est possible, si la négation de ma propre existence est pensable, l'impensable ne sera plus la marque du faux. La négation de l'existence de Dieu, même si elle est impensable, ne sera pas pour autant fausse, attendu que de ma propre existence, dont je suis absolument certain, la négation n'est pas impensable. Si, au contraire, cela m'est possible, si je dois convenir que la négation de mon existence n'est impensable, l'impossibilité de penser qu'Il n'existe pas ne sera pas le privilège de l'existence de Dieu'.[8] Ce que veut montrer Gaunilon au moyen de ce dilemme, c'est que le raisonnement dialectique d'Anselme aboutirait à la confusion de l'existence nécessaire et de l'existence contingente. Si l'existence de Dieu est nécessaire, si sa négation est indubitalement fausse, c'est parce qu'elle n'est pas intelligible, parce qu'elle contredit une définition vraie. Mais un énoncé faux, *inintelligible*, n'est pas pour autant *impensable*; s'il l'était absolument, comment pourrait-il être jugé faux?[9]

A ces vues de Gaunilon, Anselme réplique qu'il est indispensable, au contraire, si l'on veut réserver le privilège de l'existence nécessaire, de maintenir que la négation en est non seulement *inintelligible*, mais absolument *impensable*. Faute d'utiliser ce critère, on ne réussit pas à sauver, comme le voudrait Gaunilon, l'opposition entre l'existence contingente, la mienne par exemple, et celle de l'Etre nécessaire. Si en effet, suivant l'adage invoqué par Gaunilon,[10] le faux n'est jamais intelligible (*falsa nequent intelligi*), il s'ensuit que toute assertion contraire à la vérité est, au regard de l'entendement, inconcevable; tout énoncé vrai apparaîtra donc comme nécessaire; un événement, fut-il contingent, s'il est affirmé avec vérité, sera par là-même nécessaire.[11] On aboutit de la sorte au nécessitarisme mégarique.[12] Pour éviter cette conséquence, il convient de maintenir avec Anselme la distinction de l'intelligible, et du pensable.[13] Un être contingent, si je sais certainement qu'il existe, je ne puis en même temps croire (*existimare*) qu'il n'existe pas; cela serait contradictoire, inintelligible; mais je puis supposer (*fingere*) qu'il n'existe pas; c'est à cause de cela précisément qu'il est dit contingent.[14] Dieu, au contraire, l'Etre nécessaire, il est impossible de supposer, de *feindre*, qu'il n'existe pas; sa négation n'est pas seulement *inintelligible*, inconcevable pour l'entendement; elle est absolument *impensable*.[15]

Cette réplique d'Anselme est-elle convaincante? Repose-t-elle sur une argumentation irréprochable? A supposer que le critère de l'intelligible, dans son usage exclusif, conduise à tenir tout énoncé vrai pour nécessaire, à éliminer le faux comme impossible, cela signifierait-il que toute proposition vraie est *analytique*, qu'il n'y a que des *vérités de raison* ou *vérités nécessaires*, au sens leibnizien du terme, c'est-à-dire dont la négation implique contradiction intrinsèque.[16] Proclamer avec les Mégariques que le vrai est immuable, qu'une vérité saisie par l'entendement ne saurait cesser d'être vraie,[17] cela n'exclut pas qu'il y ait des *vérités contingentes*, énonçant des événements *historiques*, dont la vérité ne peut être abolie, dont on ne saurait jamais nier qu'ils se soient produits, mais qui auraient pu ne pas se produire; leur négation, dorénavant impossible, n'avait rien en soi de contradictoire.[18] On a contesté, il est vrai, le caractère absolu de cette distinction entre vérités nécessaires et vérités contingentes; on a soutenu qu'elle était relative à notre ignorance: pour un sujet omniscient, la science parfaite, contrairement à l'avis d'Anselme, ne laisse aucune place à la fiction.[19] C'est parce que j'ignore l'enchaînement infini des causes que la succession des événements me paraît contingente; c'est par là qu'il m'est possible de feindre que certains d'entre eux ne soient pas arrivés ou qu'ils n'arrivent pas, alors qu'ils sont déterminés de toute éternité. Accordons encore cette sorte de nécessité, non plus mégarique, mais spinoziste: la distinction réclamée par Anselme sera-t-elle pour autant abolie?

Pour Spinoza lui-même, cette nécessité est celle des causes secondes, d'où résultent les déterminations particulières de l'existence, autrement dit l'existence des choses singulières dans le temps;[20] mais l'existence spatio-temporelle des *modes* diffère totalement de l'existence absolue de la Substance.[21] C'est cette distinction de deux niveaux d'existence qui est requise par l'argument d'Anselme. Un objet dont l'existence est déterminée dans l'espace et dans le temps, qui existe *hic et nunc*, et non pas *toujours et partout*, il m'est possible de supposer qu'*ici-même* et *en ce moment* il ne soit pas; cette supposition n'a rien d'impensable;[22] il n'y a que l'être infini éternel, nécessaire, qui répugne à une telle supposition: la négation de son existence est absolument *impensable*.[23] D'où vient donc ce privilège, cette étonnante exception? C'est que le QMCN, défini dialectiquement, transcende tout objet de l'entendement, toute détermination spatio-temporelle, toute représentation particulière. Aussi l'Etre auprès de qui rien de plus grand ne peut être pensé ne saurait-il être conçu comme une grandeur. C'est le propre de la grandeur (étendue, nombre, quantité en général) qu'on en peut toujours considérer une plus grande; la quantité ou grandeur est *ce en quoi il y a toujours au delà*;[24] c'est seulement dans la perfection qu'il y a un *maximum*, un degré suprême et absolu,[25] en fonction duquel on peut évaluer des degrés de perfection.[26] Or c'est par cette considération que se conçoit pour Anselme le QMCN;[27] aussi son argument échappe-t-il à la critique de S. Thomas; il n'en serait atteint que si le concept du QMCN était pour lui, comme le voudrait Gaunilon, celui d'un objet strict de l'entendement; conçu au contraire dialectiquement, comme il l'est par Anselme, il est l'équivalent du *maxime ens*, de la suprême perfection, que découvre S. Thomas par la *quarta via*, l'*argumentum ex gradibus*.[28]

NOTES

1. *Proslogion*, 4, *Ans.Op.Om.*, I, 103:20-104:2: 'Nullus quippe intelligens id quod Deus est, potest cogitare quia Deus non est, licet haec verba dicat in corde aut sine ulla aut cum aliqua extranea significatione'.[1]

2. *Pro insipiente*, 7, *Ans.Op.Om.*, I, 129: 'summum vero illud, quod est, scilicet Deus, et esse et non esse non posse indubitanter intelligo'.

3. Le propos déclaré d'Anselme, dans le Prooemium du *Proslogion* (*Ans.Op.Om.*, I, 93:5), c'était d'apporter, au lieu de l'enchaînement rationnel des arguments du *Monologion* ('multorum concatenatione contextum argumentorum'), un argument unique qui se suffirait à lui-même et n'aurait pas besoin d'autre preuve ('unum argumentum, quod nullo alio, ad se probandum quam se solo indigeret').

4. *Pro insipiente*, 4, *Ans.Op.Om.*, I, 127 and 7, *Ans.Op.Om.*, I, 129.

5. *Pro insipiente*, 2, *Ans.Op.Om.*, I, 125:19-20, établit une opposition entre *cogitare vel in cogitatione habere* et *intelligere et in intellectu habere*. Il observe qu'un énoncé n'est pas à proprement parler dans l'entendement, n'est pas objet d'intellection, du seul fait que sa signification est perçue par la pensée; on ne peut dire d'un tel objet: 'quod iam sit hoc in intellectu meo, cum auditum intelligo'; car, à ce compte, bien des énoncés dont je comprends le sens seraient des connaissances de l'entendement, alors que je les juge encore incertaines ou même faux: 'in

quo (sc. intellectu meo) similiter esse posse quaecumque alia incerta vel etiam falsa ab aliquo cuius verba intelligerem dicta adhuc puto' (*Ans.Op.Om.*, I, 127).

La distinction réclamée ici par Gaunilon sera reprise par Leibniz, qui en fait un préalable à la mise en oeuvre de l'argument ontologique. Voir *Meditationes de cognitione, veritate et Ideis* (*Die Philosophischen Schriften von Gottfried Wilhelm Leibnitz*, edited by C.I. Gerhardt, 7 vols. (Berlin, 1875-90), IV, 424): 'Eodem igitur modo non sufficit nos *cogitare* de Ente perfectissimo, ut asseramus nos ejus *ideam* habere' (c'est nous qui soulignons). La requête de Leibniz est justifiée par la remarque suivante: 'Nec valet quod Cartesium alicubi dicere memini (à Mersenne, juil. 1641, *Sämtliche Schriften und Briefe*, Academy Edition (Darmstadt and Berlin, 1923 ff.), III, 392-3), nos cum de aliqua re loquimur, intelligendo quod dicimus, habere rei ideam. Nam saepe fit ut combinemus incompatibilia, velut cum de Motu celerrimo cogitamus, quem impossibilem esse constat, adeoque idea carere, et tamen concessum nobis est de eo cum intellectu loqui' (*Animadversiones in Cartesium*, I ad art. 18, *Philosophischen Schriften*, IV, 360). Dans ce texte, les termes *intelligendo quod dicimus*, et *cum intellectu loqui* sont employés en un sens large.

6. *Responsio*, 1, après avoir montré (*Ans.Op.Om.*, I, 130-2) comment de la définition de Dieu: *quo majus cogitari nequit*, se déduisent son existence nécessaire et ses attributs infinis, demande finalement (*Ans.Op.Om.*, I, 132:3-4): 'Putasne aliquatenus posse cogitari vel intelligi aut esse in cogitatione vel intellectu, de quo haec intelliguntur?' (Ne penses-tu pas qu'il puisse être en quelque mesure objet de pensée, voire d'entendement, celui de qui notre entendement saisit de telles propriétés?). Et au début du chapitre 2 (*Ans.Op.Om.*, I, 132), il renouvelle sa question: 'An est in nullo intellectu, quod necessario in rei veritate esse monstratum est?' (Comment ne serait-il pas dans l'entendement l'objet qui s'est montré compris dans une essence nécessaire, dans la vérité de la chose?) C'est de la *veritas rei*, de *l'esse in intellectu*, de la nécessité de l'essence, que l'argument d'Anselme veut conclure à l'*esse in re*, à l'existence réelle.

7. Kant, *Critique de la Raison pure. Logique transcendentale.* Introduction III.B.85, *Kant's Gesammelte Schriften*, Prussian Academy (Berlin and Leipzig, 1923).

8. *Pro insipiente*, 7, *Ans.Op.Om.*, I, 129: 'Cogitare autem me non esse quamdiu esse certissime scio, nescio utrum possim; sed si possum cur non et quidquid aliud eadem certitudine scio? Si autem non possum, non erit iam istud proprium Deo'.

9. cf. note 5 ci-dessus (*Pro insipiente*, 2, *Ans.Op.Om.*, I) et la formule: 'eo modo quo etiam falsa quaeque vel dubia, haberi possit in cogitatione' (*Ans.Op.Om.*, I, 125).

10. *Pro insipiente*, 7, *Ans.Op.Om.*, I, 129: 'Nam secundum proprietatem verbi istius falsa nequeunt intelligi, quae possunt utique eo modo cogitari quo Deum non esse insipiens cogitavit.'

11. *Responsio*, 4, *Ans.Op.Om.*, I, 133: 'Si enim dixissem rem ipsam non posse intelligi non esse, fortasse tu ipse, qui dicis, quia secundum proprietatem verbi istius falsa nequeunt intelligi, obiceres nihil quod est posse intelligi non esse. Falsum est enim non esse quod est. Quare non esse proprium Deo non posse intelligi non esse' (Si j'eusse dit que cette réalité suprême, il est inintelligible qu'elle ne soit pas, tu aurais été le premier sans doute, toi qui soutiens qu'au sens propre du terme le faux est inintelligible, à me faire cette objection: aucune chose qui est, il n'est intelligible qu'elle ne soit pas; il est faux, en effet, que ne soit pas ce qui est; et dans ces conditions, ce ne serait pas le propre de Dieu d'être inintelligible qu'il ne soit pas).

12. cf. Aristote, *De interpretatione*, 9.18b.9-15. Cicéron, *De fato*, 9.17: 'Placuit igitur Diodori id solum fieri posse quod aut verum sit aut verum futurum sit' avec ce corollaire: 'quidquid futurum sit, id dicit fieri necesse esse'. Un autre écho de cette thèse est signalé dans la communication addressée à la *Third International Anselm Conference* (Canterbury, 1979) par P.A. Streveler, 'Anselm on future contingencies: A critical analysis of the argument of the *De concordia*'. (Voir chapitre 13 de la présente édition.)

13. C'est l'objet du chapitre 5 du *Responsio* (*Ans.Op.Om.*, I, 134-6).

14. *Responsio*, 4, *Ans.Op.Om.*, I, 133-4: 'Sache donc', répond Anselme à l'indécision de Gaunilon, (*Pro insipiente*, note 8 cidessus) 'qu'il t'est possible de penser que tu n'es pas, tout en sachant très certainement que tu es . . . Il y a bien des choses, en effet, dont nous pouvons penser qu'elles ne soient pas tout en sachant qu'elles sont, et d'autres dont nous pouvons penser qu'elles soient tout en sachant qu'elles ne sont pas: nous ne *jugeons* pas, en pareil cas, qu'elles sont ou ne sont pas; nous l'*imaginons*' ('non existimando, sed fingendo ita esse, cogitamus'). 'Certes', poursuit Anselme, 'il nous est possible de penser (cogitare) qu'une chose n'est pas, tout en sachant qu'elle est, parce que nous avons à la fois ce *pouvoir* (de feindre) et ce *savoir* ('quia simul et illud possumus et istud scimus'); mais en un autre sens, il nous est impossible de penser (c'est-à-dire de *juger*) qu'elle n'est pas quand nous savons qu'elle est, car il n'est pas possible de penser (c'est-à-dire *juger*) qu'elle est et en même temps n'est pas.' Cette distinction entre *fiction* et *belief*

se retrouve chez Hume, *An Inquiry Concerning Human Under-standing*, 5.2.39, edited by L.A. Selby-Bigge (Oxford, 1902).

15. *Responsio*, 4, *Ans.Op.Om.*, I, 133-4: en distinguant ces deux acceptions du terme *cogitare*, on comprendra que: 'nihil, quamdiu esse scitur, posse cogitari (sc. *existimari*) non esse, et quidquid est, praeter id quo majus cogitari nequit, etiam cum scitur esse, posse cogitari (sc. *fingi*) non esse'. En d'autres terms (Ibid., 133:30-134:1), les choses qui sont, jamais il n'est intelligible (jamais il n'est possible de *juger*) qu'elles ne sont pas ('nulla quae sunt possunt intelligi non esse'); toujours cependant il est possible de penser (d'*imaginer*) qu'elles ne sont pas, à l'exception de ce qui est suprêmement ('omnia tamen possunt cogitari non esse, praeter id quod summe est'). En conclusion (*Ans.Op.Om.*, I, 134:16-17), c'est le propre de Dieu qu'il est impossible de penser qu'il n'est pas' ('Sic igitur et proprium est Deo non esse cogitari').

16. Voir Leibniz, *Monadologie*, 33 (*Philosophischen Schriften*, VI, 612) et aussi Leibniz, *De libertate* (Foucher de Careil, *Nouvelles lettres et opuscules inédits de Leibniz* (Paris, 1857) p. 181): 'Nimirum necessaria propositio est cujus contrarium implicat contradictionem'.

17. cf. Cicéron, *De Fato*, 9.18: 'Nec magis commutari ex veris in falsa posse ea, quae futura, quam ea quae facta sunt; sed in factis immutabilitatem apparere . . .'. Voir J. Moreau, 'Immutabilité du vrai, nécessité logique et lien causal', in *Les Stoïciens et leur logique*, Actes du Colloque (Chantilly, 1976), pp. 347-60.

18. Voir les explications de Leibniz, *Discours de Métaphysique*, 13 (*Philosophischen Schriften*, IV, 436-9).

19. cf. Spinoza, *De intellectus emendatione*, 53-4, *Spinoza Opera*, edited by C. Gebhardt, I (Heidelberg, 1926); 'Unde sequitur, si detur aliquis Deus, aut omniscium quid, nihil prorsus eum posse fingere', contrairement à la déclaration d'Anselme rapportée ci-dessus, note 14: 'quia simul et illud possumus et istud scimus'.

20. Voir Spinoza, *Ethique*, 5.6 Demonstratio: 'res omnes . . . infinito causarum nexu determinari ad existendum et operandum'. Ce qui est determiné de la sorte (per prop. 28. part 1), c'est la *series rerum singularium mutabilium* (*De intellectus emendatione*, 100), dont l'existence temporelle ne trouve cependant son fondement que dans l'essence singulière par où chacune est comprise éternellement dans la nature infinie di Dieu (*Ethique*, 2.45 scol.).
    Pareillement, chez Leibniz, la série infinie des causes et des effets suppose la transcendance d'une Cause première et absolue

(*De rerum originatione radicali; Philosophischen Schriften,* VII 302-3). C'est par cette considération que se maintient pour lui la distinction des *vérités contingentes* et des *vérités nécessaires,* encore que la vérité suppose toujours l'inclusion du prédicat dans le sujet (à Arnauld, *Philosophischen Schriften,* II, 56). Dans la proposition: 'César franchit le Rubicon', exemple de vérité historique, énonçant un événement contingent, le prédicat est contenu *analytiquement* dans la notion du sujet César, telle que Dieu l'aperçoit de toute éternité. Considérée au niveau des essences, comprises dans l'entendement divin, cette proposition est nécessaire comme une vérité de géométrie; ce qui est *contingent,* non compris dans la notion du sujet César, c'est son *existence* dans l'histoire. Dans un autre univers, qui n'eût pas été le meilleur possible, et qui pour cette raison n'a pas été produit par Dieu, César aurait pu ne pas exister, ou il aurait pu exister un *autre* César que celui qui a franchi le Rubicon. L'énoncé de cet événement n'est donc pas une vérité nécessaire, parce que cet événement dépend de l'existence du César historique, et par là de l'ordre entier du monde et du choix que Dieu a fait. Ainsi, malgré le déterminisme des causes secondes, rien de ce qui arrive en ce monde n'est nécessaire absolument, car l'*existence* de ce monde, et celle de tous les sujets, individus et choses singulières, qui sont compris en lui, dépend originairement non de l'ordre infini des causes, mais de la Cause première, de l'Etre absolu, qui seul existe nécessairement. Voir aussi J. Moreau, *Le Dieu des philosphes* (Paris, 1465), pp. 33-45.

21. Spinoza, *Lettre* 12 (à Louis Meyer), *Spinoza Opera,* IV : 'Unde clare apparet, nos existentiam Substantiae toto genere a modorum existentia diversam concipere'.

22. *Responsio,* 1, *Ans.Op.Om.,* I, 130: 'Nam quod heri non fuit et hodie est; sicut heri non fuisse intelligitur, ita numquam esse subintelligi potest. Et quod hic non est et alibi est: sicut non est hic, ita potest cogitari nusquam esse. Similiter . . . quidquid alicubi aut aliquando totum non est: etiam si est, potest cogitari non esse'.

23. *Responsio,* 1, *Ans.Op.Om.,* I, 130-1, et *Responsio,* 4, *Ans.Op.Om.,* I, 133-4: 'Illud vero solum non potest cogitaria non esse, in quo nec initium nec finem partium coniunctionem, et quod non nisi semper et ubuque totum ulla invenit cogitatio'.

24. Aristote, *Physique,* III, 6.206b.34:

οὐ γὰρ οὗ μηδὲν ἔξω, ἀλλ'οὗ ἀεί τι ἔξω ἐστι, τοῦτο ἄπειρον ἐστιν
οὗ δὲ μηδὲν ἔξω, τοῦτ'ἐστι τέλειον καὶ ὅλον

Ce en dehors de quoi il n'y a rien, ce n'est pas cela qu'il faut appeler *infini*, mais ce en dehors de quoi il y a *toujours outre*. Ce en dehors de quoi il n'y a rien, cela est le *parfait*, ce qui est *achevé* et *total'* (*perfectum atque absolutum*).

25. cf. Leibniz, *Discours de Métaphysique*, 1 (*Philosophischen Schriften*, IV, 427): 'les formes ou natures, qui ne sont pas susceptibles du dernier degré, ne sont pas des perfections, comme par exemple la nature du nombre de la figure'. C'est par cette oppposition entre le *parfait* et l'*infini quantitatif* que Leibniz résout la difficulté préjudicielle à l'argument ontologique (ci-dessus, note 5): la notion de l'*ens perfectissimum* ne recouvre pas une impossibilité, comme celle du plus grand de tous les nombres ou du mouvement le plus rapide. Dans ces conditions, 'nihil verius est quam et nos. Dei habere ideam, et Ens perfectissimum esse possibile, imo necessarium' (*Meditationes de cognitione, Philosophischen Schriften*, IV, 424).

26. Comme le précise S. Thomas, *Summa Theologica*, 1.2,3: 'Quarta via . . . Sed magis et minus dicitur de diversis secundum quod approprinquant diversimode ad aliquid quod maxime est'. Ce qui revient à dire que, dans l'ordre de la valeur, le comparatif ne peut s'appliquer à des objets que par référence à un superlatif.

27. *Responsio*, 8, *Ans.Op.Om.*, I, 137-8: 'patet cuilibet rationabili menti, quia de bonis minoribus ad maiora conscendendo, ex iis quibus aliquid maius cogitari potest, multum possumus conicere illud quo nihil potest maius cogitari'.

28. S. Thomas, *Summa Theologica*, 1.2,3: 'Est igitur aliquid quod est verissimum, et optimum et nobilissimum, et per consequens maxime ens'. Voir aussi J. Moreau, *Pour ou contre l'Insensé? Essai sur la preuve anselmienne* (Paris, 1967).

Argomento Ontologico e Ateismo Semantico

Pietro Scapin

L'argomento ontologico e l'ateismo semantico rappresentano una delle risposte più significative al problema di Dio. Ciò che li distingue – a prima vista – é il fatto che il primo si conclude con l'affermazione dell'esistenza di Dio, mentre il secondo termina con la negazione di tale esistenza.

Come mai – ci si può chiedere – una conclusione così diversa? Da che cosa può dipendere? E' possibile individuare un quadro di riferimento che consenta di analizzarne il contenuto e misurarne il valore?

Sono questi gli interrogativi ai quali vorrebbe rispondere la presente comunicazione. Per procedere in maniera graduale, proporremo anzitutto due formulazioni ormai classiche dell'una e dell'altra soluzione; ne analizzeremo quindi i presupposti e il contenuto essenziale; tenteremo infine di valutarle in rapporto a un quadro di riferimento che permetta di intravvedere l'origine e il valore del linguaggio in ordine all scoperta della verità.

1. Formulazione anselmiana dell'argomento ontologico

Come si sa, la formulazione anselmiana dell'argomento ontologico – contenuta nel *Proslogion* – si presenta sotto due forme: nella prima, Anselmo argomenta che Dio non può essere soltanto nell'intelletto, ma deve essere anche un'esistenza reale; nella seconda, dimostra che é impossibile pensare che Dio non esista.

1.1. Prima formulazione anselmiana

Noi crediamo [scrive Anselmo] che Tu [=Dio] sia qualche cosa della quale nulla si può pensare di più grande. Che forse non esiste tale natura, dal momento che lo stolto ha detto nel suo cuore: *Non esiste Dio?*

Certamente, lo stesso stolto, quando ode ciò che dico – cioé che vi é qualche cosa di cui nulla si può pensare più grande – comprende quello che ode e quello che comprende é nel suo intelletto, anche se non comprende che quello esista nella realtà. Infatti, altro é che una cosa sia nell'intelletto e altro intendere che essa realmente esista. Così, quando il pittore concepisce ciò che sta per fare, lo ha già nel suo intelletto, ma non ancora pensa che vi sia ciò non ha ancora fatto; ma quando, invece, ha già dipinto non solo ha nell'intelletto, ma anche comprende che realmente
esista quello che egli ha fatto . . . Ora, é certo che ciò di

cui nulla di più grand si può pensare non può essere soltanto nell'intelletto. Infatti, se fosse soltanto nell'intelletto, si potrebbe pensare che esistesse anche nella realtà; il che é di più. Se, dunque, ciò di cui nulla può esservi di più grande é nel solo intelletto, ciò stesso del quale non si può pensare nulla di più grande, sarebbe l'essere del quale é possibile pensare qualche cosa di più grande. Ma questo non può essere assolutamente.

Dunque, esiste certamente e nell'intelletto e nella realtà un Essere di cui nulla di maggiore si può pensare.[1]

1.2 Seconda formulazione anselmiana
Alla precedente formulazione, Anselmo fa seguire immediatamente quest'altra:

Non é possibile pensare che Dio non esista. Infatti, si può pensare che esista qualche cosa che non possa essere pensato non esistente [= ente necessario]. Ora, ciò che non può essere pensato non esistente, deve essere più grande di ciò che può essere pensato non esistente [= ente contingente]. Per tal motivo, se ciò di cui nulla di più grande si può pensare potesse essere pensato non esistente, lo stesso essere del quale nulla viè di più grande non sarebbe l'essere di cui nulla di più grande si può pensare. Il che non va. Di conseguenza, l'Essere del quale nulla di maggiore si può pensare esiste così realmente che non si può neppure pensare che non sia e questo Essere sei Tu, Signore, mio Dio.[2]

In breve: Dio é compreso dall'uomo come l'essere sommo; l'essere nel pensiero e nella realtà simultaneamente é di più che essere solo nell'intelletto. Inoltre, non poter pensare che una cosa non sia é *di più* che poter pensare che una cosa non sia. Dio, pertanto, deve essere nella realtà ed impossibile pensare che non sia perché – se non fosse nella realtà o se si potesse pensare la sua inesistenza – non sarebbe più, secondo la definizione, l'essere sommo.

2. Formulazione ayeriana dell'ateismo semantico
In un certo senso, l'ateismo semantico é un corollario della filosofia del linguaggio. Esso consiste nell'affermare che la teologia, cioé la scienza di Dio, lavora con pseudo–concetti o con parole prive di senso.[3] Di esso evochiamo la formulazione di A.J. Ayer che si può considerare emblematica per tutta la filosofia del linguaggio. Ci riferiamo a quanto Ayer scrive nel suo trattato *Language, Truth and Logic* del 1936.

Nel capitolo sesto del trattato suddetto egli svolge la critica dell'etica e della teologia.

In genere [egli scrive] oggi si ammette almeno da parte dei filosofi, che l'esistenza di un essere avente gli attributi definitori della divinità di qualsiasi religione non animistica, non si può provare per via dimostrativa. Per comprendere che la cosa sta così, dobbiamo solo chiederci quali siano le premesse donde dedurre l'esistenza di una divinità simile. Se la conclusione che esiste Dio ha da essere certa per via dimostrativa, allora queste premesse devono essere certe; infatti, siccome la conclusione dell'argomento deduttivo é già contenuta nelle premesse, qualunque incertezza sussista circa la verità delle premesse é necessariamente condivisa dalla conclusione. Ma noi sappiamo che nessuna proposizione empirica può mai esser qualcosa di più che probabile. Logicamente certe sono solo le proposizioni *a priori*. Ma non possiamo dedurre l'esistenza di Dio da una proposizione *a priori*. Poiché, come sappiamo, la ragione per cui solo le proposizioni *a priori* é il fatto che sono tautologiche. E da un insieme di tautologie non si può dedurre in modo valido null'altro che una tautologia di più. Ne consegue che non si dà nessuna possibilità di dimostrare l'esistenza di Dio . . .

Se l'enunciato 'Dio esiste' non implica altro se non che certi tipi di fenomeni hanno luogo in certe sequenze, allora asserire l'esistenza di Dio equivarrà semplicemente all'asserire che in natura vi é la regolarità suddetta; e nessun religioso ammetterebbe che ciò sia tutto quanto egli intendeva dire asserendo l'esistenza di Dio. Direbbe che, parlando di Dio, egli *parla di un essere trascendente*, che potrebbe venire conosciuto attraverso certe manifestazioni empiriche . . . Ma, in questo caso, 'Dio' é termine metafisico. E se 'Dio' é un termine metafisico, allora che esista Dio non può neppure essere probabile. Poiché dire 'Dio esiste' significa produrre un'espressione metafisica che non può essere vera o falsa. E per lo stesso criterio non possono avere nessuna significanza letterale gli enunciati in cui ci si proponga di descrivere la natura di un Dio trascendente . . . La nozione di una persona i cui attributi essenziali sono non empirici, non é neppure una nozione intelligibile. Può esserci una parola usata come se nominasse questa 'persona' ma, se gli enunciati in cui la parola figura non esprimono proposizioni verificabili empiricamente, non si può dire che essa simbolizzi alcunché. E ciò é quanto avviene nell'uso istituzionale della parola 'Dio', in cui la si intende riferita a un oggetto trascenente . . . Il punto che vogliamo fissare é che non vi possono essere verità trascendenti di fede religiosa, poiché gli enunciati cui il teista ricorre per esprimere tali 'verità' non hanno significato nel senso letterale.[4]

In breve: Dio é uno pseudo-concetto perché non ha origine empirica; l'enunciazione 'Dio esiste' non é una proposizione significativa, cioé non é né vera né falsa, perché non é verificabile; l'argomentazione *a priori* é una concatenazione di tautologie che non conduce alla conoscenza di nuova verità, intesa come realtà esistente in maniera distinta rispetto al soggetto conoscente.

3. Presupposti e contenuto essenziale
Obiettivo dell'argomento ontologico come dell'ateismo semantico é l'esistenza di Dio. Questa va intesa, in ambedue i casi, come 'esistenza nella realtà' — come dice Anselmo — o come 'essere trascendente, oggetto dell'emozione religiosa' — come dice Ayer — , cioé come esistenza extramentale da raggiungere dalla mente o da conoscere da parte dell'uomo.

Per ambedue le posizioni, tale esistenza non é 'data' in maniera diretta e immediata all'uomo, cioé non é evidente o non é un contenuto di presenza. Perciò, per essere conosciuta e, quindi, affermata, ha bisogno di essere 'dimostrata'. Ma quando sarà 'dimostrata' effettivamente? Come 'dimostrarla' in concreto?

L'unico elemento di cui dispone sicuramente l'uomo — sia credente che ateo — é l'idea di Dio. Questa fa parte dell'esperienza religiosa. Ma che cosa esprime? Ci informa e, insieme, ci mette a contatto con l'esistenza reale di Dio — d'un essere trascendente — , oppure ci dà soltanto informazione indiretta sulle proprie condizioni mentali?[5]

Per Anselmo, essa ci mette a contatto con Dio, contenuto extramentale; per Ayer, ci mette a contatto con Dio, contenuto intramentale. La convinzione del primo ha come fondamento l'esplicitazione del nesso tra il contenuto ipotetico dell'idea — essere somo — e le sue interne esigenze; la convinzione del secondo ha come giustificazione il principio di verificabilità in base al quale una proposizione é vera nella misura in cui il suo contenuto può essere sottoposto ad empirica osservazione.

Per ambedue, rimane indubbia la distinzione tra la verità che é nell'esistenza delle cose e la verità del nostro pensiero e la dipendenza di questa da quella.[6]

Noi ci permettiamo di chiamare la prima verità *ontica* e la seconda verità *logica* — se connota l'implicazione del predicato nel soggetto — e verità *ontologica*, quando la verità logica deriva e rispecchia la verità ontica. In definitiva, per Anselmo come per Ayer, l'argomentazione produce un'espansione della verità ontologica nella misura in cui la verità logica si fa strumento chiarificatore della verità ontica. In altre parole, un' argomentazione logicamente corretta può esser considerata un avanzamento nella conoscenza della verità delle cose nella misura in cui rende possibile la scoperta di nuova realtà. Ma quale fondamento occorre dare alla verità logica perché essa concorra a produrre questo risultato?

Tanto Anselmo quanto Ayer, ritengono che l'unico fondamento sia costituito dalla verità ontica? Sembra di sì. Ma nell'argomento ontologico, tale fondamento non é posto, ma presupposto; nell'ateismo semantico, invece, é postulato, ma non verificato. Come valutare, allora, la loro portata?

4. Realtà globale e verità della conoscenza

Per cogliere tale portata, ci sembra indispensabile prospettare un quadro della realtà globale con i rispettivi settori e rapporti in ordine alla nostra conoscenza. Nel suo insieme, la realtà con cui abbiamo a che fare é costituita da cose, da idee e da parole. Oppure: da realtà data, da realtà pensata e da realtà detta. Sono, questi, i tre settori che formano la realtà globale per l'uomo. Ognuno di essi costituisce un livello ben caratterizzato: il livello ontico, costituito dall'insieme dei contenuti (cose, persone, ecc.) la cui esistenza non dipende dal fatto di essere conosciuta dall'uomo; il livello onto—logico, costituito dall'insieme dei contenuti (idee, concetti ecc.) la cui esistenza si risolve nell'essere pensati dall'uomo; il livello logo—ontico, costituito in definitiva dal linguaggio.

Ora, quale di questi tre livelli fonda la verità del nostro conoscere? Tanto, per i sostenitori dell'argomento ontologico quanto per i seguaci dell'ateismo semantico, l'unico fondamento é il livello ontico. E Dio, del quale i primi affermano l'esistenza e i secondi sembrano negarla, rientra ipoteticamente nel livello ontico, anche se gli uni e gli altri concordano nel riconoscere che Egli non é un contenuto a noi accessibile nel contatto diretto e immediato, cioé come realtà empiricamente presente e, quindi, empiricamente verificabile. Egli é certamente un contenuto del nostro pensiero e, in questo senso, rientra per noi nel livello ontologico della realtà globale. Ma come appare a questo livello? Su questo punto, aprioristi e atei semantici si trovano d'accordo: l'idea di Dio o il pensiero di Dio spunta in noi sotto l'influsso del livello logo-ontico ossia a partire dal linguaggio.

In effetti, per i credente il pensiero di Dio proviene dalla Parola di Dio o dalla rivelazione; per gli atei, é suscitato dalla cultura inglobante l'esperienza religiosa (lo stolto, rileva Anselmo, ode ciò che io dico). Per il fatto di aver tale origine e di non consentire un procedimento di verifica, Egli non può divenire contenuto di vera conoscenza per l'ateismo semantico. La sua ipotetica trascendenza lo sottrae alla verifica o lo rende inaccessibile alla nostra conoscenza.

Viceversa, tale origine non solleva immediatamente alcuna difficoltà e il suo contenuto ipotetico diviene motivo che determina la certezza della sua esistenza per quanti riconoscono valore positivo all'argomento ontologico. Ma la difficoltà, per costoro, é soltanto rinviata se — con Anselmo — sono convinti che la verità del pensiero — sotto forma di concetto e di giudizio — dipenda essenzialmente dalla verità delle cose.

Così stando le cose, ci sembra di poter concludere che né l'argomento ontologico né l'ateismo semantico rappresentano una conclusione capace di allargare l'orizzonte della conoscenza umana del livello ontico. Ambedue sono corollari d'un'opzione: l'argomento ontologico é un corollario d'una opzione di fede; l'ateismo semantico é un corollario dell'opzione empirista. Chi crede, ha già deciso di esprimere il proprio consenso all'ipotesi che il livello ontico racchiuda non solo contenuti empirici — caratterizzati dalla radicale finitezza entitativa e contrassegnati dalla spazio—temporalità — , ma anche un contenuto metempirico — com'é Dio — , caratterizzato dall'infinità entitativa. L'empirista, invece, ha già deciso di dare il proprio assenso all'ipotesi contraria.

Per uscire dall'*impasse*, a nostro avviso, bisogna interrogare la realtà ontica — a noi data nell'immediatezza d'un rapporto presenziale — e coglierla non solo nella sua datità, ma anche nella sua identità, cioé nella sua finitezza entitativa, e in rapporto con la totalità.

Così interrogata, tale realtà può diventare mediatrice in due direzioni: nel senso che aiuta a comprendere la funzione ontica del linguaggio e la conseguente dimensione rappresentativa del pensiero — da una parte — e l'orizzonte globale del livello ontico — dall'altra — , orizzonte che racchiude l'esistenza di Dio come indispensabile fondamento dell'esistenza della realtà empiricamente data.

NOTES

1. cf. *Ans.Op.Om.*, I, 101: 8–9.

2. cf. *Ans. p.Om.*, I, 102–3.

3. cf. D. Antiseri, *La filosofia del linguaggi* (Brescia, 1973), pp. 164 ss.

4. cf. A.J. Ayer, *Linguaggio, verità e logica* (Feltrinelli editore, 1961), pp. 148-54

5. cf. A.J. Ayer, *ivi*, p. 156.

6. La gnoseologia anselmiana é contenuta nel dialogo *De Veritate* (*Ans.Op.Om.*, I, 176–99). In esso, Anselmo distingue tre principali forme di verità:
   i. La verità suprema — Dio — che non ha né principio né fine; in sé contiene gli archetipi a cui si conformano tutte le cose ed é soltanto causa.

ii. La verità che é nell'esistenza delle cose, effetto della somma verità ed é essa stessa causa della verità del pensiero e della proposizione.

iii. La verità del nostro conoscere, effetto soltanto della verità delle cose. A questa terza specie di verità si connettono, poi, altre più particolari forme di verità, quali:

a) La verità dell'enunciazione che si ha quando questa *dice* che é ciò che é e che non é ciò che non é.

b) La verità del pensiero, che consiste nel *giudicare* che é ciò che é e che non é ciò che non é.

c) La verità della volontà, che é rettitudine morale.

La gnoseologia ayeriana é stata recentemente riassunta dallo stesso Ayer nel suo colloquio con B. Magee in questi termini:

In sintesi, il principio fondamentale da me sostenuto nel libro [*Language, Truth and Logic*] era che le proposizioni fornite di senso potevano essere divise in due classi. La prima era formata da quelle che si riferiscono a questioni di fatto — come voleva Hume — e per queste affermai fosse essenziale la *verifica dell'osservazione*, sostenendo che esse sono insignificanti qualora la loro verità o falsità non produca differenze osservabili; la seconda classe era costituita da proposizioni formali della matematica o della logica ed esse erano considerate come tautologiche: le pensavo come pure sistemazioni di simboli che nulla dicono del mondo.

Tutto ciò che non rientrava né nell'una né ell'altra classe era metafisica e come tale era senza senso: vi includevo una gran parte di quel che nella storia della filosofia si intende, appunto, per filosofia, e tutta la teologia: tutte le proposizioni teologiche in quanto e comunque facciano riferimento ad un essere trascendente erano considerate senza senso. (B. Magee, *Colloqui di filosofia inglese contemporanea* (Roma, 1979), p. 104.)

Berkeley's Rejection of Anselm's Argument*

Desirée Park

Berkeley rejected the ontological argument only implicitly, but his grounds for not introducing it in any form can be made quite explicit. His decision is of more general philosophical interest because, as I shall argue, it was the correct one.

There can be few writers who have put more emphasis on the activities of minds finite and Infinite while still insisting on the imbalance between man and God. The relationship is not impossible to indicate, so the claim runs, but it is not measurable in any strict sense of measure, and in his philosophical writings Berkeley is quite clear about this problem.

In the *Proslogion* Anselm argues for the necessary existence of 'a being than which nothing greater can be conceived'.[1] The greatness of this being is essential because otherwise the fool could be right,[2] and such a being might be held to exist only as an idea in the minds of those who entertain the question at all. Anselm concludes that to be that 'than which nothing greater can be conceived' entails necessary existence, else in principle there could be a being greater than the being than which nothing greater can be conceived, and this is a contradiction.

Berkeley takes up the main concepts in this argument in the following manner.

> *Thing* or *being* is the most general name of all, it comprehends under it two kinds entirely distinct and heterogeneous, and which have nothing in common but the name, to wit, *spirits* and *ideas*. The former are active, *indivisible substances*: the latter are *inert, fleeting, dependent beings*, which subsist not by themselves, but are supported by, or exist in minds or spiritual substances.[3]

The minds to which this passage refers include both finite man and an Infinite God. Berkeley's task is to portray the God, which he doubts no more than does Anselm, in philosophical terms. To this end, he introduces two concepts of Infinite Mind.

The first is that of the sustainer of the ideas presented to us in sensation. The cause of these ideas we deem to be external to ourselves because we find them literally irresistible. This concept of the Berkeleyan God is of a being indispensable for the existence of the external world.

Closely allied to this notion is that of God as a fellow mind.[4] Ideas for Berkeley are passive, and we can both cause and alter

ideas of 'imagination' and of 'memory' at will. Ideas of 'sensation',
as noted, are not amenable to our preferences; hence we attribute
their occurrence to a mind more powerful than our own. From his
writings it appears that Berkeley could find no good reason to limit
this more powerful mind, and he therefore simply converted it into
the omnipotent God which orthodoxy asserted. Similarly, omniscience
was assumed to be appropriate to this external power and, again on
theological grounds, benevolence was added to the account.

Later, Berkeley combined the sustainer of ideas with the fellow
spirit and argued that those ideas or effects which lead us to
suppose that there are other finite minds are in fact many times
exceeded by those which point to the operations of an Infinite Mind.
One passage in the *Principles* runs:

> Hence it is evident, that God is known as certainly and
> immediately as any other mind or spirit whatsoever, distinct
> from our selves. We may even assert, that the existence of
> God is far more evidently perceived than the existence of
> men; because the effects of Nature are infinitely more
> numerous and considerable, than those ascribed to human
> agents. There is not any one mark that denotes a man, or
> effect produced by him, which doth not more strongly
> evince the being of that spirit who is the *Author of
> Nature.*[5]

In fact Berkeley cannot make much of this sort of argument, nor
does he try to do so in his philosophical works. Existence is not
demonstrable in his system, although it is true that the procession
of ordered ideas, no two of which are necessarily related, does
provide empirical evidence for his account of the external world.
Even so, Berkeley also asserts that hasty generalization is a
common human failing and warns us against it remarking:

> . . . we are apt to lay too great stress on analogies, and to
> the prejudice of truth, humour that eagerness of the mind,
> whereby it is carried to extend its knowledge into general
> theorems.[6]

And a few lines later he retreats further from any close argument
from observed effects to an unobservable cause in adding:

> . . . by a diligent observation of the phenomena within our
> view, we may discover the general laws of Nature, and from
> them deduce the other phenomena, I do not say *demon-
> strate*; for all deductions of that kind depend on a
> supposition that the Author of Nature always operates
> uniformly, and in a constant observance of those rules we
> take for principles: which we cannot evidently know.[7]

As to the concept of analogous mind or spirit, here too caution
prevails. Analogy once detached from its literal meaning is at best

only comparatively strong, and where there is no common measure, the conclusions are weakened to extinction. Berkeley takes up this question in the *Alciphron,* and provides Crito with the assertion:

> Every one knows that *analogy* is a Greek word used by mathematicians to signify a similitude of proportions. For instance, when we observe that two is to six as three is to nine, this similitude or equality of proportion is termed analogy.[8]

So far Berkeley and his creature are at one, but then Crito strays onto less firm ground continuing:

> And, although proportion strictly signifies the habitude or relation of one quantity to another, yet, in a looser and translated sense, it hath been applied to signify every other habitude; and consequently, the term *analogy* comes to signify all similitude or relations or habitudes whatsoever.[9]

In so far as philosophical distinctions are concerned, this looser sense of analogy is unacceptable to Berkeley. To entertain such a potentially fatal ambiguity would be to fly in the face of his known strictures on the relationship between measured quantities and infinity.[10] He had, moreover, already rejected Locke's concept of God which Locke proposed to form by the indefinite accretion of praiseworthy qualities.

The nearest approach that Berkeley makes to the establishing of a necessarily existent being remains an essentially causal claim for an immeasurably more powerful mind. And so we are told in the third of the dialogues between Hylas and Philonous:

> . . . from my own being, and from the dependency I find in my self and my ideas, I do by an act of reason, necessarily infer the existence of a God, and of all created things in the mind of God.[11]

And in the *Siris* he maintains that the presence and, therefore, the existence of any idea at this moment can be traced to an independently existing being which he simply calls 'the Deity'. No argument is given, and the historical Berkeley here simply declines to speak further as a philosopher, preferring to conclude as a cleric:

> Sense supplies images to memory. These become subjects for fancy to work upon. Reason considers and judges of the imaginations. And these acts of reason become new objects to the understanding. In this scale, each lower faculty is a step that leads to one above it. And the uppermost naturally leads to the Deity, which is rather the object of intellectual knowledge than even of the discursive faculty, not to mention the sensitive. There runs a chain throughout the whole system of beings. In this chain one link drags another. The meanest things are connected with the highest.[12]

To summarize so far, minds finite and Infinite are essentially active and have among their functions the entertaining, or perceiving, of ideas. But the Being, which Berkeley acknowledges and which Anselm's argument requires, is utterly and irretrievably remote from the human scale. Anselm, as is well-known, takes this to be a sign of greatness and praises God as one who dwells in 'unapproachable light'. Berkeley on the contrary, notices that unapproachable means just that, and admits of God that His ways are not the ways of 'impotent and saving mortals'.[13] And so it comes about that the concept of a fellow mind gives way to that of an indispensable sustainer of ideas.

It is not too fanciful, I think, to suppose that Berkeley's suspicions about any argument for a necessarily existent being are of a piece with his well-documented objections to absolute space. The basis of his opposition is that absolute space trades on the coherence of its familiar counterpart, relative space, and derives whatever content it may enjoy from the sense experience which it pretends to exclude. In 1730, Berkeley worte to Samuel Johnson, the American philosopher:

> As to Space. I have no notion of any but that which is relative. I know some late philosophers have attributed extension to God, particularly mathematicians, one of whom, in a treatise, *De Spatio Reali*, pretends to find out fifteen of the incommunicable attributes of God in Space. But it seems to me that, they being all negative, he might as well have found them in Nothing; and that it would have been as justly inferred from Space being impassive, increated, indivisible, etc., that it was Nothing as that it was God.[14]

Berkeley is able to take this stand because on his analysis the external world exhibits ideas which are spatially related, and because this perceptual space is readily distinguished from the perceptually neutral space of geometers. In fine, the spaces of perception and geometry belong to different kinds of descriptive systems and these systems are exhaustive.

The concept of necessary existence, like that of absolute space, is developed by omitting the qualifications which give it content. Berkeley's claims are quite specific as to what can count as a being, but as we have noted, he is reluctant to put much philosophical weight on the concept of a fellow mind which is infinite. Far better for him, he evidently judged, to hold orthodox views of God and cease arguing when his critical analysis had denied him a base. Analogy cannot be used literally in stating the relationship between man and God; hence 'mind' is not to be considered as a single term in strict argument. For where there is no common system of measure, there is no means of comparing the two sorts of minds by marking them against the same scale.

A slightly different way of focussing on the concept of a necessarily existent being is to notice that Berkeley was more than usually sensitive to the descriptive systems in which objects or things are to be allowed to figure. He refused, as we saw, to countenance the easy assumptions which compared, as if they were the same sorts of relationships, relative and absolute space. For not dissimilar reasons, he exploited too the several types of 'minimum sensibles' and specifically rejected the infinitesimals with which they were then frequently associated. In both cases, Berkeley argued that relative space and minimum sensibles were addressed to identifiable problems about perception, whereas absolute space and infinitesimals were a superfluous arena for an unknowable motion and a self-contradictory concept, respectively.[15]

In every instance in which either things or concepts were to be compared, Berkeley insisted that they should be genuinely comparable. The case of finite and Infinite minds fails this test because there can be no single scale of beings by which to sustain the comparison. The argument may be stated briefly. It is axiomatic that the single scale which is necessary to the drawing of such a comparison itself presupposes that the things to be compared have a common unit of measure. If there is a common unit of measure, then there is, or there may be, a systematic progression from one thing to the other thing. But progression from any finitude to arrival at infinity is impossible. Therefore there is no common unit of measure, and hence no single scale appropriate to the required beings. Accordingly, minds finite and Infinite are literally incomparable, and Anselm's 'being than which nothing greater can be conceived' is irremediably unlike any other thing.

If minds finite and Infinite cannot be compared, what then is supposed to be the relationship between a being which exists necessarily and one which exists contingently? A necessarily existent being is sometimes given a colouring of plausibility by being held to exist in every possible world. If x is a necessarily existent being, then in all circumstances, x exists. The question then becomes, what is meant by 'all circumstances' or 'every possible world'? Again, the objection is that these two phrases trade on this world and on circumstances of the sort with which we happen to be acquainted.

There is an odd, anti-empirical flavour in many discussions of possible worlds. Typically, the contents of such worlds and circumstances are borrowed, but are neither specified nor acknowledged. And this is done even though it is only the disregarded empirical observations which distinguish these possible worlds from a collection of definitions and theorems. Now it may be admitted that the concept of empirical observation has been employed too loosely in a good many discussions, but certainly it is also the case that the Berkeleyan 'ideas', strictly interpreted, bring to an end the ways of re-describing observations. For Berkeley's ideas can be shown to be quite unlike either Hume's 'impressions' or his 'ideas', and also unlike any of the theories of 'sense-data' which have been provided subsequently.[16]

This is of some moment when one comes to consider Plantinga's claim that there are propositions which enjoy 'broadly logical necessity' and that these include: (i) 'Red is a colour'; (ii) 'No prime minister is a prime number'; and the one in which he is especially interested, (iii) 'There exists a being than which it is not possible that there be a greater'.[17]

If, as Plantinga claims, the proposition, 'Red is a colour', is not true by definition, then it is essential to clarify what is meant by 'red' and to what it refers. For Berkeley, the word 'red' is employed to name an 'idea' of the most fundamental type - that is, the simplest kind of sense perception. Red is that kind of thing which is, in favourable conditions, perceived by sight and exists only as and when it is perceived. The idea red can be noticed by those who can see and can be named, but red cannot be described so as to convey what it looks like. This is not to deny that statements about red are significant. The idea red may be correctly associated with a particular wavelength or with that end of the visible spectrum which is found next to orange. But red, and any other such essentially perceived idea, remains indescribable and therefore immutable by description. According to Berkeley then, one need not say that 'Red is a colour', but it is an empirical truth that red is an idea. For those with normal colour vision, the rule *esse* is *percipi* applies in fact to red. This fundamental narrowness however belongs only to ideas, and cannot be generalized to other kinds of things.

If red is too primitive and inflexible to provide Plantinga with a suitable term to support his notion of broadly logical necessity, then the term 'prime minister' in his proposition, 'No prime minister is a prime number', is too generous. If this statement is not true by definition, it is vulnerable to a re-interpretation in which it is easily made out to be false. The objection is that Plantinga must rely on the description implicit in the stated constitutional requirements for, say, the head of Her Majesty's Government in order to make good his claim. For while it is true that, in England, 'No prime minister is a prime number', in Flatland, the head of the government, that is, the Chief Priest, is by law a circle,[18] and there is no reason in principle why, in a similar land of whole numbers, it might not be legally required that the prime minister be a prime number. Plantinga would, one imagines, object to this reading, but the question is on which grounds an objection could be sustained.

The third example mentioned, 'There exists a being than which it is not possible that there be a greater', is in no way made clearer by these two cases, nor by others not reviewed here.[19] Broadly logical necessity is introduced of course to escape the consequences of truth by definition, but it is far from apparent how this is to be accomplished. We are left then with the fact that the being to which Plantinga refers plainly is meant neither to be an idea, nor a mind which may be detected within the constraints of an observed physical body, nor yet a fiction. What then and whence may be its content?

Finally, Anselm's argument for the necessary existence of a being than which nothing greater can be conceived not only supposes that this greatness is intelligible, but that its superiority to recognized human virtues is that of the infinite to the finite. Berkeley saw clearly that the accretion of finitudes does not approach infinity, any more than the diminution of finitudes recedes from it. Consequently, he took seriously the limited powers of human minds, and argued for the existence of an Infinite Mind on the grounds that there was no known limit to the powers which produce ideas of sensation. But he pointedly resisted the additional claim that the familiar features of familiar things or beings could be recast so as to justify any argument for the necessary existence of a strictly incomparable being. And he was right.

NOTES

*   A slightly shorter version of this paper was delivered at the Third International Anselm Conference, Canterbury, England on 4 July 1979.

1. *Ans.Op.Om.*, I, 101.

2. Psalms 13:1 and 52:1, Vulgate; Psalms 14:1 and 53:1, Authorized Version.

3. George Berkeley, *Works*, edited by A.A. Luce and T.E. Jessop, 9 vols. (London, 1948-57), II, 79-80.

4. See discussion of 'Infinite Spirit' in Desirée Park, *Complementary Notions: A Critical Study of Berkeley's Theory of Concepts* (The Hague, 1972), pp. 78-97.

5. Berkeley, *Works*, II, 108.

6. Ibid., p. 87.

7. Ibid., p. 88.

8. Berkeley, *Works*, III, 169.

9. Ibid.

10. Berkeley, *Works*, IV: *The Analyst*, pp. 66-9; and *Of Infinities*, pp. 235-8.

11. Berkeley, *Works*, II, 232.

12. Berkeley, *Works*, V, 140.

13. Berkeley, *Works*, II, 111.

14. Ibid., p. 292.

15. Ibid., pp. 292-4.

16. Including the Ayerian *qualia*, which in many respects resemble 'ideas'. See A.J. Ayer, *The Central Questions of Philosophy* (London, 1973), pp. 91ff.

17. Alvin Plantinga, *The Nature of Necessity* (Oxford, 1974), pp. 1-2.

18. Edwin A. Abott, *Flatland* (New York, 1952), pp. 9ff. The correct title of this individual is 'the Chief Circle'.

19. Plantinga, *Necessity*, pp. 1-13.

III
Anselm and Language

St Anselm's Philosophy of Language Reconsidered

Marcia L. Colish

Recent studies of Anselm's philosophy of language have tended to approach this subject from one of two directions. The first, represented by my own previous work and that of R.W. Southern, Robert Pouchet, George S. Heyer, Thomas F. Torrance, and G.R. Evans, sees Anselm as standing at the end of an era and as concerned principally with the analysis of ethical and theological language.[1] The second, represented by the work of D.P. Henry and to a lesser extent by Jasper Hoskins and Herbert Richardson, emphasizes the parallels and connections between Anselmian linguistics and later scholastic and modern logic and tends to regard the theological contexts in which Anselm uses his theory of language as irrelevant.[2] Each of these perspectives has brought important features of Anselm's linguistic philosophy to light but both stand in need of correction. Neither can serve as an exclusive interpretation of his views on language.

A weakness of the first group of scholars has been their neglect of sources for Anselm apart from the eleventh-century revivals of Priscian and Boethius. There is substantial evidence to suggest that Carolingian thinkers were already heavily involved in the use of grammatical methods of analysing and structuring theological arguments.[3] Furthermore, there were sources of Stoic logic and linguistics available indirectly in the early Middle Ages by way of Augustine, Martianus Capella, and Cassiodorus that provide models for a number of Anselm's arguments, arguments that cannot be accounted for merely in terms of his familiarity with Priscian and Aristotle in Boethius' translation. Some of these Stoic themes had an enduring history in later medieval and modern logic. Several examples may be cited. There is the problem of the signification of the word *nihil*, which has no objective referent, an issue raised by Augustine's *De magistro* and by the ninth-century thinkers, Fredigisus and John the Scot, which crops up repeatedly in Anselm's writings, as well as in his well-known formula for the name of God in the *Proslogion*.[4] There is also the Stoic principle that prefacing a proposition with a negative particle negates the proposition more precisely than does simply negating the verb — a doctrine transmitted by Martianus Capella[5] which Anselm reflects in his analysis of the propositions *non possit malum facere* as applied to God, and *non posse peccare* as applied to angels.[6] Yet another case is the Stoic hypothetical syllogism, available through a number of Roman and early medieval authors,[7] which provides the basis for

Anselm's shift to an 'if/then' argument as he moves from the *Proslogion* to the *Contra Gaunilonem*.[8] A final and important example is the principle that propositions have their own natural, semantic truth, that logical intentions are distinct from objective significance, a notion that goes back to the Stoic doctrine that logical statements are *lekta* or incorporeals rather than being corporeal realities as are words and their significata.[9] This teaching was perpetuated by a number of Latin authors, most importantly Augustine, who discusses it in his *De dialectica* and who applies it in a number of his later works.[10] Augustine's *De dialectica* was copied in major Carolingian and Ottonian educational centres and there was a twelfth-century manuscript made of it at Bec.[11] Anselm's sensitivity to the issues raised by this doctrine can be seen in a number of his works and above all in his *De veritate*, which will be considered below. All of these examples suggest that Anselm was indeed much more concerned with the technical details of logic and linguistic theory than the purely theological and ethical emphasis of the first school of thought has emphasized, and that he was conversant with a wider range of classical and early medieval sources for that theory than has been appreciated.

Henry's chief contribution has been to direct attention to precisely those features of Anselm's linguistics where he was moving toward a technical language lacking the ambiguities and imprecisions of ordinary speech, as a tool for formal logic.[12] However, Henry has been inclined to ignore the fact that Anselm is concerned not only with the relation of ordinary language to formal logic but also with the relation of both ordinary language and formal logic alike to the physical and metaphysical realities to which they refer. There are numerous occasions where Anselm posits as the norm of the accuracy of propositions not their logical or grammatical cogency but their conformity to extra-linguistic or supra-linguistic criteria. Nor can the theological context in which he was operating be disregarded. Henry's emphasis leads him to treat the *De grammatico* as the paradigmatic work in Anselm's *oeuvre* and to push to one side the *De veritate* and other treatises that are of great importance for Anselmian linguistics. He also pays no attention to the chronology of Anselm's writings. In this connection it is worth noting that Anselm's most famous theological and philosophical treatises, the *Monologion*, *Proslogion*, and *Contra Gaunilonem*, were his earliest, dating to the years 1077-8. Next come the *De grammatico*, *De veritate*, and *De libertate arbitrii* (1080-5) and *De casu diaboli* (1085-90), with the rest dating to the 1190s for the most part. What this suggests is that Anselm first confronted the problem of linguistic analysis in a theological context; then he concerned himself with the more strictly technical aspects of linguistics; and then he applied it to other theological and moral issues. Both the original and eventual reasons why Anselm was interested in these questions need to be taken into account in understanding his philosophy of language and the place it occupies in his mentality, alongside of its intrinsic interest in the light of his sources or as a parallel or forerunner of what other logicians had done or would do later.

A broader and more balanced assessment of Anselm's linguistic theory can be achieved if neither of these perspectives is allowed to hold preclusive sway. An examination of the evidence in Anselm's *oeuvre*, even one that does not pretend to be exhaustive, shows that he has four main strategies as a linguistic philosopher. First, he sometimes asserts the principle that logical propriety is distinct from ordinary grammar, or the *usus loquendi*, and that, being more precise than ordinary speech, formal logic is intrinsically preferable to it. Second, he sometimes makes the *usus loquendi* the principle of explanation of other things, applying this norm to logical, ethical, metaphysical, and theological questions. Third, and on the other hand, he sometimes argues that grammar does not always correspond with real beings in the created universe and that it is those real beings and not grammar which control what may properly be said about them. Fourth, and this comprises the largest number of cases statistically, Anselm sometimes argues that grammar does not always correspond with Divine reality. In this case also, it is not the verbal cogency of theological propositions but the Being to Whom the speaker refers Who controls the linguistic and moral correctness of statements about God.

Two passages from Anselm's writings clearly illustrate the first of these strategies as cases where meaning, in a technical sense, supersedes ordinary speech. In *De casu diaboli*, 3, Anselm asserts the right of the author to create neologisms, even though they are barbarisms according to the *usus loquendi*, in order to make his meaning more precise. In this passage, accordingly, he coins the term *pervelle* to signify the perseverance of the will, the state of willing something completely, 'etiamsi non sit in usu'.[13] Even more striking is his assertion in *De grammatico*, 4, that logical cogency differs from the cogency of ordinary speech when he argues that the common term of a syllogism is to be found not so much in the form of utterance as in its meaning: 'sententia quippe ligat syllogismus, non verba'.[14]

When he uses the second strategy, however, Anselm does not hesitate to argue that grammar serves as the most cogent or useful principle of explanation for other things. Sometimes, in this connection, he means contemporary grammar as modified by Boethius and Aristotle, as in the example made famous thanks to Henry, the *De grammatico*, where he poses the question of how the word *grammaticus* signifies and how it is derived. Is it a nominal derivative from the discipline of *grammatica*? Is it a logical or chronological derivative from the flesh and blood man who happens to be a grammarian? Anselm, as we know, rules that the first of these derivations is proper, *per se*, while the second is *per aliud*, that is, the relationship deriving from grammatical declination is prior.[15]

There are times when Anselm's applications of grammar as a norm do not depend particularly on the Boethianized Aristotle current in his day. A good case is his repeated inquiry into the question of how *nihil* and other negative terms signify, a matter he considers in both a metaphysical and moral context. In *Monologion*, 8, he observes that, since *nihil* has no objective referent, the word is meaningless or self-contradictory if it is applied to something as if that thing did exist. Still, *nihil* is meaningful grammatically as the negative of *aliud*. Since it is grammatically intelligible, *nihil* is thus usable in metaphysical discourse, in explaining how God created the world *ex nihilo*.[16] Similarly, in *De casu diaboli*, 9-11,[17] *De conceptu Virginali et de originale peccato*, 6,[18] and *De potestate et impotentia Dei*,[19] he argues that, although evil as the privation of the good is non-being, the terms 'evil', or 'non-being', or specific manifestations of them, such as injustice, have a grammatical intelligibility and may hence be used in moral discourse despite their lack of objective reference. Grammatical declination also provides Anselm with principles for elucidating several other theological topics. In treating original sin in *De conceptu Virginale*, 1, he says that the term 'original' is to be understood as derived grammatically from the word 'origin': thus, he explains, original sin stems from man's original nature, not from any sins he may commit by choice.[20] Finally, in *Monologion*, 6, he explains the relations between God's essence and existence in terms of the relations between a noun and its correlative infinitive and participle in his analogy between *essentia: esse: ens* and *lux: lucere: lucens*.[21]

When he employs his third strategy Anselm feels perfectly free to turn this relationship upside down by arguing that real being in the created world is the norm of grammar and the criterion of the statements that can be properly made about man and nature. In two of his treatises on free will he notes that the term 'will' can be used in diverse senses. It may denote man's use of that faculty. And it may signify the affection that stimulates the application of the instrument to its use. According to Anselm the term 'will' properly denotes the will as an instrument or faculty of man, since this meaning points to an inherent aspect of human nature, while a man's affections or use of his will may be inconsistent in practice.[22] On a related issue, in *De libertate arbitrii*, 12, he raises the question of whether a man who sins is more properly called a 'slave to sin' or 'free'. It is more proper to call him 'free', Anselm argues, even when he is not using his freedom uprightly, because freedom of the will is intrinsic to human nature while the term 'slave' implies that man chooses to sin under constraint, which is not the case.[23] In this last example the terms 'slave' and 'free' possess equal grammatical cogency and it is not grammar but nature that governs which is to be used. The fact that grammar and nature are not isomorphic is something that Anselm underlines even more crisply in *De grammatico*, 12, where he notes that the Latin language has grammatical genders for inanimate objects that have no gender by nature and that it has neuter nouns which refer to human beings who by nature are either male or female. Grammar, thus, is no index of the real world.[24]

In the fourth and largest category of examples Anselm maintains that neither grammar nor logic is an index of the Divine reality; the nature of God often contravenes the ordinary denotations of the words that men must use in speaking about Him. In this connection Anselm insists that the criterion of theological language is not its grammatical or logical coherence but its rectitude. His basic analysis of this principle is found in *De veritate*, 2.[25] Here, he distinguishes statements that possess a natural truth from those that possess an accidental truth. The first class of statements possess *veritas* as a function of their semantic coherence. But they do not possess *rectitudo* unless they are objectively accurate as well as grammatically accurate. A statement that is grammatically well-formed retains that characteristic and possesses truth *naturaliter* even if it is a lie. Anselm thus clearly accepts the idea that statements can be significant and true in virtue of having an intelligible linguistic structure. At the same time, the chief point he makes in the *De veritate* is that the *veritas enuntiationis* ought to correspond with objective truth and that it is to be judged by its conformity to moral attitudes that promote correct judgement and action.

Armed with this doctrine, Anselm applies it to a number of theological issues. One, which he treats in several works, is how to use terminology which, when attributed to God, would appear to limit His power, freedom, goodness, or some other Divine quality.[26] If we say that God can lie, or do evil, or do something unjust, or give another being an evil will, or lead someone into temptation, he notes, we are making statements that are perfectly intelligible and grammatically accurate. However, such statements cannot properly be made about God. The criterion of theological statements, he concludes, is not their linguistic cogency but their theological fitness. Where God is concerned, apparent limitations can actually be perfections.

This conclusion holds not only for apparently privative language, but also for theological language in general. In *Monologion*, 26, Anselm supplies an *idée maîtresse* which he repeats elsewhere. He asserts that if the same term is applied to God and other beings it must signify something different in God's case: 'Unde si quando illi est cum aliis nominis alicuius communio, valde procul dubio

intelligenda est diversa significatio.'[27] Thus, he argues in
Monologion, 15-17, that it is not proper to attribute superlatives or
the terms 'substance' and 'accident' to God because they denote
beings capable of gradations and subject to change. He also asserts
in the same section of that work that it is proper to apply
infinitive statements to God although the criterion of their accuracy
is not their grammatical form but their content.[28] Thus, he argues
that propositions which may make perfect sense when applied to
human beings or natural phenomena, real or possible, do not
necessarily make sense when applied to God. He illustrates this
point in *Contra Gaunilonem*, 3, in his attack on Gaunilo's position
concerning the imaginability of the non-existence of a perfect but
necessarily contingent island,[29] and in defending the Latin doctrine
of the *filioque* against the Greek Church in *De processione spiritus
sancti*, 9-10, where he claims that the Greeks have misunderstood
the eternal procession of the Holy Spirit by extrapolating the idea
of procession from natural, and necessarily temporal processes, such
as the flow of a river from its source.[30]

In the most extreme sort of case, Anselm asserts that statements lacking an objective correspondence with God are not only
incorrect with respect to God, whatever their ostensible
grammatical cogency may be, but also that they even lack internal
linguistic coherence or natural truth, in the *De veritate* sense, when
they are uttered with the wrong moral attitude, which would be the
case if the speaker were a fool or a heretic. It is on this basis that
he castigates Roscellinus for his use of the names Father, Son and
Holy Spirit to signify God *per aliud* when they actually signify Him
per se; these names, in Roscellinus' mouth, are *flatus vocis*.[31] It is
also on the same basis, in one of Anselm's most celebrated
arguments, that he analyses the statement 'non est Deus' in the
mouth of the fool, claiming that, since the term *Deus* is com-
prehensible to anyone who knows the Latin language, it is folly to
deny its meaning and hence 'non est Deus' is gibberish.[32] These last
two examples of statements or words which are *flatus vocis*,
although they are grammatically intelligible, are characteristically
Anselmian in that they reflect his recognition of the natural truth
and the intrinsic significance of language even though in these
instances he subjects that truth and significance to the norm of
ethical and epistemological rectitude with extreme rigour.

This point leads to the only kind of conclusions which it seems
accurate to draw about Anselm's theory of language. He does not
confine himself preclusively to any of the four strategies illustrated
in this paper. He sometimes uses more than one of them in the
same work. We must therefore avoid the kind of hyper-selectivity
which would make him look exclusively like a modern linguistic
analyst and symbolic logician *avant la lettre*, on the one hand, or
like a proponent of the Platonic and Pauline doctrine of the poverty
of language, on the other. We must accept the fact that his view

of language is unsystematic, developed for its practical utility in solving the particular problems that he had on his agenda, without seeking to reduce his thought on this subject to a state of consistency or synthesis which Anselm himself was not interested in attaining.

NOTES

1. Marcia L. Colish, *The Mirror of Language: A Study in the Medieval Theory of Knowledge* (New Haven, 1968), pp. 93-111, 132 ff., 142; Marcia L. Colish, 'Eleventh-century grammar in the thought of St Anselm', *Arts libéraux et philosophie: Actes du IVe congrès international de philosophie médiévale, Montréal, 27 août − 2 septembre 1967* (Montreal-Paris, 1969), pp. 785-95; G.R. Evans, *Anselm and Talking about God* (Oxford, 1978); George S. Heyer, Jr., '*Rectitudo* in the theology of St Anselm' (unpublished Ph.D. dissertation, Yale University, 1963); Robert Pouchet, *La Rectitudo chez saint Anselme; Un itinéraire augustinien de l'âme à Dieu* (Paris, 1964); R.W. Southern, 'Lanfranc of Bec and Berengar of Tours', in *Studies in Medieval History presented to Frederick Maurice Powicke*, edited by R.W. Hunt, W.A. Pantin, and R.W. Southern (Oxford, 1948), pp. 27-48; R.W. Southern, *Saint Anselm and his Biographer* (Cambridge, 1963), pp. 12-14, 20-6; Thomas F. Torrance, 'The ethical implications of Anselm's *De veritate*', *Theologische Zeitschrift*, 24 (1968), 309-19. The most recent reprise of this position is G. Söhngen, 'Rectitudo bei Anselm von Canterbury als Oberbegriff von Wahrheit und Gerechtigkeit', in *Sola ratione: Anselm-Studien für Pater Dr. h.c. Franciscus Salesius Schmitt OSB zum 75. Geburtstag am 20. Dezember 1969* (Stuttgart, 1970), pp. 71-7. A study placing Anselm's linguistics in a primarily metaphysical and theological context is William J. Courtenay, 'Necessity and freedom in Anselm's conception of God', in *Analecta Anselmiana*, 4:2, (1975) 39-64.

2. D.P. Henry, 'Why *Grammaticus?*', *Archivum Latinitatis Medii Aevi*, 28 (1958), 165-80; D.P. Henry, 'Saint Anselm as a logician', in *Sola ratione*, pp. 13-17: D.P. Henry, 'Saint Anselm's *De grammatico*', *The Philosophical Quarterly*, 10 (1960), 115-26; D.P. Henry, *The 'De grammatico' of St Anselm: The Theory of Paronymy* (Notre Dame, 1964); D.P. Henry, *The Logic of St Anselm* (Oxford, 1967), especially pp. 24, 230-9; D.P. Henry, *Commentary on 'De grammatico': Historical-Logical Dimensions of a Dialogue of St Anselm's* (Dordrecht, 1974); Jasper Hoskins,

A *Companion to the Study of St Anselm* (Minneapolis, 1972), pp. 246-53; Anselm, *Truth, Freedom, and Evil: Three Philosophical Dialogues*, translated by Jasper Hopkins and Herbert Richardson, revised edition (New York, 1967), Introduction, pp. 12-26. The most recent effort to recast Anselm in terms of modern semantics is Wolfgang Leopold Gombocz, *Über E! Zur Semantik des Existenzprädikates und des ontologisches Argumentes für Gottes Existenz von Anselm von Canterbury* (Vienna, 1974). On the other hand, Helmut Kohlenberger, *Similitudo und Ratio: Überlegung zur Methode bei Anselm von Canterbury* (Bonn, 1972) ignores both the classical and early medieval background and treats Anselm in a historical vacuum.

3. In addition to the figures noted in Colish, *Mirror*, pp. 93-8, see E. Bertola, 'I precedenti storici del metodo del *Sic et Non* di Abelardo', *Rivista de filosofia neo-scolastica*, 53 (1961), 255-80; Leo Donald Davies, 'Hincmar of Rheims as a theologian of the Trinity', *Traditio*, 27 (1971), 455-68; Jean Devisse, *Hincmar, archevêque de Reims 845-882*, 2 vols. (Geneva, 1975-6), I, 161-70; G.R. Evans, 'The Grammar of predestination in the ninth century', *Journal of Theological Studies*, n.s. 33 (1982), 134-45; Margaret Gibson, *Lanfranc of Bec* (Oxford, 1978), pp. 42-4, 46-50, 57, 71-91; Henry, *Commentary on 'De grammatico'*, p. 336; Jean Jolivet, *Godescalc d'Orbais et la Trinité; la méthode de la théologie à l'époque carolingienne* (Paris, 1958); Jean Jolivet, 'Quelques cas de platonisme grammaticale du VIIe au XIIe siècles', in *Mélanges offerts à René Crozet*, edited by Pierre Gallais and Yves-Jean Riou, 2 vols. (Poitiers, 1968), I, 97-8; F.S. Schmitt, notes to his edition of *De casu diaboli*, *Ans.Op.Om.*, I, 249.

4. Augustine, *De magistro*, 2.3, edited by Guenther Weigel, *Corpus scriptorium ecclesiasticorum Latinorum*, 77 (Vienna, 1961); On Fredigisus, see Concettina Gennaro, *Fridugiso di Tours e il 'De substantia nihili et tenebrarum': Edizione critica e studio introduttivo* (Padua, 1963); John Marenbon, *From the Circle of Alcuin to the School of Auxerre: Logic, Theology and Philosophy in the Early Middle Ages* (Cambridge, 1981), pp. 62-4; Henry, *Commentary on 'De grammatico'*, p. 336; *Ans.Op.Om.*, I, 249; on John the Scot, see Donald F. Duclow, 'Divine nothingness and self-creation in John Scotus Eriugena', *Journal of Religion*, 57 (1977), 110-15; Gustavo A. Piemonte, 'Notas sobre la *creatio ex nihilo* en Juan Escoto Eriugena', *Sapienta*, 23 (1968), 37-58; I.P. Sheldon Williams, in the Introduction to his edition of John the Scot, *Periphyseon*, Book 3 (Dublin, 1981), pp. 5-11; on the backgrounds of the *Proslogion* formula, see Guiseppe Cenacchi, *Il pensiero filosofico di Anselmo d'Aosta* (Padua, 1974).

5. Martianus Capella, *De nuptiis Philologiae et Mercurii*, 4.402, edited by Jean Préaux and Adolfus Dick (Stuttgart, 1969). Noted

by Richard Johnson and E.R. Burge, 'A study of allegory and the verbal disciplines', in *Martianus Capella and the Seven Liberal Arts*, translated by William Harris Stahl, Richard Johnson and E.R. Burge, 2 vols. (New York, 1971), I, 108.

6. *Ein neues unvollendetes Werk des Hl. Anselm von Canterbury*, edited by F.S. Schmitt, Beiträge zur Geschichte der Philosophie und Theologie des Mittelalters, 33:3 (Münster, 1936), p. 24; *De libertate arbitrii*, 1-2, *Ans.Op.Om.*, I, 207-10; *De casu diaboli*, 25, *Ans.Op.Om.*, I, 272-3.

7. For the original Stoic background, see *Stoicorum veterum fragmenta*, edited by H.F.A. von Arnim, 4 vols. (Leipzig, 1903-24), II, 182, 207-8, 213, 215, 241-2, 245. Latin authors who perpetuate some or all of the Stoic hypotheticals include Cicero, *Topica*, 12.53-13.55, translated by H.M. Hubbell, Loeb Classical Library (Cambridge, Mass., 1960); Martianus Capella, *De nuptiis*, 4.414-22; Cassiodorus Senator, *Institutiones*, 2.3.13, edited by R.A.B. Mynors (Oxford, 1937). For a comparative analysis of these figures as transmitters of the doctrine, see Pierre Hadot, *Marius Victorinus: Recherches sur sa vie et ses oeuvres* (Paris, 1971), pp. 243-56. Isidore of Seville repeats Cassiodorus' formulation verbatim, as noted by Leslie Webber Jones in the Introduction to his translation of Cassiodorus, *An Introduction to Divine and Human Readings*, Records of Civilisation, Sources and Studies, 40 (New York, 1946), p. 167 note 44.

8. *Contra Gaunilonem*, 1, *Ans.Op.Om.*, I, 130-2.

9. For the Stoic background, see von Arnim, *SVF*, I, 93-7, 488; II, 132, 166, 168, 170, 181, 183, 331, 335, 501-2, 511, 514, 522-4, 534-46; Diogenes Laertius, *Lives of the Eminent Philosophers*, 7.63-81, translated by R.D. Hicks, 2 vols., Loeb Classical Library (London, 1925); Émile Bréhier, 'La théorie des incorporels dans l'ancien stoïcisme', *Archiv für Geschichte der Philosophie*, 22, n.F., 15 (1909), pp. 114-25; Andreas Graeser, 'A propos *huparchein* bei den Stoikern', *Archiv für Begriffs geschichte*, 15, (1971), pp. 299-305; A.A. Long, 'Language and thought in Stoicism', in *Problems in Stoicism*, edited by A.A. Long (London, 1971), pp. 90-104.
  The major recent studies that have related the logical doctrine of *lekta* to the Stoic system as a whole include Urs Egli, *Zur stoischen Dialektik* (Basel, 1967), pp. 93-104; Michael Frede, *Die stoische Logik*, Abhandlungen der Akademie der Wissenschaft in Göttingen, philosophisch-historische Klasse, 3:88 (Göttingen, 1974); Josiah B. Gould, *The Philosophy of Chrysippus* (Albany, 1970), pp. 66-88; Lorenzo Pozzi, 'Il nesso di implicazione nella logica stoica', in *Atti del convegno di storia della logica, Parma, 8-10 ottobre 1972* (Padua, 1974), pp. 177-87;

Antoinette Virieux-Reymond, *La Logique et l'épistémologie des Stoïciens* (Chambéry, 1949).

10. The Latin transmitters of this doctrine prior to Augustine include Publius Nigidius Figulus, *Operum reliquae*, Fragments 4 and 5, edited by Antonius Swoboda (Vienna, 1889), pp. 67-8, 76-7, and Aulus Gellius, *Noctes atticae*, 11.12.1 edited by P.K. Marshall (Oxford, 1968). Augustine, *De dialectica*, 5, 9, edited by Jan Pinborg, translated by B. Darrell Jackson (Dordrecht, 1975), pp. 86-90, 106-12 is the first Latin author to treat this idea in its original logical context. For an analysis of Augustine's handling of the doctrine of *lekta*, and his application of it to some of his other works, see Balduinus Fischer, *De Augustinii disciplinarum libro qui est de dialectica* (Jena, 1912), pp. 32, 36-9; B. Darrell Jackson, 'The theory of signs in St Augustine's *De Doctrina Christiana*', in *Augustine: A Collection of Critical Essays*, edited by R.A. Markus (Garden City, N.Y., 1972), pp. 123-5; Jean Pépin, *Saint Augustin et la dialectique* (Villanova, 1976) pp. 72-98; Augustine, *De dialectica*, Pinborg's commentary on his edition, pp. 123 note 2, 124 note 3, 125 note 4, 126 note 7, 131 note 2; Jan Pinborg, 'Das Sprachdenken der Stoa und Augustins Dialektik', *Classica et Mediaevalia*, 22 (1962), pp. 158-74; Alfred Schindler, *Wort und Analogie in Augustins Trinitätslehre* (Tübingen, 1965), pp. 76-81, 86-118, 250-1; Eugene TeSelle, *Augustine the Theologian* (New York, 1970), p. 225; Myra L. Uhlfelder, '"Nature" in Roman linguistic texts', *Transactions and Proceedings of the American Philological Association*, 97 (1966), 588.

11. On the manuscript tradition, see Jackson in the Introduction to his translation of Augustine, *De dialectica*, edited by Pinborg, pp. 6-20.

12. This tendency is visible throughout Henry's works but is stated most crisply in *The Logic of St Anselm*, p. 12.

13. *Ans.Op.Om.*, I, 238.

14. *Ans.Op.Om.*, I, 149.

15. *Ans.Op.Om.*, I, 157.

16. *Ans.Op.Om.*, I, 22-4.

17. *Ans.Op.Om.*, I, 246-51.

18. *Ans.Op.Om.*, II, 147.

19. Schmitt, *Ein neues unvollendetes Werk*, p. 24.

20. *Ans.Op.Om.*, II, 140-1.

21. *Ans.Opm.Om.*, I, 20.

22. *De libertate arbitrii*, 7, *Ans.Op.Om.*, I, 218-20; *De concordia praescientiae et praedestinationis gratiae Dei cum libero arbitrio*, 3. 11, *Ans.Op.Om.*, II, 278-9.

23. *Ans.Op.Om.*, I, 223-4.

24. *Ans.Op.Om.*, I, 164.

25. *Ans.Op.Om.*, I, 177-80.

26. *De potestate et impotentia Dei*, in Schmitt, *Ein neues unvollendetes Werk*, p. 24, where Anselm raises this question but does not answer it; and the following references where he does answer it: *Proslogion*, 7, *Ans.Op.Om.*, I, 105-6; *De casu diaboli*, 1, *Ans.Op.Om.*, I, 234-5; *Cur Deus homo*, 1, 6-10, *Ans.Op.Om.*, II, 53-67; *De concordia*, 2 and 4, *Ans.Op.Om.*, II, 247-50, 252-3.

27. *Ans.Op.Om.*, I, 44.

28. *Ans.Op.Om.*, I, 28-32.

29. *Ans.Op.Om.*, I, 133.

30. *Ans.Op.Om.*, II, 201-6.

31. *De incarnatione verbi*, 1-6, *Ans.Op.Om.*, II, 6-21.

32. *Proslogion*, 4, *Ans.Op.Om.*, I, 103-4; *Contra Gaunilonem*, 7, *Ans.Op.Om.*, I, 136-7.

Anselm über Sinn und Bedeutung*

Wolfgang L. Gombocz

Der philosophische Normalverbraucher verbindet den Namen Anselm von Canterbury mit dem ontologischen Gottesbeweis, und das in einer Weise, dass das *Proslogion*, welche Schrift den Beweis enthält, zu einem Symbol wird, wie z.B. der Zeushymnus des Kleanthes oder Augustins *Confessiones*. Das *Proslogion* ist die zweite Schrift Anselms in der zeitlichen Reihenfolge seiner Werke, da es 1077-8 nach Fertigstellung des *Monologion* (1076) entstand. Es ist die Arbeit eines seit mehr als 15 Jahren im Lehramt tätigen, bereits über 40 Jahre alten Forschers des 11. Jahrhunderts.

Als der Student Anselm 1059 Bec erreichte, war die Kontroverse um die Wandlungsworte der Hl. Messe zwischen Berengar von Tours und Lanfrank, dem Lehrer und Förderer Anselms, auf dem Höhepunkt. Das durch und durch theologische Problem, betreffend die reale Präsenz Christi im eucharistischen Brot und Wein, wird jedoch rein sprachphilosophisch im Stile der damals neuen Grammatik, welche u.a. unter Einfluss der *logica vetus* 'aristotelisiert' ward, abgehandelt. Berengars Argument stützt sich auf die Analyse der Wandlungsworte *Hoc est enim corpus meum* unter Heranziehung der theoretischen Unterscheidung (samt ihren Konsequenzen) des Nomens, dessen *significatio* substantiell oder akzidentell sein kann, und des Pronomens, dessen *significatio* ausschliesslich substantiell ist. *Hoc*, als Beginn und grammatisches Subjekt der Wandlungsworte, bringt nun Berengar darauf, die substantielle Wandlung von Brot und Wein in Christi Leib und Blut aufgrund logisch-grammatsicher Argumentation abzulehen, weil eben *hoc* als Subjekt des Satzes und wegen seiner ausschliesslich substantiellen Bezeichnungsfunktion, die auf Brot und Wein gerichtet ist, über *corpus meum* regiert; d.h. wäre es so, wie die Theologen sagen, würde das Subjekt des Satzes zerstört, ja in nichts aufgelöst werden. Berengar musste die Beifallspender auf seiner Seite haben, da das Argument für die gebildete Öffentlichkeit des 11. Jahrhunderts dem Standard der Wissenschaft entsprach: Logik, ja offensichtlich Logik, allerdings auf Grammatik fussend. Dennoch liess sich der Theologe Lanfrank dadurch nicht überzeugen; doch dies gehört nicht in dieses Kapitel der Philosophie des 11. Jahrhunderts, welches Anselms Bedeutungslehre darstellen möchte.

Anselm hatte die günstige Gelegenheit, mit den Methoden beider Kontrahenten vertraut zu werden, eine Gelegenheit, die Anselm wahrlich nützte. Obwohl Anselm sie schliesslich übertraf, lernte er sehr viel von beiden. So hat Anselm Lanfranks sog. Aequipollenztechnik des Beweisens ebenso weitergeführt, wie z.B. Berengars

Interesse an den sprachlichen Formen und Regeln, die bei der Entwicklung von Beweisen entscheidend sind, geteilt. Diese erste und junge Bekanntschaft mit Problemen der Grammatik und Dialektik führte offenbar frühzeitig zu einem grossen und neuen, theoretischen Entwurf innerhalb Anselms Lehrtätigkeit: Eine neue Dialektik, sprich Logik, unter Einbeziehung der Semantik. Es sei vorweg gesagt: eine *Dialectica* von Anselm gibt (und gab) es nicht; Lanfranks *Dialectica* ist ebenso wie die *Quaestiones* verlorengegangen. Was wir aber haben, ist die im gesamten Werk Anselms im Hintergrund stehende neue und moderne Logik, die bald stärker, bald schwächer, auch im Text selbst erhebbar ist. Der etwas später enstandene Dialog *De Grammatico* und die sog. *Lambeth-Fragmente* sind voll dieser Bedeutungslehre. Wir wollen hier aber, bevor wir uns diesen besonders relevanten Texten widmen, den, soweit mir bekannt, erstmaligen Versuch wagen, das später noch zu vervollständigende System Anselms aus dem allseits bekannten und gelesenen *Proslogion* zu destillieren. Dabei darf vorausgesetzt werden, dass der Nichtspezialist unter den Lesern, bekannte Texte, nämlich das *Proslogion*, Gaunilos Gegenschrift und Anselms Antwort darauf, unter einem neuen Geschichtspunkt geordnet und gedeutet findet, während allerdings der Anselmforscher, soweit er sich für die Logik und Semantik Anselms interessiert, über so viel neues Material überrascht sein wird.

Anselms Bedeutungslehre im Kontext des Proslogionbeweises

Die gewöhnliche Lektüre des *Proslogion* beginnt mit Kapitel 2 und endet mit Kapitel 4, ein Usus, der offensichtlich schon zu Anselms Zeiten einsetzt, wie das dem *Proslogion* nachgestellte *Sumptum ex eodem libello*[1] zeigt. Nun, für unsere Fragestellung finden sich *de facto* keine Hinweise vor *Proslogion* 2, womit wir dem Usus, zumindest was den Anfang der Lektüre betrifft, folgen können:

> Aliud enim est rem esse in intellectu, aliud intelligere rem esse. [. . .] Cum vero iam pinxit, et habet in intellectu et intelligit esse quod iam fecit. [. . .] Existit . . . aliquid . . . et in intellectu et in re.[2]

> Eines ist es nämlich, dass ein Gegenstand *in intellectu* ist, ein anderes [aber] einzusehen, dass ein Gegenstand existiert. [. . .] Wenn er [*sc.* der Maler] aber bereits gemalt hat, hat er es sowohl *in intellectu*, als er auch einsieht, dass das, was er bereits gemacht hat, existiert. [. . .] Etwas . . . existiert . . . sowohl *in intellectu* als auch in Wirklichkeit.

Für Anselm gibt es also mindestens zwei Existenzweisen eines Gegenstandes,[3] nämlich (1) *in intellectu* (im Verstande, im Sinne) zu sein, und (2) *in re* (in Wirklichkeit) zu sein, d.h. zu existieren. Eingangs des Zitates weist er nun darauf hin, dass es wesentlich ist, die Tatsache, dass (1), vom Einsehen, dass (2) der Fall ist, zu unterscheiden; d.h. unser Verstand kann, wenn er einen Gegenstand untersucht, sich diesem auf der Ebene des *intellectus* (des Sinnes, der Intension) nähern, er kann aber auch dessen wahre Existenz zum Ausgangspunkt nehmen. Damit zieht Anselm zu Beginn seines berühmten Beweises eine Unterscheidung an, die im Lichte von Kapitel 4, wo auch die Zeichen - bzw. Wortebene ins Spiel kommt, so gedeutet werden kann, dass sie die Aufspaltung in Intension und Extension vorwegnimmt: man kann einen Gegenstand — wie Gaunilo in seiner Gegenschrift *Pro Insipiente* 2 formuliert[4] — 'habere in intellectu' (in Sinne haben), ohne deswegen zugeben zu müssen, dass der Gegenstand auch existiere ('intelligere rem esse'). Mit anderen Worten ausgedrückt: Existenz *in intellectu* und Existenz *in re*, Intension und Extension, sind streng zu trennen, da sie 'aliud . . . aliud' sind.

Proslogion 3 arbeitet nun mit dieser Unterscheidung, während Kapitel 4 sie unter erweitertem Geschichtspunkt wieder thematisch aufnimmt:

> . . . idem sit dicere in corde et cogitare. [. . .] . . . non uno tantum modo dicitur aliquid in corde vel cogitatur. Aliter enim cogitatur res cum vox eam significans cogitatur, aliter cum id ipsum quod res est intelligitur. Illo itaque modo potest cogitari deus non esse, isto vero minime. [. . .] . . . licet haec verba dicat in corde, aut sine ulla aut cum aliqua extranea significatione.[5]

> . . . im Herzen sprechen und denken sind dasselbe . [. . .] . . . [aber] etwas wird nicht bloss auf eine Weise im Herzen gesprochen oder gedacht: eines ist es nämlich, einen Gegenstand zu denken, wenn [dabei] der Laut, der ihn bezeichnet, gedacht wird, ein anderes, [einen Gegenstand zu denken,] wenn das selbst, was der Gegenstand ist, eingesehen wird. Auf jene Weise [d.i. rein verbal] kann gedacht werden, dass Gott nicht existiert, auf diese Weise jedoch nie und nimmer. [. . .] . . . oder man spricht diese Worte im Herzen entweder ohne jeden Sinn, oder mit irgendeiner aussergewöhnlichen [d.i. fremden] Bedeutung.

Der Unterscheidung von Intension und Extension aus *Proslogion* 2 tritt hier die Unterscheidung zwischen dem Sprachzeichen (*vox, verbum*) und jenen obigen zur Seite. Die Formulierung 'id ipsum quod res est' lässt vordergründig offen, ob Anselm hier auf Intension oder Extension einer *vox significans*, eines *verbum cum significatione* anspielt, obgleich einem esse rei (vgl. *De Grammatico* 5 u. 13, sowie die Tabelle 1) für die Sinnkomponente (Intension) in den Sinn kommt.

Nach der Lektüre des Proslogionargumentes, d.h. der üblichen Kapitel 2-4, sind wir demnach in der Lage, Anselms strenge

Trennung innerhalb seiner wenigstens dreiteiligen Semantik zu rekonstruieren: einem sprachlichen Zeichen, sei es geschrieben, sei es gesprochen *(quod audit; quod dico)*, entspricht ein *intellectus* (ein *intelligere*; ein Sinn, eine Intension) und, im Falle des im *Proslogion* analysierten Begriffes eines Wesens 'quo nihil maius cogitari potest', auch eine *res* bzw. eine *natura in re* (eine Extension; Frege würde sagen, dem Zeichen, d.i. der Wortverbindung, kommt Bedeutung zu).

Wir wollen nun weiterlesen, um ähnliche Stellen aus Anselms *Proslogion* und der Diskussion mit Gaunilo zu selektieren. *Proslogion* 9 — in der Umgebung des theologisch äusserst schwierigen Problems, warum der höchst gerechte Gott sich der Bösen erbarmt — benützt diese semantische Unterscheidung, wenn Anselm dort Gott bittet, 'adiuva me, ut intelligam quod dico' (hilf mir, dass ich verstehe, was ich sage); *Proslogion* 16 gibt er dann zu, dass ihm gewisse theologische Sätze nicht mehr verstehbar sind, d.h. keinen Sinn haben, wenn er sagt: 'Non potest intellectus meus ad illam'. (Mein Sinn kann nicht an es heran.) Es ist die Konnotationsbreite von *intellectus* und *intelligere*, auf die wir besonders achten müssen, um nicht Überinterpretation zu betreiben, da auf der anderen Seite mancherlei Übersetzer dabei unterinterpretieren (vgl. *Proslogion* 18):

> Quid es, domine, quid es, quid te intelligit cor meum? [. . .] Multa sunt haec, non potest angustus intellectus meus tot uno simul intuitu videre . . . [. . .] . . . immo tu es ipsa unitas, nullo intellectu divisibilis.[6]

> Was bist du, Herr, was bist du, als was sieht mein Herz dich an? [. . .] Das ist viel, mein enger Sinn kann nicht soviel zugleich mit einem *intuitus* sehen . . . [. . .] . . . vielmehr bist du die Einheit selbst, in keinem Sinne teilbar.

Gaunilo, obgleich bereits mehr also 80 Jahre alt, erweist sich als gelehriger Schüler, wenn er, ohne den Anselmschen Umgang mit Lanfrank und Berengar geteilt zu haben, sein Semantiklesestück von *Pro Insipiente* 4[7] in Kapitel 3 bereits andeutet:

> . . . aliud sine dubio est verum illud, aliud intellectus ipse quo capitur.[8]

> . . . eines ist ohne Zweifel jener wirklich [existierende Gegenstand], ein anderes der *intellectus* selbst, mittels dessen er erfasst wird.

Hier greift er auf *Proslogion* 2 zürück, um Anselms theoretischen Hintergrund zwar zu akzeptieren, die daraus gezogenen Schlüsse bezüglich Gottes Existenz aber abzulehnen. Kapitel 4 nun ist eine Fundgrube Anselmisch-Gaunilonischer Semantik:

> . . . cum tamen ego de illo secundum veram nihilominus rem, non quae esset ille homo, sed quae est homo quilibet, cogitarem . [. . .] . . . istud omnino nequeam nisi tantum

secundum vocem [sc. cogitare], [. . .] siquidem cum ita
cogitatur, non tam vox ipsa quae res est utique vera, hoc
est litterarum sonus vel syllabarum, quam vocis auditae significatio cogitetur. [. . .] Ita [sc. secundum vocem tantum]
ergo nec prorsus aliter adhuc in intellectu meo . . .⁹

. . . dennoch würde ich von ihm gedacht haben unter
Bezugnahme auf [jenen] wirklichen Gegenstand, welcher
jeder Mensch ist, und nicht [unter Bezugnahme auf jenen],
welcher dieser Mensch ist. [. . .] . . . jenes kann ich
keinesfalls anders als nur dem Worte nach [denken], [. . .]
denn wenn man so [sc. nur dem Worte nach] denkt, dann
denkt man nicht so sehr das Wort selbst, welches [seiner-
seits] sicherlich ein wirklicher Gegenstand ist, d.h. [nicht so
sehr] den Klang der Buchstaben ober Silben, als vielmehr die
Bezeichnung des gehörten Wortes. [. . .] So, also, und nicht
anders, ist [etwas] in meinem Verstande . . .

Um Anselms Argument, und vor allem der Konklusion zu
entkommen, reduziert Gaunilo bezüglich 'quo nihil maius cogitari
potest' — nicht allgemein natürlich! — in-intellectu-sein auf
'intelligere tantum secundum vocem', was er Kapitel 5 auch
expressis verbis tut:

Si esse dicendum est in intellectu, quod secundum veritatem
cuiusquam rei nequit saltem cogitari: et hoc in meo sic esse
non denego. [. . .] . . .nec aliud ei esse concedo quam
illud, si dicendum est esse, cum secundum vocem tantum
auditam rem prorsus ignotam sibi conatur animus
effingere.¹⁰

Wenn von dem, das nicht einmal wahrheitsgetreu gedacht
werden kann, gesagt werden muss, dass es *in intellectu* ist,
dann leugne ich es nicht ab, dass es in diesem [uneigent-
lichen] Sinne in meinem [Verstande] ist [. . .] . . .ich
konzediere [aber] diesem Wesen keine andere Existenz
[weise], als jene — falls man das [überhaupt noch] Existenz
nennen kann — , die [vorliegt], wenn der Geist versucht,
ein Ding, das ihm gänzlich unbekannt ist, aufgrund des
Wortes allein, das er hört, zu erfassen.

Gaunilo, der Kapitel 6 dem 'dictum' ein 'intelligo' zuordnet,¹¹ hat
damit Anselms Instrumentarium gegen diesen zurückgewendet, da er
meint und nachzuweisen sucht, dass 'quo nihil maius cogitari potest'
eine reine Wortsammlung ('tantum prolatio') ohne möglichen Sinn
('sine ullo intellectu') bleibt. Anselm aber weiss, dass der Beweis
ohne das Verstehen der Formel (im Anselmschen Sinne) ein
Paralogismus, ja wörtlich, ein Trick mit Worten, bleibt. Anselms
Antwort, in *Responsio* 2, auf Gaunilos Reduktionismus lässt daher
auch nicht lange auf sich warten:

Utique qui non intelligit si nota lingua dicitur, aut nullum aut nimis obrutum habet intellectum.[12]

Selbstverständlich gilt, wenn in bekannter Sprache gesprochen wird, dass wer nicht versteht, entweder keinen oder ziemlich wenig Sinn hat.

Doch Anselm verlegt sich dann stärker auf inhaltliche Argumente, da Gaunilo formal nicht beizukommen ist. (Beiläufig erwähnt er aber z.B. Kapitel 4 die mehrstufige Bezeichnungsfunktion von Worten, wenn er sagt: 'Si quis igitur sic distinguat huius prolationis has duas sententias . . .'[13] (. . . diese zwei Sinne dieser Äusserung . . .).) Wir sind damit bei den ersten Synonymen für *intellectus* innerhalb der Bedeutungslehre angelangt: *sententia* und *sensus*, wie z.B. *Responsio* 7, wo Anselm *intellectus/intelligere* und *sensus* austauschbar verwendet:

. . . quia negat deum, cuius sensum nullo modo cogitat.[14]

. . . weil er Gott leugnet, wessen Sinn er in keiner Weise denkt.

Non ergo irrationabiliter contra insipientem ad probandum deum esse attuli *quo maius cogitari non possit*, cum illud nullo modo, istud aliquo modo intelligeret.[15]

Ich habe ja nicht ohne zu denken zum Beweis der Existenz Gottes gegen den Toren *quo maius cogitari non possit* herangezogen, damit er, wenn er jenes [sc. *deus*] gar nicht, dieses [sc. *quo* . . .] doch in gewisser Weise versteht.

Der Streit um das Verstehen der Formel (zwischen Anselm und Gaunilo) braucht nicht lange hin und her zu gehen, da bis heute nicht gezeigt wurde, dass der Verdacht der Widersprüchlichkeit,16 von Anselm selber bereits in *Responsio* 8 durch den Definitionshinweis auf die Menge aller Dinge, über die Grösseres gedacht werden kann, auf die Tagesordnung gesetzt, unbegründet ist.

Die Proslogionlektüre abschliessend wollen wir nun noch zwei Textstellen, nämlich *Proslogion* 7 and *Responsio* 9, wegen der darin enthaltenen allgemeineren Beiträge zu seiner Semantik, betrachten. Kapitel 7 behandelt die Frage, wie Gott allmächtig genannt werden könne, da er doch vieles nicht kann. Um die theologische Engstelle zu meistern, erinnert er sich seiner Unterscheidung von grammatischer und logischer Form einer Aussage, nach welcher wir vieles uneigentlich (*improprie*) sagen, solange wir dem Usus der Umgangsprache folgen; und was für die Philosophie gut ist, soll der Theologie nicht schaden:

Qui ergo sic potest, non potentia potest, sed impotentia. Non enim ideo dicitur posse, quia ipse possit, sed quia sua impotentia facit aliud in se posse; sive aliquo alio genere loquendi, sicut multa improprie dicuntur. Ut cum ponimus esse pro non esse, et facere pro eo quod est non facere, aut pro nihil facere. Nam saepe dicimus ei qui rem aliquam esse negat: sic est quemadmodum dicis esse, cum magis proprie videatur dici: sic non est quemadmodum dicis non esse. Item dicimus: iste sedet sicut ille facit, aut: iste quiescit sicut ille facit, cum sedere sit quiddam non facere et quiescere sit nihil facere.[17]

Wer also in der Weise [etwas] kann, kann es nicht aus Macht, sondern aus Ohnmacht. Denn nicht deshalb sagt man 'können', weil er selber kann, sondern weil seine Ohnmacht bewirkt, dass anderes gegen ihn etwas ausrichtet; oder [man sagt es gar] in einer wiederum anderen Redensart, wie vieles uneigentlich gesagt wird: So z.B. setzen wir 'sein' für 'nicht sein', und 'tun' für das, was ein Nichttun ist, oder für 'nichts tun'. Oft sagen wir nämlich zu einem, der die Existenz eines Gegenstandes abstreitet: 'So ist es, wie du sagst, dass es sich verhält', obgleich offensichtlich viel richtiger [mehr eigentlich] zu sagen wäre: 'So ist es nicht, wie du sagst, dass es sich nicht verhält'. Ebenso sagen wir: 'Jener da sitzt, so wie jener dort [auch] tut'; oder: 'Jener da ruht, so wie jener dort [auch] tut', obschon 'sitzen' 'etwas nicht tun' und 'ruhen' 'nichts tun' bedeuten.

Uns interessieren hier besonders die abschliessenden Bemerkungen über die wahre logische Form bzw. Bedeutung von Aussagen, die wir notgedrungenerweise den grammatischen Regeln entsprechend, aber damit oft uneigentlich, formulieren. (Der erste Teil von *De Grammatico* ist ausführlich diesem Thema logischer vs. grammatischer Form gewidmet.)
Nun noch zu *Responsio* 9, wo Anselm, um es vorweg zu sagen die Unterscheidung von Objekt- und Metasprache auf seine Semantik von *vox-intellectus-res* zurückführt; eine Theorie der Sprachstufen finden wir in seinem Opus nicht ausgeführt, u.a. aber hier verwendet:

Sed et si verum esset non posse cogitari vel intelligi *illud quo maius nequit cogitari,* non tamen falsum esset *quo maius cogitari nequit* cogitari posse et intelligi. Sicut enim nil prohibet dici ineffabile, licet illud dici non possit quod ineffabile dicitur; et quemadmodum cogitari potest non cogitabile, quamvis illud cogitari non possit cui convenit non cogitabile dici: ita cum dicitur *quo nil maius valet cogitari,* procul dubio quod auditur cogitari et intelligi potest, etiam si *res illa* cogitari non valeat aut intelligi, *qua maius cogitari nequit.* Nam etsi quisquam est tam insipiens, ut dicat non esse *aliquid quo maius non possit cogitari*: non tamen ita erit impudens, ut dicat se non posse intelligere aut cogitare quid dicat. Aut si quis talis invenitur, non modo sermo eius est respuendus, sed et ipse conspuendus. Quisquis igitur negat *aliquid esse quo maius nequeat cogitari*: utique intelligit et cogitat negationem quam facit. Quam negationem intelligere aut cogitare non potest sine partibus eius. Pars autem eius est *quo maius cogitari non potest.* Quicumque igitur hoc negat, intelligit et cogitat *quo maius cogitari nequit.*[18]

Selbst wenn es wahr wäre, dass jener [Gegenstand], über den Grösseres nicht gedacht werden kann, nicht gedacht oder verstanden werden kann, so wäre es dennoch nicht falsch, dass [der Ausdruck] 'über den Grösseres nicht gedacht werden kann 'gedacht und verstanden werden kann'. Denn wie nichts verhindert, 'unaussprechbar' zu sagen, obwohl man dasjenige, von dem gesagt wird, es sei unaussprechbar, nicht sagen kann; und wie weiters 'nicht denkbar' gedacht werden kann, obgleich man dasjenige, dem [das Prädikat] 'nicht denkbar' zukommt, nicht denken kann; so kann, wenn [der Ausdruck] 'über den nichts Grösseres gedacht werden kann' geäussert wird, zweifelsohne was man hört, gedacht und verstanden werden, selbst wenn jener Gegenstand, über den Grösseres nicht gedacht werden kann, [als] nicht[-existerend] gedacht bzw. verstanden würde. Denn wenn irgendjemand schon so dumm ist, dass er behauptet, etwas, über das Grösseres nicht gedacht werden kann, existert [gar] nicht, so wird er doch nicht so schamlos sein zu behaupten, er könne nicht verstehen bzw. denken, was er sage. Falls aber sogar so einer auftritt, so ist nicht nur seine Rede zu verwerfen, sondern vielmehr er selbst zu verachten. Wer immer demnach verneint, dass etwas, über das Grösseres nicht gedacht werden kann, existiert, versteht und denkt doch sicherlich die Negation, die er macht. Diese Negation aber kann nicht ohne ihre Teile verstanden bzw. gedacht werden. Ein Teil der Negation aber ist [der Ausdruck] 'über das Grösseres nicht gedacht werden kann'. Wer immer also dies verneint, versteht und denkt 'über das Grösseres nicht gedacht werden kann'.

Anselm generiert hier aus der Aussage
(1) *'Quo maius cogitari nequit* kann nicht verstanden werden', oder kurz
(2) *'Quo* ist undenkbar', die höherstufige Aussage

(3) '"*Quo* ist undenkbar" ist denkbar', bemerkt aber nicht, dass
(4) '*Quo* ist denkbar',
niemals korrekt aus (3) herzuleiten ist, damit ist aber auch, das sei am Rande vermerkt, sein Beweis *ipso facto* am Ende, weil die Forderung des Verstehens, i.e. der Denkbarkeit des 'quo . . .' nicht mehr erfüllt ist. Nicht am Ende ist Anselms Semantik, die in *Responsio* 9 eingegangen ist: Ich hoffe, wir haben bemerkt, wie präzise Anselm zwischen der *prolatio* bzw. dem *sermo* und der *res illa*, dem *illud* unterscheidet, um den Leser vor der Vermengung des Redens über Dinge mit dem Reden über Worte, die diese Dinge betreffen, zu bewahren. Beachten Sie, bitte, die im lateinischen Text jeweils kursivierten *Nomina* bzw. *Pronomina* vor der Formel, die anzeigen, dass jetzt über die Extension des Ausdrucks geredet wird, während wir überall dort, wo die Formel wegen des Fehlens eines 'Realisators' (*illud, illa res, aliquid*) allein kursiviert ist, über Zeichen oder auch deren Intension sprechen, da Anselm es im angezogenen Teil seiner Analyse auf die Trennung dieser beiden Ebenen nicht ankommt. Die Lektüre des Proslogiontextes zusammenfassend können wir sagen, dass zwar nicht die 'significatio . . . . . . huius prolationis [sc. quo . . .] tantam . . . vim . . . in se continet',[19] dass sie Gottes Existenz beweist, dass aber Anselms Semantik *tantam vim* in sich enthält, dass mit deren Instrumentarium die logisch-semantische Analyse so weit vorangetrieben werden kann, dass sie in die Auflösung dieses Wunschtraumes eines Beweises mündet.

Anselms Bedeutungslehre in *De Grammatico*

Lothar Steiger gebührt Anerkennung für eine ernstliche Wiedereinführung von Anselms *De Grammatico* in die philosophische Diskussion des deutschen Sprachraumes.[20] Zu lange hat Prantls *Geschichte der Logik im Abendlande* die akademischen Urteile über Anselms Logik und Semantik präjudiziert. D.P. Henry allerdings ist zu verdanken, dass Anselms Bedeutungslehre überhaupt (wieder) entdeckt worden ist.[21] *De Grammatico* ist eine wahre Fundgrube für Themen der Topik und Syllogistik, wie Steiger zurecht betont, aber auch eine solche für die Semantik und — dies gegen Steigers Ableugnung — für das Universalienproblem. Für Topik und Syllogistik sei der Leser auf Steiger, für das Universalienproblem auf Henry[22] und das Studium von *De Grammatico* 20 verwiesen, um hier nur die Lehre von Sinn und Bedeutung von Ausdrücken bei Anselm darzulegen.

Der zentrale semantische Text befindet sich in den Kapiteln 12-15; die ersten Kapitel erörtern im besonderen die Sinnkomponente von Ausdrücken (verschiedener Art), wobei die Notwendigkeit eines Rekurses auf die *significatio nominis*, d.i. die Bezeichnungsfunktion, durch Beispiele und Argumente erhärtet wird; Kapitel 3 bringt folgende Diskussion:

> Magister: An tibi videtur animalis nomen aliquid aliud *significare* quam substantiam animatam sensibilem? Discipulus: Prorsus nihil aliud *est* animal quam substantia animata sensibilis, nec substantia animata sensibilis aliud est quam animal.[23]

> Lehrer: *Bezeichnet*, deiner Meinung nach, der Ausdruck 'Tier' ('animal') etwas anderes als (eine) beseelte, sinnenbegabte Substanz?
> Schüler: Gewiss, Tier *ist* nichts anderes als (eine) beseelte, sinnenbegabte Substanz, und (eine) beseelte, sinnenbegabte Substanz ist nichts anderes als (ein) Tier.

In den unterschiedlichen sprachlichen Versionen von Lehrer und Schüler, die die gleiche Doktrin vertreten, kann bereits hier die Anselmsche Verwendung von *esse (est)* für *significare*, die durch das ganze Oeuvre nachweisbar ist, erhoben werden. Es handelt sich um jenes höherstufige *esse*, welches regelmässig und eindeutig dem Ausdruck (*nomen, vox, prolatio*) eine *significatio* oder *definitio* (vgl. Kapitel 5, 8 u. 13) zuordnet, wobei der Bezeichnungsinhalt in die sprachliche Variante von z.B. *esse hominis, esse albi* oder *esse grammatici* (Kapitel 5, 8 u.9) im Sinne von *essentia* (vgl. Kapitel 6) gekleidet wird. Kapitel 4, wo es um die Bezeichnung von Aussagen und Termen in Syllogismen geht, bringt für die *significatio* dieser die Fachausdrücke *sententia*, *sensus* und *intellectus*, wobei nachdrücklich darauf hingewiesen wird, dass das sprachliche Kleid der Prämissen (*in prolatione, in voce; non verba ligat syllogismum*) völlig irrelevant ist, da es allein auf die Bedeutung der Terme ankommt: sententia quippe ligat syllogismum, non verba.[24]

Die auf Aristoteles bezugnehmenden Einschübe in Kapitel 9 u. 17-18 sind allerdings vorsichtig zu studieren, da sie zumindest terminologisch der strengen *vox-res*-Semantik, die z.B. auch in Augustins *De Magistro* vorfindlich ist, verpflichtet sind. Es muss offen gesagt werden, dass der durch Boethius vermittelte Aristoteles ein Hemmnis für Anselm ist, da dieser den Gepflogenheiten seiner Zeit entsprechend die *auctores=auctoritates* Aristoteles und Augustinus, gelegentlcih sogar ängstlich, jedenfalls aber als unbestreitbar zitiert, was hier auf eine Fixierung auf die simple Wort-Sache-Semantik ohne ausgeführte Bezeichnungstheorie hinausläuft. Wir sind somit beim zentralen Text angelangt:

> Nempe nomen hominis per se et ut unum significat ea ex quibus constat totus homo. [. . .] Quapropter quamvis omnia simul velut unum totum sub una significatione uno nomine appellentur homo, sic tamen principaliter hoc nomen est significativum et appellativum substantiae . . . [. . .] Grammaticus vero non significat hominem et grammaticam ut unum, sed grammaticam per se et hominem per aliud significat. Et hoc nomen quamvis sit appellativum hominis,

non tamen *proprie* dicitur eius significativum; et licet sit significativum grammaticae, non tamen est eius appelativum. Appelativum autem nomen cuiuslibet rei nunc dico, quo res ipsa usu loquendi appellatur . . .[25]

Gewiss bezeichnet der Name 'Mensch' direkt [*per se*] und als eine Einheit [all] das, woraus ein ganzer Mensch besteht. [. . .] Daher gilt, [dass], obgleich [diese] alle zugleich und als ein einziges Ganzes mittels eines Ausdrucks durch eine Bedeutung (ein) Mensch genannt werden, dieser Ausdruck dennoch und zu allererst Substanz bedeutet und benennt . . . [. . .] 'Grammaticus' aber bezeichnet nicht Mensch und Grammatik in gleicher Weise, sondern Grammatik direkt [*per se*] und Mensch indirekt [*per aliud*]. Und wenn auch dieser Ausdruck ein Appellativum von Mensch ist, [d.i. Mensch benennt,] so kann er dennoch nicht *eigentlich* dessen Signifikativum [Bedeutung] genannt werden. Und obgleich [der Ausdruck] Grammatik bedeutet, benennt er dennoch nicht [Grammatik]. 'Appelativ' nenne ich nämlich einen Namen irgendeiner Sache dann, wenn [durch ihn] in der gewöhnlichen Umgangssprache die Sache selber benannt wird . . .

Die im *Proslogion* nachgewiesene semantische Aufspaltung in Intension und Extension (von Ausdrücken) wird hier terminologisch klar durchgeführt. Zunächst wird mittels des allgemein verwendeten Terminus *significatio* eine *significatio per se* (direkte Bedeutung; Bezug auf die Intension des Ausdruckes) und eine *significatio per aliud* (Benennung; Bezug auf die Extension des Ausdruckes) unterschieden, um sodann die *significatio per se* eines Ausdruckes als das *significativum* (im eigentlichen Sinne) zu stipulieren, wärend der referentielle Bezug auf die Extension *appellativum* genannt wird: Bedeuten (*esse significativum nominis*; *significatio per se*) wird dem Benennen (*appellare*; *nominare*; *esse appellativum nominis*) gegenübergestellt, wobei Anselm der Umsgangssprache vorrechnet, sie schaue nur auf die Benennungsfunktion der Ausdrücke. Der Philosoph dagegen stützt seine Analyse auf die rein logische Bedeutung, die *significatio per se*, womit er den Verkürzungen der Umgangssprache — aber auch einer aristotelischen Semantik, wie sie z.B. zu Anfang von Augustins *De Magistro* auftritt — entflieht. Nach Kapitel 15 ist die *significatio per se* eines Ausdrucks *substantialis*, während die *significatio per aliud accidentalis* genannt wird, da sie nur eine *aliquo modo significatio* ist. Erst diese semantische Unterscheidung ermöglicht es Anselm, das sei kurz angemerkt, in der Frage der Universalien die extreme Position eines Roscelin ebenso wie die der Realisten zu vermeiden. Der Ausweg ist die dritte Komponente im Bezeichnungssytem, die *significatio per se*. Wer wie Roscelin nur den *voces* oder *nomina* Wirklichkeit zuspricht, muss ebenso scheitern, wie die Realisten, die in einer allzu simplen *vox-res*-Semantik überall eine Substanz oder *natura* suchen, während Anselm sich hier, wie später ähnlich Abaelard und Thomas, eine Lösung über die Sinnkomponente der Ausdrücke sichern kann.

In den *Lambeth-Fragmenten* ist Anselm diese seine Semantik von so grosser Hilfe, dass er das seit Augustin und Fredegisus ungelöste Problem der *significatio* von *nihil* lösen kann. *Aliquid* gebrauchen wir nach Anselm in vierfacher Weise: (Vgl. die Erstausgabe der Fragmente von F.S. Schmitt.).[26]

(a) In erster Linie dürfen Objekte 'etwas' genannt werden, wenn sie 'suis . . . vocabulis nominantur et mente concipiuntur et sunt in re', d.h. wenn einem entsprechenden Ausdruck Intension und Extension zukommen.

(b) Aber auch extensionslose Ausdrücke berechtigen zum Gebrauch von *aliquid*, zumindest in der Umgangsprache: 'Dicitur enim aliquid, quod et nomen habet et mentis conceptionem, sed non est in veritate, ut chimera'.

(c) Die dritte Art des Gebrauchs von *aliquid* liegt bei Ausdrücken vor, die nach Anselms Auffassung, der hier in der Tradition der Augustinischen Privationstheorie steht, weder Intension noch Extension haben, wie z.B. *nihil* und *iniustitia*: 'Solemus quoque dicere aliquid, quod solum nomen habet sine ulla euisdem nominis in mente conceptione et est absque omni essentia, ut est iniustitia et nihil'.

(d) Die vierte Art, etwas dunkel bleibend, verneint sogar das Vorliegen eines Namens: 'Nominamus etiam aliquid, quod nec suum nomen habet nec conceptionem nec ullam existentiam . . .'.

Für Anselm ist aber nur (a) ein *aliquid proprie dictum*, während (b)-(d) *quasi aliquid*, i.e. *vero non aliquid*, sind. Nach Anselm wäre also, wenn wir seine zunächst gegebene Analyse von *nihil* ganz ernst nehmen, dieser Ausdruck ein Name ohne Sinn und Bedeutung. Ihm selbst aber kommt im Nachsatz diese durch die Privationstheorie vorgegebene Extremposition bereits problematisch vor, sodass er einschränkt, *nihil* konstitutuiere zwar keinesfalls *etwas* im Intellekt, es gäbe aber dem Intellekt doch Information (*constitutere intellectum*), insofern es 'removet aliquid et non ponit aliquid in intellectu'. Das heisst dass Anselm hier wieder der zweiteiligen *vox-res*-Semantik den Vorzug gab. Demnach ist weiters die Unterscheidung von (b) und (c) nur bedingt gültig, da sie Anselms Ontologie, die durchaus platonisch ist, voraussetzt. Auf der anderen Seite kommt ihm die Möglichkeit sogenannter intensionsloser Ausdrücke aber mit Extension nicht in den Sinn; ich meine die nach manchen als intensionslos anzusetzenden genuinen Eigennamen, z.B. 'Sokrates' oder 'Snoopy'.

Anselms Bedeutungslehre ist, sieht man von vereinzelten Rückfällen in die enge *vox-res*-Deutung ab, durch das gesamte Werk

Tabelle 1

De Grammatico

significatio (significare)
(. . . duas has significationes distinguere) — Kap.14

nomen, vox, prolatio

significatio per se
significatio substantialis

significatio per aliud
significatio accidentalis
appellatio (appellare) — Kap.4, 12

significare per se

appellare, nominare, ostendere
` significare aliquo modo — Kap.15

quod est esse rei
(essentia, definitio)

res ipsae — Kap.6, 13

significat animal

an de rebus — Kap.9

de hoc nomine

significativum

appellativum — Kap.3

animalis nomen

appellativum — Kap.12

Tabelle 2

Proslogion

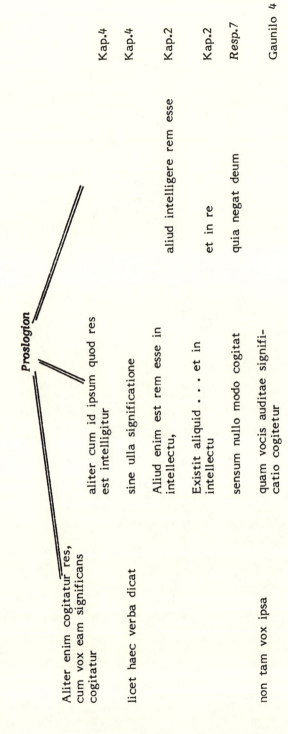

Aliter enim cogitatur res, cum vox eam significans cogitatur	aliter cum id ipsum quod res est intelligitur	Kap.4
licet haec verba dicat	sine ulla significatione	Kap.4
	Aliud enim est rem esse in intellectu,	aliud intelligere rem esse	Kap.2
	Existit aliquid . . . et in intellectu	et in re	Kap.2
	sensum nullo modo cogitat	quia negat deum	Resp.7
non tam vox ipsa	quam vocis auditae significatio cogitetur	Gaunilo 4

Tabelle 3

Philosophische Fragmente 42-3

suo nomine profertur	et mente concipitur	et est in re	42:23-5
quod nomen habet	et mentis conceptionem	sed non est in veritate	42:27-8
suis namque vocabilis nominantur	et mente concipiuntur et sunt in re		42:25-6
significatur hoc nomine	quaedam mentis conceptio	quae non existit in rerum natura	42:28-30

hindurch eine dreiteilige Semantik, die den Ausdrücken sowohl Intension wie Extension zuordnet.[27] Wenn dies in verschiedenen Schriften auch teilweise zu terminologischen Unterschieden führt, so ist doch der theoretische Entwurf derselbe, ob er nun *Proslogion*, *De Grammatico* oder die *Fragmente* betrifft. Man kann aus den Tabellen 1, 2 und 3 ersehen, wie die einzelnen sprachlichen Varianten zur Deckung zu bringen sind.

ANMERKUNGEN

Diese ist eine überarbeitete und erweiterte Fassung meines Vortrages am Anselmkongress in Canterbury 1979: 'Interpreting Anselm on sense and reference'. Ich möchte für ausführliche Diskussion und Hinweise William C. Carroll (New York), H.L. Dazeley (Manchester), D.P. Henry (Manchester) und Helen S. Lang (Trinity College, Hartford) danken. Alle Zitate folgen der Werkausgabe, *S. Anselmi Cantuariensis Archiepiscopi Opera Omnia*, herausgegeben von F.S. Schmitt, 6 vols. (Rome/Edinburgh, 1938-61). Nachdruck 1968; die Übersetzungen stammen vom Verfasser.
* In memoriam Jan Pinborg († 1982).

1. *Ans.Op.Om.*, I, 123-4.

2. *Ans.Op.Om.*, I, 101-2.

3. Vgl. die sehr allgemeine Verwendung von *res* in *De Grammatico*, 17, wo selbst die Sinnkomponente darunter fällt. Solche terminologische Unschärfen sind durchaus nichts Ungewöhnliches bei Anselm; vgl. dazu die Zusammenstellungen in W.L. Gombocz, 'Anselm von Canterbury. Ein Forschungsbericht über die Anselm-Renaissance seit 1960', *Philosophisches Jahrbuch*, 84 (1980), 109-34, dazu 117-19.

4. *Ans.Op.Om.*, I, 126.

5. *Ans.Op.Om.*, I, 103-4.

6. *Ans.Op.Om.*, I, 114.

7. *Ans.Op.Om.*, I, 126-7.

8. *Ans.Op.Om.*, I, 126: 25.

9. *Ans.Op.Om.*, I, 127: 8-10, 13, 15-17, 21-22.

10. *Ans.Op.Om.*, I, 127: 28-29; 128: 5-7.

11. *Ans.Op.Om.*, I, 128: 20-21

12. *Ans.Op.Om.*, I, 132: 11-13.

13. *Ans.Op.Om.*, I, 134: 13-14

14. *Ans.Op.Om.*, I, 136: 31 - 137: 1.

15. *Ans.Op.Om.*, I, 137:3-5.

16. Wie J. Vuillemin, *Archiv für Geschichte der Philosophie*, 53 (1971), 279-99 und H.L. Dazeley u.a. *Synthese*, 40 (1979), 71-96 zu zeigen versuchen, enthält die Anselmsche Formel einen widerspruchsvollen Begriff.

17. *Ans.Op.Om.*, I, 105: 15-23.

18. *Ans.Op.Om.*, I, 138: 4-19. (Kursivierung von mir. Vgl. den nachfolgenden Kommentar.)

19. *Ans.Op.Om.*, I, 138: 30-31.

20. *Analecta Anselmiana*, 1 (1969), 107-43.

21. D.P. Henrys diesbezügliches Werk ist seit den Fünfzigerjahren in vielen Aufsätzen und Büchern zugänglich; vgl. die Angaben in Gombocz, 'Anselm von Canterbury', 109-12, wo auch entsprechende Hinweise zur deutschen Anselmrezeption im 19. Jahrhundert zu finden sind.

22. D.P. Henry, 'War St. Anselm wirklich ein Realist?', *Ratio*, 5 (1963), 178-83.

23. *Ans.Op.Om.*, I, 147: 1-4. (Meine Kursivierung.)

24. *Ans.Op.Om.*, I, 149: 11-14.

25. *Ans.Op.Om.*, I, 156: 21 - 157:8.

26. F.S. Schmitt, *Eines neues, unvollendetes Werk des Hl. Anselm von Canterbury*, Beiträge zur Geschichte der Philosophie und Theologie im Mittelalter, 33:3 (Münster, 1936).

27. Jan Pinborg — verstorben am 24. September 1982 — hat neben D.P. Henry zur Promulgation dieser Wissenserweiterung betreffend die Geschichte der Semantik beigetragen. Vgl. J. Pinborg, *Logik und Semantik im Mittelalter* (Stuttgart, 1972).

Anselmian Agency in the *Lambeth Fragments*:
A Medieval Perspective on the Theory of Action

Eileen F. Serene

The *Lambeth Fragments*, preserved in a codex containing Anselm's late letters and sermons, reveals his most elaborate thoughts regarding the analysis of causation and agency, the semantics of predication, and the interpretation of modality.[1] These fragments are valuable not only because their topics are pivotal in Anselm's system of philosophical theology but also because they frequently modify or extend his earlier treatment of issues involving these concepts.[2] His reflections on the verbs 'to do' (*facere*) and 'to will' (*velle*), which can be understood both as a nuanced addition to his previous views of agency and responsibility and as a provocative contribution to the theory of human action, comprise the most intriguing segment of the text. A demonstration of exactly how this account develops his earlier ideas would involve a review and interpretation of Anselm's account of the pre-eminence of correctness of will (*rectitudo*) in morality and of the role of grace in the restoration and preservation of this *rectitudo*.[3] Since that undertaking involves explicating several subtle theological issues, I shall limit the focus of the present discussion to the implications of the account of agency and responsibility for the the theory of action in the *Fragments*, deferring the question of how significantly this view might diverge from the rest of Anselm's moral theory.

The rationale for taking these remarks as a medieval contribution to the theory of action requires some comment. With one qualification, it is natural to consider Anselm's analysis a counterpart to our current theories of action, since he claims to present an exhaustive account of the bases for ascribing the general predicate 'to bring something about' (*facere aliquid esse*).[4] Anselm holds that this account applies to agency in general on the grounds that any sentence which ascribes an action or omission to a subject can be paraphrased as the subject's bringing about the occurrence of a specifiable outcome.[5] He also argues, less persuasively, for an extension of this causal theory to all predicates, including passive and existential verbs and so-called 'verbs of state' which ascribe properties such as colour, disposition, position and so forth. He motivates this generalization of his theory by suggesting that in some context or other any verb can be used as an acceptable reply to the question, 'What is he doing?' (*Quid facit?*).[6] But his fundamental reason in support of the putative substitutivity of *facere* for any predicate is his idea that every subject is either an efficient or a non-efficient cause of whatever is predicated of it.[7]

Because the analysis of *facere* is meant to apply to all instances of agency, whether or not the subject is human, rational, conscious or even an efficient cause of the outcome, it does not constitute a complete or a specific account of human action. His full theory of human agency also includes some explanation of the nature of willing, and of the bases for ascribing various types of volition to human agents. The qualification that Anselm's discussion of willing must be taken together with his account of doing, in order to understand his view of human agency, enriches the account of human action we can reconstruct from the *Fragments*.

There is an important sense, however, in which Anselm's reflections differ from contemporary action-theory, if the theory of human action is considered a fundamental, self-sufficient, metaphysical inquiry which might contribute to the clarification of normative issues when fully developed. His account of human action is ancillary to his fundamental interest in the correct appreciation and practice of Christian morality; indeed, his analysis of action is well-designed to complement the norms of Benedictine monasticism.[8] In the *Monologion*, he holds that, insofar as we can, rational agents ought to discern differing degrees of goodness and badness wherever they occur, so that we can will and act accordingly.[9] Like Augustine, Anselm stresses the importance of willing correctly, sternly insisting that ' . . . whoever does not will . . . what he ought . . . does badly'.[10] These points, together with his distinction between dispositional and occurrent willing (to be discussed below), suggest that Anselm accepts something like the following principle of moral obligation:

(1) One ought to will dispositionally to promote morally preferable states of affairs, and

(2) One ought in practice to will to do whatever one can to promote the occurrence of morally preferable states of affairs and to impede the occurrence of morally worse ones, unless an excusing condition is satisfied, for example, if one is unconscious or has relinquished autonomy to an appropriate authority.[11]

While this formulation of what I call the Mandate for Moral Perfection (MMP) leaves open several crucial questions which, in my opinion, are not settled in texts, I believe that it is a plausible representation of his basic view of moral obligation.[12]

In conjunction with the *Fragments'* treatment of doing and willing, the MMP appears stringent in two noteworthy respects. As we shall see below, maintaining correctness of will can entail action as well as volition, since one type of willing, which *rectitudo* sometimes requires by definition, must activate its bearer.[13] Secondly, Anselm stipulates virtually no bounds with respect to what one can be required to will; where subsequent medieval thinkers and modern philosophers emphatically adduce ignorance, or at least invincible ignorance, and lack of intentionality as excusing conditions, Anselm's *Fragments* are curiously silent.[14] Because Anselm approaches the analysis of human action from a moralist's perspective, he is well aware that bad consequences and blame can accrue from omissions, even unintentional ones. This awareness, together with his *penchant* for unravelling theoretical knots by semantic analysis, naturally leads him to adopt an ascriptivist approach to action. Thus he attends to the possible kinds of bases for ascriptions of agency and willing which are furnished by subjects' actions and omissions: this strategy easily accommodates attributions of causal and moral responsibility in virtue of omissions. Anselm's treatment of human action as a relationship between a subject and an outcome which can be ascribed on the basis of facts, together with background assumptions about causal and normative responsibility, differs in focus from the popular current treatment of action as a special type of event causally related to the agent's intention.[15] Thus it is possible that by contrast Anselm's view and these theories of action can manifest and complement each other's strengths and short-comings.

I

In the *Lambeth Fragments*, Anselm elaborates what he claims are all the possible bases for ascribing agency to a subject with respect to some state of affairs.[16] It is important to realize that this analysis starts from the assumption that not all instances of ascription of 'bringing something about' are cases in which the agent directly and literally does what he is said to do — for example, the assertion that Jones brought about Smith's death might base itself on his direct act of killing the victim, or alternatively on his arranging the murder. The main challenge is to clarify the variety of such alternative bases for what Anselm calls indirect ascriptions of agency. His central claim will be that any ascription of a 'bringing about' relation will have a basis in at least one of the two direct or four indirect modes he distinguishes.[17] In the direct, or *per se* modes, the relation is said to hold either in virtue of the agent's immediately producing the outcome, or in virtue of his directly failing to prevent the outcome ascribed. In the indirect, or *per aliud* modes, a causal role is ascribed to an agent in virtue of something he either does or fails to do which in turn helps to bring about the outcome ascribed to him. Anselm identifies four indirect modes, since he distinguishes cases in which the agent acts from cases in which he fails to act; and further distinguishes cases in which he effects the pertinent intermediate outcome from occurring.[18]

A refreshingly clear section of Anselm's often cryptic *Fragments* illustrates each mode of predication in terms of the example, 'He brings it about that the victim is dead'.[19] In the first mode, the ascription is based on the agent's doing the deed himself, by means of a sword. After admitting difficulty in finding a plausible example of an ascription of this particular predicate in the second mode, Anselm resorts to the case of a miracle-worker's forbearing to revive a dead person when he could have done so. In the third mode, the agent brings about some outcome which then contributes to the victim's death, for example he orders the murder or arms the killer. Should the agent fail to do something which would have prevented the murder, for example, arming the victim or restraining the killer, his agency with respect to the victim's death is ascribable in the fourth mode. The examples of the remaining two modes follow similar patterns; in the fifth mode, the agent might prevent the barring of the victim's door, thereby allowing the killer access, and in the sixth mode the agent simply fails to bar the door, with the same result.

A more precise elaboration of Anselm's scheme is not necessary for beginning to appreciate its philosophical interest. A reader versed in recent debates over the ontological status of action and criteria for individuating actions will notice that Anselm takes no firm stand on these issues in the *Fragments*.[20] He presents the modes as a disjunctive necessary condition for ascriptions of agency, but he does not to my knowledge assert that any relationship, no matter how remote, between a subject and a state of affairs provides a sufficient condition for agency. If he does think so, there must be an enormous number of instances of Anselmian agency, especially since his scheme can count omissions as bases for agency. Although the textual evidence from the *Fragments* does not dictate the exact extent of the realm of agency, Anselm's examples indicate that it is capacious enough to include many indirect and even somewhat remote effects of direct actions and omissions.[21] Another striking feature is the generality of this account: a subject need not be be rational, animate, or even material to bring about an outcome. Anselmian agency is much more inclusive than current conceptions of human agency which typically require intentional action or forbearance as a condition for agency. Anselm's account of ascription of agency applies to human behaviour in its particularity only in conjunction with his treatment of the will and ascriptions of volition.

Following his usual strategy, Anselm presents his views on willing in a series of distinctions which cumulatively yield a rather subtle theory. Naturally he assumes that willing can be ascribed in each of the six modes identified in the analysis of *facere aliquid esse*, since a well-informed agent can will both direct and indirect effects of his actions and omissions.[22] But willing and ascriptions of volition need not mirror agency and its ascription, since at least the indirect effects of our actions and omissions are often unforeseen, and sometimes unforeseeable. We typically will outcomes under certain descriptions or depictions, and regularly modify our intentions if the portrayal of the direct effect changes, or if we expand the initial characterization of the outcome to include additional indirect effects. While it may be plausible to maintain that one is always an agent with respect to the consequences or at least foreseeable consequences of his actions and omissions, it is certainly problematic to insist that one wills all these consequences.

Anselm's thinking minimizes this apparent asymmetry in the extension of ascriptions of agency and of willing in several ways. He notes that the assertion '*A* wills *s*', where *A* is an agent and *s* is a state of affairs, may be ambiguous since it could refer either to an instance of *A*'s operationally willing to bring about *s*, or his dispositional inclination toward bringing about *s*. He terms the former a use (*usus*) of the will, the latter a disposition of it (*affectio*).[23] The knowledge that *A* has an habitual inclination to will outcomes of *s*'s type provides some justification for attributing volition to *A* when his acts or omissions bring about *s*. According to this ascriptivist treatment of willing, if I dispositionally will to protect my child, then it is plausible to say that I willed to save him when I did so in a flash of panic. On this view, the number of cases in which an instance of willing can be correlated with an instance of bringing something about is larger than one might initially have expected.

In another line of reasoning, Anselm presents a detailed account of the varieties of willing, ranging in degree of strength from the efficient will through the approving and conceding to the merely permitting will.[24] To explain the differences among these types of volition, he refers to both the attitudes and the actions of the subject of the ascription. Someone whose will is efficient with respect to an outcome does whatever he can to ensure that it occurs; one whose will is only approving welcomes the outcome without doing everything possible to make it happen. A person whose will is conceding has a neutral or even a negative view toward the outcome, but perhaps for ulterior reasons accepts it nonetheless; finally, someone whose will is merely permitting does nothing to prevent an outcome, although he has or ought to have an aversive will toward it.[25] In the *Fragments*, Anselm straightforwardly presents efficient, approving, and conceding volition as ways in which people will outcomes, but he describes the permitting will only as a type of volition we can ascribe to someone, without explicitly insisting that whenever an agent omits to prevent an evil from occurring, he has at least a permitting will toward it.[26] His example of an ascription of a permitting will — a prince's allowing pirates to plunder his territory — suggests that a standard case for ascription of a permitting will involves a subject who is cognisant that he is allowing something to occur which he could and should prevent. But insofar as Anselm espouses a general obligation to bring about morally preferable states of affairs, it seems that we can ascribe at least a permitting will to anyone who is an Anselmian agent with respect to any morally relevant outcome he should prevent. In other words, the obligation not to bring about worse outcomes rests with a person at all times, and creates at least a presumption that he willingly lets all the foreseeable effects of his agency happen. On this view, having done something unintentionally could count as a mitigating but not an excusing condition. Thus Anselm's account tries to respect the intuitions that a person is strictly liable for what he does and fails to do and that the locus of responsibility is the will.

How extensively and stringently would Anselm invoke this notion of the permitting will? If we are responsible for any permittng will ascribable to us, then his conception of moral responsibility appears rigorous in the light of his remark that, 'The root and principle of all actions which are in our power is in the will, and even if we cannot do what we will, we are still judged all the same by God with respect to the proper disposition of our will'.[27] To readers immersed in utilitarian ethical theory, the strategy this strict notion of moral responsibility suggests is to promote the greater welfare of the greatest number of individuals. Such a view of Anselm's theory does not obviously square with his reported reluctance to use his miraculous powers to stop a fire or to cure a mad person, with his apparent attraction to monastic life as a haven from worldly opportunities for sin, and with his reliance on conventional monastic and ecclesiastical determinations of the boundaries of responsibilities and rights.[28] Since Anselm's view of morality emphasizes our obligation to conform to God's will, it is natural for him to regard monastic life, with its concern to avoid sin and to promote spiritual ends rather than to maximize tangible goods for individuals, as the best strategy for salvation. In his view, according to R.W. Southern, 'Every step away from the cloister was a step further from salvation'.[29] Although Anselm's responsibilities at Bec and Canterbury placed him in positions of authority, he continued to prize the virtue of obedience; indeed, one of the few excusing conditions he introduces to mitigate the rigour of his MMP is submission of the individual's will to an appropriate authority.[30] While we cannot overlook the hortatory character of his remarks about our obligations, neither can we interpret his treatment of moral perfection as simply rhetorical. Since he believes that even the smallest violation of God's infinite dignity deserves infinite recompense, it is hard to imagine Anselmian grounds for asserting that anything short of an utmost effort to will and act as we ought satisfies our obligation to God.[31] Although Anselm must recognize that certain sorts of ignorance diminish blame, and must in charity dissuade us from judging our fellows, he can set no limits to our possible moral responsibility for the effects of our actions and omissions. Thus the open-ended category of the permitting will can be understood as an acknowledgement of the point, soon to be developed by Abelard, that God is the ultimate moral arbiter.[32] Of course Anselm's complete account of Christian moral life would include discussions of divine mercy and grace as well as justice and obligation; but his treatment of the possible scope of obligation in the *Fragments* is not tempered by these additional elements.

An application of Anselm's various distinctions to a person's behaviour in a given situation provides the framework for a nuanced description of what he does and wills which specifies the agent; a state of affairs which occurs; a 'bringing about' relation in one of the six modes of ascription; and whether he wills the outcome efficiently or merely by approval, concession, or permission. This framework facilitates discrimination of degrees of responsibility if, for example, a person who murders someone in mode one, with an efficient will, bears more or less direct responsibility than a bystander who fails to intervene to save the victim, but who has only a conceding or permitting will toward the outcome. Anselm's analysis clearly separates causal from moral responsibility, and provides a way of conceptualizing moral choice. For example, suppose that some hikers converge on a path where a falling tree has just hurled an innocent victim into a lake. The tree, the lake and the hikers are all Anselmian agents with respect to the incipient drowning. Assuming that the hikers can swim and the victim cannot, that rescue is the morally preferable alternative, and that the excusing conditions of the MMP are not satisfied, the MMP requires the hikers to will efficiently to save the victim. If they ignore the crisis, they can be blamed for having at least a permitting will with respect to the worse outcome. What distinguishes their action or inaction from the other agents' is the disposition and exercise of the will, subject to the obligation expressed in the mandate for moral perfection.

II

To assess the philosophical cogency of Anselm's approach to agency and human action in the *Fragments*, it is appropriate to focus on his strategy, since the full details of his account are not settled in this text. One appealing feature of this treatment of agency is its generality. Many modern theorists assume that an important part of the problem of human action is to explicate the contrast between what an agent does and what merely happens to him. One line of response is to explain human agency in terms of intentionality, or in terms of the characteristic causation of action by our desires and beliefs. But whatever explains the difference between a person's raising his arm and his arm simply rising, or being raised, by an external cause should hold, *mutatis mutandis*, for any animal or machine.[33] Anselm's generic treatment of agency provides a simple initial response to this fact; in the first case the ascription of agency to any type of subject would typically be made in the first direct mode, and in the latter cases the basis of the ascription would be one of the subsequent modes. While this is only a first step in elucidating what has recently been considered the 'problem of human action', it is sensible as far as it goes. The difficulties universally encountered in formulating accounts of intentionality indicate the prudence of postponing reliance on this problematic concept.

A second attractive feature of Anselm's strategy is its recognition that ascriptions of agency and volition are sometimes based on the subject's omissions, in conjunction with certain causal and normative assumptions. Suppose, for example, that a philosopher is unintentionally day-dreaming on a weekend afternoon, and that the philosopher's spouse indicates that he or she is wasting time, shirking household duties, insulting a house-guest and angering the spouse. These remarks certainly sound like ordinary ascriptions of actions, even though much of their basis is an unintentional omission on the subject's part. Especially if we expect an account of action to provide a standard framework for normative evaluations, it is important to make a perspicuous place for unintentional omissions and their consequences within a general theory of human action. From the perspective of teleological ethical theories, there should, in principle, be no difference between the consequences of actions, forbearances, and unintentional omissions which we could have avoided or rectified. The moral importance of unintentional omissions need not be limited to teleological theories. The importance of omissions, even unintentional ones, is obvious in the realms of prudence and convention. If, for example, someone is a hazardous driver with a long record of collisions and near-misses, yet he heedlessly fails to fasten his seat-belt, then he deserves criticism on prudential grounds; and if a person fails to thank his host, then he deserves criticism on conventional grounds. Why should morality differ in this respect? If someone fails to convey a message that a critically ill person requires medical attention, he merits moral blame. Anselm's characterization of agency, joined with suitable normative premises, provides a good account of the basis for assignment of blame in such cases. It is also well-suited for moral instruction since it directs the moral laggard's attention to both the direct and the indirect consequences of his actions and omissions.

In the *Lambeth Fragments'* study of the predicates *facere* and *velle*, Anselm presents suggestive reflections on the issues of agency and responsibility, adopting a perspective which is broad in two interesting respects: the treatment of agency is not limited to intentional human acts, and the discussion of volition includes the open-ended category of the permitting will. Presumably, at least part of the motivation and justification of these features is the Mandate for Moral Perfection, a dictum whose foundation and qualifications are not fully clarified in the *Fragments*. Anselm appears to regard this mandate, like the famous definition of God in the first premise of the ontological argument, as self-evident. Is it put forward as a principle of reason, a semantic truth, a matter of sacred duty, or a summary of monastic aspirations? A philosophically self-sufficient version of an Anselmian theory of agency and responsibility would have to clarify the foundation of its normative premises; but if this could be done, we would have a theory with notable utility for moral instruction and the discrimination of degrees of responsibility.[34] Today, many philosophers believe that human actions ought to be placed in the ontological category of events rather than of relations; it is typically considered necessary for an action to have a distinct spatio-temporally specifiable origin in the agent's intentional bodily movement or intentional forbearance from moving. Even if this approach yields significant metaphysical results, its utility for certain sorts of normative judgements is limited. If we hope that the theory of action will help clarify the broad range of assignments of normative responsibility, and if we think that unintentional omissions or their consequences have moral significance, then Anselm's remarks provide more than a simulating counterpoint to some contemporary theories of action. Despite their shortcomings, they direct attention to some appealing features of an ascriptivist approach to human action, and raise the issue of the appropriate relationship between theory of action and ethics.[35]

NOTES

1. The *Fragments*, found in Lambeth Codex 59, were edited and re-ordered by F.S. Schmitt under the title, *Ein neues unvollendetes Werk des Hl. Anselm von Canterbury'*, in Beiträge zur Geschichte der Philosophie und Theologie des Mittelalters, 33:3 (Münster, 1936). The text appears in the manuscript's original ordering in *Mem.Ans.*, pp. 333-51; it has been translated in J. Hopkins, *A Companion to the Study of St Anselm* (Minneapolis, 1972), and more literally translated in E. Serene, 'Anselm's Philosophical Fragments: A Critical Examination' (unpublished Ph.D. dissertation, Cornell University, 1974). It may be possible to question how directly Anselm was involved in the composition and compilation of these fragments, but it is impossible to doubt that they represent his thinking.

2. For a discussion of the treatment of possibility and necessity in the *Fragments*, see E. Serene, 'Anselm's modal conceptions', in *Reforging the Great Chain of Being: Ancient and Medieval Modal Concepts*, edited by S. Knuuttila (Dordrecht, 1980).

3. Accounts of these topics may be found in Hopkins, *A Companion* and in R. Pouchet, *La Rectitudo chez saint Anselme: Un itinéraire augustinien de l'âme à Dieu* (Paris, 1964).

4. *Mem.Ans.*, pp. 343-6, especially p. 344.11: 'Sex ergo modis "facere" pronuntiamus . . .'. (Therefore we assert 'to do' in six ways . . .) Recent treatments of Anselm's *Fragments* as a philosophical theory of action include D. Walton, 'Logical form and agency', *Philosophical Studies*, 29 (1976), 75-89; A. Danto, *Analytical Philosophy of Action* (Cambridge, 1973), p. 199; and D.P. Henry, *The Logic of St Anselm* (Oxford, 1967), Chapters 6 and 8. I believe that my account of these texts distinguishes more sharply between Anselm's view of agency and his view of human action than other commentaries, and puts more stress on the role of Anselm's account of willing in his theory of human action.

5. 'Verbum ad hoc quod est "facere" solet poni pro omni verbo cuius libet significationis finito vel infinito, etiam pro "non facere".' (The verb 'to do' may be put for every finite or infinite verb of any signification whatever, even for 'not to do'.) *Mem.Ans.*, p. 337.8-9 and p. 342.26-7; 'Quidquid autem "facere" dicitur, aut facit ut sit aliquid, aut facit ut non sit aliquid. Omne igitur "facere" dici potest aut facere esse aut facere non esse . . .'. (Moreover whenever 'to do' is said, either it makes something be the case, or it makes something not be the case. Therefore, every 'to do' can be said either to make something be or to make something not be . . .) *Mem.Ans.*, p. 343.34-6.

6. 'Potest ergo omne verbum aliquando responderi interroganti "quid facit", si sit qui hoc facere convenienter sciat.' (Thus every verb can be used at some time in reply to someone asking 'What is he doing?', if there is someone who knows how to do this appropriately.) *Mem.Ans.*, p. 343.4-5.

7. See *Mem.Ans.*, pp. 337.32-338.18, especially p. 337.32-4: 'Denique omne, de quo aliquod verbum dicitur, aliqua causa est ut sit hoc quod verbo illo significatur; et omnis causa usu loquendi "facere" dicitur illud cuius causa est.'. (Finally, everything of which a verb is said is some cause of the occurrence of what is signified by that verb; and in common parlance every cause is said 'to bring about' that of which it is a cause.) See also *Mem.Ans.*, pp. 338.35-339.2, especially p. 338.35-8: 'Quamvis aliae causae dicantur efficientes, sicut artifex . . . aliae vero ad comparationem illarum non vocentur efficientes, sicut

materia ex qua fit aliquid . . .'. (Although some causes are called efficient, such as an artisan . . . others by comparison with these are not called efficient, such as the material from which one makes something . . .)

8. Southern points to Anselm's 'deep pessimism', his 'utter abhorrence of sin even down to the smallest detail', and the 'passionate intensity' of his commitment to monastic obedience as the best hope for salvation. See R.W. Southern, *Saint Anselm and his Biographer* (Cambridge, 1963), pp. 101-3.

9. 'Quis enim neget quaecumque meliora sunt in potestate, ea magis esse debere in voluntate? Denique rationali naturae non est aliud esse rationalem, quam posse discernere iustrum a non iusto, verum a non vero, bonum a non bono, magis bonum a minus bono. Hoc autem posse omnino inutile illi est et super-vacuum, nisi quod discernit amet aut reprobet secundun verae discretionis iudicium.' (For who would deny that whatever better things are in our power ought with better reason to be in the will? Certainly for a rational nature to be rational is nothing other than to be able to distinguish the just from the unjust, the true from the untrue, the good from the not-good, the greater good from the less good. But this ability is totally useless to him, and superfluous, unless he loves and rejects what he distinguishes in accordance with judgement of true discernment.) *Ans.Op.Om.*, I, 78:19-25.

10. ' . . . qui nec vult . . . quod debet . . . male facit'. Schmitt, *Ein neues unvollendetes Werk*, p. 44.5-7.

11. For the first excusing condition, see *Ans.Op.Om.*, II, 283:7-13; for a suggestion of the second, see *Ans.Op.Om.*, 336:6-10 and *The Life of St Anselm, Archbishop of Canterbury, by Eadmer*, edited by R.W. Southern (London, 1962), pp. 10-11 and pp. 80-1.

12. In formulating this principle, I recast Anselm's usual phrases 'facere esse bona' and 'facere esse mala' as 'to promote morally preferable (or worse) states of affairs'. Together with a specification of individuating conditions for states of affairs, this recast principle would be slightly more precise than Anselm's texts clearly require. But I think his view is that we should not only do good and avoid evil, but that we should try our utmost to do good, given the likelihood, horror, and cost of sinning. See Eadmer, *Life of Anselm*, pp. 84-5.

13. 'Haec voluntas potest vocari efficiens, quoniam, quantum in ipsa est, efficit ut sit quod vult.' (This will can be called efficient, since, insofar as is in it, it brings it about that what it wills is the case.) *Mem.Ans.*, p. 334.4-5.

14. 'De his autem quae fieri non debent quam sepe abseque peccato fiant, cum per uim scilicet aut ignorantiam committantur . . . '. (Moreover, I think everyone knows how often things that should not be done are done without sin, when, that is, they are committed under coercion or through ignorance . . .) *Abelard's Ethics,* edited by D.E. Luscombe (Oxford, 1971) p. 24.9-10 and p. 25.

15. For this view, see, for example, Donald Davidson, 'Agency', in *Agent, Action and Reason,* edited by R. Binkley, R. Bronaugh, and A. Marras (Toronto, 1971), p. 7; and A. Goldman, *A Theory of Human Action* (Englewood Cliffs, N.J., 1970), Chapter 3.

16. 'Isti modi quos dixi in "facere", in aliis quoque verbis per quandam similtudinem inveniuntur; etsi non omnes in omnibus, aliquis tamen aut plures in singulis, et magis in illis verbis quae transitionem faciunt ad verba, ut sunt "debere" et "posse".' (The modes I presented here in connection with 'to do' are found in other verbs as well, by virtue of a certain similarity. Although not all the modes are found in all verbs, one or more is in each verb, especially in those verbs, such as 'ought' and 'can', which effect a transition to other verbs.) *Mem.Ans.,* p. 346.22-5.

17. *Mem.Ans.,* pp. 344.8-346.21.

18. Anselm's insistence on the latter distinction explains why his division of actions contains two more modes than the counterpart analysis in G.H. von Wright, *Norm and Action* (London, 1971), Chapters 3 and 4, especially p. 49.

19. *Mem.Ans.,* pp. 344.18-345.4.

20. For a clear presentation of two positions, see Goldman, *Human Action,* Chapter 1.

21. In addition to the examples given in connection with the ascription of bringing about a victim's death, Anselm cites the agency of remote causes in saying: 'Si vero dicitur ille facere lucidam domum qui fenestram fecit, aut facere tenebrosam qui fenestram non fecit, aut si dicit aliquis quia terra sua pascit eum, longinqua causa est . . .'. (But if the person who made the window is said to do so that the house is lighted, or if a person who did not make a window is said to do so that it is dark, or if someone says that his land feeds him, it is a remote cause . . .) *Mem.Ans.,* p. 350.10-12.

22. '"Velle" eisdem sex modis dicimus quibus "facere esse".' (We say 'to will' in the same six modes in which we say 'to do so that something is the case'.) *Mem.Ans.,* p. 351.6.

23. 'Dicitur autem "volantas" et instrumentum volendi, et affectio eius, et usus eius.' (The instrument of willing, a disposition of

it, and a use of it are, however, called 'the will'.) *Ans.Op.Om.*, II, 280:1-2. The distinction introduced here is elaborated throughout *De concordia*, 3, 2, and is discussed in *De potestate*, PL 158.487.

24. *Mem.Ans.*, pp. 334.1-335.22.

25. 'Habet etiam frequens usus ut dicatur aliquis velle quod nec approbat nec concedit, sed tantum permittit, cum prohibere possit. Nam cum princeps in potestate sua non vult cohibere latrones et praedones, clamamus illum velle mala quae faciunt, quamvis illi displiceant, quoniam vult ea permittere.' ([To will] is also used frequently when one is said to will what he neither approves nor concedes but merely permits, when he could prevent it. For when a ruler in power does not will to restrain thieves and pirates, we complain that he wills the bad things they do, even though they displease him, because he wills to permit them.) *Mem.Ans.*, p. 335:10-14.

26. Apparently Anselm thinks that God in his omniscience must have at least a permitting will toward everything that happens in the world; for example, he permits some individuals to be reprobate, but only in the weak fourth mode of willing. See *Mem.Ans.*, p. 335.31-3.

27. 'In voluntate namque est radix et principium omnium actionum quae sunt in nostra potestate, et si non possumus quod volumus, iudicatur tamen apud deum unusquisque de propria voluntate.' *Mem.Ans.*, p. 269:4-7.

28. These incidents are reported in Eadmer, *Life of Anselm*, pp. 65-6, 120-1.

29. Southern, *Anselm*, p. 187.

30. See note 11.

31. For Anselm's view of the gravity of any violation of divine dignity, see *Cur Deus homo*, 1, 21, *Ans.Op.Om.*, II, 88-9.

32. Abelard writes, 'Deus uero unius cuiusque penam secundum culpae quantitatem disponit. Et quicumque ipsum equaliter contempnunt, equali postmodum pena puniuntur, cuiuscumque conditionis aut professionis sint.'. (God, however, distributes everyone's punishment according to the amount of fault, and all who offer equal contempt to him are later punished with an equal punishment whatever their condition or profession.) Luscombe, *Abelard*, p. 44.13-16 and p. 45.

33. For a more detailed discussion of this point, see Harry G. Frankfurt, 'The problem of action', *American Philosophical Quarterly*, 15:2 (April 1978), 157-62.

34. Unless we can provide an independent defence of appropriate normative premises, Anselm's theory of agency and responsibilty rests embedded in Christian ethics. In part because of the difficulty of this project, I can concur only partially with Arthur Danto's remark that, 'Anselm's brilliant discussion of the concept of action . . . is an overpoweringly subtle analysis, as one would expect from the framer of the Ontological Arguments . . . in view of the impoverished history that the philosophical theory of action has . . . it is difficult not to speculate upon the counterfactual historical development of philosophy had Anselm's analysis entered the discussion and not have been mislaid.'. Danto, *Analytical Philosophy*, p. 199.

35. For their especially helpful comments, I would like to thank Michael Bratman, Bonnie Dorrick, D.P. Henry, Norman Kretzmann, R.W. Southern, and G.H. von Wright.

IV
Anselm's Later Writings

Anselm and the *Filioque:*
A Responsio pro Graecis

Alasdair Heron

Anselm's *De processione spiritus sancti* generally receives relatively little attention from theologians and philosophers alike. I would not wish to suggest that it compares either in historical influence or in depth of creative reflection with such writings as the *Proslogion* or the *Cur Deus homo.* Yet, together with the *Epistola de incarnatione verbi Dei,* it offers an approach to the understanding of the Trinity which in its own way illustrates Anselm's characteristic style, method and genius; while the argument in the *De processione* laid the foundations of the medieval (as opposed to the earlier) defence of the *filioque* in the Western form of the Nicene Creed. Aquinas' subsequent analysis in the *Summa Theologica* I, Question 36, certainly covers the topic from more angles than does Anselm's, but his indebtedness to Anselm is patent, as is that of the Councils of Lyons (1274) and Florence (1439).

In this brief paper, I should like to develop a little further, and in a fresh way, some critical reflections upon Anselm's assumptions and procedure which I first attempted to formulate some years ago,[1] for I find myself both fascinated by and dissatisfied with his form of argument. My suspicions doubtless have to do in part with my own theological views, and with a certain personal concern for the modern dialogue between Eastern and Western Christianity — a dialogue in the *filioque* which inevitably bulks large and in which Anselm's arguments and their influence are of more than purely archaeological or speculative interest. But I should like here to attempt to show that they are objectively grounded in weaknesses in Anselm's argument which can perhaps be brought out by the application of a method of questioning similar to his own. What follows is advanced as if it were the opening of an answer to him by one of the 'Greeks' against whom he wrote, composed in not unconscious imitation of his own style. Inevitably, only certain key points can be touched upon in the space available, but they are, I believe, crucial ones.

Pro Graecis

The Latins believe, confess and teach a doctrine which we Greeks deny, namely that the Holy Spirit proceeds not only from the Father but also from the Son. Now, Anselm of Canterbury has argued that this doctrine follows by rational necessity from those things which Greeks and Latins hold in common, and that it is re-

futed by no opposing reason; and he presents 'most certain arguments' to demonstrate it. 'Higher matters' than this he leaves to
'more learned men'; and in this he shows the proper humility of a
Christian who, even as archbishop, knows that his duty is to believe
the teaching of the Church, and to search for the reasons which
show why that teaching is true, as he has also written in his
response to the ideas of a certain cleric in France concerning the
blessed Triad.[2] For this teaching of the *filioque* has been accepted
and approved by the Pope of Rome, and must accordingly be most
certainly believed by all Latins.

I too can search out no higher matters, but ask only this
question. What is the rational necessity by which Anselm under-
stands the doctrine that the Holy Spirit proceeds also from the Son
to follow from that which Greeks and Latins alike believe? For here
only two things are possible. Either this rational necessity has been
demonstrated or it has not been demonstrated. If it has been
demonstrated, the Latin doctrine is sound; but if it has not been
demonstrated, that doctrine remains uncertain in itself and must be
admitted to be an innovation. Let us, therefore, see how the
archbishop defends his belief; and that the argument may be
clearer, let us cast it in the form of a dialogue in which Anselm
affirms his opinions and a Greek questions him.

Anselm   The Latins and the Greeks believe alike in one God,
            Father, Son and Holy Spirit; and the same whole and
            perfect God is spoken of whether one speaks of one
            person, or of two, or of all three together. Yet there is
            also a plurality in God signified by the names Father, Son
            and Holy Spirit. By these God is designated as existing as
            God in three ways: as God from nothing, as God from
            God by begetting, and as God from God by procession.
            These distinctions of origin constitute the relations by
            which the persons are distinguished as diverse from each
            other; for he who begets, or from whom another pro-
            ceeds, is thereby distinguished from him who is begotten
            or him who proceeds from him, and the two poles of
            these relations cannot be confused, for the relations are
            irreversible and the two poles mutually exclusive. Thus all
            that is truly and properly said of God *as God* is said
            equally of each and all of the three persons; but the
            oppositions constituted by the relations prevent what is
            said peculiarly *of one person* from applying also to the
            other persons. Therefore, the unity of God is to be
            maintained throughout, except where the plurality of re-
            lation opposes it; while the plurality is to be maintained,
            except in those things which belong to the simplicity of
            the divine unity.

Greek   I do not yet wish to challenge what you say, though to
          my ears this Latin dialectic of unity and plurality sounds
          somewhat strange, as does your use of the term
          'relation'. It may be that here already there are hidden
          traps concealed in the form of your affirmations. But as
          to the material content of what you state, it is good and
          orthodox; for the Father, Son and Holy Spirit are indeed
          distinguished from each other in this way, as we too
          affirm when we speak of the *tropoi tes hyparxeos*. For
          the Father is uncaused and unbegotten; the Son is
          begotten; and the Spirit he who proceeds from the
          Father; and so each hypostasis is distinguished from the
          others. But how from these true distinctions do you
          propose to show that the Holy Spirit proceeds also from
          the Son? For it appears to me that you have rightly
          shown that his *hypostasis* is constituted solely by his
          procession from the Father.

Anselm   Nothing could be easier to show. You have not yet
          considered the full import of what has been said.

Greek   Pray instruct me further.

Anselm   Gladly. Just as the Son exists from the Father, and not
          the Father from the Son, and so it is that they are dis-
          tinguished from each other; and similarly as between the
          Father and the Spirit; so too I affirm that either the Son
          must exist from the Holy Spirit or the Holy Spirit from
          the Son. And as it is manifest from Scripture that the
          Spirit as the Spirit is the Spirit of the Son as well as of
          the Father, and as the person of the Son is perfectly
          constituted by his being begotten from the Father, it is
          impossible to believe that the Son exists from the Spirit
          as well as from the Father. The only remaining poss-
          ibility, therefore, is that the Spirit proceeds also from
          the Son. And that this indeed is so can be further
          demonstrated and confirmed by the beauty and elegance
          of the conclusions which follow from it. For the relation
          of origin in every case establishes two poles. On the one
          side, so to speak, is 'God from whom God exists', and on
          the other, 'God who exists from God'. Now, the Father is
          'God from whom God exists', but not 'God from God'.
          The Son is both 'God from whom God exists' and 'God
          from God'. The Spirit is not 'God from whom God exists',
          but only 'God from God'. Indeed, even more complex and
          harmonious patterns of relational attributes may be seen
          to distinguish the three divine persons, as I have shown in
          the sixteenth chapter of my little book on the subject.
          For there are six distinct attributes, viz. (1) to have a

father (2) not to have a father (3) to have a son (4) not
to have a son (5) to have a spirit proceeding from oneself
(6) not to have a spirit proceeding from oneself. And
each of the three persons possesses three and only three
of these attributes, one unique to himself, and one shared
with each of the other two. Thus, the Father . . .

Greek   Yet pause a moment! Pause before we are quite over-
whelmed with the enchanting dance of logical abstractions. The conclusions which you are now offering do
indeed appear so rational that nothing more rational could
be conceived. But not all that appears to be rational is
necessarily true, as you yourself have so often and so
well reminded us. There lies a point far back where as it
seems to me your flow of thought has left its proper
channel and spread into diffused speculation. By what
reason or necessity must it be said that either the Son
exists from the Spirit or the Spirit from the Son? You
have indeed asserted this, but how is to be shown to be
true? To leap from the relations between the Father and
the Son, or the Father and the Spirit, to assert a similar
relation between the Son and the Spirit is a *metabasis eis
allo genos*. The Father alone is 'God from whom God
exists'; the Son and Spirit alike are 'God from God', the
one by begetting and the other by procession, and it is in
this way, and not by the origination of the one by the
other, that they are distinguished. Are you any longer
speaking of the Holy Triad or perhaps only of a picture
painted upon the air?

Anselm   What you dismiss as a leap, a speculation, a *metabasis eis
allo genos* is but the necessary consequence of
irrefragable arguments by which nothing more is asserted
than is already implicit in what you and we alike believe
concerning the blessed Trinity.

Greek   I should very much like you to show me this for I find
your claim very strange.

Anselm   It will no longer seem so to you when you have discerned
its necessity.

Greek   I beg you, unfold that reality to me, for I am eager to
understand further.

Anselm   I shall do so, so far as my meagre powers permit. First
paint in your mind this thought, that the Holy Spirit is
God, as the Father is God, and the Son is God, and these
are one and the same God. Then paint beside it what has
already been said concerning unity, plurality and relation.
Now consider this also, remembering that the simplicity

of the divine unity is to be maintained except where the opposition of relations stands against it. The Son and the Spirit are each 'God from God'; but who is the 'God from whom God exists' in each case?

Greek   The Father alone.

Anselm   Not so, for the divine being which the Son and the Spirit receive from the Father, they also hold in common with each other. Therefore, either the Son receives that being from the Spirit as well as from the Father, or the Spirit receives it from the Son as well as from the Father. If neither of these is the case, the godhead of the Son or of the Spirit must be denied, and thereby their existing as God from the Father will also be denied. The unity of the divine being permits no other conclusion than that either the Son receives from the Spirit or the Spirit from the Son. And this can be shown in another way as well. That same unity and simplicity requires that there be an opposition of relation between the Son and Spirit in order that they be suitably and necessarily distinguished from each other; for otherwise as each is 'God from God' they would appear to be identical with each other. As it is patent that they are not identical, for the one is begotten, and the other proceeds, one must receive from the other as well as from the Father. And as has already been shown, the Son is begotten from the Father alone: therefore, the order of the relation must necessarily be that the Spirit proceeds from the Father and the Son.

Greek   Now, at last, the nature of your argument is clear, but its necessity is by no means apparent. For it is not necessary that anything which is shared by two must be given by one and received by the other; nor is it necessary that there be a relation between the Son and the Spirit of the same kind as those between the Father and each of them. Their relations to the Father are themselves sufficient to establish both that each is fully God, and that each is distinct from the other, but this you have obscured by describing both the Son who is be-gotten and the Spirit who proceeds as 'God from God' and this has made it necessary for you to establish some further relation between them in order to distinguish them. The necessity is not absolute, but relative to the terms in which you have cast the enquiry.

Anselm   Surely you do not deny that the Son is 'God from God' and that the Spirit is also 'God from God'?

Greek   I do not deny, but strongly affirm and believe it. But it
is one thing for a statement to be true, and another for
it to be the whole truth. And especially in such deep
matters, we must beware of partial affirmations which,
by what they do not say, distort our questioning and open
the path to doubtful assertions. . .

NOTES

1.   Alasdair Heron, "'Who proceedeth from the Father and the Son":
the problem of the *filioque'*, *Scottish Journal of Theology,* 24:2
(1971), 149-66.

2.   *Epistola de incarnatione verbi Dei,* I, *Ans.Op.Om.,* II, 6:10-7:4

Anselm on Future Contingencies:
A Critical Analysis of the Argument of the *De concordia*

Paul A. Streveler

I am mainly concerned in this paper with Anselm's resolution of the apparent inconsistency of maintaining both that God knows all things and that some events should occur contingently. The problem was an ancient one, even by the time Anselm set his mental powers to its resolution, he having inherited it from Augustine and Boethius, and the latter from Aristotle in a slightly different form. I do not wish here to become involved in the complications with respect to the theological excrescences of divine predestination and grace considered by Anselm in the later sections of the *De concordia*. My concern will only be with the 'minimal thesis' of foreknowledge and contingency — any problems residing in that thesis being applicable, *mutatis mutandis*, to the more complicated theses as well. So too, my concern will be mainly with the position of part one of the *De concordia*; although some reference to other works will be made.

The paradigm of a contingent action is free choice, and the paradigm of a free choice is sin. Does God's foreknowledge that I will sin take away the freedom of choice, since what God foreknows must necessarily occur? Anselm's initial response is typically Augustinian:[1] God's foreknowledge includes the fact that I will sin *freely*.[2] That is, God foreknows that I will sin without necessity; although that truth is itself necessary. It is necessary that God knows that I will sin without necessity. The opponent is not satisfied, and Anselm introduces various senses of 'necessity' in order to clarify what is being claimed. The crux of Anselm's solution to the problem of future contingencies hinges upon his distinction between *necessitas subsequens* and *necessitas praecedens* — a distinction which later fourteenth-century logicians will use in their solutions to the problem under the terminology of a *necessitas consequentiae* and *necessitas consequentis* — although it is not at all clear that the Anselmian distinction precisely parallels the more modern distinction.[3] We shall attempt to define the two senses of necessity in the formal rather than material mode, acquiescing to the contemporary bias that necessity, like truth, is a characteristic of sentences rather than things.

A proposition, P, is necessary by *necessitas subsequens* if, and only if, there exists no power which can bring about not-P.[4] This definition of necessity is in terms of some impossibility with respect to the denial of P. Thus, the primitive modality seems to be 'possibility', and not necessity — and this seems to be Anselm's position. Thus, our analysis must elucidate the sense of possibility (or impossibility-over-the-opposite, in this case) involved here. From Anselm's remarks and examples, it seems clear that the reason why there exists no power which *can* bring about the denial of a proposition which is necessary by subsequent necessity is because the sentence, not-P, is self-contradictory. Thus, he says, for example, 'God is immortal' is necessary by subsequent necessity because 'nothing can cause Him not to be immortal' — the reason being, presumably, that the sentence 'God is mortal' is self-contradictory and thus not able to be made true by any force or power. Or, even more clearly, Anselm says:

> Indeed, (if someone considers the meaning of the word), by the very fact that something is said to be 'foreknown', it is declared to be going to occur. For only what is going to occur is foreknown, since knowledge is only of the truth. Therefore, when I say, 'If God foreknows something, it is necessary that this thing be going to occur', it is as if I say, 'If this thing will occur, of necessity it will occur'. But this necessity neither compels nor prevents a thing's existence or non-existence. For because the thing is presumed to exist, it is said to exist of necessity; or because it is presumed not to exist, it is said to not-exist of necessity. (But our reason for saying these things is) not that necessity compels or prevents the thing's existence or non-existence. For when I say 'If it will occur, of necessity it will occur', here the necessity follows, rather than precedes, the presumed existence of the thing. The sense is the same if we say, 'What will be, of necessity will be'. For this necessity signifies nothing other than what will occur will not be able not to occur at the same time.[5]

It is clear then that the idea of *necessitas subsequens* is purely logical in the sense that the denial of a subsequently necessary sentence will be a sentence of the form, or reducible to the form, (P.-P).[6] Anselm also seems aware that the sentences necessary by subsequent necessity are either identity sentences or reducible to such.[7] And he suggests that these are necessary by definition or 'by the meaning of the terms in the sentence'.[8]

Anselm clearly realizes that all events, past, present, and future can be said to be necessary by subsequent necessity, although strictly speaking it is not the event that is necessary but only the hypothetical conditional which really has the logical form, $(P \supset P)$, where the 'P' can be a past, present, or future tensed statement.[9]

The idea of subsequent necessity is, thus, fairly clear but there are a few curiosities with the way in which Anselm defines this sense of necessity. It may be instructive to note one of these. It seems curious to me that Anselm should define subsequent necessity in terms of the lack of any power able to bring about the denial of the sentence said to be subsequently necessary. For, it seems quite superfluous to note that, in addition to not-P being self-contradictory, there exists no power able to bring it about that it is true. It is as if I were to say that the reason why a bachelor cannot be married is because there is no one available who can perform this feat — suggesting, perhaps, that this is some physical or legal 'cannot', which someone, if he had the power, could overcome. This idea of 'power over x' as the primitive notion of 'possibility' and the analysis of other senses of 'possibility', including 'logical possibility', in its terms is clearly an inheritance from Aristotle's idea of 'potentiality' as somehow primitive. Although even Aristotle seems to recognize 'non-potential' senses of 'possibility', they seem parasitic upon the idea of 'potency'.[10]

Thus, we encounter the idea of 'power over the past' which plays an essential role in this discussion of future contingencies. The medievals are fond of quoting the Aristotelian text:

> For this alone is denied even to God, to make undone things that have once been done.[11]

Although there is some debate about the truth of Aristotle's claim,[12] the great majority of medieval philosophers are in agreement. There is, however, a good deal of confusion about how and in what sense the past is necessary; and, I think, the confusion is heightened because of the analysis of logical necessity in terms of this idea of 'power over x'.

In the *De concordia*, Anselm says, as we have already noted, that there is a legitimate sense in which past, present, and future are all necessary. But, in addition, Anselm has this to say about the past:

> Now a past event has a characteristic which a present or a future event does not have. For it is never possible for a past event to become not-past, as a present event is able to become not-present, and as an event which is not necessarily going to happen has the possibility of not happening in the future.[13]

Anselm does not return to this peculiarity concerning past events in this treatise, although it is notable that when he speaks about the nature of God's eternal present — this being the mode in which, strictly speaking, God knows all things — Anselm notes that the analogy is with the temporal past, not the temporal present.[14] The reason being, presumably, that the kind of necessity applicable to propositions in God's eternal present is analogous to the necessity peculiar to the past. Now, in what sense is the past necessary, and the present and future not necessary? It would appear that since subsequent necessity applies equally to past/present/future, the additional necessity peculiar to the past cannot be subsequent. But, elsewhere, Anselm frequently uses the example of the impossibility of undoing the past (as presumably distinct from 'undoing the present or future') as an example of something self-contradictory, as indeed it is frequently argued by other medieval philosophers.[15] And we noted above that subsequent necessity is fundamentally logical. But, then, this would not show the past as necessary in any sense that the present and future are not.[16] The fact of the matter seems to be that it is no less contradictory to 'undo the present' or to 'undo the future', on the basis of the hypothesis that these are 'done' (i.e. are what they are), a hypothesis which is also made of the past.

Thus, unless there is some third sense of necessity, the necessity peculiar to the past is *necessitas praecedens*. But, I think we can show that, if this is so, the distinction between subsequent and precedent necessity breaks down. Precedent necessity is defined by Anselm as a necessity applicable to events, (rather than sentences), because there exists some power or force that brings about the event in question, while the event is itself not capable of preventing that power from causing it. It seems that this latter clause is necessary, since every event is brought about by some other event. But, if we include the clause, it seems that the distinction breaks down because there is no event which is capable of preventing the power that causes it because this would entail a power over the past, the event being after the cause that brings it about.

Another possible way of reading Anselm's definition is this: An event, E, is precedently necessary if it is caused to occur by some power, P; and there exists no power, P-1, prior to P, which can bring about the non-occurrence of P. If the distinction between subsequent and precedent necessity is not to break down, the sense of 'can' in our second definition must itself be precedent. That is, the proposition 'P does not occur' is not self-contradictory. So it is simply an accident that there exists no power over P, and logically at least, P could be prevented, and so too, E. Anselm's example is 'Tomorrow the sun will rise'.[17] This is an unfortunate example for it is taken from Aristotle, and yet the sense in which it is necessary for Aristotle cannot be precisely the sense in which it is necessary for Anselm.[18] For Anselm it appears that the sentence is necessary by precedent necessity because there is some power which brings about tomorrow's sunrise, and there exists no further power which can prevent the power from bringing about tomorrow's sunrise. But once again, this latter is to be taken in a qualified sense, for, strictly speaking, there does exist a power which can prevent tomorrow's sunrise, viz., the power of God. For, assuming 'Tomorrow there will be a sunrise' is not logically necessary, then God's power extends over it. It is here that the later medieval distinction between *potentia dei absoluta* and *potentia dei ordinata* is relevant.[19] *De potentia absoluta,* God can prevent tomorrow's sunrise. *De potentia ordinata,* He cannot. The distinction is, roughly, between logical necessity and causal necessity. Once again, however, the distinction is blurred within Anselm's discussion, for the analysis is in terms of the common notion of 'power over x'. Furthermore, the definition of precedent necessity is itself in terms of precedent necessity, and thus is circular.[20] No clear difference has been marked between the sense in which God has power over the event in question, and the sense in which no *other* thing has power over the event in question. If it is logically possible to imagine (*sic!*) God preventing tomorrow's sunrise, then it is logically possible that there be no sunrise tomorrow and thus, logically possible to imagine (*sic!*) any power at all preventing tomorrow's sunrise. God may be, in some peculiar sense, the instrument for our imagination's task, but, with respect to logical necessity, it is clear that this 'instrument' is really superfluous and misleading.

While interpreting some scriptural passages, Anselm finds it helpful to introduce a further element into his solution to the problem of future contingents — an element which Boethius had used and which Thomas Aquinas will also use — the notion of the 'eternal present' as being the mode in which all events are known to God.[21] The point is simply that, strictly speaking, God does not know events as they occur temporally and with all their temporal modalities; God knows them in the aspect of their unchangeable eternity. One must, presumably, imagine a kind of isomorphism between the events known, while noting a difference in the mode of knowing. Yet, it is the mode of knowing that itself 'shapes' the object known, according to the principle of Boethius that 'quidquid concipitur, concipitur per modum concipientis'.[22]

There are several aspects of this idea of the eternal present as outlined by Anselm that are confusing and curious. I think it can be shown that there is an inconsistency within Anselm's position, if he wishes to take this idea of the eternal present seriously. The inconsistency can be easily seen in the following way.

According to Anselm's previous remarks, the very freedom of my sinning is part of what God knows and, thus, God knows that I will sin freely.[23] Now, 'to sin freely' entails, I assume, 'to sin mutably', that is, sinning in such a way that there exists a power over the sinning which could, prior to the event, prevent the sin. 'To sin mutably' is then intimately tied up with the temporal mode, and so is 'to sin freely'. To know that someone will sin freely, then, must also be tied to the temporal mode. Otherwise, what one knows will not be truly the event in question, and this is impossible. But God is now said to know events only in the eternal present. In what sense do I 'sin in the eternal present freely'? That is, in what sense can I sin *mutably* in the eternal present, such that there exists a power over the sinning which could, *prior* to the event, prevent the sin in the eternal present? Clearly, this description is barely intelligible. Thus, it would seem, that if God knows all things in His eternal present, then He cannot know that I will sin *freely*. Anselm cannot have both of these theses as parts of a consistent analysis of the problem of divine foreknowledge and future contingents, for they are mutually inconsistent.

In closing, I would like to note two further difficulties with this idea of the eternal present as outlined by Anselm. Anselm does not deny that the eternally present statements of divine knowledge are necessary; but since their necessity does not 'reach', as it were, from past to future, they pose no problem for future contingencies.[24] The question arises, are these statements subsequently or precedently necessary? Clearly, precedent necessity must be ruled out, for this is a temporal mode of necessity involving causality. Yet later, Anselm does insist that God's knowledge is the cause of why events occur, rather than the reverse.[25] Nevertheless the cause and effect must here be 'simultaneous' (*sic!*) since no 'priority' can be allowed in the modality of the eternal present. The necessity involved here is a peculiar hybrid of both causal and logical necessity.

Anselm compares the necessity peculiar to God's eternal present to the necessity peculiar to the past.[26] We have already noted the difficulties involved in understanding this 'spilt-milk necessity', as Anscombe has labelled it.[27] The principal point we wish to make, however, is that one cannot help but feel that the free actions which are performed without this necessity attached to them are 'free' in a rather non-genuine sense, since these actions are occurring in God's eternal present, and necessarily so — not merely by virtue of the logical relationship between 'truth' and 'knowledge', but also by virtue of the 'fact' of their being known by God.

NOTES

1. Augustine's remarks on this subject can be found in several places, for example, *De Civitate Dei*, 5.9.

2. *De concordia praescientiae et praedestinationis et gratiae Dei cum libero arbitrio*, 1, Ans.Op.Om., II, 245-7. I have used the translation of Jasper Hopkins in Volume II of *The Works of St Anselm* (New York, 1976). This 'solution' itself poses certain puzzles. Presumably, 'I will sin freely at T^1', means 'I will sin at T^1 or I will not sin at T^1', the disjunction being exclusive since I cannot do both at T^1. Now, if God knows that I will sin freely at T^1, then He knows that I will sin at T^1 or I will not

sin at T^1. But this disjunctive fact is an empty piece of knowledge, since it is trivially true. Thus, if God is to know something more than anyone who knows logic can know, He must know which disjunct is true. Therefore, God knows not only that I will sin freely, but also that I will sin, if this is true; or that I will not sin, if this is true. And we are right back at the original problem.

3. The distinction can be found in the works of numerous fourteenth-century writers. Robert Holkot, for example, notes Anselm himself as the author of the distinction. See Robert Holkot, *Commentaria in Sententiarum*, 2.2, 'Utrum Deus ab aeterno sciverit se producturum mundum'.

4. 'We must realize that we often say "necessary to be" of what is not compelled-to-be by any force, and "necessary not to be" of what is not excluded by any preventing factor.' Hopkins, *St Anselm*, II, 183.

5. Ibid., pp. 183-4.

6. Or, more exactly, the form $(P \supset -P)$.

7. 'Similarly whenever we predicate something of itself, (the statement is true). For when we say "Every man is a man", or "If he is a man, he is a man", or "Every white thing is white", or "If it is white thing, it is white", these statements must be true (because something cannot both be and not be the case at the same time). Indeed, if it were not necessary that everything which is going to happen were going to happen, then something which is going to happen would not be going to happen – a contradiction. Therefore, necessarily, everything which is going to happen is going to happen; and if it is going to happen, it is going to happen'. Hopkins, *St Anselm*, II, 185.

8. Ibid., p. 183. One should note, however, that there is a difference between a sentence being true by virtue of the meaning of the terms, and a sentence being logically identical. Perhaps Anselm was unaware of this distinction.

9. 'Likewise, the following statements are equally true: (1) that some thing did exist and does exist and will exist, but not out of necessity, and (2) that all that was, necessarily was, all that is, necessarily is, and all that will be, necessarily will be. Indeed, for a thing to be past is not the same as for a past thing to be past; and for a thing to be present is not the same as for a present thing to be present; and for a thing to be future is not the same as for a future thing to be future.' Hopkins, *St Anselm*, II, 184.

10. cf. Aristotle, *Metaphysics*, 5.12.

11. Aristotle, *Nichomachean Ethics*, 1139b:5-10; cf. also Aristotle, *De Coelo*, 283b:13.

12. For an interesting discussion of exceptions to this rule, see W.J. Courtenay, 'John of Mirecourt and Gregory of Rimini on whether God can undo the past', *Recherches de théologie ancienne et medievale*, 40 (1973), 147-74.

13. Hopkins, *St Anselm*, II, 184.

14. Ibid., p. 190.

15. *Proslogion*, 7, *Ans.Op.Om.*, I, 105-6; see also Petrus de Rivo, 'Quaestio quodlibetica disputata', in *La Querelle des futurs contingents*, edited by L. Baudry, Études de philosophie medievale, 38 (Paris, 1950) 70-8.

16. The popular belief is that the past is necessary in a way that the future is not, or that the future is contingent in a way that the past is not, has been persuasively questioned by Anthony Kenny, 'Divine foreknowledge and human freedom', in *Aquinas, A Collection of Critical Essays* (New York, 1969).
    This idea has also been questioned by some medieval writers. For example, Robert Holkot in certain unedited *quodlibetal* questions, argues that there is a sense in which I can, today, make certain statements which were said of me in the past, true or false. Thus in a sense, I can 'affect the past'. See Paul Streveler, 'Robert Holkot on future contingents: a preliminary account', in *Studies in Medieval Culture*, 8 and 9 (1975), 163-72

17. Hopkins, *St Anselm*, II, 185.

18. The thesis that the sun will rise tomorrow is tied in Aristotle to the thesis that the world is eternal, and thus necessary in both directions of past and future. Since Anselm does not apparently have the distinction between things necessary *a se*, and being necessary *per se*, as in Aquinas, it is unclear how the sun's rising could, for him, be necessary in any sense close to Aristotle's.

19. The distinction is, roughly, between 'logical' and 'causal' necessity. Any event, the description of which is not logically impossible, can be brought about by God, *de potentia absoluta*. So, events, the description of which is not logically impossible, would, nevertheless, if they did not occur, run counter to the ordinary course of nature and, thus, God could not bring them about, *de potentia ordinata*.

20. One might argue that this circularity is unavoidable because the primitive modality involves the idea of 'power over x', which can itself not be analysed in other terms.

21. Hopkins, *St Anselm*, II, 188-9. cf. Boethius, *De Consolatione Philosophiae*, 5.5. 401-11, edited by E.K. Rand and S.J. Tester, Loeb Classical Library (Cambridge, 1968). Thomas Aquinas, *Summa Theologica* I, Q. 14, a. 13, ad. obj. 2.

22. Boethius, *De Consolatione*, 5.5.388-9. Clearly, this principle is merely an instance of the Aristotelian principle, 'quidquid recipitur, recipitur per modum recipientis'. But a serious problem arises as to whether we are even permitted to say that God knows the same thing that we know, if this principle is taken seriously. Indeed, some passages in Anselm indicate that the objects known are not the same (see, for example, Hopkins, *St Anselm*, II, 190). The question then will arise of whether we have two different 'truths'; or is the temporal mode of knowing merely illusory?

23. Hopkins, *St Anselm*, II, 182.

24. Ibid., pp. 189, 190-1.

25. God's willing, knowing, and causing are all identical within his nature, which is absolutely simple. Thus, in knowing X, God causes X. Evil is to be ruled out as, strictly speaking, not real and thus not an effect of God's causality. cf. Hopkins, *St Anselm*, II, 193-4, 189.

26. 'Thus we can recognize that for lack of a verb signifying the eternal present, the apostle used verbs of past tense; for things which are temporally past are altogether immutable, after the fashion of the eternal present. Indeed, in this respect, things which are temporally past resemble the eternal present more than do things which are temporally present'. Hopkins, *St Anselm*, II, 190.

27. G.E.M. Anscombe, 'Aristotle and the sea battle', *Mind*, 65 (1956), 1-15.

V
The Devotional Works

'Inward feeling and deep thinking':
The Prayers and Meditations of St Anselm Revisited

Benedicta Ward

Imitation, it is said, is the sincerest form of flattery. If this is so, it is an attention which has been lavished upon one small part of the works of Anselm of Canterbury far in excess of that given to his main theological writings. From the first, the prayers were used and misused, collecting around them a host of lesser works which went under the name of Anselm. The separation of the genuine prayers from the rest was undertaken by Dom Wilmart, and the small nucleus of three meditations and nineteen prayers which survived was edited by Dom Schmitt in 1946. These prayers have, therefore, received a good deal of attention, perhaps more than is good for them, since they are at best early and minor compositions of Anselm, somewhat apart from the main body of his works. Yet, they were popular and entered the mainstream of medieval devotion. There can be no doubt that the element of emotion used in a particularly personal way as a goad for the will in prayer was a notable innovation by Anselm in these meditations. But the very novelty of it, now as then, appears to have obscured the full context in which such emotion is used, so that the true balance within Anselm's prayers has not been fully appreciated. The question which arises in looking at the prayers and the later imitations of them, is whether the latter represent a true continuation of the method of prayer espoused by Anselm, or whether they actually prolong and exaggerate only *one* element within his prayers, an element which appealed to a particular style of devotion, itself shaped by quite different influences. In order to demonstrate how the second of these possibilities seems to be true, I would like to give an example of the use made, in a different century and devotional climate, of Anselm's prayers, not through an imitation of his style but through translations of the genuine prayers themselves.

The example I have chosen is the Middle English prose treatise, *A Talking of the Love of God*,[1] a minor part of the body of mystical writing which evolved in England in the thirteenth and fourteenth centuries and found its greatest expression in the work of Richard Rolle, Walter Hilton, Julian of Norwich and the author of *The Cloud of Unknowing*. That the prayers of Anselm, and the method of prayer he recommended, were known to these writers is apparent from their writings. Julian, in particular, makes use of the three states of compunction which are found in Anselm's prayers and echoes many of his images and phrases in her writings,[2] and Richard Rolle has been seen as the author of a translation of

Anselm's first meditation.[3] The *Talking* is a composite treatise, and one of far less depth than the writings of these four mystics, but precisely because it is more popular, less weighty and less universal in its appeal, it shows more clearly the way in which the prayers of Anselm were understood and used in general. Moreover, one section of the *Talking* is a translation into English of several of the prayers: the prayer of St John the Baptist, the prayer to St Paul, the second prayer to St Mary and the third meditation, as well as the preface. It is, furthermore, of some interest to see how a translation into another language can also mean a translation into an altogether different style of prayer.

The complete text of the *Talking* is preserved in two manuscripts of the fourteenth century,[4] both of which contain many more devotional works of a similar nature, and which seem designed for use in private prayer for individuals. In that sense, they belong to the kind of prayer *in cubiculum meum* which was proposed by Anselm. They are texts to be used as a way into prayer and they are meant to be read privately. The *Talking* itself can be divided into three sections with a preface: the first part is a free and somewhat enlarged version of an earlier meditation on Jesus Christ as the lover of the soul, *An Orison to God Almighty,*[5] and the last section takes its main theme from another earlier work, *The Wooing of our Lord.*[6] These are linked by a section based on several of the genuine prayers of Anselm, and the whole work is prefaced by a version in English of the Preface to Anselm's prayers and meditations in which is outlined the way in which the prayers were to be used.

The Preface to the *Talking* is recognizably a version of Anselm's Preface, but a comparison of the texts shows at once that a world of difference lies between them.

Orationes Sive Meditationes

Prologus

Orationes sive meditationes quae subscriptae sunt, quoniam *ad excitandam legentis mentem* ad Dei *amorem vel timorem,* seu ad suimet discussionem editae sunt, non sunt *legendae in tumultu* sed *in quiete,* et *cursim et velociter,* sed paulatim cum *intenta* et *morosa meditatione.* Nec debet intendere lector ut quamlibet earum totam *perlegat,* sed quantum sentit sibi Deo adiuvante valere *ad accendendum affectum orandi,* vel quantum illum delectat. Nec necesse habet aliquam semper a principio incipere, sed ubi magis illi placuerit. Ad hoc enim ipsum paragraphis sunt distinctae per partes, ut ubi elegerit incipiat aut desinat, ne prolixitas, aut frequens eiusdem loci repetitio generet fastidium, sed potius aliquem inde colligat lector propter quod *factae sunt pietatis affectum.*

Heer is a Tretys.
A Talkyng of þe Loue of God.

þis tretys Is a talkyng of þe loue of God And is mad for to
sturen hem þat hit reden to louen him þe more And to
fynde *lykyng* and *tast* in his loue. Hit falleþ for to reden hit
esyliche and *softe*. So as men may mest in *Inward elyng
and deplich þenkyng sauour* fynden. And þat not beo dene
But bi ginnen and leten in what paas so men seoþ þat may
for þe tyme ȝiunen *mest lykynge*. And whon men haþ con-
ceyued þe maters wiþ redyng *Inward þenkyng* and *deoplich
sechyng* wiþouten eny redyng vppon þe selue maters and of
such oþere þat god wol senden. Hose wole sechen schal
ȝiunen *in ward siȝt* and *felyng in soule*. And *swetnes
wonderful* ȝif preyere folwe. But hose wole in Meditacion
swete fruit fynden hit mot be taken in wone wiþ þreo
poyntes þat folewen: Affyaunce, And continuaunce, And louh
herte and clene þat he truste sikerliche to fynden þat he
secheþ And þat his pouȝt beo harde i set And ful bisyliche
I.kept And holden him self vn worþ out of godes ȝifte. And
wlate on him seluen.þorw siht of his fulþe Men schal fynden
lihtliche þis tretys in Cadence After þe bigynninge ȝif hit
beo riht poynted & Rymed in sum stude To beo more
louesum to hem þat hit reden.God ȝiue vs grace so for to
rede þat we mowen haue heuene to vre Mede.Amen.

For Anselm, the aim of the prayers was to increase the ability of
the reader to love and fear God and to know himself; for the
author of the *Talking*, it was to love God more and enjoy this sensation. Both recommend that the prayers should be read thought-
fully, quietly and slowly, but the words and phrases used by Anselm
in his prayer — 'quiet', 'slow', 'thoughtful', and 'meditative reading'
— are transformed during translation and represented in the *Talking*
as 'easily', 'softly', 'enjoyment', and 'inward feeling'. Both writers
suggest that selections should be made in using the material in
preparation for prayer, but while for Anselm the guideline in such
selection is that the reader should use only as much as leads him to
prayer, in the old tradition of *lectio divina*, the author of the
Talking says he should choose what pleases him and holds his
interest. Perhaps the difference can be summarized by saying that
while Anselm himself writes in the tradition of ascetical prayer, the
author of the *Talking* transposes Anselm's words into the tradition
of mystical prayer.

Comparing the texts themselves, this difference is clearly
apparent wherever there is a parallel between the prayers of
Anselm and those in the *Talking*. I shall discuss three instances
where this occurs. In the first case we shall look at that section of
the *Talking* which is most closely based on Anselm's prayers and

which uses his prayer to St John the Baptist. The whole of the prayer by Anselm has a clear and precise basis in the Bible, and revolves around the concept of John the Baptist's recognition of Christ as the Lamb of God, which is linked with the use of a phrase in the liturgy, the 'Lamb of God who takes away the sin of the world'. The prayer is presented as a conversation between three participants — Anselm, St John the Baptist and Christ. The theme of the prayer passes between these three and the reader goes through definite stages of prayer: self-abasement and grief at sin; the possibility of trust in the aid of the saint; and confidence and adoration of Christ as the saviour of the sinner who repents.

In the *Talking*, only one element of Anselm's prayer has been selected and the result is an intense and self-concerned monologue, in which the person praying dwells at depressing length on his own sins and condemnation. Those mighty Anselmian contrasts between the sin of Adam, or the sin of Lucifer, and the sin of those who have known redemption, appear in the *Talking* as the almost hysterical exclamations of a man concerned with his own unworthiness, as if the more sinful he makes himself sound the more he will merit help. The controlled use of emotion has here been distorted by being taken out of its context.

In the second example, it is this concern with personal emotion for its own sake and the attempt to arouse as much of it as possible in the reader which distinguishes Anselm's meditation on the Passion of Christ from the section on the Passion found in the *Talking*. It is not Anselm's 'Prayer to the Cross', an austere and beautiful prayer based on the liturgy, which is the parallel for the text in the *Talking* but his longer and more passionate 'Prayer to Christ'. This prayer might well be considered the most emotional of Anselm's meditations on a scriptural theme, but it is precisely here that the contrast with the 'inward feeling' of the fourteenth-century mystics is most apparent. Anselm describes with emotional intensity the details of the sufferings of Christ on the cross — the buffeting, the scourging, the wounds, the piercing with a lance, and the tears of the Virgin — but, in doing so, he does not go beyond the information found in the Gospels, and he gives the account reserve and dignity by placing the scene at a remove. 'Would that I with happy Joseph might have taken down my Lord from the cross', Anselm writes, and it is this passionate regret at *not* having been present at the crucifixion that gives the scene its reality and dignity while simultaneously adding, through the expression of his longing, an emotional dimension to the situation. Moreover, the meditation on the details of the Passion leads to an equally strongly felt apprehension of the resurrection of Christ and into a prayer, as in the *Proslogion,* to see the face of Christ in heaven.

In the *Talking*, what do we have? A direct involvement with the lurid details of crucifixion at first hand: limbs twisted in agony, joints wrenched apart, blood, wounds and pain. The difference between this and Anselm's own prayer is the difference between the crucifixion scene as portrayed in the St Alban's Psalter and the representation by Heironymous Bosch of the deposition of Christ from the Cross. Moreover, where the reaction provoked in Anselm by the scene is that of repentance, adoration and desire for greater apprehension of the mystery of God, in the *Talking* it is a very different matter. Here an overflow of what can only be called erotic emotion is released, involving leaping upon the cross and sucking blood from the wounds: 'I leap at him as a greyhound at an hart — I fold him in my arms — I suck the blood from his feet'.[7] This is neither the method of prayer devised by Anselm nor is it the theology of the *Cur Deus homo*. Again, emotion has been isolated and distorted through exaggeration.

A third example shows the same divergence. The *Talking* lists the qualities that all men desire: beauty, generosity, wisdom, courage, riches, noble birth and gentleness. The writer sees each one as finding its perfection in Jesus Christ, portrayed as the lover of the individual soul: 'Who would not love you, sweet Jesus? For within you are gathered all things that may ever make anyone worthy of another's love'.[8] The aim here is to stir emotion in the reader towards the person of Jesus, making him desired with the emotions of human affection. Where these qualities are evoked in the *Proslogion*, it is with a very different intention. At the end of the *Proslogion*, Anselm presents the same qualities as finding their full flowering in the vision of God in heaven: 'whatever you love, whatever you desire, it is there, it is there indeed'.[9] Beauty, generosity, wisdom, friendship, riches and pleasures — these are not set out as the attributes of a person who is to be desired because he possesses them, but as the fulfilment of all human qualities in the shared vision of God. The *Proslogion* represents a deeply felt expression of a profound theological truth about God and the purpose of Man, and its aim is to stir the reader to attain to that end throughout his whole life.

There, is then, a wide difference between the 'inward feeling' of the *Talking* and the 'deep thinking' of Anselm. Yet it is Anselm who provided the model for the later writer. In one of his very rare references to his sources, the name 'Anselmus' appears.[10] In this respect, the writer stands as one in a series of devotional writers who took this one isolated theme of emotion and personal involvement with the subject of prayer from Anselm, and produced thereby some masterpieces of a certain type of personal devotion, for example, the *Stabat Mater dolorosa*, or that treasure of Protestant hymnody, 'When I survey the wondrous cross'. But this should not obscure from our view the fact that Anselm's total approach to prayer, in those few prayers which are certainly his own, was different. There is in each of them a firm apprehension of theological and scriptural reality, and the use he makes of emotion is subservient to these themes. What is most significantly in Anselm but lacking elsewhere is the dimension of 'the others': whether it is St Mary Magdalene, St Peter, St Paul, or the whole company of the redeemed, he demonstrates in his prayers a continual awareness of others, of a 'great cloud of witnesses'. Where prayer, for the author of the *Talking*, is an intensity of personal emotion — essentially private and inward — for Anselm, it is never a private matter, even when conducted in the small inner chamber. That which is most personal to each is in some sense common to all, and in the perfection of charity he sees the emotions of each as a source of unity rather than divisiveness.

Let me end with two quotations which illustrate these differences between Anselm and his translator. The first is from the end of the *Talking*: 'Ah sweet Jesus, sweet love, my dear heart, love of my life, my death, my bliss, because you made me your dear lover, I place myself between your arms and embrace you. Now give me awareness of you for ever and keep me in your care, sweet Jesus, King of heaven, amen'.[11] The second concludes Anselm's prayer to the evangelist St John who has been pictured as pre-eminently the friend beloved of Christ: 'See, he [Christ] shows how much he loves me, he comes near to me so that I may love him. So I press on and hope not in myself but in him, for he listens to my desire who thus crowns my prayer. My heart and my flesh rejoice in him and love him and all that is within me blesses him, amen'.[12]

Perhaps all I have shown in this paper is that to translate is to betray ('traducere tradere est'), but perhaps I have also indicated the particular kind of betrayal which a partial appreciation of Anselm caused, and which led his name to be linked, in spirituality as in theology, with a tradition very far from his own understanding and faith.

NOTES

1. *A Talkyng of the Loue of God*, edited with introduction and notes by M. Salvina Westra (The Hague, 1950).

2. See Benedicta Ward, 'Faith seeking understanding: Anselm of Canterbury and Julian of Norwich', in *Julian of Norwich*, edited by A.M. Allchin (Oxford, 1973; reprinted 1978).

3. 'Here is a good meditation which Saint Anselm made', in *Yorkshire Writers: Richard Rolle of Hampole and his Followers*, edited by C. Horstman, 2 vols. (London, 1895-6), II, 443-5.

4. Oxford, Bodleian Library, MS Vernon 3938, ff. ccclxvii–ccclxxi; British Library, MS Simeon, Add. MS 22283, ff. 171v and 172.

5. *On Wel Swude God Ureisun of God Almihti*, edited by W. Meredith Thompson, Early English Text Society, O.S. 241 (London, 1958).

6. *The Wohunge of Ure Lauerd*, edited by W. Meredith Thompson, Early English Text Society, O.S. 241 (London, 1958).

7. Westra, *A Talkyng*, p. 60.

8. Ibid., p. 26.

9. *Ans.Op.Om.*, I, 118.

10. Westra, *A Talkyng*, p. 20. The actual words referred to ('Ah, sorrow and sighing, crying and groaning, where are you abundant if here you are absent? Where are you ardent if here you abate?') are not a direct translation of Anselm but a paraphrase of the kind of sentiment and phraseology the writer looked for in him.

11. Ibid., p. 68.

12. *Ans.Op.Om.*, III, 49.

St Anselm, the Monastic Community at Canterbury, and Devotional Writing in Late Anglo-Saxon England

Thomas H. Bestul

St Anselm began an active association with the affairs of England on his first visit there in 1079, shortly after his consecration as Abbot of Bec. The purpose of the journey was to survey the English holdings of his abbey, which by this time were considerable, and were soon to become extensive. From this time forward, Eadmer tells us, England was familiar to him; and he must have made other visits before 1093, when he became Archbishop of Canterbury.[1]

Although the usual opinion is that Anselm had no very profound relationship to England, and in particular to the monastic community at Canterbury, there are a few direct indications of Anselm's interest in Anglo-Saxon culture, even before his arrival in England. He had asked Lanfranc for a copy of a monastic code, presumably the *Regularis concordia*, which he attributed to Dunstan, and had sent to Canterbury in search of correct texts of Bede's *De Temporibus*.[2] During the visit of 1079, he took pains to defend the veneration of Alphege as a saint and martyr, and spent considerable time in conversation with the monks of Canterbury, living among them as one of their number.[3] After his assumption of the pontificate in 1093, Anselm was associated with those who made the second half of the eleventh century a great age of Anglo-Saxon hagiography, most notably, of course, with Eadmer, who wrote lives of Dunstan, Oswald, Wilfred, and Oda. At the time of Anselm's visit in 1079, the community at Christ Church had received a Norman implantation and was ruled by Lanfranc and Prior Henry, a former monk of Bec, but the Anglo-Saxon element must still have been quite vital at this time.[4] It is useful to consider how that house and its traditions might have appeared to Anselm at the time of his sojourn there, in order to better understand the context of the visit.

In considering Anselm's literary career and his intellectual development, it seems that Anselm would have found most in common with the monastic culture of Christ Church in his role as a devotional writer. By this time, he had probably substantially completed his *Orationes sive meditationes*, with the exception of the *Meditatio redemptionis humanae*.[5] The likelihood of this supposition is strengthened by the contrast between Anselm's house of Bec and Christ Church. Bec was a recent foundation, noted first for the austerity and simplicity of its life and then for the high level of its theological learning. Orderic Vitalis declares that the monks of Bec were so devoted to their studies that almost all of them seemed to be philosophers ('Ut paene omnes videantur philosophi').[6] The situation at Christ Church was quite different. The English house did not participate at all in the new advances in philosophy and theology, but was devoted, from an intellectual standpoint, as David Knowles has remarked, 'to the laborious transmission of an attenuated legacy that had been exploited for five hundred years'.[7] At Canterbury, the considerable energy released by the Benedictine reform movement of the tenth century resulted in a great number of Gospel books, psalters, missals, and benedictionals. In contrast to Bec, which had no importance from an artistic standpoint, the prevailing interest at Canterbury, as well as at Winchester and elsewhere, seems to have been in the production of sumptuously executed and skillfully illuminated liturgical books. Closely related to the production of manuscripts of this kind, and perhaps even a by-product of it, is the formation of collections of private devotional prayers, which are most often found in psalter manuscripts.

We are fortunate in possessing a considerable number of manuscripts from the first half of the eleventh century containing private devotional prayers which can be attributed with some certainty to Christ Church, Canterbury. It is well to recall that as N.R. Ker's thorough study shows, the number of surviving manuscripts of all kinds from this period from Christ Church exceeds that of any other house, including the two great houses at Winchester and St Augustine's, Canterbury.[8] The number of extant manuscripts is quite probably an accurate index of the amount of activity in the production of manuscripts, but one must always be aware that the accidents of survival may present a somewhat distorted picture. In the case of houses with a relatively large number of surviving manuscripts, such as Christ Church, one must also remember that the attributions themselves vary greatly in their certainty. Nevertheless, the manuscripts offer evidence of a kind that repays careful examination, and an insight into the intellectual and devotional climate of the monastic community at Christ Church in the years before Anselm's visit can be gained through a study of them. Rather little is known about monastic life at Christ Church in the period before the Conquest, except for the general impression that there was a decline during the reign of Edward the Confessor.[9] While discipline may have relaxed, I believe the evidence shows considerable vitality in the production of manuscripts generally, including those with devotional works. These manuscripts enable us to appreciate Anselm's devotional writings in a broader context — we are in a better position to recognize his originality, the power of his thought and expression, and to see his prayers and meditations as part of a common tradition which was nurtured diligently at Christ Church.

Christ Church received devotional materials from two sources. The first is an earlier generation of English prayer books from the eighth, or early ninth centuries, such as the *Book of Cerne* (Cambridge, University Library, MS Ll.1.10), the *Book of Nunnaminster* (British Library, MS Harley 2965), and the collection in British Library, MS Royal 2 A.xx.[10] These large collections, not attached to psalters, seem to be especially influenced by Irish piety. A small number of the prayers in the *Book of Cerne* became extremely popular and spread throughout Europe over the period of the ninth to the twelfth centuries. Two examples are those prayers attributed variously to Augustine, Gregory, or less frequently, to Jerome: 'Domine deus omnipotens, qui es trinus et unus', and 'Mane cum surrexo'.[11] The compilers of collections of private prayers at Christ Church, as elsewhere in England at this time, were also much influenced by Carolingian models. One particular psalter written in Northern France in the ninth century (Cambridge, Corpus Christi College, MS 272), came to Canterbury at an early date and undoubtedly influenced the development of collections of private prayers there. The psalter contains, among others, the prayers 'Domine deus meus qui non habes dominum' (f. 178b), 'Domine exaudi orationem meam quia iam cognosco quod tempus meum prope est' (f. 181b), and 'Clementissime deus qui me inutilem famulum tuum' (f. 183a), all of which are found in the later Christ Church collection, British Library, MS Arundel 155, which will be discussed below. In dealing with the question of influence, it is not always easy to tell whether a particular eleventh-century prayer reached Canterbury from native sources or from the Continent, since there was a wide diffusion of certain prayers in the early English collections, particularly those of the *Book of Cerne*. The prayer, 'Domine deus meus qui non habes dominum', for example, found in the Canterbury manuscripts Arundel 155 (f. 181b) and Corpus Christi College 272 (f. 178b), is also found in the *Book of Cerne*,[12] which contains the oldest known text of the prayer. As it happens, the Arundel text is closer to the Corpus Christi manuscript than to the *Book of Cerne*, so it seems reasonable to suppose that this English prayer travelled to the Continent in the eighth or ninth century, acquired changes in the text, and was then re-introduced to England in the eleventh century, rather than passing directly into the Arundel collection from the *Book of Cerne* through exclusively English intermediaries.

Those surviving manuscripts which were written at Christ Church show considerable concern for the cultivation of private prayer of the kind Anselm himself was to carry to new heights. Around the turn of the eleventh century, the Bosworth Psalter manuscript of about 980 (British Library, Add. 37517) had devotional prayers added to it, a very common practice in England throughout that century. At Christ Church, as well as elsewhere, earlier manuscripts were modified by the addition of fresh material in order to make them suited to the new devotional requirements of the age. MS Royal 2 A.xx has a series of collects in its margins which were added in the late tenth century; the *Book of Cerne* has one prayer which was probably added during the same century; and the Old English glossed Psalter, MS Royal 2 B.v, written at Winchester in the middle of the tenth century contains an office to the Virgin and three Old English devotional prayers appended to the manuscript in the eleventh century at Christ Church.[13] The prayers in the Bosworth Psalter are liturgical prayers that seem to have been intended for devotional use. One of them, 'Omnipotens sempiterne deus, qui dedisti famulis tuis in confessione', is a collect to the Trinity found also in a ninth-century prayerbook from Tours (Paris, Bibliothèque Nationale, MS lat. 13388).[14]

The earliest major collection of private prayers from Christ Church is in the psalter manuscript, British Library, MS Arundel 155, which can be dated somewhere between 1012 and 1023.[15] This large and eclectic collection begins with four liturgical collects adapted for devotional use by the change of first person plural references to the singular, a practice found elsewhere, for example, in the series of private prayers appended to Aelfric's Catholic Homilies, where liturgical forms are similarly modified.[16] Three of the Arundel collects, 'Omnipotens mitissime deus, respice propitius ad precem meam' (f. 171a), 'Ure igne sancti spiritus renes meos' (f. 171a), and 'Inveniat quesumus domine animae famulorum famular-umque' (f. 171a), are either found in their entirety or by their incipits in the two surviving manuscripts of the *Regularis concordia*, both of which are eleventh-century texts connected with Christ Church.[17] All three of these have their origins in Carolingian service books and two are found in other contemporary English manuscripts in addition to those of the *Regularis*.[18] The fourth prayer, 'Omnium sanctorum intercessionibus', is found in the contemporary manuscript from the New Minster, Winchester, British Library, MS Cotton Titus D.xxvi (f. 65a), and in other English manuscripts from the second half of the eleventh century.[19]

The collects are immediately followed by a series of forty-five prayers glossed in Old English, which form the heart of the collection.[20] Included are a number of prayers found in the earlier *Book of Cerne*, and also in other eleventh-century English prayer-books, such as 'Omnipotens dilectissime deus, sanctissime atque amantissime salvator' (f. 173a; no. 14),[21] 'Sancta et gloriosa dei genitrix semperque virgo maria' (f. 182b; no. 28),[22] and the popular prayer to St Michael, 'Sancte Michael archangele domini nostri iesu christi' (f. 183a; no. 29), a prayer which is found in some twelfth-century manuscripts of Anselm's *Orationes sive meditationes*.[23] Since these prayers do not appear to be found in continental collections (with the exception of the prayer to St Michael), it is perhaps justified to think of them as belonging to a specifically English tradition, although the text of most of the Arundel prayers varies considerably from that in the *Book of Cerne*.

The Arundel collection also, as is typical, includes many prayers which can be traced to continental Carolingian sources: the first glossed prayer, 'Domine deus omnipotens, aeterne et ineffabilis' (f. 171a; no. 1), is from the *De psalmorum usu* of the pseudo-Alcuin (*PL* 101.468); the prayer, 'Domine Jesu Christe gloriosissime conditor mundi' (f. 172b; no. 10), is from an early ninth-century prayerbook from Tours (Troyes, Bibliothèque Municipale, MS 1742);[24] and the widely diffused prayer attributed to St Augustine, 'Deus inaestimabilis misericordiae' (f. 175b; no. 17), seems to come from the Carolingian *Officia per ferias* (*PL* 101.524).

The most original part of the Arundel collection includes a prayer to the Holy Cross, 'Domine Jesu Christe, pro sancta cruce tua' (f. 173b; no. 15), reflecting perhaps the increasing interest throughout Europe during the eleventh century in devotions to the Cross, of which Anselm's own 'Prayer to the Cross' is also evidence,[25] and three lengthy personal confessional prayers, 'Confiteor tibi, domine, quia ego peccavi' (f. 179b; no. 19), 'Confiteor tibi domino deo celi, omnia peccata mea' (f. 180a; no. 20), and 'Clementissime deus, qui me inutilem famulum tuum' (f. 180b; no. 23), all of which seem to respond to the needs of the times for longer, more intensely personal, forms of devotion. Also seemingly original to this collection is a large group of full-scale prayers to such saints as John the Baptist, Peter and Paul, Stephen, Maurice, Cecilia, Dunstan, and the very recent Anglo-Saxon saint, Alphege, who is also mentioned, along with Edward, in a prayer to martyrs (f. 187a; no. 36). This is a type of devotion brought to culmination a generation later in the prayers of Anselm. One indication of the advanced nature of this part of the collection is that two of the confessional prayers (nos. 19 and 23), found otherwise only in this manuscript, are copied in a late twelfth-century manuscript of Anselm's prayers, Oxford, Bodleian Library, MS Laud Misc. 508 (f. 38a, f. 34b). The prayer to St Alphege seems to have been used at Christ Church in the twelfth century and beyond — a later hand has changed references from Alphege to 'Thoma' (f. 186a; no. 35), undoubtedly Thomas à Becket.

A similar collection is found in Vatican, MS Reg. lat. 12, a psalter intended for use at Bury St Edmunds. The manuscript was possibly written at Christ Church betwen 1025 and 1050, although the attribution is somewhat speculative.[26] The full analysis of the twenty-one prayers in the Vatican manuscript published by André Wilmart shows that the collection has much in common with MS Arundel 155.[27] There are a number of prayers from continental Carolingian sources, such as the prayer attributed to St Augustine, 'Domine Iesu Christe qui in hanc mundum propter nos' (no. iii), which is found also in MS Arundel 155 (f. 177b; no. 18), and comes originally from the *De psalmorum usu* attributed to Alcuin (*PL* 101. 476). The Vatican collection also preserves devotional material from early English or Anglo-Irish sources. The most remarkable instance of this is the prayer 'Omnipotens sempiterne deus, respice propitius' (no. i), which is found elsewhere only in the Bobbio missal, a seventh-century text of Irish origin. The manuscript also has the prayer to the twelve apostles, 'Domine Iesu Christe qui dedisti potestatem' (no. xi), found in the *Book of Cerne*,[28] and also in MS Arundel 155 (f. 184a; no. 32), as well as in the contemporary prayerbook from Winchester, British Library, MS Cotton Galba A.xiv (f. 28b). The collection includes lengthy diffusive personal prayers, among them a prayer attributed to St Gregory, 'Domine exaudi orationem meam quia iam cognosco' (no. xvi). This prayer, which seems to be continental in origin (the oldest texts are early ninth century), was popular in eleventh-century England: besides appearing in this manuscript, it is found in MS Arundel 155 (f. 174a; no. 16), in MS Cotton Galba A.xiv (f. 21a) and in the '*Portiforium* of Wulfstan'.[29] The other example of a personal confessional prayer is, 'Omnipotens sempiterne deus rex regum et dominus dominantium' (no. xviii), which is drawn partly from the *Synonyma* of Isidore of Seville, and is found also in the nearly contemporary psalter manuscript, possibly from Winchester, British Library, MS Cotton Tiberius C.vi (f. 22a). There are four seemingly original prayers (nos. iv, xii, xx, xxi), including one addressed to St Edmund, 'Domine rex angelorum et susceptor peccatorum' (no. xii), and another invoking Edmund and Botulf, which has a particularly effective and beautiful opening petition: 'Audi domine deus meus ymnum anime et gemitum cordis mei, quem ante conspectum maiestatis tuae hodie effundo' (no. xxi). The prayer to St Dunstan in the Arundel collection (f. 187b; no. 38) is here addressed to St Benedict, appropriately for use at Bury: 'Sancte ac beatissime domine et pater Benedicte' (no. xiii).

Perhaps the most remarkable of the surviving Christ Church devotional manuscripts is British Library. MS Cotton Vespasian A.i. This celebrated, splendidly written and decorated psalter of the eighth century has had a quire with private devotions added to it in the first half of the eleventh century, possibly in the decade between 1030 and 1040, according to T.A.M. Bishop.[30] This collection deserves comment, not only for the intrinsic interest of what it contains, but also because the prayers in it are unedited for the most part, although they are accessible in the reproduction of the Vespasian psalter in the series Early English Manuscripts in Facsimile.[31]

The collection begins with a metrical prayer of Eugenius of Toledo, 'Rex Deus immense' (f. 156a), which is found in Carolingian collections, such as the *Officia per ferias* (*PL* 101.579) and the Fleury prayerbook (*PL* 101.1397), but in no other surviving pre-Conquest English manuscript. The second item is the widely circulated Carolingian prayer, 'Deus inaestimabilis misericordiae'

(f. 156b), found in MS Arundel 155 and the Vatican collection and which eventually appears in the early printed editions of Anselm's *Orationes sive meditationes.*[32] The collection is concluded by five extraordinary prayers to the Holy Cross, unique to this manuscript and presumably composed at Christ Church:

(a) 'O sanctum et verabile [sic] nostri redemptoris signum' (f. 157b)
(b) '[O] iesu christe crucifixe domine qui pro nobis factus' (f. 158a)
(c) 'Salve crux sancta et veneranda, gloriosa et laudanda' (f. 158b)
(d) 'Ave sancta crux omnium arborum gloriosissma' (f. 159a)
(e) 'Te sancta dei crux humiliter adoro' (f. 160a).

These prayers fully reflect eleventh-century subjectivism and effusiveness, and invite comparison with Anselm's own 'Prayer to the Cross'. The prayer (d) became part of the Anselmian apocrypha, and is printed in the Migne edition of Anselm's *Orationes sive meditationes* (PL 158.937). The Vespasian manuscript is the earliest-known authority for the prayer. As might be expected, the oldest manuscripts which combine this prayer with the genuine work of Anselm are English. The prayer clearly entered the apocrypha through the medium of English Anselm manuscripts of the twelfth century: it is found in London, Society of Antiquaries, MS 7 (f. 37a), a manuscript from Durham from the first half of the twelfth century; and in Oxford, Bodleian Library, MS Laud Misc. 79 (f. 108b), a manuscript from Reading from the second half of the century. It is interesting to note that the printed version of the prayer, which is close to the text in the Laud and Antiquaries manuscripts, is rather pale in comparison with the much lengthier Vespasian text. The Vespasian version makes greater use of rhymed cadences, in a fashion similar to Anselm, and has a concluding section not found in the printed edition, the diction of which is close to Anselm's usage:

> Per te confractum est iugum captivitatis nostrae. Per te est deletum cyrographum dampnationis nostrae. Per te venit salus mundi et redemptio totius seculi.[33]

> Per te infernus spoliatur et omnibus per te redemptis obturatur. Per te daemones terrentur, comprimuntur, vincuntur, conculcantur. Per te mundus renovatur atque veritate in illo lucente et iustitia regnante decoratur.[34]

The prayer (c) 'Salve crux sancta et veneranda', has a series of questions addressed to the Cross lamenting the inadequacy of human efforts to adore it properly, in a way similar to Anselm's 'Prayer to the Cross':

> Quid digne de te dicere, qua laude te competenter predicare? Quibus verbis fragilitas humana te congrue potest adorare quam distinctae angelicorum dignitates spirituum

suppliciter adorant et venerantur, glorificantemque velud insuperabile regis sui vexillum et gloriosum creatoris triumphum? Quid tuae sanctitati in creaturis potest comparari, sine qua nullus ab initio seculi licet sanctus esset et iustus potuit salvus fieri? Quis tui misterii profunditatem et sanctitatis magnitudinem sensu comprehendere vel verbis plene potest enarrare? Cum signum tuae imaginis tantam in se contineat virtutem ut quocumquemodo exprimatur adverse potestates et dibolica [sic] fantasmata inde fugentur?[35]

Quo ergo affectu gloriabor in te, sine qua non solum nulla mihi esset gloria, sed insuper aeterne me possideret infernalis luctus et miseria? Qua delectatione iucundabor in te, per quam pro servitute tartarorum haereditas mihi data est regni caelorum? Quo gaudio gratulabor in te, sine qua futurum erat ut horrerem me vel ad momentum esse, et per quam expecto quia gaudebo me in aeternum esse? Nam etsi adhuc inter spem et metum deo serviam, certus tamen sum quia ad haec bona, si gratias agendo, amando, vivendo in te gloriabor, per te perveniam.[36]

Besides these three collections of prayers, other manuscripts testify to the interest in devotional writing at Christ Church. The well-known British Library, MS Cotton Tiberius A.iii, from about 1050, contains the Rule of St Benedict glossed in Old English (f. 118a), as well as several documents relating to the Benedictine reform, such as the *Capitula* of Aachen (f. 169a), part of the *Memoriale* of Benedict of Aniane (f. 164a), and the *Regularis concordia* (f. 3a), which itself includes several prayers used liturgically which are also found in contemporary devotional collections. For example, the prayer, 'Domine iesu christe, gloriosissme conditor mundi', is also contained in MS Arundel 155 (f. 172b; no. 10), in British Library, MS Galba A.xiv (f. 112a), and in the twelfth-century English Anselm manuscript, Oxford, Bodleian Library, MS Laud Misc. 79 (f. 109b).[37] The manuscript also has four confessional prayers in Old English, apparently intended for private use.[38] One of them is a translation of the popular prayer mentioned above, 'Deus inaestimabilis misericordiae' (f. 44a). The same prayers are in the psalter manuscript, British Library, MS Royal 2 B.v, a Winchester product which reached Canterbury during the eleventh century.[39] The Paris psalter manuscript of about the middle of the eleventh century (Paris, Bibliothèque Nationale, MS lat. 8824) has a short series of private prayers which seem unique; its drawings have some affinities to those of MS Arundel 155, and it may have been written at Christ Church.[40] Another mid-eleventh-century manuscript which may be from Christ Church is also significant: Lambeth Palace, MS 204 contains a text of the *De compunctione cordis* of Ephraim the Syrian. While this work is a fourth-century sermon addressed to monks, its effusiveness of style, its use of vivid language and imagery to evoke a powerful emotional response, and its insistent emphasis on tears, penitence, and the horrors of the Last Judgment, make it thematically and stylistically close to the new devotions of the eleventh century. of which Anselm's own first meditation, 'Terret me vita mea', is an excellent example.

It is legitimate to ask whether the interest in devotional writing was unique to Christ Church, or common to other English houses at that time. The manuscript evidence suggests, in fact, that the greatest activity was conducted at Christ Church, but it is also clear, as might be expected, that manuscripts with private prayers were collected and produced at Winchester and, to a lesser extent, at St Augustine's, Canterbury. One of the most important Winchester manuscripts is the so-called 'Athelstan Psalter' (British Library, MS Cotton Galba A.xviii), produced on the Continent around the turn of the tenth century and probably given to the Old Minster by King Athelstan.[41] The manuscript contains a number of devotional prayers which became popular in England, among them the series of devotions to the Holy Cross, 'Domine iesu christe, adoro te in cruce ascendentem', found, for example, in the *Regularis concordia*.[42] Written at Winchester itself is the large heterogeneous collection of prayers from the early eleventh century in MS Cotton Galba A.xiv, which probably belonged to the Nunnaminster, and a similarly diverse collection of prayers from the New Minster, the companion MSS Cotton Titus D.xxvi and xxvii, which belong to the years 1023 to 1035.[43] Both of these collections include continental prayers as well as those from the earlier Anglo-Irish tradition. From the second half of the eleventh century, and of uncertain attribution to Winchester, is the collection of prayers in the '*Portiforium* of Wulfstan' (Cambridge, Corpus Christ College, MS 391).[44] Also from later in the century is the important collection of prayers in the Winchester psalter, British Library, MS Arundel 60. This manuscript is of special interest because new prayers were added to it late in the eleventh, or early in the twelfth, century, probably at Christ Church rather than at Winchester. One of these prayers borrows heavily from Anselm's 'Prayer to Christ', and later becomes part of the Anselmian apocrypha.[45]

From St Augustine's, Canterbury, a smaller number of manuscripts has survived. A psalter manuscript from the last quarter of the tenth century, Cambridge, Corpus Christi College, MS 411, which was once thought to be of continental origin, has now been assigned to St Augustine's.[46] This manuscript has a series of prayers, one of which, 'Suscipiat pietas tua Domine Deus meus' (f. 137a), is found in the later Christ Church manuscript, Arundel 155 (f. 182a; no. 26), and two of which are found in the late eleventh-century '*Portiforium* of Wulfstan'.[47] Some other St Augustine's manuscripts may be mentioned briefly. The ninth-century Cambridge,

Gonville and Caius College, MS 144, has the 'Oratio Prudentii' ('O dee cunctipotens anime dator'), which is found in continental devotional collections;[48] and the tenth-century MS Cotton Vespasian D.vi contains the Old English Kentish Hymn and an Old English metrical paraphrase of Psalm 50.[49] The Vespasian poems were perhaps intended for devotional use, and may be compared with the Old English prose prayers in MSS Cotton Tiberius A.iii and Royal 2 B.v. The production of paraphrases of biblical or liturgical texts is one of the characteristics of late Old English poetry, paralleled by the Latin metrical paraphrases of the Lord's Prayer, Creed, and *Te Deum* in a St Augustine's manuscript from the second half of the eleventh century, Cambridge, University Library, MS Gg.5.35.[50] Also from the late eleventh century is a collection of thirty-one prayers in the psalter manuscript, Rouen, Bibliothèque Municipale, MS A.44.[51]

The manuscript evidence thus suggests that there was consider-able interest in the collection and production of private prayers in eleventh-century England and, more particularly, that at Christ Church the period from 1020 to 1070 stands out as a time of great activity, even innovation, in the field of devotional writing. No direct evidence indicates that Anselm was aware of this enterprise prior to or during his visit of 1079, and certainly none suggests that his own prayers and meditations were influenced by what was done in the monastic community of Christ Church. However, it is impor-tant to note that neither the products of Christ Church nor Anselm's own devotional writings existed in isolation. Pursuits of the kind I have described at Canterbury went on elsewhere in England — at St Augustine's and most notably at Winchester, and quite probably at Norman houses as well — although manuscript evidence is sparse. As is well-known, there were contacts between Normandy and England before the Conquest, as the career of Robert of Jumièges, Bishop of London and Archbishop of Canterbury in the reign of Edward the Confessor, illustrates. Moreover, it should be emphasized that, throughout northern Europe during the eleventh century, a new devotional idiom was being created, the finest expression of which is the prayers and meditations of Anselm.[52] The manuscripts of the *Orationes sive Meditationes* produced in the century after his death show that his successors regarded his work as at one with this larger devotional tradition. The interpolated twelfth-century English manuscripts of the *Orationes sive Med-itationes* combine the genuine work of Anselm himself with Caro-lingian prayers and newer devotions found in such pre-Conquest Christ Church collections as MS Cotton Vespasian A.i (the 'Prayer to the Holy Cross' is a notable example), MS Arundel 155, and Vatican, MS Reg. lat. 12.[53] Moreover, there were those at Canterbury, Rochester and elsewhere who, in the generation after Anselm's death, continued writing in this same tradition. One thinks of Ralph of Battle, Elmer of Canterbury, Osbert of Clare, and the author of the prayer in MS Arundel 60, who borrows both from a Carolingian prayer and Anselm's 'Prayer to Christ'.[54] In the development of the new devotional sensibility that occurred in the eleventh century, Christ Church played a part, and our knowledge of this helps us to see Anselm's entire relationship to English culture in a new light, and offers a fresh perspective on the visit of 1079, when Anselm sojourned among the monks of Canterbury.

NOTES

1. See *The Life of St Anselm, Archbishop of Canterbury, by Eadmer*, edited by R.W. Southern (London, 1962), pp. 48-57; on the possessions of Bec, see Marjorie Chibnall, 'The relations of Saint Anselm with the English dependencies of the Abbey of Bec: 1079-1093', *Spicilegium Beccense*, 1 (1959), 521-30.

2. *Ans.Op.Om.*, III, 151, 154 (*Epistolae* 39, 42). In *Epistola* 39, he also asks for a life of Dunstan.

3. Eadmer, *Life of Anselm*, pp. 50-4.

4. See David Knowles, *The Monastic Order in England* (Cambridge, 1940), pp. 100-27; R.W. Southern, *Saint Anselm and his Biographer* (Cambridge, 1963), pp. 277-84.

5. On the date, see Southern, *Anselm*, pp. 34-6; F.S. Schmitt, 'Zur Chronologie der Werke des Hl. Anselm von Canterbury', *Revue bénédictine*, 44 (1932), 322-50.

6. *The Ecclesiastical History of Orderic Vitalis*, edited by Marjorie Chibnall, 6 vols. (Oxford, 1969-80), II, p. 296.

7. Knowles, *Monastic Order*, p. 94.

8. N.R. Ker, *Medieval Libraries of Great Britain: A List of Surviving Books*, second edition (London, 1964), s.vv.

9. Southern, *Anselm*, pp. 242-5; Knowles, *Monastic Order*, pp. 31-82; R.R. Darlington, 'Ecclesiastical reform in the late Old English period', *English Historical Review*, 51 (1936), 385-428.

10. The prayers from these manuscripts are printed in *The Prayer Book of Aedeluald the Bishop, Commonly Called the Book of Cerne*, edited by A.B. Kuypers (Cambridge, 1902); *An Ancient Manuscript of the Eighth or Ninth Century* [*Nunnaminster*], edited by Walter de Gray Birch, Hampshire Record Society (London, 1889); the prayers from the MS Royal 2 A.xx are in an appendix to the *Book of Cerne*.

11. Kuypers, *Book of Cerne*, pp. 103 and 89 respectively.

12. Ibid., p. 117.

13. See N.R. Ker, *Catalogue of Manuscripts Containing Anglo-Saxon* (Oxford, 1957), no. 249.

14. Printed in André Wilmart, *Precum libelli quattuor Aevi Karolini* (Rome, 1940), p. 102.

15. Ker, *Catalogue*, no. 135; Elzbieta Temple, *Anglo-Saxon Manuscripts, 900-1066* (London, 1976), no. 66.

16. See Donald G. Bzdyl, 'The source of Aelfric's prayers in Cambridge University Library, MS Gg.3.38', *Notes and Queries*, 222 (1977), 98-102.

17. Printed in *Regularis Concordia*, edited by Thomas Symons (London, 1953), see pp. liii-lix, 13, 15, 24.

18. The second is in the mid-eleventh-century British Library, MS Arundel 60, f. 133b; the third in the late eleventh-century MS known as the *'Portiforium* of Wulfstan' (Cambridge, Corpus Christi College, MS 391), p. 582. The latter is printed in the *The Portiforium of Wulstan*, edited by Anselm Hughes, Henry Bradshaw Society, 96 (1960), p. 2; cf. Wilmart, *Precum libelli*, p. 101; *Liber sacramentorum*, PL 101.453.

19. Hughes, *The Portiforium of Wulstan*, p. 2; Cambridge, University Library MS, Ff.1.23, f. 281a.

20. One of the glossed prayers from this MS is printed in H. Logeman, 'Anglo-Saxonica minora', *Anglia*, 11 (1888), 115-19; the rest are in Ferdinand Holthausen, 'Altenglische Interlinearversionen lateinischer Gebete und Beichten', *Anglia*, 65 (1941), 230-54; and Jackson J. Campbell, 'Prayers from MS Arundel 155', *Anglia*, 81 (1963), 82-117. Campbell counts 44 prayers, but his prayer no. 44 in reality combines two prayers, as the manuscript clearly shows at f. 191b. Prayer no. 45 begins, 'Deus omnipotens, bone et iuste'.
    The numbers in the following citations in my text refer to the editions of Holthausen (nos. 1-28); Campbell (nos. 28-44); and Logeman (no. 17 only).

21. cf. Kuypers, *Book of Cerne*, p. 135; British Library, MS Cotton Titus D.xxvii, f. 89a.

22. cf. Kuypers, *Book of Cerne*, p. 155; British Library, MS Cotton Titus D.xxvii, f. 83a.

23. cf. Kuypers, *Book of Cerne*, p. 152; Oxford, Bodleian Library, MS Douce 296, f. 125a; British Library, MS Arundel 60, f. 136a. The prayer is in the twelfth-century, English Anselm manuscript,

British Library, MS Cotton Vespasian D.xxvi, f. 48b, and in the fourteenth-century Cambridge, Corpus Christi College, MS 284. On the latter MS, which belongs to St Augustine's, Canterbury, see André Wilmart, *Auteurs spirituels et textes dévots du Moyen Age latin* (Paris, 1932), pp. 209-13; on the former, see T.H. Bestul, 'The collection of Anselm's prayers in British Library, MS Cotton Vespasian D.xxvi', *Medium Aevum*, 47 (1978), 1-5.

24. Wilmart, *Precum libelli*, p. 13.

25. See André Wilmart, 'Prières médiévales pour l'adoration de la Croix', *Ephemerides Liturgicae*, 46 (1932), 22-65.

26. See Temple, *Anglo-Saxon Manuscripts*, no. 84.

27. André Wilmart, 'The Prayers of the Bury Psalter', *Downside Review*, 48 (1930), 198-216. Citations of prayers from the Bury Psalter in my text are given by Roman numeral and refer to Wilmart's article.

28. Kuypers, *Book of Cerne*, p. 127.

29. See Hughes, *Portiforium*, p. 12; for early manuscript tradition, see Wilmart, 'Bury Psalter', p. 209; on the personal characteristics of this prayer, see Edmund Bishop, *Liturgica Historica* (Oxford, 1918), pp. 384-91.

30. T.A.M. Bishop, *English Caroline Minuscule* (Oxford, 1971), no. 25; see also Ker, *Catalogue*, no. 203.

31. *The Vespasian Psalter*, edited by David Wright, Early English Manuscripts in Facsimile, 14 (Copenhagen, 1967); see also the diplomatic text in the *Vespasian Psalter*, edited by Sherman M. Kuhn (Ann Arbor, 1965), pp. 315-21.

32. The prayer is in the twelfth-century Anselm manuscript, Oxford, Bodleian Library, Laud. Misc. 508, f. 32b, and is printed in the Migne edition of Anselm's *Orationes sive meditationes*, PL 158. 876; see André Wilmart, 'La Tradition des prières de saint Anselme', *Revue bénédictine*, 36 (1924), 52-71.

33. British Library, MS Cotton Vespasian A.i, f. 160a.

34. *Oratio ad sanctam crucem*, Ans.Op.Om, III, 11-12:25-8.

35. British Library, MS Cotton Vespasian A.i, f. 158b.

36. *Oratio ad sanctam crucem*, Ans.Op.Om, III, 12:42-9.

37. Symons, *Regularis*, p. 43.

38. See Ker, *Catalogue*, no. 186.

39. The prayers are printed from this manuscript in H. Logeman, 'Anglo-Saxonica minora', *Anglia*, 12 (1889), 497-518.

40. See Temple, *Anglo-Saxon Manuscripts*, no. 83.

41. See Bishop, *Liturgica*, p. 141.

42. Symons, *Regularis*, p. 43; see also Kuypers, *Book of Cerne*, p. 114; these devotions are found in British Library, MS Cotton Galba A.xiv, f. 110a, and in MS Arundel 155, f. 172a (nos. 4-9).

43. Ker, *Catalogue*, no. 202; Temple, *Anglo-Saxon Manuscripts*, no. 77.

44. The prayers have been edited in Hughes, *Portiforium*; see Ker, *Catalogue*, no. 67.

45. The text of the apocryphal prayer is in *PL* 158.885-7; the Arundel text is printed in T.H. Bestul, 'St Anselm and the continuity of Anglo-Saxon traditions', *Annuale Mediaevale*, 18 (1977), 39-40; on the Arundel manuscript, see Ker, *Catalogue*, no. 134; Temple, *Anglo-Saxon Manuscripts*, no. 103; T.H. Bestul, 'British Library, MS Arundel 60, and the Anselmian Aprocrypha', *Scriptorium*, 35 (1981), 271-5.

46. Temple, *Anglo-Saxon Manuscripts*, no. 40.

47. 'Deus qui patriarchas et prophetas caelesti' (f. 138b) and 'Deus qui lapso lucifero' (f. 138b); cf. Hughes, *Portiforium*, p. 9.

48. *PL* 101.544, 1396.

49. Ker, *Catalogue*, no. 207.

50. See Ker, *Catalogue*, no. 207; A.G. Rigg and G.R. Wieland, 'A Canterbury classbook of the mid-eleventh century', *Anglo-Saxon England*, 4 (1975), 113-30.

51. The collection is analysed in Lili Gjerløw, *Adoratio Crucis: The Regularis Concordia and the Decreta Lanfranci* (Oslo, 1961), pp. 132-47.

52. See Southern, *Anselm*, pp. 34-47; G.R. Evans, '*Mens devota*: the literary community of the devotional works of Jean of Fécamp and St Anselm', *Medium Aevum*, 43 (1974), 105-15.

53. See Bestul, 'Anglo-Saxon devotional traditions', pp. 35-8; Bestul 'The collection of Anselm's prayers', pp. 1-5.

54. See Wilmart, *Auteurs sprituels*, p. 270; *The Prayers and Meditations of St Anselm*, translated by Benedicta Ward (Harmondsworth, 1973), pp. 275-86; T.H. Bestul, 'The Verdun Anselm, Ralph of Battle, and the formation of the Anselmian Apocrypha', *Revue bénédictine*, 86 (1977), 383-9.

VI
Anselm's Influence

Ratio bei Rodulfus Monachus:
Ein Versuch aus der Sicht historischen Anthropologie

Helmut Kohlenberger

Mit dem ausgehenden 11. Jahrhundert werden die Weichen für das neuzeitliche westeuropäische Jahrtausend gestellt. Wir, die wir uns aus dieser Epoche herausanalysieren, blicken mit Wehmut und Neid auf eine Zeit, die in allen Bereichen und auf allen Ebenen neue Wege ging. Das Stichwort des Neuen war *ratio*. Dieses Wort war selbst keineswegs unbekannt, aber als Anzeige für das kulturelle Niveau war es neu. Unter dem Zeichen der *ratio* wurde aus der Schriftgelehrsamkeit rationale Theologie, aus dem traditionellen Vertrauen in gelebte Ordnung rationale Legitimation der Politik. Der neue Anspruch durchzieht alle Länder Westeuropas, das dem Zangengriff des Islam zwar erfolgreich Widerstand geleistet hat, aber keineswegs konsolidiert war.

Dies zeigt sich erstens in dem Bemühen, eine neue — eben rationale Basis — zu finden, auf der mit jenen kommuniziert werden kann, die nicht an die Schrift glauben. Ausdruck dieses Bemühens sind die einsetzenden Religionsgespräche z.B. der *Cur Deus homo*, des Gilbert Crispinus Disputation mit einem Juden. Erst mit Abaelard erhält diese Auseinandersetzung ihre auf spätere Jahrhunderte vorausweisende Form. Parallel zu diesem Bemühen wird zweitens energisch zu den Kreuzzügen aufgerufen, in einer der Nachwelt genügend bedeutsamen Form bpsw. bei Bernhard von Clairvaux, hier übrigens nicht ohne Kontext zu der gruppenegoistisch gesteigerten Idee der Freundschaft in Christo. Im Lager des westeuropäischen Christentums wie im Lager des Islam gab es die Propagandisten des Heiligen Krieges und die irenischen Philosophen. Liebe und Freundschaft waren die Stichworte der Krieger, *ratio* war das Stichwort der Nachdenklichen. Beide Parteien standen jedoch im Widerspruch zu ihrer Tradition: Wer die Liebe mit dem Schwert ausbreiten will, ist ebenso wenig vom Vertrauen auf die Kraft des allmächtigen Gottes bestimmt wie der, der es im Namen der *ratio* besser weiss als die Schrift, die autoritative Vorgabe existentieller Deutung des Lebenssinnes. Zwar besass der Islam mit dem Gebot des *dschihad* eine eindeutig aggressive Note, die aus dem Evangelium nicht herauszulesen ist, ausser man löst Worte wie Mt 10, 34 ('Ich bin nicht gekommen, Frieden zu bringen, sondern das Schwert') aus ihrem Kontext. Und es bleibt die Frage, ob in den Privilegien für Juden und Christen, die im Islamgebiet wohnen, nur ein erweiterter Gruppenegoismus der 'Leute der Schrift' zu sehen ist. Was letztlich die Frage nach dem Zusammenhang von Gruppenegoismus und Liebe stellt, eine nicht nur rational, sondern vor allem emotional unbewältigte Problematik.

Jedenfalls, Benjamin Nelson folgend, können wir sagen: nur im Bereich des westeuropäischen Christentums kommt es mit dem Stichwort *ratio* zu einer Zurückdrängung religiös-lebensgemeinschaftlicher Tradition. Nur hier wird Universalität in den Bezugsbegriffen und in den Diskursgemeinschaften möglich.[1] Nelson stellt mit Recht fest, das Westeuropas intellektuelle Überlegenheit trotz der weit grösseren Fortschrittlichkeit der Einzelwissenschaften im Islambereich eben auf diesem Grund beruht. 'Nur im Christentum, wo der Durchbruch zur natürlichen Theologie früh erfolgt war, wo der beschleunigte Ubergang zu universalistischen Strukturen mit der neuen Logik und der neuen Wissenschaft des 12. und 13. Jahrhunderts kam, nur dort war der Weg frei für die besonderen Muster der westlichen Zivilisation, für den beschleunigten Vorstoss in Richtung auf Modernisierung, Rationalisierung und Universalisierung'.[2]

Heute stehen wir am Ende des rationalen Universalismus. Nur mühsam werden szientismusanaloge Philosopheme aufrechterhalten. Wir fallen zurück auf lebensform- und sympathiegebundene Gruppenbildungen. Die rationalen Strukturen unserer Gesellschaft, traditionelle Kirchen, unabhängige Gerichtsbarkeit, politische Parteien, Gewerkschaften stören. Wir sind dabei, sie von innen her aufzulösen. Dieser Analyse-Prozess, parallel zur Psychoanalyse als Weltbewegung, der sich auch Moskau nicht mehr entziehen kann, geht keineswegs kampflos vor sich. Aber die Widerstandskraft der europäischen Rationalität ist mit der Symbolkraft der Aussagen Franz Kafkas und mit der stummen Sprache der Lager in Auschwitz und Dachau und anderswo gebrochen. Westeuropa steht auf der Anklagebank, mit ihm alle Kompromisse von Religion und Rationalität. Es erwacht das Erstaunen über den Bann des alten Denkens, es wird als Metaphorik wiederentdeckt.[3] Das Interesse der sog. analytischen Philosophie am ontologischen Argument ist ein Zeichen für die Sehnsucht nach dem Ursprung in der Zeit der Gefährdung einer Denkstruktur. Das ontologische Argument ist nur ein besonders prominentes Beispiel für die Übersetzung der *fides* auf den kulturellen Standard der *ratio*. Das Wort *intellectus* dient gewissermassen als Übergangschiffre, die verdecken konnte, dass *fides quaerens intellectum* tatsächlich nicht mehr der lebensformgebundene Glaubensvollzug einer Gemeinschaft war. Das Argument muss in den gesamten Kontext des intellektuellen Aufbruchs im England nach Hastings, im Zeitalter Gregors VII. und seines monastisch-monarchistischen Ekklesialimperialismus unter dem Stichwort *libertas ecclesiae* und in der beginnenden Neuformierung der Bildungsgesellschaft besonders im französischen Raum gestellt werden. Ein guter Weg zum Studium des intellektuellen Milieus um 1100 ist die Untersuchung des Kontextes von Verwendungsweisen des Begriffes *ratio* bei 'Durchschnittsautoren'.

Ein solcher Autor ist Rodulfus Monachus. R.W. Southern schildert ihn als ein typisches Beispiel für Mönche mit administrativer Verantwortung, die in eher geringem Masse am intellektuellen Leben ihrer Zeit teilnahmen und vor allem in unmittelbar lebenskontextgebundenem Zusammenhang Schriften mit geringer Wirkungsgeschichte verfassten.[4] Gering war die Wirkung dieser Schriften schon deswegen, weil ihre Autoren keine Lehrtätigkeiten grösseren Stiles ausübten. Beschränken wir uns im folgenden auf den *Libellus de peccatore qui desperat et de ratione quae peccatorem ne desperet confortat* und die *Meditatio cuiusdam christiani de fide et quia multa quae secundum fidem credimus etiam secundum rationem intelligimus.* Schon in den Titeln wird die prominente Stellung von *ratio* deutlich. *Ratio* steht im Kontext von *fides* und *intellectus*, sie ist Kriterium dessen, was gelten soll und hat daher auch lebensgestaltende Bedeutung für den *peccator*. Die *ratio* deckt die Konstitution des Menschen auf, sie verschärft die Probleme. Ihrer Problemverschärfung auszuweichen würde Furcht vor der Problemlage selbst bedeuten. Der Engpass der *ratio* zeigt sich in dem Problem, dass die Sünde gerechte Bestrafung erfordert, diese aber dem Menschen nicht möglich ist. Rational ist dieser Engpass nicht zu verlassen. Er fordert die Einführung neuer Gesichtspunkte: der Notwendigkeit einer *satisfactio congrua* tritt der universale Heilswille Gottes entgegen. Zwischen diese beiden rational nicht zu vermittelnden Gesichtspunkte tritt der Rekurs auf Gottes Allmacht, bzw. Gottes Barmherzigkeit. Allerdings ist *ratio* bemüht, die Rationalität dieses Gesichtspunktes zu betonen: 'Sed quamvis deus peccatori propter magnam misericordiam suam peccata dimittat, non fit ista misercordia peccatori sine iustitia, quia et hoc ipse deus secundum aequitatem iustitiae suae rectum esse iudicat, ut qui ex toto corde de malis quae fecit paenitendo se macerat, iuste misericordiam faciat.[5] Das Netz der *ratio*, das den privilegierten Zugang zur Welt durch das Wort der Schrift filtert, ist auch noch in dem Rat gegenwärtig: der Sünder solle ganz ruhig sich an Gott wenden und nicht verzagen: 'Securus ergo ad eum accede eique securus tuas infirmitates ostende quia te vult secundum potentiam suam salvare.[6] Gefahren für die Zuständigkeit der *ratio* werden dadurch abgewehrt, dass die Begriffe, von denen her diese Gefahren drohen — *misericordia, potentia* — als besonderer Ausdruck von Rationalität gelten. Die *ratio* immunisiert sich gegenüber der Begrenzung ihres Herrschaftsbereiches dadurch, dass sie Begriffe mit Sprengkraft zu von ihr unabhängigen Zeugen für Rationalität macht. Es liegt die Denkstruktur vor, die aus dem *id quo maius cogitari nequit* das *maius quam cogitari possit* werden lässt.

Wie ist aber die Konstitution des ratiobestimmten Menschen gesehen? Der Mensch steht vor Gott als einer, der einem Gesetz unterworfen ist, diesem nicht genügt und — nach Recht und Gesetz gesehen — keine Chance hat. Die *ratio* also Kriterium des Weltzuganges verschärft diesen Aspekt, indem sie Gottes Handeln selbst dem Gesetz des Menschen unterwirft, wenn auch mit Vorbehalten, wie sich an dem *iuste misericordiam facere* zeigt. Der Mensch ist durch und durch von Recht und Gerechtigkeit her gesehen, aber so, dass er selbst Recht und Gerechtigkeit unterworfen ist. Daher resultiert aus der Rechtskonstitution des Menschen die Forderung der *humilitas.* Also nicht der anspruchberechtigte Mensch, sondern der Mensch, der trotz durchgängiger Rechtsbestimmtheit dieser seiner Konstitution nicht genügt und daher konsequenterweise auf *misericordia* angewiesen ist, ist der Sinnzusammenhang von *ratio* bei Rodulfus.

Der Sinn des Rekurses auf *misericordia*, bzw. *potentia dei*, ist der Gedanke, dass die Intention des Schöpfers erhalten bleiben muss. Sie kommt z.B. in dem auch bei Rodulfus aufgenommenen Gedanken vom Ersatz der Zahl der gefallenen Engel durch die Menschen zum Ausdruck.[7] Dieser Gedanke zeigt in mehr als einer Hinsicht den Kontext und die Problematik von *ratio*: Kriterium dafür, ob die Intention des Schöpfers gewahrt ist, ist die Zahl derer, die sich der ewigen Seligkeit erfreuen; alle Geschöpfe stehen miteinander in einem Zusammenhang der Negation der Schöpfungsintention; der Mensch findet sein Urbild im Engel ('ex natura animae iungens se cum angelo qui est animal rationale').[8] In diesem Kontext fällt der Freiheit des Menschen von selbst eine Schlüsselstellung zu. Rodulfus spricht von *propria voluntas* und *liberum arbitrium*, die zwischen den beiden Naturen des Menschen, *anima* und *caro*, vermitteln. *Voluntas* ist eine Art Verlängerung der *ratio* über ihren Ursprungsbereich (*anima*) hinaus. Insofern *anima* über ihren Bereich hinaus Einfluss hat, herrscht sie; daher kann Rodulfus sie am Ende der *Meditatio* 'nostra regina' nennen. Überschreiten einer zunächst gegebenen Grenze ist Herrschen. Wir müssen hier die Fragen übergehen, die mit der Anerkennung eines selbständigen *liberum arbitrium* zusammenhängen: die Diskussion der *praedestinatio*, die auf die zeitliche Dimension der Konstitution des Menschen führt.

Die Lektüre der Schriften des Rodulfus zeigt, wie selbstverständlich der Konsens darüber war, dass *ratio* das letzte Wort über den Menschen hat. Trotz der prononcierten Weise des Gebrauches dieses Wortes kann von einer Isolierung der *ratio* aus dem Kontext kultureller Selbstverständlichkeiten um 1100 keine Rede sein. Der Programmcharakter der Rede von *ratio* weist jedoch auf eine Tendenz hin, die *ratio* an die Stelle des Schrift gewordenen Wortes Gottes zu setzen. Dies konnte dadurch geschehen, dass sie gewissermassen Garant und Abbreviatur der Intention der Schöpfung — in der Erlösung — war. Wer über die Intention der Schöpfung genau Bescheid weiss, sie zur Formel gerinnen lassen kann, steht in der Versuchung, den Sinn der Schöpfung festzulegen. Stellt sich die Frage: wie gross ist der Spielraum zwischen der kulturellen Grundgestalt im Kontext der Bibel und der unterschiedlichen Akzentsetzung innerhalb dieser Grundgestalt? Hat *ratio* im Gebrauch des 11. Jahrhunderts diesen Spielraum im Sinne einer Infragestellung der Grundgestalt selbstverständlicher kultureller Identität gesprengt? Worin besteht die Kontinuität der christlichen Kultur ab 1100?

ANMERKUNGEN

1. Benjamin Nelson, *Der Ursprung der Moderne, Vergleichende Studien zum Zivilisationsprozess.* Übersetzt von M. Bischoff (Frankfurt a.M., 1977).

2. Ibid., S.88.

3. Vgl. Hans Blumenbergs Studien, z.B. 'Paradigmen zu einer Metaphorologie', *Archiv für Begriffsgeschichte*, 6 (1960), 7-143 und *Arbeit am Mythos*, (Frankfurt a.M., 1979).

4. R.W. Southern, *Saint Anselm and his Biographer* (Cambridge, 1963), bes. S.206 ff.

5. Oxford, Bodleian Library, MS Laud Misc. 363, f. 14b.

6. Ibid., f. 4b.

7. Ibid., f. 38a.

8. Ibid., f. 54a.

St Anselm and Abelard

D.E. Luscombe

In what ways and how extensively did Anselm of Canterbury shape the thought and influence the writings of Abelard? No adequate answer could be given to such a question, but useful comparisons between the two men may be drawn and differences may be noted. R. Thomas has skilfully and profitably juxtaposed Abelard's views on logic and faith, as they are found in his *Dialogue*, and Anselm's views on *argumentum* and on faith as contained in the *Proslogion*.[1] Thomas rightly emphasizes that Abelard was a younger contemporary of Anselm: Abelard was born in 1079 when Anselm was Abbot of Bec, and he was thirty years old when Anselm died.[2] One could, in a similar way, study the affinities between statements regarding the understanding of faith that Abelard made in his *Theologia* and Anselm's own remarks in the *Epistola de incarnatione verbi* and elsewhere.

In the prologue to his *Theologia 'Scholarium'*, Abelard justifies the study of the secular arts and of the literature of the Gentiles because these provide assistance with the understanding of Scripture and with the defence or proof of truth, especially against the attacks of so-called philosophers. He presents the reasons why his *scholares* have pressed him to write an introduction to Scripture. They say that Abelard can arrive at an understanding of the divine page: '. . . ut multo facilius divinae paginae intelligentiam, sive sacrae fidei rationes nostrum penetraret ingenium'. They also state that where Christian faith leads to questions it should be fortified with reasons:

> 'Quo enim fides nostra, id est Christiana, inquiunt, diffi-
> cilioribus implicita quaestionibus videtur, et ab humana
> ratione longius absistere; validioribus utique munienda est
> rationum praesidiis, maxime vero contra impugnationes
> eorum, qui se Philosophos profitentur'.

Abelard goes on to say that he has finally agreed to their request but he begs pardon if he culpably departs from a Catholic understanding or a Catholic expression: 'si culpis meis exigentibus a Catholica (quod absit!) exorbitavero intelligentia vel locutione, ignoscat ille mihi . . .'[3]

Anselm, too, saw the role of understanding as ancillary to faith and as an objective to which faith itself invites us to aspire: '. . . sacra pagina nos ad investigandam rationem invitat: ubi dicit: "nisi credideritis, non intelligetis", aperte nos monet intentionem ad intellectum extendere . . .'.[4] In *De incarnatione verbi*,[5] Anselm dismisses those who dispute the Catholic faith without having an understanding of it, they should seek instead the reason for this faith. Objections arise through misunderstanding and through weakness of faith.[6]

Both stressed, therefore, the fruitful alliance that could be formed between faith and reason. But if we ask how consciously Abelard was affected by the example of Anselm, or how deliberately he distanced himself from Anselm in the growth of his appreciation of the role of logic in the study of Christian belief, we enter the realm of uncertainty.[7] Let us, therefore, look elsewhere.

There are three occasions in his writings on which Abelard named Anselm of Canterbury. This is a small number of direct references from such a large corpus of works and all three references are concerned with questions of theology only not with logic. It would be wrong, however, to infer from this that Anselm contributed only peripheral stimuli to the development of Abelard's theological views. To appreciate the significance of these mentions we must, first of all, consider each of them in turn.

The first mention of Anselm by name comes in a letter which Abelard wrote to Bishop Girbert of Paris while he was still a clerk of the Church of Paris sometime after 1116. This letter is one of three stormy letters arising out of a quarrel between Abelard and his former teacher, Roscelin of Compiègne, the other two letters being a letter from Roscelin to Abelard and a lost letter from Abelard to the Canons of St Martin of Tours to which Roscelin's is a reply. In his letter to the Bishop of Paris, Abelard complains that Roscelin has slandered both Abelard's own book on the Trinity and Anselm of Canterbury. Abelard salutes Anselm as a magnificent doctor of the Church and Archbishop of Canterbury and declares that he had written his own book on the Trinity in opposition to the heresy of Roscelin. He adds that Roscelin had been expelled from England following his attack on Anselm.[8]

In his letter to Abelard, Roscelin defends himself against Abelard's charge, apparently made in a lost letter to the Canons of Tours, that he has been unjust and vindictive with respect to Anselm of Canterbury.[9] Roscelin wrote after Abelard had become a monk at Saint Denis and before Abelard's book on the Trinity was condemned, that is, between 1118 and 1121. This is over twenty years after Anselm had completed his *De incarnatione verbi* and the *Cur Deus homo*, which lies at the heart of this division of opinion between Abelard and his former teacher. Roscelin declares his esteem for Anselm as a man of good conduct and reputation but he admits that he has found some of Anselm's sayings and actions to be reprehensible. The central issue is the omnipotence of God and it is clear from all we know of Abelard's later teaching on this matter that he had challenged Roscelin on a central point and not just on the ground that he lacked personal respect for a venerable name. Roscelin criticizes the argument of the *Cur Deus homo* that God cannot save mankind in any way other than the one which he has used, namely that of the incarnation and passion. This, says Roscelin, is contrary to the mind of the saints, and he cites passages from Leo, and from Augustine's *De trinitate*, which support the contrary view, that God can choose any one of innumerable means to save mankind — a view which is essentially that of Boso in *Cur Deus homo*.

Neither Roscelin nor Anselm was named in Abelard's book on the Trinity, nor in the account of the condemnation of that work at Soissons in 1121 which Abelard gave in his autobiography.[10] But, in his letter to Bishop Girbert, Abelard had named Roscelin as one of the book's critics, and had mentioned Roscelin's own earlier trial for error at Soissons. The issue which had faced the Council at Soissons between 1090 and 1093 was similar to that which was later discussed in 1121, namely the omnipotence of God. Besides this, there are some other noteworthy, if incidental, similarities between the ways in which Roscelin and Abelard were treated. Abelard says that he was afraid of being stoned by the people on his arrival at Soissons, and Roscelin too went there in fear of being lynched by the crowd.[11] Abelard complained that he was condemned without any discussion or hearing, while Anselm had, in Roscelin's case, asked that he should neither be heard nor given the opportunity to justify his error or to be told what is the truth.[12] Moreover, Abelard states that he was accused of not submitting his book to the Pope or the Church before lecturing on it. Anselm, on the other hand, had dedicated his *De incarnatione verbi*, to Pope Urban II between 1092 and 1093 on the ground that a reply to error concerning the Catholic faith could not be shown to any better authority.[13] In contrast, however, stands the fact that whereas Abelard was, in 1121, condemned, placed in confinement, and his book burned, Roscelin (although he exiled himself to England) was not condemned and was later welcomed in Rome.

Abelard felt out of sympathy with Roscelin's teachings and in fact his *Theologia 'Summi boni'* — as the book on the Trinity that was criticized by Roscelin and condemned in 1121 is currently known — carries some circumstantial traces of Anselm's polemics against Roscelin, particularly those against Roscelin's tritheism and pseudo-dialectic.[14] He describes his foes — the *professores dialecticae* — as 'singulari superbiae cornu erecti', just as Anselm criticized those who 'coeperint quasi cornua confidentis sibi scientiae producere . . .'[15]

After Soissons, Abelard adapted his book and produced a new one — the *Theologia Christiana*. We can see clearly in it how

Roscelin's attack on what one might call the 'Anselmianism' of
Abelard was still in the forefront of his thinking: the three
quotations from St Augustine's *De trinitate* which Roscelin had
produced in his letter to Abelard, and which had not appeared in
the condemned book, now appear in Book 5.38 of the *Theologia
Christiana* and also in the early versions of the *Sic et non*.[16] The
quotations are not presented in *Theologia Christiana* in the same
order, or with the same wording that they have in Roscelin's letter,
and Abelard adds other passages to show that there is wider
patristic support for Roscelin's view that God has the power to
choose different means of acting from the ones he actually chose.[17]
But it is striking that the texts used by Roscelin to show that God
could have chosen another way than the incarnation and the passion
to save mankind appear together in the same place at the opening
of Abelard's discussion in *Theologia Christiana* of the question of
whether God must do all that he does.[18] Abelard admits that all
the quotations he has collected make it difficult for him to sustain
his argument that God can only do what he does,[19] although he
adds that whenever questions are hotly controversial their solutions
inevitably become more difficult.[20]

Abelard proceeds to make a distinction between what God does
(that which he must necessarily do) and what is done by him (that
which need not necessarily be done). In himself God is immutable;
in the world of other natures everything is mutable.[21] Peter Damian
had also upheld the inalterability of God's power in his letter on
divine omnipotence,[22] but Abelard shows no marked reliance upon
Damian or upon any particular text of Anselm. The thesis that God
can only do what he does, and its corollary that God cannot do
anything better than he does, forms a major item in Abelard's
Theologia Christiana,[23] and also in his later *Theologia*, known now
as the *Theologia 'Scholarium'*.[24] Here, he dispenses with the
patristic documentation found earlier in Roscelin's letter, but
Abelard agrees with Roscelin that his thesis is contrary to the mind
of the saints.[25] He also uses the incarnation as an illustration of
the argument that God can only act in the way and at the time he
actually does act.[26] Criticism was heaped upon Abelard for his
teaching at the time of his second condemnation at the Council of
Sens in 1140.[27] Although fifty years separate Roscelin's trial at
Soissons from Abelard's at Sens, it seems altogether likely that the
beginnings of Abelard's own speculations on these issues may be
traced back to the clashes between Anselm and Roscelin.

In *Theologia Christiana*, Abelard had already mentioned Anselm by
name. Book 4 consists of a lengthy examination of the relationship
between the three divine persons in one substance, with special
attention being paid to the generation of the Son and the
incarnation.

This subject had already been broached in the *Theologia 'Summi boni'*, where Abelard introduced the notion of analogy (*similitudo*). Since creation resembles the creator, a *similitudo* or *exemplum* may help men to understand God and also to refute the pseudo-dialecticians, even though every analogy must presuppose that there is a degree of dissimilarity between the subjects of the comparison.[28] Thus Abelard introduced the analogy of a waxen image with which he hoped to illustrate the generation of the Son (the Word of God) from the Father (the omnipotence of God), the wax and the image which is formed by it being identical in essence, like a species and its genus such as a man and animal. But the wax image comes into being later than the wax itself, whereas the Son is eternal with the Father and his generation is not a development taking place in time. An example of generation that does not involve a succession of developments in time is the brightness of the sun: brightness and the sun exist simultaneously.[29] When Abelard came in later life to look back on the writing of his first *Theologia ('Summi boni')*, he described it, not unreasonably, as an attempt to explain the basis of faith by means of analogies (*similitudines*) invented by human reason.[30]

Abelard returned to this discussion and developed it when he wrote his *Theologia Christiana*.[31] Now he mentions Anselm. He does so only briefly but he mentions him shortly after the outset of his discussion and gives him prominence.[32] He offers a criticism of Anselm's own use of analogies but, as we shall see shortly, it is *via* Anselm's recourse to analogies that Abelard comes to re-state and amplify what he had more briefly indicated in the earlier *Theologia 'Summi boni'*.

Abelard explains in the *Theologia Christiana* that some conventional analogies had lately been criticized. He mentions the analogies of the cithara and of the sun, ascribing both to St Augustine.[33] The latter analogy, of the sun which emits both warmth and light, had been adopted and defended by Anselm in his *De processione spiritus sancti*,[34] and it had, as we have just seen, also been used approvingly in the *Theologia 'Summi boni'*. It was, in fact, very familiar at the time.[35] But Abelard admits that critics of both analogies allege that they illustrate the differences between the divine persons better than they show the identity of the divine essence; neither analogy illustrates how only one and not all three persons became incarnate when the divine substance assumed human flesh.[36]

Abelard goes on to say that in recent times Anselm, the metropolitan of Canterbury, has provided a better analogy which safeguards the oneness of the divine substance.[37] Abelard does not name a particular work by Anselm but he refers to the analogy of the watercourse which is found in Anselm's *De processione spiritus sancti*,[38] and which had been used earlier by Anselm in the form of

the analogy of the River Nile in his *De incarnatione verbi*.[39]
Abelard says on this occasion that Anselm's analogy comes from
Augustine.[40] The watercourse consists of a spring, a river, and a
pool. The water is the same throughout but the river comes from a
spring, like the Son from the Father, and the pool comes from the
river and the spring, as the Spirit proceeds from the Father and the
Son. Moreover, this analogy illustrates the incarnation because the
river which is produced by the spring flows through a gap or
passage just as the Son enters human flesh. Nonetheless, Abelard
finds Anselm's analogy defective because the spring, the river and
the pool succeed each other temporally whereas the three persons in
God are not separated in time.[41] In fact Abelard says that Anselm's
analogy, although the best available at the time, perhaps lends itself
particularly to a heretical view of the Trinity ('Immo fortassis haec
similitudo illi maxime suffragatur haeresi . . .').[42] Thus Abelard
again advances his own analogy, that of wax which contains an
imprinted image.[43] There is only one substance here — wax — but
the image comes from the wax. The analogy therefore illustrates
the generation of the Son. It does not, however, illustrate the
procession of the Spirit.

When Abelard next referred to Anselm by name he reproduced
substantially the passage which had appeared in the *Theologia
Christiana*. He did this in the second book of the *Theologia
'Scholarium'* which is a new work replacing the *Theologia
Christiana*.[44] Here, Abelard repeats Anselm's analogy of the
watercourse and again criticizes it for possibly creating the
heretical impression that the divine persons succeed one another in
time ('fortassis haec similitudo illi potius suffragatur haeresi').
However, the context in which this passage reappears is markedly
different from that found earlier in the *Theologia Christiana*. In the
latter, Abelard presented his analogy of the waxen image after first
evaluating Anselm's analogy of the watercourse. Now, perhaps more
confidently, he introduces and gives a prominent place to a new
analogy of his own before mentioning Anselm's. Abelard's new
analogy — of a bronze seal — copes with the procession of the
Spirit as well as with the generation of the Son, and it is explained
at length. Book 2 of the *'Scholarium'* is largely organized around it.
Like the analogy of the wax, it enables Abelard to apply the
concept of matter and form: bronze is the matter of which a seal
is made; the figure or design on the bronze seal is the form which
is impressed on the wax in the act of sealing. The seal itself has
three properties in one essence: it is bronze (*aes*); it has the ability
to seal (*sigillabile* or *aptus ad sigillandum*); and it does actually seal
(*sigillans*). These three properties in one essence may serve as a
model for presenting the doctrine of the Trinity. But, whereas in
the *Theologia Christiana* Abelard could not apply his more limited
analogy of the wax to the procession of the Spirit, in the

'Scholarium', the analogy of the bronze seal makes this possible, for the action of sealing *(sigillans)* results from the bronze and the ability to seal *(sigillabile)* together.[45]

Anselm's use of analogies does seem to have been a factor in prompting Abelard to develop discussion of the value of analogies. In the *Theologia 'Scholarium'* he seems to be more firm in his opposition to Anselm because he insists that only analogies drawn from the *artes* — grammar and philosophy — can achieve probability.[46] He appears to mean by this that the analogy of the bronze seal, in terms of which Abelard discusses matter and form, properties and essence, has advantages that are not shared by either Anselm's analogy or other traditional analogies. There is, here, a 'direct personal influence' by Anselm upon Abelard, even though Abelard is in opposition to this aspect of Anselm's influence upon him.[47] However, not all contemporaries were convinced by Abelard's innovation and some were incensed to the point of singling out his 'horrenda similitudo' for special execration at the time of the Council of Sens.[48] Perhaps their indignation was heightened by the way in which Abelard presented his own dialectical discussion as a conscious attempt to transcend the shortcomings of Anselm's own argument.

A further occasion when Anselm appears to make an entry into Abelard's writings is one on which he is not named. His shadow falls over a part of the second book of Abelard's *Commentaria in Epistolam Pauli ad Romanos* which was written by 1137.[49] Here, Abelard rejects, as Anselm had done before, the theory that the Devil had acquired rights over sinful man and, with it, the theory that Christ, out of regard for the Devil's rights, became incarnate in order to pay a ransom to him thereby securing the release of captive mankind from subjection and slavery.[50]

The incarnation had not been overlooked in the *Theologia* where Abelard had earlier shown why only the Son, and not the Father and the Spirit, is said to be incarnate: it is the Wisdom of God which shines among men through the incarnate Son. Abelard had assembled passages from Scripture on the theme of light shining among men to show that divine wisdom was incarnate in order to instruct men in the doctrine of true justice by means of preaching and by setting an example in this physical life.[51] Abelard's view was that all Christ did in the flesh was intended to teach men to believe and to lead them to love what they learn, and this view was clearly present in the *Theologia* before Abelard completed his *Commentaria*.[52]

Discussion of the redemption in the *Commentaria* is fuller but by no means exhaustive. It occurs chiefly in a *quaestio* which Abelard inserts into the course of his exposition of the text at

Romans, 3.26. On reading the *quaestio* it is not clear whether Abelard knew Anselm's own writings on the redemption, or how far he wished to reinterpret what Anselm himself had thought. Indeed, R. Peppermüller in his study of Abelard's *Commentaria* is sceptical of the view which is normally subscribed to, that it was Anselm whom Abelard had in his mind when writing his *quaestio*.[53] There are resemblances of theme and there are even some close verbal similarities between passages in the *quaestio* and in Anselm's *Cur Deus homo*, but Abelard might have echoed teachers other than Anselm himself. When Abelard asks what necessity there was for God to assume manhood and to redeem mankind by a physical death:

> Primo itaque quaerendum videtur qua necessitate Deus hominem assumpserit ut nos secundum carnem moriendo redimeret . . .[54]

he echoes, as Weingart noted,[55] Anselm's own question:

> . . . qua scilicet ratione vel necessitate deus homo factus sit, et morte sua, sicut credimus et confitemur, mundo vitam reddiderit, cum hoc aut per aliam personam, sive angelicam sive humanam, aut sola voluntate facere potuerit.[56]

There are also parallels in the following:

> Quae itaque necessitas aut quae ratio uel quid opus fuit, cum sola iussione sua divina miseratio liberare hominem a diabolo potuisset . . .?[57]

> Plures mecum petunt: qua necessitate scilicet et ratione deus, cum sit omnipotens, humilitatem et infirmitatem humanae naturae pro eius restauratione assumpserit.[58]

Again, Abelard resembles Anselm in his attack on the theory of the Devil's rights over man. He uses the example of the slave (Mankind) who is lured away from the service of his lord (God) by a fellow slave (the Devil) who then proceeds, without justification, to assume authority over his disobedient companion.[59] Abelard further resembles Anselm in saying that although the Devil was allowed by God to torture fallen man, he gained thereby no right to do this.[60]

Abelard's *quaestio* consists of a cascade of varied queries concerning the necessity and purport of redemption. He asks, for example, whether the Crucifixion of Christ ought to have made God more angry with men than did Adam's sin; how the sinful putting to death of the innocent Son of God could possibly have been pleasing to God, and to whom the price of blood is paid, if the theory is discarded that it is paid to the Devil? Peppermüller has rightly observed that the problem of whether Abelard's queries are implied criticisms of Anselm's *Cur Deus homo* is more important than the question whether he echoes actual passages of Anselm's work.[61] Abelard certainly struck a polemical and topical note when he wrote 'Et dicitur . . .'.[62] But the questions are brief; they are not obviously linked to particular passages in the *Cur Deus homo* and it is difficult to follow the direction of Abelard's reasoning from his questions alone. It is clear that Abelard rejected the theory of the Devil's rights, as Anselm had done, but his questions also bore upon the 'satisfaction theory' (the theory that Christ made satisfaction to God).[63] In pointing to the paradox that the atonement appears to have been procured by a new sin (the Crucifixion), Abelard may have wished to imply some doubt about Anselm's particular view of satisfaction. On the other hand, he seems more concerned to heighten his readers' curiosity and to prepare them for his own presentation of the redemption in the *solutio* which follows immediately.

If the *solutio* showed disagreement with Anselm then the questions leading up to it might justly be read as directed against Anselm. But this does not appear to be the case. Abelard in his *solutio* and Anselm in his *Cur Deus homo* share common ground. The *solutio* contains the famous sketch of Abelard's 'exemplarist theory' of the redemption: that Christ's life on earth and the Crucifixion were examples of divine love that were designed to prompt and stimulate men to love God in return and abandon sin. But already in the *Cur Deus homo* Anselm had alluded to this very theme — that Christ demonstrated to men the love of God: 'quanto nos mirabilius . . . restituit, tanto maiorem dilectionem erga nos et pietatem monstravit'.[64]

Boso too is made to speak of Man's redemption by God in terms of a demonstration of how much God loves mankind, although Boso goes on to argue, as Anselm and Abelard do not, that the incarnation was not a unique or necessary means of redemption, and that therefore another means of showing divine love could have been adopted:

> Quippe quod dicitis deum taliter ostendisse quantum vos diligeret, nulla ratione defenditur, si nullatenus aliter hominem potuisse salvare non monstratur. Nam si aliter non potuisset, tunc forsitan necesse esset, ut hoc modo dilectionem suam ostenderet. Nunc vero cum aliter posset salvare hominem: quae ratio est, ut propter ostendendam dilectionem suam ea quae dicitis faciat et sustineat? An enim non ostendit bonis angelis quantum eos diligat, pro quibus talia non sustinet? . . . Haec nobis infideles objicere posse videntur.[65]

We have then three indications that Abelard here offers strong support for Anselm's approach to the redemption: he asks some of the same initial questions in virtually the same words; he rejects the theory of the Devil's right, using Anselm's analogy with slaves or serfs; and his exemplarist theory is also already contained, as in a nutshell, in Anselm's work.

Before continuing we must look further at R.E. Weingart's excellent study of Abelard's soteriology. Weingart's tragic death removed all possibility that he might develop the views he advanced so eruditely in his book, and in offering a disagreement with one small part of his study I wish in no way to subtract from my admiration for the rest.[66] Weingart presents Abelard's discussion of the necessity of the incarnation as a critical reaction against Anselm's search for necessary reasons why God became incarnate.[67] He reads Abelard's questions not only as indications that Abelard is sceptical of talk about necessity but also as direct attacks upon Anselm. Weingart finds suppport for his interpretation of the direction of Abelard's argument in the *Theologia*,[68] where he believes that Abelard shows his objection to necessary reasons and indicates his preferences for discovering 'worthy' reasons.[69] Therefore, Abelard can be presumed to have regarded Anselm's *Cur Deus homo* unfavourably in so far as Anselm had set out to prove the necessity of Christ's death, whereas Abelard distrusted talk of necessary reasons. Weingart further quotes a remark in Abelard's *Theologia Christiana*: 'it is written that God could have redeemed the human race in a way other than he did'.[70] Abelard here produced quotations from Scripture which seem to confirm this view.

Now, Weingart's interpretation of Abelard's anti-Anselmianism appears to be wrong for two reasons. The first is that Abelard and Anselm speak with a similar voice about divine necessity. In the *Cur Deus homo*, Anselm himself defined necessity in the sense of God's unalterable *honestas* rather than in terms of any extrinsic constraint upon divine omnipotence or freedom.[71] He admits that the word 'necessity' is only used of God *improprie*, in an ill-fitting way. He assesses the type of necessity by which God acts; necessity in God means the immutability of divine *honestas*. Anselm, therefore, is close to agreement with Abelard in his application of a notion of necessity to the Godhead.[72] Secondly, Abelard, far from concluding that God might have redeemed man in a way other than the way he chose, in fact argues the opposite. One of the most salient features of Abelard's *Theologia* is the thesis that God does not and cannot act in any other way or in any better way than the one in which he does act. The reason Abelard gives for his view is that God, being supremely reasonable and wise, chooses the most fitting way in which to act. Hence, Abelard, in fact, writes of the incarnation in terms of its necessity, not otherwise:

. . . ut necessario Christus ad auferendam quoque abundantiam peccatorum descenderet[73]

necesse erat ut ueniret Christus qui est finis et consummatio legis . . .[74]

He does, it is true, admit that Scripture and the Fathers appear to lend support to the opposite view — that God did not have to choose incarnation — but he plainly resists this. It is hard to see any sign here of Abelard moving away from Anselm on this point. Moreover, when we take into account the strikingly unusual character of their common viewpoint and also bear in mind the other resemblances noted earlier, we must conclude that an onus of proof lies on those who disbelieve that Abelard was powerfully persuaded either by Anselm or at least by reports of a teaching that was so singular that only a very badly informed master could have been unaware of the identity of its foremost exponent. Otherwise we should have to admit (what is possible in principle but in fact unlikely, since Abelard was Anselm's younger contemporary) that it is a coincidence that the two thinkers advanced largely overlapping arguments. Finally, it may be noted that the chapter on the redemption in one of the most detailed sentence collections of the 'school' of Abelard (the Sentences attributed to one Hermann) is entitled *Cur Deus homo.*[75]

Abelard's exemplarist thesis of the atonement is linked, then, to his theory that God only acts in the way in which he does. The latter theory had already been debated, with special reference to the incarnation, by Roscelin, and it is not possible fully to understand Abelard's *quaestio* in his *Commentaria* or his repeated reference to the question of the necessity of the incarnation without bearing in mind Abelard's earlier polemics against Roscelin in support of Anselm. Moreover, the examples given above of Anselm's contributions to the development of Abelard's thought should not be considered in isolation from each other; Anselm did not provide Abelard with one argument about omnipotence, another about analogies and a third, unlinked, about the redemption. Both Abelard's view of God's power and his use of analogies in discussion of the Trinity support his discussion of the incarnation and already in the *Theologia Christiana*, Abelard promised to discuss the incarnation more fully on a later occasion.[76] It is true that Abelard seems more aware of the themes that appear in the *Epistola de incarnatione verbi* and *Cur Deus homo* than those which appear in the *Monologion* and *Proslogion*, and that his handling of Greek views regarding the procession of the Spirit in *Theologia Christiana*, 4 and *Theologia 'Scholarium'*, 2 is quite independent of Anselm's *De processione sancti spiritus*. But Abelard clearly derives from Anselm an insight into the links between divine omnipotence and the incarnation as well as an added interest in belief in the Trinity. In his quarrels with Roscelin, Abelard provided an early vindication of sympathies for Anselm that were never wholly to be laid aside. Anselm's magnetism enlivens Abelard's thinking on the properties and power of God not only in his early career when Roscelin was still alive and active but right up to the Council of Sens and Abelard's withdrawal from the schools.

   If it is right to perceive in Abelard's writings the signs of an extensive and pervasive submission to some of Anselm's deepest thoughts, then Anselm's standing on the twelfth-century scholastic scene may deserve to be valued more highly than it usually is. Abelard was in and out of schools in France between about 1100 and 1140; he keenly followed debates and, although his written references to other contemporary masters are (like his explicit references to Anselm) brief, they are not peripheral or incidental. On the contrary, they indicate his widespread involvement in many lively disputes with influential rivals which so impressed contemporary commentators. Roscelin, William of Champeaux, Anselm of Laon, Vasletus, Garmundus and others were anvils on whom Abelard sharpened his arguments and forged his reputation. Anselm of Canterbury was of greater stature than any of these masters and his name was honoured, despite the fact that he was not alive after 1109 and had not taught in the 'open' schools. It would be a meaningless exaggeration to label Abelard (who did not imitate anyone) as a disciple of Anselm, but he did approvingly recognize Anselm's standing in the confederation of modern teachers. Abelard generally had sharp words of personal criticism and scorn for other masters but, significantly, he stops short of this with Anselm.

By way of conclusion, mention may be made of the enigmatic *Ysagoge in theologiam*.[77] This systematic survey of theological teaching, with its special emphasis on exegesis of the Hebrew Scriptures, may have been written by someone with English connections. The author (one Odo, if the preface attached to the manuscript really is a preface to this work), was clearly a thoughtful writer and no hasty abbreviator or *reportator*.[78] He wrote, in all likelihood, in the 1130s,[79] and combined the reflections of the Victorine school with those of Abelard and St Anselm, though he does not name his recent sources and they have to be identified by means of comparisons of texts. The editor of the *Ysagoge*, the late A.M. Landgraf, noticed in his edition how the author followed Anselm on free will,[80] and on original sin,[81] and he listed summarily the main parts of Anselm's writings which were used by him.[82] But since Landgraf did not examine so carefully the mingling of Anselmian with Abelardian features and phraseology in the course of the discussion of the redemption, the author's juxtapositions deserve to be signalled here.[83]

   To put the matter briefly, the *Ysagoge* supported both Anselm and Abelard in arguing that Man was not redeemed from the Devil, and that the Devil had no rightful possession of mankind.[84] There are some close verbal links with the *quaestio* in Abelard's *Commentaria* and the two works also share Biblical quotations.[85] But the *Ysagoge*[86] soon turns to Anselm's *Cur Deus homo* for arguments in favour of the necessity of God-man to achieve the redemption,[87] whereas Abelard's *quaestio* proceeds, unlike the *Ysagoge*, to develop the exemplarist theory.[88] The *Ysagoge* in arguing further on that Christ is the son of Adam,[89] again follows the *Cur Deus homo*.[90]

Although we cannot be certain of the identity of the author of the *Ysagoge*, it is worth bearing in mind his interest in Anselm of Canterbury since Odo, one possible candidate, was Prior of Canterbury from 1175 to 1200.[91]

NOTES

1. R. Thomas, 'Anselms Fides Quaerens Intellectum im Proslogion und Abaelards Rationibus Fides Astruenda Et Defendenda im Dialogus Inter Philosophum, Iudaeum et Christianum. Eine Vergleichserörterung', *Analecta Anselmiana*, 5 (1976), 297-310. This study also appeared under the same title in the *Bulletin de la Societe academique, religieuse et scientifique de l'ancien duche d'Aoste*, 47 (1974/5), 297-310. On the links between Anselm's and Abelard's discussions of logic, see D.P. Henry, *The Logic of St Anselm* (Oxford, 1967), pp. 65-6, 89-90, 141-2.

2. Ibid., pp. 297, 307.

3. *PL* 178.979AB, 980A.

4. *Cur Deus homo*, commendatio operis, *Ans.Op.Om.*, II, 40:7-9.

5. *Ans.Op.Om.*, II, 6-8.

6. For the quotation which Anselm uses here and elsewhere — 'nisi credideritis, non intelligetis' — see note at *Ans.Op.Om.*, II, 7:11-12. It is an adaptation of Isaiah 7:9 which Anselm found in Augustine. Compare the prior recension of Anselm's letter, *Ans.Op.Om.*, I, 283:26-284:8. See also *Proslogion*, 1, *Ans.Op.Om.*, I, 100:18-19, 'Neque enim quaero intelligere ut credam, sed credo ut intelligam. Nam et hoc credo: quia "nisi credidero, non intelligam"'.

7. The closest Abelard comes to writing something that appears to contest Anselm's views on the relationship between faith and understanding is a report he gives of the views of his *scholares* for whom he wrote the earliest version of his *Theologia* (known

now as the *Theologia 'Summi boni'*): ' . . . quendam theologie tractatum *De Unitate et Trinitate divina* scolaribus nostris componerem, qui humanas et philosophicas rationes requirebant, et plus que intelligi quam que dici possent efflatigabant: dicentes quidem verborum superfluam esse prolationem quam intelligentia non sequeretur, nec credi posse aliquid nisi primitus intellectum, et ridiculosum esse aliquem aliis predicare quod nec ipse nec illi quos doceret intellectu capere possent'. Abelard, *Historia calamitatum*, edited by J. Monfrin, third edition (Paris, 1967), lines 692-700; *PL* 178.141-2. Bernard of Clairvaux accused Abelard of abandoning the priority of faith over reason: '. . . Et quid magis contra fidem quam credere nolle quidquid non possit ratione attingere? . . . At contra theologus noster: "Quid", inquit, "ad doctrinam loqui proficit, si quod docere volumus exponi non potest ut intelligatur?"' 'Sed iste, Deum habens suspectum, credere non vult, nisi quod prius ratione discusserit. Cumque Propheta dicat: "Nisi credideritis, non intelligetis", iste fidem voluntariam nomine redarguit levitatis, abutens illo Salomonis testimonio: "Qui credit cito, levis est corde"'. *Epistolae* 190 and 338, *S. Bernardi Opera*, edited by J. Leclercq and H. Rochais, 8 vols. (Rome, 1957-77), VIII, 18, 278; *PL* 182.1055BC, 543B.

8. *Epistola 14*, *PL* 178.355-8. On Roscelin, see especially F. Picavet, *Roscelin, philosophe et théologien* (Paris, 1911). On Roscelin's relationship with Anselm, see R.W. Southern, *Saint Anselm and his Biographer* (Cambridge, 1963), pp. 78-82; also, L. Ott, *Untersuchungen zur theologischen Briefliteratur der Frühscholastik*, Beiträge zur Geschichte der Philosophie und der Theologie des Mittelalters, 34 (Münster, 1937), pp. 19-21, and J. Hofmeier, *Die Trinitatslehre des Hugo von St. Viktor dargestellt im Zusammenhang mit den trinitarischen Strömungen seiner Zeit*, Münchener theologische Studien, II. Systematische Abteilung, 25. (Munich, 1963), pp. 18-26. An attempt to reconstruct Roscelin's philosophical teaching has been made by E.-H.W. Kluge, 'Roscelin and the medieval problem of universals', *Journal of the History of Philosophy*, 14 (1976), 405-14.

9. *Epistola 15*, *PL* 178.357-72, here 360D, 362A-D. This is better edited by J. Reiners, *Der Nominalismus in der Frühscholastik. Ein Beitrag zur Geschichte der Universalienfrage im Mittelalter. Nebst einer neuen Textausgabe des Briefes Roscelin an Abälard*, Beiträge zur Geschichte der Philosophie des Mittelalters, 8:5 (Münster, 1910) pp. 62-80, here pp. 66-8.

10. Abelard, *Historia calamitatum*, lines 690-909. In his *Dialectica*, 5.1, Abelard openly dismissed one of Roscelin's *sententiae* as insane: 'Fuit autem, memini, magistri nostri Roscellini tam insana sententia ut nullam rem partibus constare vellet, sed

sicut solibus vocibus species, ita et partes adscribebat', *Petrus Abaelardus. Dialectica*, edited by L.M. de Rijk, Wijsgerige Teksten en Studies (Assen, 1956), pp. 554.37-555.2.

11. Abelard, *Historia calamitatum*, lines 721-5. *De incarnatione verbi*, 1, *Ans.Op.Om.*, II, 4-5; Ivo of Chartres, *Correspondance*, edited by J. Leclercq (Paris, 1949), p. 24.

12. Abelard, *Historia calamitatum*, lines 868-70, 895, 900. *Epistola* 136 to Fulk, Bishop of Beauvais (before the Council of Soissons 1090-3), *Ans.Op.Om.*, III, 280.

13. Abelard, *Historia calamitatum*, lines 848-51. *De incarnatione verbi*, *Ans.Op.Om.*, II, 3-4; *The Life of St Anselm, Archbishop of Canterbury, by Eadmer*, edited by R.W. Southern (London, 1962), pp. 72-3. The practice of submitting works to the pope for inspection was coming to be expected of authors. See the important remarks of P. Classen, *Burgundio von Pisa*, Sitzungsberichte der Heidelberger Akademie der Wissenschaften. Philosophisch-historische Klasse, 1974:4 (Heidelberg, 1974), p. 61 and note. Also, H. Jürgen von Miethke, 'Theologenprozesse in der ersten Phase ihrer institutionellen Ausbildung: Die Verfahren gegen Peter Abaelard und Gilbert von Poitiers', *Viator*, 6 (1975), 87-116, here p. 94, note 36.

14. '. . . cum unaquaeque trium personarum sit deus sive substantia, non tamen ideo plures dii sunt sive substantiae', Abelard, *Theologia 'Summi boni'*, 3.1, in *Peter Abaelards Theologia 'Summi boni'*, edited by H. Ostlender, Beiträge zur Geschichte der Philosophie und der Theologie des Mittelalters, 35:2/3 (Münster, 1939), p. 75. cf. Abelard, *Theologia Christiana*, 4.22, in *Petri Abaelardi opera theologica*, edited by E.M. Buytaert, Corpus Christianorum, Continuatio Mediaevalis, 11 and 12, 2 vols. (Turnhout, 1969), II, 275. 'Roscelinus clericus dicit in Deo tres personas esse tres res ab invicem separatas . . . et tres deos vere posse dici, si usus permitteret', *Epistola* 136, *Ans.Op.Om.*, III, 279. cf. Abelard, *Theologia 'Summi boni'*, 2.2, p. 42; *Theologia Christiana*, 3.89, p. 230.

In *Theologia 'Summi boni'*, 3.1, pp. 84-5, where Abelard defends the proposition that the Son of God became incarnate but not the Father or the Spirit (cf. *Theologia Christiana*, 4.60-4, pp. 290-3), he resembles Anselm in the *De incarnatione verbi*, 3, *Ans.Op.Om.*, II, 14-16. The importance of Anselm's criticisms of Roscelin in *De incarnatione verbi* for Abelard's *Theologia 'Summi boni'* was suggested by Picavet, *Roscelin*, p. 41 and Appendix XVI, pp. 124-7 in his notes, where he compares a number of passages, and by Ostlender in his edition of Abelard's *Theologia 'Summi boni'*, p. xxvi.

15. Abelard, *Theologia 'Summi boni'*, 2, p. 32 (cf. Abelard, *Theologia Christiana*, 3.25, p. 205). *De incarnatione verbi*, 1, *Ans.Op.Om.*, II, 7.

16. Abelard, *Theologia Christiana*, 5.38, p. 364. Buytaert did not notice in this edition that these passages had appeared in Roscelin's letter. Abelard, *Sic et Non*, *quaestio* 35, in *Peter Abailard*, *Sic et Non*, edited by B. Boyer and R. McKeon (Chicago, 1976/7), p. 185. The *quaestio* is entitled 'Quod ubi deest velle Dei desit et posse et contra'. Some other passages common to the *Theologia Christiana* and *Theologia 'Summi boni'* and touching this debate have been indicated in the foregoing notes.

17. Abelard, *Theologia Christiana*, 5.39-40, pp. 364-5.

18. Ibid., 5.38, p. 364.

19. Ibid., 5.41, p. 366.

20. Other attacks on Roscelin noticed by Buytaert in his edition of the *Theologia Christiana* are found at 3.93, p. 231; 3.131, p. 244; 3.135, p. 246; and 4.25, p. 276.

21. Abelard, *Theologia Christiana*, 5.57-8, pp. 371-2.

22. *Pierre Damien. Lettre sur la toute-puissance divine*, edited and translated by A. Cantin, Sources chrétiennes, 191, Série des textes monastiques d'Occident, 11 (Paris, 1972), for example p. 388.

23. Abelard, *Theologia Christiana*, 5.18, p. 354; 5.29-35, pp. 358-62.

24. Abelard, *Theologia 'Scholarium'*, 3.4-5, *PL* 178.1091C-1104B.

25. Abelard, *Theologia 'Scholarium'*, 3.5, *PL* 178.1098D.

26. Abelard, *Theologia 'Scholarium'*, 3.5, *PL* 178.1102B, 1102D, 1103D-4A.

27. The *capitula* which Bernard of Clairvaux asked the prelates at Sens to condemn included the following (No. 7): 'Quod ea solummodo possit Deus facere vel dimittere vel eo modo tantum vel eo tempore quo facit, non alio', Leclercq and Rochais, *Bernardi Opera*, VIII, 39 (*Epistola* 190). cf. Thomas of Morigny, *Disputatio Catholicorum Patrum adversus Dogmata Petri Abaelardi*, 3, *PL* 180.310D-21B, also new edition by N.M. Häring in *Studi medievali*, third series, 22:1 (1981), 299-376, here pp. 356-68; *Anonymi Capitula Haeresum Petri Abaelardi*, 3, in Buytaert, *Abaelardi opera theologica*, II, 474. See further, D.E. Luscombe, *The School of Peter Abelard*, Cambridge Studies in Medieval Life and Thought, new series, 14 (Cambridge, 1969), pp. 134-6.

28. Abelard, *Theologia 'Summi boni'*, 2.2, p. 43; 2.3, pp. 48, 52-3; 3.2, pp. 94-6. cf. Abelard, *Theologia Christiana*, 3.95, 118, 133-5, pp. 231, 237-8, 245-6, and also Abelard, *Theologia 'Scholarium'*, 2.10, *PL* 178.1063D-4D.

29. Abelard, *Theologia 'Summi boni'*, 3.2, pp. 87-90, 93.

30. '. . . ad ipsum fidei nostre fundamentum humane rationis similitudinibus disserendum primo me applicarem, et quendam theologie tractatum *De Unitate et Trinitate divina* scolaribus nostris componerem', Abelard, *Historia calamitatum*, lines 690-4.

31. Abelard, *Theologia Christiana*, 4.82, pp. 303-4.

32. Abelard, *Theologia Christiana*, 4.83, p. 304. Anselm is one of only three post-patristic writers to be mentioned by name in the whole work, the others being Pope Hadrian I and 'Rabanus Maurus' (in fact, Atto of Vercelli); E.M. Buytaert in his edition of the *Theologia Christiana*, p. 29. Ostlender in his edition, pp. xxvi and 32, notes 20-1, surmised that Anselm was in Abelard's mind when he wrote the *Theologia 'Summi boni'*.

33. Abelard, *Theologia Christiana*, 4.82, pp. 303-4. cf. 1.104a, p. 115, citing Cassiodorus, and 4.137, p. 335.

34. *De processione spiritus sancti*, 8, *Ans.Op.Om.*, II, 199:30-201:9. Schmitt cites as Anselm's source, Cassiodorus, *Expositio in Psalterium*, *Psalmus L*, *versus* 13, *PL* 70:367; cf. Abelard who inserts this passage from Cassiodorus into the last version of his *Theologia Christiana* at 1.104a, p. 115. In *Epistola* 128, lines 13-16, John the Monk writing to Anselm (c. 1090) ascribed the sun analogy to Augustine. So did William of Champeaux, *De essentia Dei et de tribus personis*, in *Psychologie et morale aux XIIe et XIIe siecles*, edited by O. Lottin, 6 vols. (Louvain, 1942-60), V, 192.101. Buytaert in his edition of *Theologia Christiana* was unable to find the sun analogy in Augustine's works (see p. 303, note). A.M. Gietl in his edition of *Die Sentenzen Rolands* (Freiburg, 1891), p. 25, note, had, however, already found the analogies of the sun and the cithara in pseudo-Augustine, *Sermo* 245, *PL* 39.2196-7. Augustine uses an analogy of fire, light and warmth (*ignis, splendor, calor*) in *De Symbolo*, 3.9, *PL* 40.660 etc.; cf. Augustine, *Sermo de quarta feria*, 6, *PL* 40.692. For the sun analogy, see also the Anselm miscellany in British Library, MS Royal 8. D. viii, edited in *Mem.Ans.*, pp. 302-3 (here the analogy is extended to include the incarnation). Anselm does not use the analogy of the cithara.

35. In a *Tractatus de trinitate* of the circle of Thierry of Chartres, the analogy of the sun is passed over because it is known to everybody, see *Commentaries on Boethius by Thierry of Chartres and his School*, edited by N.M. Haring, Pontifical Institute of

Medieval Studies, Studies and Texts, 20 (Toronto, 1971), p. 307.64.

36. For criticism by Roscelin of another of Anselm's analogies used in the *De incarnatione verbi*, *Ans.Op.Om.*, I, 282:12-283:16, see G.R. Evans, *Anselm and Talking about God* (Oxford, 1978), pp. 97-9, and also G.R. Evans, 'St Anselm's analogies', *Vivarium*, 14:2 (1976), 81-93, here p. 92. In her article, Evans underlines the rhetorical features of Anselm's analogies.

37. Abelard, *Theologia Christiana*, 4.83, p. 304. cf. 4.135, pp. 333-4.

38. *De processione spiritus sancti*, 9, *Ans.Op.Om.*, II, 203:7-205:16.

39. *De incarnatione verbi*, 13-14, *Ans.Op.Om.*, II, 31:10-33:8.

40. Augustine, *De fide et symbolo*, 8 (9), no.17, edited by J. Zycha, Corpus Scriptorum Ecclesiasticorum Latinorum, 41 (Vienna, 1900), pp. 18ff.; *PL* 40.189ff. Also, Augustine, *De Genesi ad litteram*, 5.9.25, *PL* 34.329. cf. also Tertullian, *Liber adversus Praxeam*, 8, *PL* 2.163. Abelard states that the analogy is found 'Augustino scribente ad Laurentium papam', see A. Pézard, 'Le sceau d'or: Dante, Abélard, saint Augustin', *Studi Danteschi*, 45 (1968), 28-93, here pp. 83-91, suggests ingeniously how *Laurentius papa* may have earlier come to replace Aurelius to whom the *De trinitate* was addressed and why Abelard assumed that the image was contained in this work. Pézard's essay also appears in A. Pézard, *'La Rotta gonna'. Gloses et corrections auz textes mineurs de Dante*, 2 vols. (Florence and Paris, 1967/69), II, 96-160, here pp. 149-57.

41. In *De processione spiritus sancti*, 9, *Ans.Op.Om.*, II, 204:22-7, Anselm answers the objection concerning a temporal sequence by referring to his letter, *De incarnatione verbi*, 13, (*Ans.Op.Om.*, II, 32) where he admits that God is totally freed from constraints of time and of place. G.R. Evans, 'St Anselm's images of Trinity', *Journal of Theological Studies*, new series, 27 (1976), 46-57, emphasizes Anselm's reluctance to follow the convention of using analogies because they might be criticized for unintended implications on points of detail; she also observes that the answers Anselm gives to objections to analogies in *De processione spiritus sancti* suggest that 'Anselmian images of the Trinity were the subject of current debate in the schools' (p. 52). On the use of the Nile image by Anselm's disciple, Gilbert Crispin, see G.R. Evans, *Anselm and a New Generation* (Oxford, 1980), pp. 205-8. G.R. Evans also underlines (here, pp. 106-10) Abelard's concern for 'technical propriety' in his use of the Nile and other analogies.

42. In a stimulating paper entitled 'Abelard's mockery of St Anselm', which is to appear in the 1983 issue of *Paideia: An*

International Journal of General Culture, edited by G.C. Simmons, M. Clanchy argues that Abelard's reference to Anselm in his *Theologia Christiana* is highly scornful, not merely critical. On the basis of a supposedly significant deterioration in the tone of his references to Anselm, Clanchy argues that Abelard's previous esteem for Anselm in his letter to the Bishop of Paris evaporates in the face of an attempt in the *Theologia Christiana* to make Anselm 'look a fool'. In fact, the terms *fistula* and *infistulatus* which Abelard uses somewhat apologetically ('ac si . . . dicamus', Abelard, *Theologia Christiana*, 4.83, lines 1218-19, p. 304) in the course of his discussion of Anselm's analogy of the watercourse in order to describe the Son passing through human flesh, do not necessarily have a foul meaning. Abelard is here echoing the *De incarnatione verbi*, 14, *Ans.Op.Om.*, II, 33:5-8 ('Si enim rivus per fistulam currat a fonte usque ad lacum: nonne solus rivus, quamvis non alius Nilus quam fons et lacus, ut ita dicam infistulatus est, sicut solus filius incarnatus est, licet non alius deus quam pater et spiritus sanctus?'). Although Clanchy elucidates well Abelard's tendency to mock the objects of his criticism, he appears to read too much into this passage, particularly since Roscelin's two antagonists shared a striking community of ideas. Clanchy speculates that Abelard felt, when writing his *Theologia Christiana*, that his condemnation at Soissons was caused by Anselm's part in securing the earlier condemnation of Roscelin at Soissons. But not only is Abelard more likely to have felt that he had supported Anselm in his own attack on Roscelin in the *Theologia 'Summi boni'*; he also probably saw his criticism in the *Theologia Christiana* as a criticism of one particular aspect of Anselm's reasoning. This criticism does not read like a sharp or vindictive attack. I am particularly grateful to Dr Clanchy for his kindness in showing me both his paper and an earlier version of it.

43. Abelard, *Theologia Christiana*, 4.84, 86, 87, pp. 304-5, 306-7. cf. also 3.140-1, p. 248; 4.58, p. 290; 4.102, p. 315; 4.106, pp. 317-18. Augustine uses the analogy of a signet ring to show how God impresses his image on creatures (i.e. wax) without losing it, *De trinitate*, 14.15, PL 42.1052. cf. Augustine, *Sermo 265*, alias *De Tempore* 215, PL 39.2237. Augustine diversified his analogies easily; for man as the coinage of Christ, bearing the image of Christ, see *Sermo* 90.10, PL 38.566; *Enarratio in Psalmum*, 4.8, PL 36.81.

44. For another analogy — the bronze statue — see Abelard, *Theologia Christiana*, 4.51, p. 288. Also, Abelard, *Logica 'Ingredientibus'*, in *Peter Abaelards Philosophische Schriften*, 1, Beiträge zur Geschichte der Philosophie und Theologie des

Mittelalters, 21 (Münster, 1919), p. 79. cf. Augustine, *De trinitate*, 7.6, *PL* 42.943ff. on golden statues. The shorter versions of the *Theologia 'Scholarium'*, edited by Buytaert in *Abaelardi opera theologica*, II, 401-451, do not comprise more than Book 1 of the whole work and, therefore, do not concern us here; a typed edition of the longer versions was prepared by the late E.M. Buytaert, but this has not yet been published. I am indebted to R. van der Plaetse of *Corpus Christianorum* for kindly allowing me to consult the typescript. The passage concerning Anselm is 2.120, *PL* 178.1071BD. The analogy of the watercourse is briefly used later at 2.164, *PL* 178.1079C, and the analogy of the sun appears at 2.118-19, *PL* 178.1070C-71A and at 2.164, *PL* 178.1080A.

45. Abelard, *Theologia 'Scholarium'*, 2.13, *PL* 178.1068C-70A; 2.141-7, *PL* 178.1073B-75A. Buytaert indicates no sources for the bronze seal, but see the references to Augustine collected above at note 43. Master Roland in his *Sentences*, in *Die Sentenzen Rolands*, edited by A.M. Gietl (Freiburg, 1891), pp. 25-9, lucidly explains why Abelard introduced the analogy of the bronze seal as an improvement upon the other Augustinian analogies. In the *Epitome theologiae christianae* (or *Sententiae Hermanni*), a work of the 'school' of Abelard, analogies of a golden seal, a bronze ring and a bronze seal are used, see Chapters 12, 15, 17, *PL* 178.1715C, 1717B, 1720BC.

46. Abelard, *Theologia 'Scholarium'*, 2.91-3, 121, *PL* 178.1064AD, 1071D.

47. Evans, 'Anselm's images of Trinity', overlooks the case of Abelard when she suggests that there was no 'traceable pattern of direct personal influence' by Anselm on the development of theological debate in the twelfth century (p. 56). She is also on doubtful ground (ibid.) — in view of Abelard's frequent recourse to Augustine's *De trinitate* — in seeing a movement away from reliance on Augustine to commentary on Boethius between the eleventh and twelfth centuries.

48. William of St Thierry, *Epistola* 326, *PL* 182.532, and also his *Disputatio*, *PL* 181.255AB. Bernard of Clairvaux, *Epistola* 190, in Leclercq and Rochais, *S. Bernardi opera*, VIII, 22-3. Bernard cites Abelard, *Theologia 'Scholarium'*, 2.116, *PL* 178.1070A. *Anonymi Capitula Haeresum Petri Abaelardi*, 1, in Buytaert, *Abaelardi opera theologica*, II, 473.

49. Abelard, *Commentaria in Epistolam Pauli ad Romanos*, in Buytaert, *Abaelardi opera theologica*, I, 37.

50. Abelard, *Commentaria*, pp. 113-28; *Cur Deus homo*, 1, 7, *Ans.Op.Om.*, II, 57.

51. Abelard, *Theologia 'Summi boni'*, 3.1, p. 84; Abelard, *Theologia Christiana*, 4.60-9, pp. 290-7. Earlier in the *Theologia*, Abelard had announced his intention to discuss the incarnation of the Word, *Theologia Christiana*, 1.129, p. 128; Abelard, *Theologia Scholarium* (recensiores breviores), 59, in Buytaert, *Abaelardi opera theologica*, II, 424-5; Abelard, *Theologia 'Scholarium'*, 1.21, *PL* 178.1032B. The question why the second person of the Trinity is incarnated was considered by many contemporaries; for some references, see R.E. Weingart, *The Logic of Divine Love: A Critical Analysis of the Soteriology of Peter Abailard* (Oxford, 1970), p. 101, note 1. For Anselm of Canterbury on this, see *Cur Deus homo*, 2, 9, *Ans.Op.Om.*, II, 105-6.

52. Abelard, *Theologia Christiana*, 4.63, pp. 292-3; Abelard, *Theologia 'Scholarium'*, 1.10, *PL* 178.995CD.

53. R. Peppermüller, *Abaelards Auslegung des Römerbriefes*, Beiträge zur Geschichte der Philosophie und der Theologie des Mittelalters, n.F., 10 (Münster, 1972) pp. 91-2. Peppermüller gives references to other scholars who have held that Abelard was indebted to Anselm here.

54. Abelard, *Commentaria*, pp. 113-14.

55. Weingart, *Divine Love*, p. 92.

56. *Cur Deus homo*, 1, 1, *Ans.Op.Om.*, II, 48.

57. Abelard, *Commentaria*, p. 116.

58. Boso in *Cur Deus homo*, 1, 1, *Ans.Op.Om.*, II, 48.

59. Abelard, *Commentaria*, pp. 114-15, *Cur Deus homo*, 1, 7, *Ans. Op.Om.*, II, 57.

60. Abelard, *Commentaria*, p. 115; *Cur Deus homo*, 1, 7, *Ans. Op.Om.*, II, 57. cf. Weingart, *Divine Love*, pp. 84-7, 89.

61. Peppermüller, *Abaelards Auslegung des Römerbriefes*, p. 91.

62. Abelard, *Commentaria*, p. 114; corrected to 'Et quidem dicitur . . .' by R. Peppermüller, 'Zur kritischen Ausgabe des Römerbrief-Kommentars des Petrus Abaelard', *Scriptorium*, 26 (1972), 82-97, here p. 89.

63. cf. Weingart, *Divine Love*, pp. 88-9.

64. *Cur Deus homo*, 1, 3, *Ans.Op.Om.*, II, 50-1.

65. *Cur Deus homo*, 1, 6, *Ans.Op.Om.*, II, 54-5.

66. For a review of the book as a whole, see D.E. Luscombe in *The Downside Review*, 89:294 (1971), 96-7.

67. Weingart, *Divine Love*, pp. 91-3.

68. Ibid., pp. 91-2.

69. 'Magis autem honestis quam necessariis rationibus nitimur . . .', Abelard, *Theologia Christiana*, 5.15, p. 353; Abelard, *Theologia 'Scholarium'*, 3.2, PL 178.1090C.

70. Abelard, *Theologia Christiana*, 5.38, p. 364.

71. *Cur Deus homo*, 2, 5, Ans.Op.Om., II, 100:20-8.

72. cf. Peppermüller, *Abaelards Auslegung des Römerbriefes*, p. 90, note 496, where he notes that Abelard means by 'necessity' either *convenientia* in God, i.e. what is fitting for God, or our necessity, i.e. what is inescapable for man.

73. Abelard, *Commentaria*, p. 175.

74. Ibid., p. 191.

75. *Epitome theologiae Christianae*, 23, PL 178:1730B.

76. Abelard, *Theologia Christiana*, 1.129, p. 128.

77. *Ecrits théologiques de l'école d'Abélard: Textes inédits*, edited by A.M. Landgraf, Spicilegium sacrum lovaniense. Etudes et documents, 14 (Louvain, 1934), pp. 61-289.

78. The preface is printed in an appendix by Landgraf, *Ecrits théologiques*, pp. 287-9. For discussion, see Landgraf's introduction, pp. xliv-xlvi (where he questions the link between the preface and the work) and, for a contrary view, see D.E. Luscombe, 'The authorship of the *Ysagoge in theologiam*', *Archives d'histoire doctrinale et littéraire du Moyen Age*, 35 (1968), 7-16.

79. See R.W. Southern, *Medieval Humanism and Other Studies* (Oxford, 1970), p. 159, note.

80. *Ysagoge in theologiam*, in Landgraf, *Ecrits théologiques de l'école d'Abélard*, pp. 93-5.

81. Ibid., pp. 117ff.

82. Ibid., pp. lii, 310.

83. R. Blomme has drawn attention to the connections between the *Ysagoge*'s teaching on sin and Anselm's *De conceptu virginali et originali peccato*, in his *La Doctrine du péché dans les écoles théologiques de la première moitié du XIIe siècle* (Louvain, 1958), pp. 238-43.

84. Landgraf, *Ysagoge in theologiam*, pp. 155-8.

85. Landgraf, *Ysagoge in theologiam*, p. 155, lines 20 et seq., 28 et seq.; p. 157, lines 26 et seq.; p. 158, lines 4 et seq., 10 et seq. cf. Abelard, *Commentaria*, p. 114, lines 146 et seq., 154 et seq.; p. 115, lines 179 et seq.; p. 116, lines 202 et seq.; p. 117, lines 239 et seq.

86. Landgraf, *Ysagoge in theologiam*, pp. 161-2.

87. *Cur Deus homo*, 2, 7, *Ans.Op.Om.*, II, 101-2.

88. Abelard's *quaestio* in Buytaert, *Abaelardi opera theologica*, pp. 117-18.

89. Landgraf, *Ysagoge in theologiam*, pp. 165-6, especially p. 165, line 24.

90. *Cur Deus homo*, 2, 8, *Ans.Op.Om.*, II, 104.

91. See C.N.L. Brooke and W.J. Millor, *The Letters of John of Salisbury, Volume II: The Later Letters (1163-1180)*, Oxford Medieval Texts (Oxford, 1979), p. 546, note, citing the *Chronica de Bello*, edited by J.S. Brewer (London, 1846), p. 148, where this Odo is said to be 'doctus lege divina'. See further *The Heads of Religious Houses: England and Wales, 940-1216*, edited by D. Knowles, C.N.L. Brooke and V. London (Cambridge, 1972), p. 29.

Anselm and Thomas of Buckingham
An Examination of the *Questiones super Sententias*[1]

Arthur R. Lee

The widespread influence of St Anselm on fourteenth-century theologians has often been noted.[2] In this paper, an attempt will be made to assess the extent and nature of that influence in a particular work of one such theologian: the *Questiones super Sententias* of Thomas of Buckingham — an Oxford scholar, later Chancellor of Exeter Cathedral, who flourished during the second quarter of the fourteenth century.[3]

In common with many other fourteenth-century commentaries *in libros sententiarum*, Buckingham's *Questiones super Sententias* (written between 1335 and 1343)[4] treats only a limited number of topics, here discussed under six principal questions with a number of subordinate questions, articles and conclusions. Because of this form, the work resembles more a collection of long *questiones quodlibetales* than a traditional sentence-commentary. From this, we may assume that the topics discussed by Buckingham were matters of some concern to him and that the influences of St Anselm which we find in them are of some importance.

In an earlier study of a small portion of the *Questiones super Sententias*, it has been shown that the references to St Anselm in the first two Conclusions of Question I, '. . . demonstrate Buckingham's familiarity with Anselm's works and ideas, but they do not here indicate any intellectual dependence'.[5] This distinction between familiarity and influence is important: while familiarity is indicated by the frequency and variety of citation, significant influence is shown only by the acceptance or rejection of ideas.[6] In examining Anselm's influence on Buckingham, it will be useful to begin by surveying Buckingham's familiarity with Anselm's works, but the assessment of influence must rest upon an examination of Buckingham's use of Anselm's ideas:

Buckingham's familiarity with Anselm's works may be gauged from the number of references to them which occur in the body of the text of the *Questiones super Sententias*: some 139 direct citations of specific works and passages, a large proportion of which include either clear quotations or accurate summaries, plus a number of more general references. This is probably the largest number of references in the *Questiones super Sententias* to any single author apart from St Augustine. The citations occur in the following order of frequency: *Cur Deus homo* (48); *De casu diaboli* (23); *De concordia* (17); *De conceptu virginali* (15); *De similitudinibus* [a work of

'Anselmian' authorship, attributed directly to St Anselm] (6); *Monologion* (6); *Proslogion* (5); *Contra responsionem pro insipiente* (5); *De veritate* (5); *De libertate arbitrii* (5); *Responsionem pro insipiente* [by Gaunilo] (1); *De processione spiritus sancti* (1); *Meditatio redemptionis humane* (1); *Meditatio ad concitandum timorem* (1). A detailed listing of these citations is given in the supplementary Index at the end of this chapter.

In addition to suggesting a wide familiarity with the works and ideas of St Anselm and an extensive use of these materials in discussion, these citations also suggest strong concentrations of interest. A third of the references are to the *Cur Deus homo*; half are to the two works *Cur Deus homo* and *De casu diaboli*; and approximately three-quarters are to the four works *Cur Deus homo*, *De casu diaboli*, *De concordia*, and *De conceptu virginali*, works which particularly discuss the nature of sin and evil and their relation to free will. Within these works, further concentrations may be observed (see Index), notably, *Cur Deus homo*, 1, cc. 11, 21, 24, and 2, cc. 14, 15, 16 and, particularly, 17; *De casu diaboli*, 1, cc. 12, and 16; *De concordia* 1, cc. 2 and 6; *De conceptu virginali*, 24 and 29; and *Monologion*, 78.

Both the arrangement and, to some degree, the use of these materials are influenced by the ordering of the six principal questions of the *Questiones super Sententias*, which superficially follows the arrangement of these topics in the *Book of Sentences*:

Q. I.   Utrum deo frui sit summa merces cuiuslibet creature beate?

Q. II.   Utrum essentia divina generet vel generetur?

Q. III.   Utrum deus sit omnipotens? (Utrum deus potest velle mundum nunquam fuisse?; Utrum omne futurum sit necessario futurum?)

Q. IV.   Utrum sic dare primum instans meriti vel demeriti?

Q. V.   Utrum deus sit omnipotens? (de infinito)

Q. VI.   Utrum pro omni et solo peccato mortali pena eterna debeatur?

Question 1, 'Utrum deo frui sit summa merces cuiuslibet creature beate?', is discussed under eight conclusions. In Conclusion I, 'Sola privatio boni est per se malum', five references support the opening argument that evil is simple privation,[7] and a sixth — understood in an objection as implying the existence of positive evil — is refuted.[8] In Conclusion II, 'Omnis privatio rei debite inesse est tantum malum quantum est bonum quod ipsa per se et essentialiter privat si esset bonum', four references are found in the solution: one to the sense in which God is the cause of punishment,[9] one to the gravity of the least mortal sin,[10] and two to the counter-argument that punishment should be in proportion to the amount of sin.[11] In Conclusion III, 'Nulla privatio est per se et essentialiter alicui magis mala quam bonum cuius est privatio si esset bonum', one reference is found in the initial list of authorities,[12] and a second — that all sin is injustice — is used to support an objection.[13] In Conclusion VI, 'Quantum eligenda est aliqua res, tantum fugibilis est eius perfecta privatio, et econtra', two references to the extreme gravity of sin support an objection;[14] in the refutation, the references are affirmed, while the objection is denied. In Conclusion VII, 'Nullum miserum esse miseria que non est culpa est tam fugiendum quam fugiendum est non esse', two references to sin as dishonouring God support an affirmative argument,[15] one to sin as meriting great privation supports a negative argument,[16] which is refuted by means of another reference concerning the unreasonableness of annihilation as punishment for sin,[17] and one on the extreme gravity of sin is used in a final objection.[18] In Conclusion VIII, 'Deo frui est creature rationali maximum bonum possibile', three references with extensive quotations are used to argue the objection that total privation is to be preferred to sin,[19] supported by three references on the importance of doing God's will;[20] one partial, misleading reference[21] is used to support an objection which is later refuted by means of the remainder of the quoted passage;[22] and, to the question 'An omne peccatum sit magis fugibile quam aliquod bonum citra deum sit eligibile?', four supporting references are given,[23] followed later by four references in opposition;[24] and one reference re-introduces an objection to the conclusion.[25]

    Question II, 'Utrum essentia divina generet vel generetur?', is discussed as the simple question, 'Utrum essentia divina generat?'. One reference on the unity of the divine substance is given in support,[26] but is refuted at the end of the question by means of itself;[27] and, in the solution, one reference — is given on the nature of the divine persons,[28] while another supports both their unity and their individuality.[29]

    Question III, 'Utrum deus sit omnipotens?', is argued under two articles. In Article I, 'Utrum deus potest velle mundum nunquam fuisse?',[30] two references in denial are given in the preliminary argument to the principal question;[31] one reference is given in oblique support of God's power to undo the past;[32] five are given at some length in the arguments against;[33] and two are given in the refutation,[34] in opposition on the subsidiary question of whether Christ could deceive. In Article II, 'Utrum omne futurum sit necessario futurum?', after initial arguments for and against, the question is decided in a series of five conclusions of a projected seven. Four references are included in a list of authorities given in an initial argument for the question;[35] two given in the arguments against the question distinguish between antecedent and consequent necessity;[36] two support a definition of consequent necessity;[37] and two support a weak relationship between God's foreknowledge and the necessity of future contingents.[38] In Conclusion II, 'Volitio divina non est cuiuslibet effectus sui necessitas antecedens', two references in the arguments in favour support the contingency of consequent necessity upon antecedent necessity;[39] two are used in discussion of necessity and the divine will;[40] three affirm that the divine will is consequent necessity;[41] and one, in the refutation of the arguments against the conclusion, is used to define the term 'per se'.[42] In Conclusion V, 'Nec per se nec per accidens meritum nec demeritum necessitati repugnat', two references form the basis of an argument for the conclusion.[43]

Question IV, 'Utrum sic dare primum instans meriti vel demeriti?', is treated as a *dubium*, with full arguments and responses both to the affirmative and to the negative. In the second, negative, initial discussion, one reference forms the basis for an argument against the question;[44] another supports an additional argument against the question;[45] and two are used in the refutation of a negative argument in the initial discussion.[46]

Question V, 'Utrum deus sit omnipotens?', is a continuation of Question III, considered under a series of subsidiary questions. In the first of these, 'Utrum sit possibile quod aliquod continuum sit secundum se totum in aliquo situ indivisibili?', an utterly misleading reference is adduced in support,[47] a quotation of a position which Anselm himself immediately refutes. To the final subsidiary question, 'Utrum sit possibile infinitum esse?', Buckingham presents a fairly long, careful examination of the ontological argument, utilizing some ten references (including one to Guanilo)[48] with extensive quotations.[49]

Finally, Question VI, 'Utrum pro omni et solo peccato mortali pena eterna debeatur?' the longest of the six questions, is argued under six articles. In Article II, 'Utrum actus exteriores aggravant peccata?', two references are given to support an argument that actions committed while one is inebriate or angry are no less culpable because of that circumstance.[50]

In Article III, 'Utrum si deus crearet creaturam rationalem cum privatione gratie gratum facientis sine demerito ipsius vel alicuius alterius nunquid talis privatio esset culpa mortalis eodem modo si iam creature dicto modo auferat gratiam', the question is argued by two series of arguments, for and against, followed by a solution to which objections are brought and refuted. In the opening arguments, which deny that such a privation would be a mortal fault, one reference supports the argument that God would be the cause of the privation, which then would not be the fault of the creature;[51] two form the basis for an argument that God's privation of grace in a creature cannot be counted as sin in the creature;[52] two references support a similar argument, that injustice is the privation of a justice previously given, but not the simple lack of a justice not yet given;[53] one is included among the authorities for another argument;[54] three with substantial quotations argue another, that

God is not able to remove righteousness by removing grace;[55] two provide minor support for another argument;[56] and two are used to refute a significant counter-argument, that the righteousness of an act is contingent upon God's continuing to impute righteousness to it, by affirming that the goodness of the will consists in willing what God wills it to will.[57] In the objections to the solution, one reference is given to explain the occasion of an opinion of Duns Scotus;[58] and two, in another objection, affirm Adam's original justice before the Fall.[59]

In Article V, 'Utrum voluntas possit cogi ad actum?', which is argued much as was Article III, Buckingham poses two series of opening arguments, for and against the question, argues his solution, and responds to each series of initial arguments. In the first, affirmative arguments, one reference supports the argument that knowledge is necessary for the will to desire blessedness;[60] four references form the basis for another which argues that the angels are moved to love by knowledge,[61] while in the refutation of this argument — that to will love is not always in the power of the will — another reference is given;[62] one reference is the basis for the argument that thought necessarily preceded the fall of the angels;[63] and one supports the argument that the ability to discriminate is the foundation of all punishment.[64] In the arguments against the question, three references support the argument that free will cannot be subject to external influence.[65] In the solution, one reference is given on the tripartite nature of the soul;[66] one on evil as affecting the will, rather than the appetite;[67] and one to the affirmation that angels must have some volition.[68] In the responses to the negative arguments, two references are used as minor proof-texts.[69]

In Article VI, the question 'Utrum deus voluntate beneplaciti vult peccatum fieri et esse?', is the first in a series of questions which lead to a solution of the principal question of Question VI. In the arguments for this subsidiary question, one reference is used in support of an argument that God wills sin;[70] and a second supports a subsidiary argument, that sin is volition contrary to the will of God.[71] In a second question, 'Quid sit peccare?', in the initial arguments, one reference is used as a proof-text for the statement that sin is the violation of the law or the will of God;[72] one with a substantial quotation forms the basis of the argument that sin is the non-payment to God of a debt which is owed;[73] one to the effect that sin is the privation of justice gives support to another argument;[74] and, in the summation, one reference is given in support of the solution.[75] In a third sub-question, 'Utrum quelibet creatura rationalis habeat infinitam bonitatem et et iusticiam privabilem per peccatum?', one reference supports the initial assumption that sin is the privation of justice;[76] one is used in an opposing argument, that the quantity of original sin is immutable;[77] and one, that right volition proceeds from righteousness, and not the converse, supports another opposing argument.[78] In the solution, which is argued primarily by Anselm, two references are adduced to prove that original sin is the equal and absolute privation of original justice.[79]

Finally, Buckingham turns to the question, 'Utrum pro peccato temporali et momentaneo debeatur pena eterna propter aliquam circumstantiam infinite aggravantem?'. In the initial list of authorities for the infinite gravity of sin, there is one reference to Anselm;[80] three references occur in a discussion of the infinite and, thus, equal gravity of all sin;[81] and, in the solution, one reference is used as a proof-text on the nature of eternal punishment.[82] A subsidiary question on the gravity of the murder of Christ is argued almost entirely from Anselm, using three references with long quotations and extensive discussion.[83] Finally, at the end of the question, one reference supports differences in the relative gravity of sins.[84]

Both from our examination of Buckingham's familiarity with Anselm's works, and from our survey of his use of Anselm's ideas, it is clear that Anselm exercised a definite influence on Buckingham's thought. In particular, we may conclude:

(1)   that Buckingham had a wide and detailed knowledge of Anselm's works, including the Anselmian book, *De similitudinibus*, which he applied frequently in the course of his own arguments.

(2)   that Buckingham's use of Anselm is notably careful and precise: most of the references are supported by exact quotations or by accurate summaries of Anselm's arguments. Indeed, in the two instances of misleadingly partial quotations, it is quite clear that these were deliberate: each is the citation of a position later rejected by Anselm (or pseudo-Anselm) as though it were his final position and, in one case, the counter-argument is quoted by Buckingham in his refutation.[85]

(3)   that Buckingham was influenced deeply by Anselm in a number of questions in the *Questiones super Sententias*. In Question III, Article I, on the question of God's ability to undo the past, Buckingham's negative conclusion is strongly influenced by Anselm, as is his negative conclusion on the subsidiary question of whether Christ could deceive. Article II, on God's foreknowledge of future contingents, shows a similarly strong influence,[86] the arguments suggesting that Anselm's thought (particularly in *Cur Deus homo*, 2, 17, and *De concordia*, 1, 2-3) was highly formative in the establishment of Buckingham's position. In Question V, Buckingham's discussion of the ontological argument appears to be conducted entirely within Anselm's framework and, although he does give some weight to the divine revelation of the argu-

ment, Buckingham's decision on its validity is based entirely on the internal merits of Anselm's reasoning. Buckingham initially accepts that 'the arguments of Anselm are good and sufficiently prove God to be the highest good, omnipotent, and thus of similar things'.[87] Next, he affirms Anselm's inspired authority: 'Nevertheless, many say that Anselm was sophistically deceived in these arguments, but I believe that they do not understand his arguments, which were revealed to him by inspiration'.[88] Finally, after critical examination, Buckingham concludes that Anselm's course of argument is sufficient to lead beyond the purely mental concept and, thus, to demonstrate the existence of God. His references to Anselm are taken from *Proslogion,* 2-4; the *Responsionem pro insipiente* of Gaunilo; and the book *Contra responsionem pro insipiente.* In Question VI, Article III, on the possibility of an intermediate state between grace and sin, while there are several references to Anselm in the course of the discussion, there is also the definite possibility that the initial impetus to Buckingham's affirmative position is to be found in Anselm's discussion in the *De casu diaboli,* 16. Finally, in Question VI, Article VI, strong Anselmian influences are found in the subsidiary questions on the nature, quantity, and gravity of sin; and in the question of the gravity of the murder of Christ, argued from *Cur Deus homo,* 2, 14-15.

(4)   that Buckingham had a profound, but not uncritical, regard for Anselm as an authority. Although he treats Anselm with the respect due to a nearly patristic authority, there is also present a personal regard for the man and his work which is greater than merely conventional. One may glimpse this, and the critical nature of of Buckingham's respect, in the discussion of the ontological argument when, having quoted from Anselm's reply to the *Responsionem pro insipiente,* Buckingham exclaims, 'See! how confidently and presumptuously Anselm speaks of these arguments!'[89] Yet, a few lines later he disagrees with those who think that Anselm is mislead in his reasoning, saying that they do not understand Anselm's arguments. There is in this something of the regard of a disciple for his master: an emotional commitment which is more than simple regard for an authority.

This would not be inappropriate: Buckingham himself was a devout priest, as well as a scholar, and was moved by the material he studied. Anselm's evident faith may well have drawn Buckingham to him: certainly, as with Anselm, faith seems to have been Buckingham's theological starting-point; a particular concern with sin and its consequences, a major area for the exploration of that faith; and his theological explorations, a quest to inform that faith with understanding.

NOTES

1. This article is a revised version of a paper read at the Third International Conference on 3 July 1979 at Canterbury. The research for this study was carried out with the support of a grant from the Johnson Fund of the American Philosophical Society.

2. For example, '[St Anselm] for whom the Moderns and the Modernists have so much affection'. D. Trapp, 'Augustinian theology of the fourteenth century', *Augustiniana*, 6 (1956), 149.

3. The principal works on Buckingham include: K. Michalski, 'Les courants philosophiques à Oxford et à Paris pendant le XIVe siècle', *Bulletin international de l'Académie polonaise des sciences et des lettres, classe d'histoire et de philosophie* (Cracow, 1922-4), pp. 59-88; K. Michalski, 'Le Criticisme et le scepticisme dans la philosophie du XIVe siècle', *Bulletin international de l'Académie polonaise des sciences et des lettres, classe d'histoire et de philosophie* (Cracow, 1927), pp. 41-122; K. Michalski, 'Les Courants critiques et sceptiques dans la philosophie du XIVe siècle', *Bulletin international de l'Académie polonaise des sciences et des lettres, classe d'histoire et de philosophie* (Cracow, 1927), pp. 192-244; K. Michalski,'Le Problème de la volonté à Oxford et à Paris au XIVe siècle', in *Studia Philosophica*, 2 (1936), 233-365; M.-D. Chenu, 'Les Quaestiones de Thomas de Buckingham', in *Studia medievalia in honorem R.J. Martin* (Bruges, 1948), pp. 229-41; A.B. Emden *A Biographical Register of the University of Oxford to A.D. 1500*, 3 vols. (Oxford, 1957-9); W.A. Pantin, *The English Church in the Fourteenth Century* (Cambridge, 1955); J.A. Robson, *Wyclif and the Oxford Schools* (Cambridge, 1966); J.A. Weisheipl, 'Early fourteenth-century physics and the Merton "School"' (unpublished D.Phil. dissertation, University of Oxford, 1957); J.A. Weisheipl, 'Repertorium Mertonese', *Medieval Studies*, 21 (1969), 174-224.

   Two especially significant analyses are given in: H.A. Oberman, *Archbishop Thomas Bradwardine* (Utrecht, 1957); G. Leff, *Bradwardine and the Pelagians* (Cambridge, 1957).

   The most recent studies are in W.J. Courtenay, 'John of Mirecourt and Gregory of Rimini on whether God can undo the past', Part 2, *Recherches de théologie ancienne et médiévale*, 40 (1973), 150-7; W.J. Courtenay, *Adam Woodham* (Leiden, 1978); A.R. Lee, 'Thomas of Buckingham' (unpublished B.Litt. dissertation, University of Oxford, 1975); Z. Kaluza, 'La prétendue discussion parisienne de Thomas Bradwardine avec Thomas de Buckingham', *Recherches de théologie ancienne et médiévale*, 43 (1976), 219-36; J.-F. Genest, 'Le De Futuris Contingentibus de Thomas Bradwardine', *Recherches augustiniennes*, 14 (1979), 249-

336; B.R. de la Torre, 'Thomas Buckingham's *Ostensio Meriti Liberae Actionis,* Conclusions to 1 to 15: *De Contingentia Futurorum et Arbitrii Libertate:* an edition and study' (unpublished Ph.D. dissertation, University of Toronto, 1979).

4. Lee, 'Thomas of Buckingham', pp. 44-7.
   For full bibliographical details of the twelve surviving manuscripts and one printed edition (edited by Augustinus Perez de Olivano and printed by Jean Barbier in Paris in 1505) of the text of the *Questiones super Sententias,* see Lee, 'Thomas of Buckingham', pp. 146-66. Abridgments and extracts are noted on pp. 50-3. The surviving texts (both the manuscripts and Perez's printed edition) are corrupt: reliance is to be placed on none of them in isolation. A critical edition of 'Question I, Conclusions I and II', is to be found in Lee, 'Thomas of Buckingham', and has been used in this study. For the remainder of the *Questiones super Sententias,* the Perez edition has been used because of its relative accessibility, but it has always been corrected against one, and usually several, of the manuscripts.

5. Lee, 'Thomas of Buckingham', p. 97.

6. This is well stated in Courtenay, *Adam Wodeham,* pp. 39-40.

   The following references to the 'Questiones super Sententias' in notes 7-11 are to Lee, 'Thomas of Buckingham'. (For example Q.I, C.I: C.I., 90 refers to Question 1, Conclusion I of the 'Questiones super Sententias' in Lee, 'Thomas of Buckingham', Conclusion I, p. 90.)

7. Q.I, C.I: C.I, 90 (*De casu diaboli,* 9); C.I, 93 (*De casu diaboli,* 16); C.I, 94 (*De casu diaboli,* 20); C.II, 94-5 (*De conceptu virginali,* 5); C.I, 95 (*De concordia,* 1, 7 [given as 1, 13]).

8. Q.I, C.I: C.I, 181 (*De casu diaboli,* 26).

9. Q.I, C.II: C.I, 402 (*De casu diaboli,* 1).

10. Q.I, C.II: C.I, 415 (*Cur Deus homo,* 2, 16).

11. Q.I, C.II: C.II, 496-7 (*De conceptu virginali,* 23); C.I, 499 (*Cur Deus homo,* 1, 20).

    The following references to the 'Questiones super Sententias' are to the Perez edition (see note 4 above).

12. Q.I, C.III: b.iii^{va}, 30-5 (*Cur Deus homo,* 2, 14).

13. Q.I, C.III: b.iiii^{rb}, 40-4 (*De conceptu virginali,* 3).

14. Q.I, C.VI: c.iii^{rb}, 4-5 (*Cur Deus homo,* 1, 21); c. iii^{rb}, 5-6, *Cur Deus homo,* 2, 14).

15. Q.I, C.VII: c.vi^{ra}, 28-33 (*Cur Deus homo*, 1, 11-15); v.vi^{ra}, 32-3 (*De similitudinibus*, 8 [given as 9]).

16. Q.I, C.VII: c.vi^{vb}, 15-20 (*Cur Deus homo*, 2, 16).

17. Q.I, C.VII: d.v^{ra}, 6-10 (*Monologion*, 71).

18. Q.I, C.VII: d.v^{rb}, 36-9 (*Cur Deus homo* 1, 21).

19. Q.I, C.VIII: d.v^{vb}, 38-41 (*Cur Deus homo*, 1, 21); d.vi^{ra}, 2-15 (*Cur Deus homo*, 1, 21); d.vi^{ra}, 15-16 (*Cur Deus homo*, 2, 14).

20. Q.I, C.VIII: d.vi^{ra}, 38-43 (*De libertate arbitrii* £*De libero arbitrio*$: *De concordia*; *De veritate*).

21. Q.I, C.VIII: d.vi^{rb}, 23-8 (*De similitudinibus*, 191 [given as *penultimo*]).

22. Q.I, C.VIII: e.ii^{ra}, 17-23 (*De similitudinibus*, 191 [given as *penultimo*]).

23. Q.I, C.VIII: d.vi^{va}, 43 - d.vi^{vb}, 1 (*Cur Deus homo*, 2, 14); d.vi^{vb}, 1-6 (*Cur Deus homo*, 1, 21); d.vi^{vb}, 6-8 (*Cur Deus homo*, 1, 22 et seqq.); d.vi^{vb}, 9-13 (*Cur Deus homo*, 2, 6).

24. Q.I, C.VIII: e.i^{va}, 16-26 (*De casu diaboli*, 8); e.i^{va}, 40 plus manuscript material omitted in the Perez edition (*Cur Deus homo*, 2, cc. 11, 14, 20).

25. Q.I, C.VIII: e.ii^{rb}, 14-16 (*Cur Deus homo*, 1, 21).

26. Q.II: e.iii^{rb}, 14-26 (*Monologion*, 78).

27. Q.II: e.vi^{rb}, 28-31 (*Monologion*, 78).

28. Q.II: e.iiii^{rb}, 13-15 (*Monologion*, 78).

29. Q.II: e.iiii^{va}, 18-19 (*De processione spiritus sancti*).

30. Discussed in Courtenay , 'John of Mirecourt', pp. 105ff.

31. Q.III, Art.I: e.vi^{va}, 11-15 (*Cur Deus homo*, 2, 17; *Proslogion*, 7).

32. Q.III, Art.I: e.vii^{va}, 36-40 (*Cur Deus homo*, 2, 17).

33. Q.III, Art.I: e.viii^{va}, 16-26 (*Cur Deus homo*, 2, 17; *Proslogion*, 7); e.viii^{vb}, 9-18 (*De concordia*, 1, 2 [given as 1, 4]); e.viii^{vb}, 18-27 (*De concordia*, 1, 5 [given as *et post*]); f.i^{vb}, 8-16 (*De casu diaboli*, 1).

34. Q.III, Art.I: f.iii^{vb}, 19-24 (*Cur Deus homo*, 2, 10); f.iiii^{va}, 11-16 (*Meditatio redemptionis humanae*).

35. Q.III, Art.II: f.vii^{rb}, 23-6 (*De concordia*, 1, 3 [given as 1, 4]); f.vii^{va}, 36-9 (*Cur Deus homo*, 2, cc. 5, 17; *De concordia*, 1, 3 [given as 1, 3]).

36. Q.III, Art.II: f.viii^{ra}, 19-21 (*De concordia*, 1, 2 [given as 1, 4]; *Cur Deus homo*, 2, 17).

37. Q.III, Art.II: f.viii^{rb}, 6-10 (*Cur Deus homo*, 2, 17; *De concordia*, 1, 2 [given as 1, 4]).

38. Q.III, Art.II: f.viii^{va}, 26-30 (*De concordia*, 1, 2 [given as 1, 4]); f.viii^{va}, 30-5 (*Cur Deus homo*, 2, 17 [given as 2, 7]).

39. Q.III, Art.II: g.i^{ra}, 35-41 (*Cur Deus homo*, 2, 17); g.i.^{ra}, 41-5 (*De concordia*, 1, 2-3 [given as 1, 3-4]).

40. Q.III, Art.II: g.i.^{rb}, 27-32 (*De concordia*, 1, 2 [given as 1, 4]; *Cur Deus homo*, 2, 17).

41. Q.III, Art.II: g.ii^{ra}, 5-7 (*Cur Deus homo*, 2, 16-17); g.ii^{ra}, 7-8 (*De concordia*, 1, 2 [given as 1, 4]).

42. Q.III, Art.II: g.iii^{vb}, 35-7 (*De casu diaboli*, 12).

43. Q.III, Art.II: g.vi^{va}, 12-17 (*Cur Deus homo*, 1, 24); g.vi^{va}, 17-22 (*De conceptu virginali*, 29).

44. Q.IV: h.v^{va}, 6-15 (*De casu diaboli*, 5).

45. Q.IV: h.v^{va}, 16-21 (*De casu diaboli*, 12).

46. Q.IV: h.vii^{rb}, 36-42 (*Cur Deus homo*, 1, 24; *De conceptu virginali*, 29).

47. Q.V: i.i^{ra}, 46 - i.i^{rb}, 3 (*Monologion*, 21).

48. Q.V: i.viii^{ra}, 29-33 (*De concordia*, 3, 9 [given as 3, 34]); i.viii^{ra}, 37-41 (*Proslogion*, 2-4); i.viii^{rb}, 14 - i.viii^{va}, 10 (*Proslogion*, 2); i.viii^{rb}, 36 - i.viii^{va}, 4 (*Contra responsionem pro insipiente*, 1 [no capitula given]); i.viii^{va}, 4-10 (*Contra responsionem pro insipiente*, 4 (no capitula given]); i.viii^{va}, 10-17 (*Contra responsionem pro insipiente*, 3 [no capitula given]); i.viii^{va}, 17-27 (*Contra responsionem insipiente*, 1 [no capitula given]); i.viii^{va}, 31 - i.viii^{vb}, 4 (*Responsionem pro insipiente*, 6 [given as *in principio*]); i.viii^{vb}, 19-33 (*Contra responsionem pro insipiente*, 10 [no capitula given]); i.viii^{vb}, 46 - k.i^{ra}, 13 (*Proslogion*, 4).

49. The text of this discussion is extremely confused, both in the manuscripts and in the Perez edition. It is hoped that a future article, containing a critical edition and an examination of the historical context of the discussion, will clarify both the text and its setting.

50. Q.VI, Art.II: l.i^{ra}, 5-7 (*Cur Deus homo*, 1, 24; *De conceptu virginali*, 29).

51. Q.VI, Art.III: l.iiii^{rb}, 35-9 (*De casu diaboli*, 1).

52. Q.VI, Art.III: l.iiii^{va}, 5-20 (*De casu diaboli*, 2-4).

53. Q.VI, Art.III: l.iiii^{va}, 30 - l.iiii^{vb}, 2 (*De casu diaboli*, 16); l.iii^{vb}, 4-9 (*De casu diaboli*, 18 [no capitula given]).

54. Q.VI, Art.III: l.v^{ra}, 18-21 (*De conceptu virginali*, 19).

55. Q.VI, Art.III: l.v^{rb}, 8-13 plus manuscript material omitted in the Perez edition (*De concordia*, 1, 6 [given as 1, 10]; *De concordia*, 1, 6 [given as 1, 11]; *De libero arbitrio*, 8).

56. Q.VI, Art.III: l.v^{rb}, 43 - l.v^{va}, 1 (*De veritate*, 10 [no *capitula* given], 13 [given as *versus finem*]).

57. Q.VI, Art.III: l.vi^{ra}, 25-31 (*Cur Deus homo*, 1, 11); l.vi.^{ra}, 31-6 (*De concordia*, 1, 6 [given as 1, 10]).

58. Q.VI, Art.III: m.ii^{va}, 4-9 (*De casu diaboli*, 16).

59. Q.VI, Art.III: m.ii^{vb}, 6-8 plus manuscript material omitted in the Perez edition (*De conceptu virginali*, 24; *Cur Deus homo*, 1, 18).

60. Q.VI, Art.V: n. ii^{rb}, 31-6 (*Monologion*, 70).

61. Q.VI, Art.V: n.ii^{va}, 32-8 (*De casu diaboli*, 12-13 [given as 13]; n.ii^{vb}, 1-6 (*De casu diaboli*, 12); n.ii^{vb}, 11-25 (*De casu diaboli*, 13); n.ii^{vb}, 25-8 (*De casu diaboli*, 23 [given as 13 or 33]).

62. Q.VI, Art.V: n.vi^{ra}, 27-30 (*De casu diaboli*, 13).

63. Q.VI, Art.V: n.ii^{vb}, 35-41 (*De casu diaboli*, 21 and 23).

64. Q.VI, Art.V: n.iiii^{vb}, 1-5 (*De conceptu virginali*, 4).

65. Q.VI, Art.V: n.v^{ra}, 30-5 (*De libero arbitrio*, 5); n.v^{rb}, 6-9 (*De libero arbitrio*, 5); n.v^{rb}, 6-18 (*De libero arbitrio*, 6-7 [given as 6-8]).

66. Q.VI, Art.V: n.v^{va}, 30-5 (*De similitudinibus*, 170 [given as 189]).

67. Q.VI, Art.V: n.v^{vb}, 2-6 (*De similitudinibus*, 122 [given as 130]).

68. Q.VI, Art.V: n.v^{vb}, 19-24 (*De casu diaboli*, 12-13 [given as 13]).

69. Q.VI, Art.V: n.vii^{vb}, 23-30 (*Cur Deus homo*, 2, cc. 10, 17).

70. Q.VI, Art.V: n.viii^{va}, 7-21 (*De veritate*, 8).

71. Q.VI, Art.VI: o.i^{rb}, 38 - o.i^{va}, 2 (*Cur Deus homo*, 1, 11).

72. Q.VI, Art.VI: o.iiii^{va}, 5-6 (*De veritate*).

73. Q.VI, Art.VI: o.iiii^{va}, 36 - o.iiii^{vb}, 3 (*Cur Deus homo*, 1, 11).

74. Q.VI, Art.VI: o.v^{ra}, 20-5 (*De conceptu virginali*, 4-5).

75. Q.VI, Art.VI: o.vi^{ra}, 9-17 (*Cur Deus homo*, 1, 12).

76. Q.VI, Art.VI: o.vi^{rb}, 10-13 (*De conceptu virginali*, 4-5).

77. Q.VI, Art.VI: o.viii^{rb}, 26-34 (*De conceptu virginali*, 24).

78. Q.VI, Art.VI: o.viii^{va}, 4-10 (*De concordia*, 3, 3 [given as 3, 23]).

79. Q.VI, Art.VI: o.viii^{va}, 16-23 (*De conceptu virginali*, 24); o.viii^{va}, 23-7 (*De conceptu virginali*, 2).

80. Q.VI, Art.VI: p.ii^{ra}, 13-21 (*Cur Deus homo*, 1, 21).

81. Q.VI, Art.VI: p.iii^{rb}, 4-15 (*Cur Deus homo*, 1, 11; *Meditatio ad concitandum timorem*; *De similitudinibus*, 8 [given as 9]).

82. Q.VI, Art.VI: p.iiii^{vb}, 25-31 (*De conceptu virginali*, 13).

83. Q.VI, Art.VI: p.vi^{rb}, 23-5 (*Cur Deus homo*, 2, 14); p.vi^{va}, 5-20 (*Cur Deus homo*, 2, 15); p.vi^{va}, 21 - p.vi^{vb}, 4 (*Cur Deus homo*, 2, 15).

84. Q.VI, Art. VI: p.viii^{vb}, 9-14 (*Cur Deus homo*, 2, 15).

85. In Q.I, C.VIII: d.vi^{rb}, 23-8 (see note 21 above), a partial quotation from the Anselmian book *De similitudinibus* is refuted by the remainder of the passage at e.ii^{ra}, 17-23 (see note 22 above). In Q.V: i.i^{ra}, 46 - i.i^{rb}, 3 (see note 47 above), Buckingham gives a very misleading partial quotation from the *Monologion*, 21. A similarly misleading partial quotation from William of Auxerre in the *Questiones super Sententias* is recorded in Courtenay, 'John of Mirecourt', pp. 151-2.

86. See H. Oberman, *Archbishop Thomas Bradwardine*, pp. 70-2, for Bradwardine's use of Anselm on this subject.

87. 'Respondeo et dico quod argumenta Anselmi sunt bona et sufficienter probant deum esse summum bonum, omnipotentem, et sic de consimilibus.' Perez, i.viii^{vb}, 6-9, corrected by the manuscripts.

88. 'Dicunt tamen multi quod Anselmus fuit in istis argument-ationibus sophistice deceptus, sed credo quod tales non intelligunt argumenta sua, que sibi per inspirationem fuerunt revelata.' Perez, i.viii^{vb}, 33-8, corrected by the manuscripts.

89. 'Ecce quam confidenter et presumptuose loquitur Anselmus de istis argumentis.' Perez, i.viii^{vb}, 17-19, corrected by the manuscripts.

An index to the references to St Anselm
in the *Questiones super Sententias* of Thomas of Buckingham

*Boldface references to passages in the 'Questiones super Sententias'
are to Lee, 'Thomas of Buckingham'; references in normal type are
to the printed Perez edition.*

Cur Deus homo	*Questiones super Sententias*	References in Perez or **Lee**
1, 11	Q.VI, Art.III	l.vi^{ra}, 25-31
	O.VI, Art.VI	o.i^{rb}, 38 - o.i^{va}, 2
		o.iiii^{va}, 36 - o.iiii^{vb}, 3
		p.iii^{rb}, 4-151
1, 11-15	Q.I, C.VII	c.vi^{ra}, 28-33
1, 12	Q.VI, Art.VI	o.vi^{ra}, 9-17
1, 18	Q.VI, Art.III	m.ii^{vb}, 6-8
1, 20	Q.I, C.II	**C.II, 499**
1, 21	Q.I, C.VI	c.iii^{rb}, 4-5
	Q.I, C.VII	d.v^{rb}, 36-9
	Q.I, C.VIII	d.v^{vb}, 38-41
		d.vi^{ra}, 2-15
		d.vi^{vb}, 1-6
		e.ii^{rb}, 14-16
	Q.VI, Art.VI	p.ii^{ra}, 13-21
1, 22 *et seqq*	Q.I, C.VIII	d.vi^{vb}, 6-8
1, 24	Q.III, Art.II	g.vi^{va}, 12-17
	Q.IV	h.vii^{rb}, 36-42
	Q.VI, Art.II	l.i^{ra}, 5-6
2, 5	Q.III, Art.II	f.vii^{va}, 36-9
2, 6	Q.I, C.VIII	d.vi^{vb}, 9-13
2, 10	Q.III, Art.I	f.iii^{vb}, 19-24
	Q.VI, Art.V	n.vii^{vb}, 23-30
2, 11	Q.I, C.VIII	e.i^{va}, 40 + MS material
2, 14	Q.I, C.III	b.iii^{va}, 30-5

Cur Deus homo (cont.)	Questiones super Sententias	References in Perez or Lee
2, 14 (cont.)	Q.I, C.VI	c.iii^rb, 5-6
	Q.I, C.VIII	d.vi^ra, 15-16
		d.vi^va, 43 - d.vi^vb, 1
		e.i^va, 40 + MS material
	Q.VI, Art.VI	p.vi^rb, 23-5
2, 15	Q.VI, Art.VI	p.vi^va, 5-20
		p.vi^va, 21 - p.vi^vb, 4
		p.viii^vb, 9-14
2, 16	Q.I, C.II	C.II, 415
	Q.I, C.VII	c.vi^vb, 15-20
	Q.III, Art.II	g.ii^ra, 5-7
2, 17	Q.III, Art.I	e.vi^va, 11-15
		e.vii^va, 36-40
		e.viii^va, 16-26
2, 17	Q.III, Art.II	f.vii^va, 36-9
		f.viii^ra, 19-21
		f.viii^rb, 6-10
		f.viii^va, 30-5
		g.i^ra, 35-41
		g.i^rb, 27-32
		g.ii^ra, 5-7
	Q.VI, Art.V	n.vii^vb, 23-30
2, 20	Q.I, C.VIII	e.i^va, 40 + MS material

De casu diaboli

1	Q.I, C.II	C.II, 402
	Q.III, Art.I	f.i^vb, 8-16
	Q.VI, Art.III	l.iiii^rb, 35-9
2	Q.VI, Art.III	l.iiii^va, 5-12

De casu diaboli (cont.)	*Questiones super Sententias*	References in Perez or **Lee**
3, 4	Q.VI, Art.III	l.iiiiva, 11-20
5	Q.IV	h.vva, 6-15
8	Q.I, C.VIII	e.iva, 16-26
9	Q.I, C.I	**C.I, 90**
12	Q.III, Art.II	g.iiivb, 35-7
	Q.IV	h.vva, 16-21
	Q.VI, Art.V	n.iivb, 1-6
12, 13	Q.VI, Art.V	n.iiva, 32-8
		n.vvb, 19-24
13	Q.VI, Art.V	n.iivb, 11-25
		n.vira, 27-30
16	Q.I, C.I	**C.I, 93**
	Q.VI, Art,III	l.iiiiva, 31 - l.iiiivb, 2
		m.iiva, 4-9
18	Q.VI, Art.III	l.iiiivb, 4-9
20	Q.I, C.I	**C.I, 94**
21, 23	Q.VI, Art.V	n.iivb, 25-41
23	Q.VI, Art.V	n.iivb, 25-8
26	Q.I, C.I	**C.I, 181**

De concordia

To the work as a whole	Q.I,C.VIII	d.vira, 38-43
1, 2 [1,4]	Q.III, Art.I	d.viiivb, 9-18
	Q.III, Art.II	f.viiira, 19-21
		f.viiirb, 6-10
		f.viiiva, 26-30
		g.irb, 27-32
		g.iira, 7-8
1, 2-3 [1,3-4]	Q.III, Art.II	g.ira, 41-5

De concordia (cont.)		Questiones super Sententias	References in Perez or **Lee**
1, 3	[1, 4]	Q.III, Art.II	f.vii^{rb}, 23-6
	[1, 3]		f.vii^{va}, 36-9
1, 5	[et post]	Q.III, Art.I	e.viii^{vb}, 18-27
1, 6	[1,10]	Q.VI, Art.III	l.v^{rb}, 8-13
	[1,11]		l.v^{rb}, 13 MS material
	[1,10]		l.vi^{ra}, 31-6
1, 7	[1,13]	Q.I, C.I	C.I, 95
3, 3	[3,23]	Q.VI, Art.VI	o.viii^{va}, 4-10
3, 9	[3,34]	Q.V	l.viii^{ra}, 29-33

De conceptu virginali

2		Q.VI, Art.VI	o.viii^{va}, 23-7
3		Q.I, C.III	b.iiii^{rb}, 40-4
4		Q.VI, Art.V	n.iiii^{vb}, 1-5
4-5		Q.VI, Art.VI	o.v^{ra}, 20-25
			o.vi^{rb}, 10-13
5		Q.I, C.I	**C.I, 94-5**
13		Q.VI, Art.VI	p.iiii^{vb}, 25-31
19		Q.VI, Art.III	l.v^{ra}, 18-21
23		Q.I, C.II	**C.II, 496-7**
24		Q.VI, Art.III	m.ii^{vb}, 6-8
		Q.VI, Art.VI	o.viii^{rb}, 26-34
			o.viii^{va}, 16-23
29		Q.III, Art.II	g.vi^{va}, 17-22
		Q.IV	h.vii^{rb}, 36-42
		Q.VI, Art.II	l.i^{ra}, 6-7

De similitudinibus (Anselmian)

8	[9]	Q.I, C.VII	c.vi^{ra}, 32-3
		Q.VI, Art.VI	p.iii^{rb}, 4-15

De Similitudinibus (cont.)		Questiones super Sententias	References in Perez or **Lee**
122	[130]	Q.VI, Art.V	n.v^{vb}, 2-6
170	[189]	Q.VI, Art.V	n.v^{va}, 30-5
191	[*penultimo*]	Q.I, C.VIII	d.vi^{rb}, 23-8
			e.ii^{ra}, 17-23

Monologion

	Q.V	i.i^{ra}, 46 - i.i^{rb}, 3
21	Q.V	i.i^{ra}, 46 - i.i^{rb}, 3
70	Q.VI, Art.V	n.ii^{rb}, 31-6
71	Q.I, C.VII	d.v^{ra}, 6-10
78	Q.II	e.iii^{rb}, 14-26
		e.iiii^{rb}, 13-15
		e.vi^{rb}, 28-31

Proslogion

2	Q.V	i.viii^{rb}, 14 - i.viii^{va}, 10
2-4	Q.V	i.viii^{ra}, 37-41
4	Q.V	i.viii^{vb}, 46 - k.i^{ra}, 13
7	Q.III	e.vi^{va}, 11-15
		e.viii^{va}, 16-26

Contra responsionem pro insipiente
(No *capitula* given in references)

1	Q.V	i.viii^{rb}, 36 - i.viii^{va}, 4
		i.viii^{va}, 17-27
3	Q.V	i.viii^{vb}, 10-17
4	Q.V	i.viii^{va}, 4-10
10	Q.V	i.viii^{vb}, 19-33

De veritate

To the work as a whole	Q.I, C.VIII	d.vi^{ra}, 38-43

De vertitate (cont.)	*Questiones super Sententias*	References in Perez or **Lee**
	Q.VI, Art.VI	o.iiii^{va}, 5-6
8	Q.VI, Art.VI	n.viii^{va}, 7-21
10	Q.VI, Art.III	l.v^{rb}, 43-l.v^{va}, 1
13 [*versus finem*]	Q.VI, Art.III	l.v^{rb}, 43-l.v^{va}, 1

De libero arbitrio (De libertate arbitrii)

To the work as a whole	Q.I, C.VIII	d.vi^{ra}, 38-43
5	Q.VI, Art.V	n.v^{ra}, 30-5
		n.v^{rb}, 6-9
6-7 [6-8]	Q.VI, Art.V	n.v^{rb}, 6-18
8	Q.VI, Art.III	l.v^{rb}, 8-13

De processione spiritus sancti

To the work as a whole	Q.II	e.iiii^{va}, 18-19

Responsionem pro insipiente (Gaunilo)

6 [*in principio*]	Q.V	i.viii^{va}, 31-i.viii^{vb}, 4

Meditatio redemptionis humanae	*Questiones super Sententias*	References in Perez or **Lee**
To the work as a whole	Q.III	f.iiii^{va}, 11-16

Meditatio ad concitandum timorem
(including 'Terret me vita mea')

To the work as a whole	Q.VI, Art.VI	p.iii^{rb}, 6-9

VII
The Texts

The Hereford *Proslogion*

G.R. Evans

One of the main factors which has made it possible for Anselm's modern editors to distinguish genuine Anselm from unpolished or misreported or imitation Anselm, is the relatively clear trail left by the early manuscript tradition. Anselm seems to have taken care to ensure that his treatises were copied exactly. It is unlikely that any new discoveries will substantially alter the picture or throw seriously into question the work of A. Wilmart and F.S. Schmitt in establishing the texts of his works. The interest of the *Libellus* which was first published half a century ago by E. Druwé lies, not as its editor first supposed, in what it has to tell us about Anselm himself, but in the light it throws on the way in which his works were studied after his death.[1]

This is the case, too, with two texts which occur in a manuscript of the first half of the twelfth century, now Hereford Cathedral Library, MS O.I.vi: some hitherto unnoticed 'sayings' of Anselm, and a text of the *Proslogion* which has been substantially abbreviated. This is a 'plain text' *Proslogion*, stripped of its devotional material, with a number of omissions, re-phrasings and syntactical changes. It must have been composed within a few decades of Anselm's death, or possibly within his lifetime, but its author has defied Anselm's intentions and condensed the *Proslogion* into a pocket-book version.

MS O.I.vi has long been known to contain the text of the *De Motione Altaris* which is edited from this manuscript and two others in the *Memorials of St Anselm*.[2] In 1927, A.T. Bannister noted this work in his catalogue of the Hereford manuscripts,[3] but did not mention the Anselmian material which occurs later, beginning on f. 81. It is easy to understand how it has come to be overlooked. The scribe draws attention to it with a heading in small capitals only at the very end of f. 81. The text itself, which begins on f. 81^V has therefore, at first glance, no heading to indicate the beginning of a new work, and the *incipit* consists of a sentence which occurs in the middle of Chapter 2 of the Schmitt text of the *Proslogion*.

The manuscript was given to the Augustinian Abbey of Cirencester within a generation of so of Anselm's death, by 'Canon Joscelin', during the abbacy of Serlo. A note on f. 89^V states: 'Hunc librum D. Joscelinus Canonicus dedit Deo et ecclesiae beate Marie de Cyrencestre, D. Serlone ibidem tunc Abbate primo'. Hence, the gift can be dated between 1131 and 1147, although there is no reason why the book should not have been copied even earlier.[4] The manuscript contains a dozen items, chiefly homiletic and pastoral writing, notably sermons of Caesarius, Eusebius, Gregory, (Ps.) Augustine, and Jerome, but also some unusual mathematical items which may help to link the collection with the work of the mathematicians of the Severn Wye areas in the late eleventh and early twelfth centuries.[5] The whole has about it the look of a 'school-book' – workmanlike, compact and portable – of the kind used by schoolmasters such as Joscelin himself may have been if it was he who was responsible for compiling the collection, or of adding to it (more than one hand is identifiable).

Some pieces, particularly the mathematical ones, appear either to derive from fragmentary or incomplete exemplars, or to have been abbreviated by the compiler. Diagrams are missing or unfinished; there is no indication of the point at which one piece ends and the next begins, where we move from instruction in the use of the abacus to the rules for playing the *rithmomachia*, for example. The Anselm items are run together, too, with nothing to show that the *Proslogion* has come to an end and the *dicta* begun except a marginal note: 'De rotulo' on f. 83^V, which may suggest that these 'sayings' were copied from a loose membrane.

The Anselm pieces do not form a self-contained unit which could have been bound in with this collection. Whoever filled the notebook put them in as he went. There is nothing to indicate whether he made his abbreviation as he wrote, or whether he copied an existing abbreviation.

It is perhaps of some significance that the manuscript came from Cirencester and is now at Hereford. Some important and unusual early Anselmian manuscripts are to be found in Hereford Cathedral Library (in particular, a unique test of the *De incarnatione verbi*), and some of the earliest manuscripts of the *De humanibus moribus* come from the Hereford and Llanthony area.[6] The Anselmian 'sayings' in Hereford MS O.i.vi include analogies which are closer to those in the *De humanibus moribus* than to any other known accounts of Anselm's sayings. The two earliest manuscripts of this work date from the second or third decade of the twelfth century.[7] Both come from Llanthony. Llanthony Prima was founded in 1103, in Monmouthshire; Llanthony Secunda, which shared a single prior with Llanthony Prima, was founded in 1136 just outside Gloucester. This geographical coincidence, together with the fact that Llanthony Secunda and Cirencester were among the few Augustinian foundations in the area, provides a possible link between Canon Joscelin of Cirencester and the Anselmian manu-scripts at Llanthony. A further coincidence lies in the fact that Robert de Bethune, second Prior of Llanthony Prima, was made Bishop of Hereford in 1131, and continued to take an active interest in the welfare of the house thereafter. All this is far from conclusive, but it does suggest that the ultimate source of the Anselmian material in MS O.I.vi may have been Anselm's texts available at Llanthony.

The *Proslogion* Text[8]

This begins on f. 81^v, following the heading at the bottom of f. 81: 'Anselmi Archiepiscopi de Dictis Quaedam'. No note of the manuscript appears in Schmitt's apparatus, or in the *Ratio Editionis* to the *Anselmi Opera Omnia*, and it seems likely that that he did not know of it. The variant readings of the Hereford version appear to be quite unrelated to the known variants of the *Proslogion* text. The Hereford text has some curious features: almost the whole work is set in the third person, instead of alternately in the second and third person, and most of the devotional material is missing, so that only the central argument and some of its ramifications are there. In places, portions of the argument itself are distinctively phrased. There are no chapter headings, and although the paragraph marks generally correspond with Schmitt's chapter divisions, they do not always do so, and in one place a 'chapter heading' forms part of the sequence of the argument. This may offer a clue as to the date of the abbreviation since Bodleian Library, MS Rawl. A392, one of the most important of the early manuscripts, lacks the chapter headings, and there seems a strong possibility that they do not derive from Anselm or were, at any rate, added some time after the completion of the treatises.

The *Anselmiana*[9]

Some Anselmian 'sayings' follow at the marginal note: 'De Rotulo', on f. 83^v, without any preliminaries other than this indication that these items originally came from a separate leaf. The Anselmian material does not exactly match anything in the *Memorials*, but it introduces in a modified form some of the analogies to be found in the *De humanibus moribus*. The next heading occurs on f. 87^v: 'Incipit Brevarium Apostolorum', but the echoes of Anselm's writings and teaching have ceased to sound long before that — unless some of these items preserve sayings which have not been written down elsewhere. The selection resembles a 'commonplace-book' of *florilegia*, put together from notes made of Anselm's conversation and preaching, perhaps, and from other, non-Anselmian sources, almost certainly. There is no way of telling whether these scraps of Anselm have been retold again and again before they were written down, or whether they are reasonably close to Anselm himself.

It is difficult to do more than guess at the relationship between the *Proslogion* text and the *Anselmiana*. Since he interposes no additional heading, the scribe presumably intended the heading on f. 81 to cover what follows. It is strange that he only made use of the *Proslogion*, since the best of the early manuscripts contain several or all of the treatises.[10] The presence of one work on its own may indicate that the copy our compiler used was of particularly early origin, but the notes of Anselm's sayings could have been made well before Anselm became Archbishop, or at various times afterwards. Anselm made his first visit to England in 1079, and already his gift for talking to the communities he visited made an impression on English listeners.[11] Eadmer describes such occasions.[12] The only detail which suggests that the sayings may have been collected earlier rather than later is the fact that the few quotations from the treatises which they contain are drawn from works completed before Anselm became Archbishop.

These pieces are not to be compared in importance with the material in the Canterbury manuscript which contains the *Philosophical Fragments*. Lambeth Palace Library, MS 59 seems to have been compiled by someone with access to Anselm's literary remains;[13] our compiler cannot have been so close to Anselm. (The fact that the two collections may be roughly contemporary points the contrast sharply.) Their significance lies in the contribution they make to the evidence for the early diffusion of Anselm's treatises immediately outside the ambit of his friends and household. No one who knew Anselm well enough to understand and respect his wishes about the copying of his treatises could have compiled this collection. And yet the compiler had access to Anselmian material which has not survived elsewhere. His source was not by any means remote from Anselm.

NOTES

1. E. Druwé, *Libri Sancti Anselmi: 'Cur Deus homo' Prima Forma Inedita*, Rome, 1933). The publication of this text led to a prolonged correspondence. See J. Rivière, 'Un premier jet du *Cur Deus homo?*', *Revue des sciences religieuses*, 14 (1934), 1-41; E. Druwé, 'La première rédaction du *Cur Deus homo* de S. Anselme', *Revue d'histoire ecclésiastique*, 31 (1935), 501-40; J. Rivière, 'La question du *Cur Deus homo*', *Revue des sciences religieuses*, 16 (1936), 1-32. See also *Ans.Op.Om.*, I, 93-139.

2. *Mem.Ans.*, pp. 320-2.

3. For a detailed description of the manuscript, see A.T. Bannister, *A Descriptive Catalogue of the Manuscripts in Hereford Cathedral Library* (Hereford, 1927) pp. 9-10. See, too, a brief reference to the manuscript in W. St. Clair Baddeley, *A History*

of Cirencester (Cirencester, 1924), and a longer description in T.W. Williams, 'Gloucestershire mediaeval libraries', *Transactions of the Bristol and Gloucestershire Archaeological Society*, 21 (1908), 105-6. On the way in which the manuscript came to be at Hereford, see N.R. Ker, *The Library*, fifth series, 10 (1955), 1-24.

4. Joscelin seems to have given a number of books to the library. See Williams, 'Mediaeval libraries', p. 104 on British Library, MS Cotton Vespasian A XV, and p. 106 on Hereford Cathedral Library, MS O.1.x.

5. Of especial note is a copy of Garlandus Compotista's, *Liber de Abaco*, which begins on f. 70^V and is followed by part of Hermannus Contractus' instructions for using a fraction table (f. 76), a piece of a commentary on Gerbert of Aurillac's, *Regulae Abaci* (also on f. 76) and a *rithmomachia*, or number-game (ff. 76-8). The Garlandus text begins in a new hand, under a line drawn across the page, and after the mathematical pieces three folios have been excised. See G.R. Evans, 'The *rithmomachia*: a mediaeval mathematical teaching aid?', *Janus*, 63 (1976), 257-73 on the number-game.

6. *Mem.Ans.*, p. 11, and see p. 361 for a list of Anselmian manuscripts at Hereford. Of special note is MS P.I.i, which contains an important early recension of the *De incarnatione verbi*, see *Ans.Op.Om.*, II, 2.

7. *Mem.Ans.*, pp. 15-17.

8. See p. 258 for the text of the Hereford *Proslogion*.

9. See p. 264 for the text of the *Anselmiana*.

10. See Schmitt's, *Indices Siglorum* and the *Ratio Editionis* to Vol. I of the *Ans.Op.Om.*

11. R.W. Southern, *Saint Anselm and his Biographer* (Cambridge, 1963), pp. 217-26.

12. *The Life of St Anselm, Archbishop of Canterbury, by Eadmer*, edited by R.W. Southern (London, 1962), Chapter 31.

13. *Mem.Ans.*, pp. 34, 272-88, 333-53.

The Proslogion

[f. 81] ANSELMI ARCHIEPISCOPI DE DICTIS QUAEDAM

[II]
[f. 81^V] Aliud est rem esse in intellectu, aliud intelligere rem esse. Nam cum pictor praecogitat que facturus est, habet quod [for: quidem] in intellectu, sed nondum intelligit esse, quod nondum fecit. Cum vero iam pinxit, et habet in intellectu, et intelligit esse, quod iam fecit. Similiter insipiens homo convincitur esse vel in intellectu aliquid, quo nihil maius cogitari potest, scilicet deum, quia cum audit hoc dici intelligit aliquo modo, et quod intelligit, in intellectu eius aliquatenus est, etsi non intelligat illud esse, quia quicquid intelligitur in intellectu est. Et certe id quo maius cogitari nequit, non potest esse, in [solo] intellectu. Si enim vel in solo intellectu esset, posset cogitari esse, et in re, quod maius est. Sed si id quo maius cogitari non potest, esset in solo intellectu, id ipsum quo maius cogitari non potest, esset quo maius cogitari potest. Sed hoc de deo esse non potest.[1]

[IV]
Non uno tantummodo dicitur aliquid in corde [vel] cogitatur. Aliter enim cogitatur res cum vox eam significans cogitatur, aliter cum id ipsum quod res est intelligitur. Illo itaque modo potest cogitari deus non esse, isto vero minime. Nullus quippe intelligens id quod deus est, potest cogitare quia deus non est, licet haec verba dicat in corde, aut sine ulla, aut cum aliqua extranea significatione. Deus enim est id quo maius cogitari nequit. Quod qui bene intelligit, utique intelligit id ipsum sic esse, ut nec cogitatione queat non esse. Qui ergo sic deum intelligit esse, nequit eum non esse cogitare.[2]

[VI]
Cum melius sit esse sensibilem, omnipotentem, misericordem, impassibilem, quam non esse, quomodo est deus sensibilis, si non est corpus, aut omnipotens, si omnia non potest, aut misericors simul et impassibilis? Nam si sola corporea sunt sensibilia, quoniam sensus circa corpus et in corpore sunt; quomodo est sensibilis deus cum non sit corpus sed summus spiritus, qui corpore melior est? Sed si sentire non nisi cognoscere est, qui enim sensit, cognoscit secundum sensum proprietatem, ut per visum colores, per gustum sapores, non inconvenienter dicitur aliquo modo sentire, quicquid aliquo modo cognoscit. Ergo deus quamvis non sit corpus, vere tamen eo modo sensibilis est quo summa omni cognoscit, non quo animal corporeo sensu cognoscit.[3]

[VII]
Et omnipotens quomodo est, si omnia non potest? Nam si non potest corrumpi nec mentiri nec facere verum esse falsum, aut quod factum est nec esse factum, et plura similiter, quomodo potest

omnia? Sed haec posse non est potentia, sed impotentia. Nam qui hoc potest, quod sibi non expedit, et quod non debet potest, quod quanto magis potest, tanto magis adversitas et perversitas possunt in illum, et ipse minus contra illas. Qui ergo sic potest, non potentia potest, sed impotentia. Non enim ideo dicitur posse, quia ipse possit, quia suam impotentiam [for: *sua impotentia*] facit aliud in se posse; sine [for: sive] aliquo alio genere loquendi, sicut multa improprie dicuntur. Ut cum ponimus, esse non pro [for: pro non] esse, et facere pro eo quod non est facere, aut pro nihil facere. Nam [f. 82] saepe dicimus ei qui rem aliquam esse negat, sic est quemadmodum dicis esse, cum magis proprie videatur dici sic non est quemadmodum dicis non esse. Item dicimus: 'Iste sedet' sicut: 'Ille facit', aut: 'Iste quiescit' sicut: 'Ille facit', cum sedere sit quiddam non facere, et quiescere sit nihil facere. Sic itaque cum quis dicitur habere potentiam faciendi aut patiendi quod sibi non expedit aut quod non debet, impotentia intelligitur per potentiam, quia quo plus habet hanc potentiam, eo adversitas et perversitas in illum sunt potentiores, et ille contra eas impotentior. Et non ergo deus verius est omnipotens, quia nihil potest per impotentiam, et nihil potest contra eum.[4]

[VIII]
Et quomodo est deus misericors simul et impassibilis? Nam si est impassibilis, non compatitur; si non compatitur, non est ei miserum cor ex compassione miseri, quod est misericordem. Aut si non est misericors, unde miseris est tanta consolatio? Quomodo ergo est et non misericors, nisi quia est misericors secundum nos, et non secundum se? Est quod secundum nostrum sensum, et non est secundum suum. Etenim cum ipse respicit nos miseros, nos sentimus misericordis effectum, sed ipse non sentit affectum. Et misericors est, quia miseros salvat et peccatoribus suis parcit, et misericors non est, quia nulla miseriae compassione afficitur.[5]

[IX]
Cum deus sit summe iustus et totus quare parcit malis, cum parcere illis iniustum esse videatur? Quae enim iustitia est merenti mortem aeternam dare vitam sempiternam? Unde ergo, bono deo procedit salvare et malos, si hoc non est iustum, et ipse non facit aliquod iniustum? Sed sciendum est quia bonitas dei est incomprehensibilis, et hoc latet in luce illa inaccessibili quam ipse bonus inhabitat, unde manat fluvius misericordiae ipsius. Nam cum totus et summe iustus sit, tamen idcirco et malis benignus est, quia totus summe bonus est. Minus namque bonus esset, si nulli malo esset benignus. Melior enim est qui et bonis et malis bonus est, quam qui bonis tantum bonus est. Et melior est qui malis et puniendo et parcendo est bonus, quam qui puniendo tantum. Ideo ergo misericors est, quia totus et summe bonus est. Et cum forsitan videatur cur bonis bona, et malis mala retribuat, illud certe penitus mirandum est, cur deus

ipse totus iustus et nullo egens, malis et reis suis bona tribuat. O
altitudo bonitatis tuae, deus, et videtur unde sis misericors, et non
pervidetur. Cernitur unde flumen manat, et non perspicitur unde
fluminis fons nascatur. Nam et de plenitudine bonitatis est quia
peccatoribus tuis pius es, et in altitudine bonitatis latet, qua ratione
hoc es. Etenim domine licet bonis bona et malis mala ex bonitate
retribuas, ratio tamen iustitiae hoc postulare videtur. Cum vero
malis vel bona tribuis, et scitur quia summe bonus hoc facere
voluit, et mirum est cur summe bonus vel iustus hoc velle potuit. O
immensitas bonitatis dei, quo affectu amanda es peccatoribus. Justus
enim salvas, iustitia comitante, peccatores vero liberas iustitia
dampnante. [f. 82a] Illo meritis adiuvantibus, istos meritis
repugnantibus. Illos bona quae dedisti cognoscendo, istos mala quae
odisti ignoscendo.[6]

Et cum difficile sit intelligere, quomodo misericordia des
numquam absit a bonis, iustitia tamen necesse est credi, quia
numquam absit ab eius iustitia, necesse tamen est, quia numquam
adversatur iustitiae, quod exundat ex eius bonitate, quae nulla est
sine iustitia, immo vere concordat iustitiae. Ideo enim deus
misericors est quia iustus est, et quodammodo oritur misericordia
eius ex ipsius iustitia. Quod cum ita sit, quaeritur an ex iustitia
parcat deus malis, quod sic esse dicitur. Est et enim iustum deum
sic esse bonum, ut nequeat intelligi melior, et sic potenter operari,
ut non possit cogitari potentius? Quod utique non fieret, si ipse
esset bonus tantum retribuendo et non parcendo, et si faceret de
non bonis tantum bonos, et non etiam de malis. Hoc itaque modo
iustum est ut parcat malis, et faciat et bonos de malis.[7]

[X]
Et iterum iustum est, ut deus malos puniat. Quid namque iustius
quam ut boni bona, et mali mala recipiant? Quomodo ergo et iustum
est ut malos puniat, et iustum est ut malis parcat? An alio modo
iuste punit malos, et alio modo iuste parcit malis? Cum enim punit
malos, iustum est, quia illorum meritis convenit; cum vero parcit
malis, iustum est, non quia illorum meritis, sed quia bonitati dei
condecens est. Nam parcendo malis ita iustus est secundum se et
non secundum nos, sicut misericors, est secundum nos et non
secundum se. Nam salvando nos quos iuste perderet, sicut misericors
est non quia ipse sentiat affectum, sed quia nos sentimus effectum.
Ita iustus est non quia nobis reddat debitum, sed quia facit quod
decet se summe bonum. Sic itaque sine repugnantia iuste punit, et
iuste parcit.[8]

[XI]
Iustum est et, scilicet in ipsum deum, ut malos puniat. Justum
quippe est illum sic esse iustum, ut iustior nequeat cogitari. Quod
nequaquam esset, si tantum bonis bona, et non malis mala redderet.
Iustior enim est qui et bonis et malis, quam qui bonis tantum

merita retribuit. Iustum igitur est secundum deum iustum et
benignum, et cum punit et cum parcit. All[   ] universae viae
domini misericordia et veritas, et tamen iustus dominus in omnibus
viis suis. Et hae utique sine repugnantia, quia quos vult perire vel
punire, non est iustum salvare, et quibus vult parcere, non est
iustum dampnare. Nam id solum iustum est quod vult, et non iustum
quod non vult. Sic ergo nascitur de iustitia dei misericordia ipsius,
quia iustum sic esse bonum, ut et parcendo sit bonus. Et hoc est
forsitan, cur summe iustus potest velle bona malis. Sed si utcumque
capi potest, cur malos potest velle salvare deus, illud certe nulla
ratione potest comprehendi, cur de similibus malis hos magis salvet
quam illos per summam bonitatem, et illos magis dampnet quam
istos per summam iustitiam. Sic ergo vere est deus sensibilis,
omnipotens, misericors et impassibilis, quemadmodum vivens, sapiens,
bonus, beatus, aeternus, et quicquid melius est esse quam non esse.[9]

[XII]
[f. 83] Sed certe quicquid est deus, non per aliud est quam per
seipsum. Est igitur deus vita ipsa qua vivit, et sapientia qua sapit,
et bonitas ipsa qua bonis et malis bonus est; et ita de similibus.[10]

[XIII]
Sed omne quod clauditur aliquatenus loco aut tempore, minus est
quam quod nulla lex loci aut temporis coercet. Quoniam ergo maius
deo nihil est, nullus locus aut tempus illum cohibet, sed ubique et
semper est. Quod quia de deo solo dici potest, ipse solus
incircumscriptus. Quomodo ergo dicuntur et alii spiritus
incircumscripti et aeterni? Et quidem solus deus est aeternus, quia
solus omnium sicut non desinit, sic non incipit esse. Sed solus
quomodo est incircumscriptus? An creatus spiritus ad eum collatus
est circumscriptus, ad corpus vero ut circumpscriptus? Nempe
omnino circumscriptum est quod cum alicubi totum est, non potest
simul esse alibi; quod de solis corporeis cernitur. Incircumpscriptum
vero, quod simul est in quibus totum; quod de deo solo intelligitur.
Circumscriptum autem et incircumscriptum simul est, quod cum
alicubi sit totum, potest simul esse totum alibi, non tamen ubique;
quod de creatis spiritibus agnoscitur. Si enim non esset anima tota
in singulis membris sui corporis, non sentiret tota in singulis. Est
ergo deus singulariter incircumscriptus et aeternus, et tamen etiam
alii spiritus sunt incircumscripti et aeterni.[11]

[XV]
Deus non solum est quo maius cogitari nequit, sed est quiddam
maius quam cogitari possit. Valet namque cogitari esse aliquod
huiusmodi, quod si deus non est, potest cogitari aliquid maius ipso;
quod fieri nequit.[12]

[XVIII]
In illo omnes perdidimus, qui facile tenebat, et male sibi et nobis
perdidit, quod cum volumus quaerere nescimus, cum quaerimus non

invenimus, cum invenimus non est quod quaeramus. Cum deus sit vita, sapientia, veritas et cetera his similia, videndum est quomodo ipse omnia haec sit. Scilicet utrum haec talia est sint partes ipsius an unumquodque horum est totum quod deus est. Sed partes ipsius esse non possunt. Nam quicquid partibus est iunctum, non est omnino unum, sed quodammodo plura et diversum a seipso, et vel actu vel intellectu dissolvi potest. Nullae igitur partes sunt in deo, nec ipse est plura, sed sic est ipse unum quiddam et idem sibi ipsi, ut in nullo sibi ipsi sit dissimilis, immo ipse est ipsa unitas, nullo intellectu divisibilis. Ergo vita et sapientia et cetera non sunt partes dei, sed omnia sunt unum, et unumquodque horum est totum quod deus est et quod sunt reliqua omnia. Quoniam ergo nec deus habet partes, nec eius aeternitas quae ipse est nusquam et numquam est pars eius aut aeternitatis eius, sed ubique totus est, et aeternitas ipsius tota est semper.[13]

[XIX]
Sed si per aeternitatem suam fuit deus et est et erit, et fuisse non est futurum esse, et esse non fuisse vel futurum esse, quaerendum est quomodo aeternitas dei tota est semper? Si enim semper est ergo heri fuit et cras erit. Sed de eternitate dei nichil praeterit ut iam non sit, nec aliquid futurus est quasi nondum sit. Non ergo dicendum est de deo fuit, aut erit cras, sed heri nec hodie nec cras est, sed simpliciter est extra omne tempus. Nam nihil est aliud hodie heri, et cras, quam esse in tempore, deus autem licet nihil sit sine eo, non est tamen in tempore aut in loco, sed omnia sunt in eo. Nihil enim deum continet, sed ipse continet omnia.[14]

[XX]
Deus vero implet et complectitur omnia, et ipse est ante et ultra omnia. Ante omnia est, quia antequam fierent ipse est. Ultra omnia vero quomodo est? Qualiter enim est ultra ea quae finem non habebunt? Hoc modo scilicet quia illa sine deo nullatenus esse possunt, deus autem nullo modo minus est, etsi illa redeant in nihilum? Sic enim quodammodo est deus ultra illa. Vel hoc modo, quia cogitari possunt habere finem, deus vero nullo modo, et certe quod nullo modo habet finem, ultra illud est quod aliquo modo finitur. Vel hoc modo transit deus omnia etiam aeterna, quia eius et illorum aeternitas tota ipsi deo praesens est, cum illa nondum habeant de sua aeternitate quod venturum est, sicut iam non habent quod praeteritum est. Sic quippe semper est ultra illa, cum semper ibi sit praesens, seu cum semper illud sit ei praesens, ad quod illa nondum pervenerunt.[15]

[XXI]
Hoc et est saeculum saeculi sive saecula saeculorum. Sicut enim saeculum temporum continet omnia temporalia, sic tua aeternitas continet etiam ipsa saecula temporum. Quae eternitas dicitur secundum quod propter indivisibilem unitatem, saecula vero propter

interminabiliem immensitatem. Quamvis deus ita sit magnus, ut omnia sint eo plena et in eo sint, sic tamen est sine omni spatio, ut nec medium nec dimidium nec ulla pars sit in eo.[16]

[XXII]

Est igitur deus quod est, et est qui est. Nam quod aliud est in toto et aliud in partibus, et in quo aliquid est mutabile, non omnino est quod est. Et quod incepit a non esse et potest cogitari non esse, et nisi per aliud subsistat redit in non esse, et quod habet fuisse quod iam non est, et futurum esse quod nondum est, id non est proprie et absolute. Deus vero proprie est quod est, quia quicquid aliquando aut aliquomodo est, hoc totus et semper est, et ipse simpliciter est, quia nec habet fuisse nec futurum esse, sed tantum praesens esse, nec potest cogitari aliquando non esse. Est itaque vita et lux et sapienta, et beatitudo et aeternitas et multa huiusmodi bona et tamen non est nisi unum et summum bonum, quo omnia indigent ut sint, et ut bene sint.[17]

NOTES (to the *Proslogion*)

All references are to *Ans.Op.Om.*, I.

1. 101:7-20.

2. 101:18-102:4.

3. 104:20-105:6.

4. 105:9-106:2.

5. 106:4-14.

6. 106:18-107:26.

7. 108:2-16.

8. 108:23-109:6.

9. 109:10-110:3.

10. 110:5-8.

11. 110:12-111:5.

12. 112:14-17.

13. 114:5-115:4.

14. 115:7-15.

15. 115:18-116:3.

16. 116:6-12.

17. 116:15-117:2.

The Anselmiana

DE ROTOLO

[f. 83^v] Sicut paterfamilias aliquam herbam nimium dulcem prohibente medico biberet, unde ipse et tota eius progenies lepram contraheret, ac demum medicus volens infirmitati eius consulere, iuberet herbam nimium austeram bibere, ut post parvam dormitionem perfectam recuperaret sanitatem. Sic Adam pater noster dulcem herbam proprie voluntatis bibit; unde ipse et tota eius successio interiit, quia eandem bibere non desistit. Volens autem deus verus medicus huic morbo mederi, prohibuit propriae voluntatis dulcedinem et adhibuit obedientis voluntatis austeritatem, ut post somnum mortis perfectae gloriae sanitatem mereretur manscisci.

Sic trium ramorum ex eadem radice procedentium medius huic vel huic fisso cortice, unum cum eo efficitur; [f. 84] sic voluntas toto nisu cohaerendo ratione vel appetitui non solum unum cum eo efficitur, sed et alterum secum trahit ad obsequium illius cui adhiberet.

Quamvis iustus non semper actum iustitiae exerceat, tamen nihilominus iustus reputatur, ex bono mentis habitu, virtus namque non ex actu sed ex habitu iudicatur. Unde dicitur: 'Virtus est habitus bene constituae mentis'.[1] Inde Horatius: 'Virtus est fugere vitium, sapientia prima, stultitia caruisse'.[2] 'Iustitia est rectitudo voluntatis propter se servata'.[3] 'Unde idem Horatius: 'Oderunt peccare boni virtutis amore'.[4] 'Justititia vero est absentia debitae iniustitiae'.[5] Iustus ergo dicitur propter habitum etsi numquam actus appareat. Sic mater propter habitum filii etsi numquam [ei] lac praebeat.

Duo sunt genera virtutum. Unum interius, aliud exterius. Unum laboriosum et fallax et saepe sine praemio. Aliud facile, veras et utile. Hoc est animum mitem, humilem, patientem, dilectionem ferventem habere. Aliud, corpus ieiuniis afficere, vilibus induere, vocam summam mittere, obstippo capite incedere. Haec sine his quae in animo fiunt, potius nocent quam iuvent. Sine his vero multa bona animi valeat, coniuncta vero perfectio est.

Duobus modis habetur invidia exercitia, vel cum quod aliquis iuste possidet, etsi non habituri quaeramus, tamen eum non possidere optamus, vel ut nos habeamus. Duobus et ex iustitia, cum iniuste possessum ab aliquo vellemus eum non habere ut nos idem habemus, vel ut neuter. Unde Horatius: 'Invidus alterius marcescit rebus optimus'.[6]

Sicut uni domino tres agricolae de fructu pomorum suorum servirent, diverso modo tamen, ita ut unus sine aliquo pacto, sed per libitu suo expectans maturitatem domino suo partem offeret, et sibi partem reservaret. Alius vero videtur sine conventione omnia tamen pomarum velle proprium eidem domino exhiberet. Alius tamen autem totum fructum cum arbore, sive maturum sive immaturum domino traderet ut ipse secundum pacitum summ de fructu cum arbore faceret. Et poma sive matura sive immatura custode suo adhibito tractaret. Ita tripartito ordine deo offerentur homines. Quidam namque sine professione aliqua in opportuno tempore, dum eis placet, obedientiae precumque suarum munus deo offerent, ut saeculares. Alii vero totam vitam suam deo offerent, sed tamen secundum libitum suum hoc faciunt, ut heremitae. Alii vero totam vitam sub professione deo offerent, se ipsos et albati quasi custodi ortus dei tradunt, ut secundum dispositionem suam et actus et voluntates ipsorum deo quasi domino suo preparent et excolant eos. Quod monachi faciunt. [f. 84^V]

Curiositas est studium sciendi ea quae non iuvant ad eternam gloriam, ut mathematica et incantationes mulierum, vel etiam quilibet rumusculi.

Superbia habetur vel in opinionem vel in voluntate, vel in actu simpliciter vel coniunctim.

Naturales appetitus sunt curiositas, superbia, delectatio sensualis et cetera talia. Non naturales sunt ut frangere domum, aggredi hostem.

Tria sunt genera hominum ad similitudinem monetae diversa. Sicut enim quaedam de puro argento vel paveam[7] copri admixtionem habentes, vel etiam usque ad medietatem, sic monachi vel purae oboedientiae militantes, nec in aliquo suae proprie deserviunt voluntati, sed clerici saeculares non puram sed aliquantulum propriae voluntati mixtam oboedientiam servant. Laici vero quasi usque ad medium [ ] dum uxores ducunt et bella committunt, et cetera. Sed tamen sicut moneta in statuto ordine suo non iudicatur falsa, sic in illis ordinibus in institutione sua servatis, non falsitas. Laicus enim in ordine suo si iuste vixerit, non falsus sed verus est Christianus, et sicut rex aliquis nollet pro debito viliorem monetam pro meliore recipere, sic deus pro vita monachi vitam laici vel clerici non suscipiet, sed sicut in denario puritas pondus et imago sunt observanda, sic in monacho ne quaequam propriae voluntatis admisceatur oboedientiaem et ut pondere firmae stabilitatis animum roboret et ut in omnibus imago monachi appareat in eo, ut in tonsura et ceteris.

Ex propria voluntate et angeli et primus homo ceciderunt, ex qua omnia mala fiunt. Omnis enim peccati causa est et sicut alicui regi iniuriam faceret qui in regno eius illo nesciente corona eius coronaretur, sic deo iniuriam facit qui quod eius proprium est id est sequi propriam voluntatem suam sequitur. Sua autem est hominis voluntas quae contra deum est. Si autem dei voluntati via concordet, non iam propria dicenda. Deus autem nec aequalem nec superiorem habet. Illius autem proprie est propria voluntas qui super est omnibus. Omnium ergo aliorum obediens est voluntas. Nascitur autem malum propriae voluntatis ex occulatione vel defensione delicit. Diabolus enim temptans cor hominis per concelationem et defensionem peccati ibi se occultat. Sicut vulpes astutum alis foveam sibi faciens ibi abscondit.

Imago dei est in anima hominis hoc modo quod sicut deus unus semper ubique totus est omnia vivificans, movens et gubernans, in illo enim vivimus, movemur et sumus; ita anima in suo corpore ubique tota viget, vivificans illud movens et gubernans suo modo. Non enim in maioribus membris [f. 85] maior et in minoribus minor sed ubique membrorum sui corporis aequaliter tota.[8] Velut sicut deus est, vivit et sapit, ita anima suo modo est, vivit et sapit. Velut sicut unus deus est pater et filius et spiritus sanctus, ita unius naturae anima tres habet in se quasi dignitatum personas, scilicet, intellectum, voluntatem, memoriam.[9] Ex quibus anima iubetur deum diligere. 'Diliges deum dominum tuum ex toto corde tuus et ex tota anima tua et ex tota mente tua',[10] id est, ex toto intellectu et voluntate et memoria. Nam sicut ex patre generatur filius et ab utroque procedit spiritus sanctus, ita per intellectum verum gignitur recta voluntas et ab utroque memoria. Non enim perfecta anima sine his tribus potest esse, nec unum sine ceteris valet ad cultum dei. Et sicut deus pater et filius et spiritus sanctus non tres dii, sed unus deus habens tres personas, ita anima una habet tres dignitates illas, ex quibus iubetur colere domini, ut quantum intelligit, velit memoriter semper deum diligere. Similitudo autem dei consideratur in anima secundum qualitatem bonorum morum, ut sicut deus bonus et iustus est ita et anima sit suo modo.

Ecclesiae sanctae tres esse patres [for: partes] dicuntur, angelorum bonorum et sanctorum virorum cum deo iam in animabus quiescentium, et eorum qui adhuc peregrinantur in corpore et in dei servitio laborant. Ad quarum partium designationem sacrosancti panis in altari fiunt tres partes. Quarum maior designat sanctos angelos, altera vero de paribus quae cum maiori extra calicem tenetur, designat animas beatorum iam cum deo quiescentium. Tercia vero qui in calico ponitur, et cum sanguine sumitur, significat illos qui adhuc in certamine fidei laborantes, passionibus Christi convincant.

Prima statio ad altaris dexteram innuit primum statum primi hominis in paradiso antequam peccaret. Secunda vero ad sinistram designat lapsum eius de bonis in hac misera vita, ubi diutius moram fecit. Media vero significat interpositionem passionis Christi per cuius misericordia a sinistra vita reditur ad dexteram.

Gratias deo agere est sentire et confiteri omnia bona ab eo data esse, et pro his corde, voce, opere, eum laudare.

Iusticia dei est qua gratis iustificat quemquam sine operibus legis.

Malitia est quaequam damnum molitur alicui. Nequitia est temeritas quando suadet quod nequit, vel intemperantia sui.

Contentio est impugnatio veritatis, per confidentiam clamoris. Malignitas est mala voluntas cum ultra non potest, vel de beneficiis gratias non referre.

Detractores sunt qui bona aliorum vel negant parva animo, vel invertunt. Detrahere autem est vel dicere vel facere unde alius inhonoretur, vel minus ametur.

Contumeliosi sunt qui dictis vel factis turpia inferunt; elati sunt [f. 85ᵛ] qui nolunt pares vel priores.

Consentire est tacere cum possis arguere, vel errori favere.

Passiones dicuntur delictorum voluptates, quae etsi delectent tamen passiones sunt vel conscientiae cel naturae.

Tria sunt genera visionum, unum corporale aliud spirituale, aliud mentuale vel intellectuale. Primum est quo per carnis oculos videmus, secundum est quo in exstasi positi vel dormientes, vel vigilantes intuentur similitudines corporalium rerum futura presangantes misteria. Quod convenire bonis et malis, sicut Nabugod[nezzar] et Phara, qui hoc modo multa viderunt, sed mali non intelligunt. Boni aliquando intelligunt, aliquando non, sicut Da[niel] qui non intellexit quid significarent quatuor venti qui pugnabant in mari, sed accessit ad unum de astantibus et quaesivit ab eo super his.[11] Tercium est quo interius in mente veritas manifestatur, quod est electorum tamen, quia intelligebant. Unde et videntes et intelligentes olim vocabantur, et prophetiae illorum visiones, unde est visio Isaiae fili Amos et cetera.

Due sunt ablutiones peccatorum, una in baptismo alia in lacrimis penitentialibus, quibus lota e[s]t Maria et multi alii.

Consilium divinae scripturae aliud est correctionis aliud perfectionis. Correctionis ut est: 'Declina a malo et fac bene',[12] perfectionis, ut est: 'Si vis perfectus esse, vende omnia quae habes et da pauperibus',[13] et cetera.

Tres mortes esse dicuntur, una carnis alia animae, tercia supplicium aeternae damnationis, quae tamen non tercia sed secunda dicitur in apocalypsi: 'Qui vicerit non laedetur a morte secunda'.[14] Prima autem quae laedit peccatum est, secunda aeterna damnatio. Mors vero carnis non laedit bonos.

Fornicatio quadripartita est. Alia enim sit animo, alia effectu corporis, alia adorando demones, alia diligendo terrena plus quam deum. De prima est: 'Qui viderit mulierem ad concupiscendam eam iam moechatus est'.[15] De secunda est: 'Fugite fornicatio'.[16] Et: 'Qui fornicatur in corpus suum peccat'.[17] De tertia contra Jerusalem est: 'Moechata est cum ligno et lapide'.[18] De quarta est: 'Et avaritia quae est idolorum servitus'.[19]

Scire deum tripliciter dicitur, scilicet pro approbare ut: 'Scio opera tua',[20] vel pro scientes reddere, ut est: 'Temptat vos deus vester ut sciat si diliges eum',[21] vel pro penetrare, ut est: 'Tu solus nosti corda fidelium hominum'.[22]

Temptatio alia qua deus temptat, alia qua diabolus, alia quo homo vel se vel deum. De prima est: 'Temptavit deus Abraham',[23] scilicet probatum ostendet; de diabolica ne inducamur, oramus: 'Et ne nos inducamur in temptationem'.[24] De ea qua homo a seipso temptatur: 'Unisquisque temptatur a concupiscentia, sua abstractus et illectus'.[25] De ea qua deum: 'Et temptaverunt deum in cordibus suis'.[26]

Quinque modis flagellantur homines a deo, vel ad augmenta virtutum, ut Job, et Tobias, vel ad custodiam virtutum, ut Paulus, vel pro peccatis, ut paraliticus [f. 86] ad hoc ut corrigeretur, aliquando non ut fiat correctio, sed damnatio, ut Antiochus, et Herod, qui dupplici damnatione corporis et anima perierunt. De quibus est et duplici contritione contere eos. Aliquando ut dei gloria per hoc ostendatur, ut Lazarus, et caecus natus.

Septem modis loquitur scriptura, aut indicativo modo, ut: 'Ego dominus docens te utilia',[27] aut promissimo, ut: 'Indicabo tibi quod sit bonum',[28] aut imperativo, ut: 'Audi Jacob, serve nostris',[29] aut optativo, ut: 'Utinam audisses verba mea',[30] aut coniunctivo, ut: 'Si audieritis vocem mean, et custodieritis pactum meum, eritis mihi in populum de cunctis populis',[31] aut infinitivo, ut: 'Timere deum intelligentia est',[32] aut impersonalium: 'Quis loquetur potentia dei'.[33]

Duo gladii sunt, unus diaboli, alter dei qui de suo duobus modis interficit spiritualiter et corporaliter, per se interius, per suos exterius. Unde est: 'Datus est ei gladius magnus'.[34] Est autem iste gladius parva persuasio quae sit per diabolus. De gladio quae ipse possidet in membris suis est exacuerit ut gladium vel suus quo interficit et spiritualiter et corporaliter.

Duobus modis se praeparent praedicatores ad praedicandum vel quando praecogitant quod cui qualiter quantum et quando dicant, vel quando prius opera exhibent, prius ea ore proferant. Unde est: 'Quod ceperit Jesus facere et docere'.[35]

N.B. The text continues to the foot of f. 87 without a break, but there is nothing among the remaining items with any Anselmian flavour at all. The material which has been included here after the piece on the powers of the soul will, it is hoped, give a sufficiently clear picture of the character of this later part of the collection.

NOTES (to the *Anselmiana*)

1. cf. Cicero, *De inventione*, 2.53.159, edited by H.M. Hubbell (London, 1960); Boethius, *De Differentiis Topicis*, 2, *PL* 64.1188.

2. Horace, *Epistola*, 2.1.41-2, edited by E.C. Wickham (Oxford, 1900).

3. *De veritate*, 12, *Ans.Op.Om.*, I, 194:26.

4. Horace, *Epistola*, 1.16.52.

5. *De conceptu virginali, Ans.Op.Om.,* II, 146:23; cf. *De concordia,* 1, 7, *Ans.Op.Om.,* II, 258:8-10.

6. Horace, *Epistola,* 1.2.57.

7. The reference here may possibly be to a coin of Pavia. The scribe has corrected himself above and is evidently not very sure of the word. A parallel example occurs in the *Ruodlieb,* edited by G.B. Ford (Leiden, 1966), Fragment 4, lines 211-12, referring to a coin of Pisa:

    > Is mihi deponit, sibi me deponere nil vult
    > et dat quae posuit, pisa quod non una remansit.

8. cf. Augustine, *De Quantitate Animi,* PL 32.1035-80, especially Chapters 2-7.

9. cf. *Mem.Ans.,* p. 306.

10. Matthew 22:37.

11. Daniel 7:2.

12. I Peter 3:11.

13. Matthew 19:21.

14. Revelation 2:11.

15. Matthew 5:28

16. I Corinthians 6:18

17. Ibid.

18. Ezekiel 20:32(?)

19. Ephesians 5:5.

20. Revelation 2:2.

21. Deuteronomy 13:3.

22. Acts I:24.

23. Genesis 22:1.

24. Luke 11:4.

25. James 1:14.

26. Psalm 77:18.

27. Isaiah 48:17.

28. Micah 6:8.

29. Isaiah 44:1.

30. Isaiah 48:18(?)

31. Exodus 19:5
32. Job 29:8(?)
33. Psalm 105:2
34. Revelation 6:4.
35. Acts 1:1.

Appendix

De Humanis Moribus
Rursus de Propria Voluntate

38. Similitudo inter propriam voluntatem et venenosam herbam

Rursus propria voluntas cuidam herbae venenosae atque mortiferae assimilatur, quam medicus quidam peritissimus progeniei cuiusdam primis interdixit parentibus, comminans eis quia si ex ea comederent leprosi effecti procul dubio interirent. At illi praeceptis cius oboedire noluerunt, sed ex eadem herba comederunt. Unde et leprosi effecti leprosos quoque filios genuerunt, atque ut medicus comminatus eis fuerat mortui sunt. Quorum filii, licet patres suos agnoverint herba illa infirmatos fuisse et mortuos, seque ipsos lepra percussos atque morituros, eandem tamen herbam super omnes alias diligunt indeque cibos suos universos condiunt. Manc quoque surgentes ex eadem quasi pro medicamento accipiunt, sed et somnum sero capturi similiter faciunt. Hi igitur quam sint dementes, omnis qui audit advertere potest. Sed nec minus dementantur, qui propria voluntate utuntur. Ipsa etenim est herba diaboli, venenosa suggestione venenata et omnibus ea utentibus pestifera. Hanc deus, qui nostris pie medetur peccatis, primis humani generis parentibus interdixit, cum eos comedere pomum sub mortis comminatione prohibuit. Qui quia praeceptum eius transgressi ex eo comederunt, mox peccatores effecti et in anima mortui, postquam alios peccatores genuerunt et carne mortui sunt. Homines tamen eandem voluntatem prae ceteris diligunt et eam immiscent omnibus paene quae agunt. Nihil itaque illis dementius, qui nihil utuntur sua morte libentius.

[*Mem.Ans.*, p. 52]

. . .

84. Similitudo inter monachum et arborem

Utenim rursus a simili potest videri, acceptabilius est deo bonum opus monachi quam hominis cuiusquam saecularis. Solet quippe accidere duos esse homines sub domino uno singulas habentes arbores in proprio solo. Arbores autem illae fructum bonum ferunt utraeque. Verum illi, quia dominum inaequaliter diligunt, et ei de fructu earum impariter serviunt. Unus enim eorum, quia eum minus diligit, cum arboris suae fructus fuerit maturus, colligit fertque inde domino suo quantum sibi visum fuerit. Alius vero dominum adeo amat, ut ad eum veniens arborem ipsam sic ei offerat dicens, 'Domine, arborem habeo quandam, bonum valde fructum ferentem. Quae quia vestrae congruit dignitati, malo eam vestri esse iuris quam mei. Eam igitur offero vobis, ut amodo vobis fructificet soli. Ipsam quoque vestro assignabo praeposito, ut ex ea fructum colligat, indeque vobis prout vos velle noverit diligenter deserviat. Sed et ego, quanta diligentia potero, eandem vobis custodire curabo. Cuius igitur horum obsequium domino illi magis videtur acceptum? An illius qui quando quantumque voluerit dat ei de fructu propriae arboris? Immo magis illius, qui arborem totam dat ei cum fructu.

Sic ergo et servitium monachi deo est magis acceptum quam hominis saecularis. Ipsi enim sunt homines duo, qui sub deo velut arbores quasdam habent seipsos. Ipsi quoque utrique sunt apti ad ferendum fructum operis boni. At quia non eodem modo diligunt deum, nec ei pariter bene operando deserviunt. Saecularis enim, quia eum minus diligit, tunc tantum cum habuerit animum bene operandi, boni operis offert deo quantum voluerit. Monachus vero eum dilexit in tantum ut ad eum accedens totum ei offerret seipsum, factis ac si verbis alloquens eum: 'Domine', inquit, 'meae hactenus potestatis eram, quodque mihi libebat bonum malumve, faciebam. Verum quia tuus omnino debeo esse tibique soli bona tantum opera fructificare, me totum tuae trado potestati, ut amodo tibi fructificem soli. Quod ut melius facere valeam, uni ex ecclesiae tuae praelatis me subdam, qui me custodiens ea tantum opera doceat agere, quae tibi noverit magis placere. Sed et ego pro modulo meo custodire meipsum studebo.' Cuius igitur munus deo est acceptabilius? An illius qui sibi offert quaedam ex operibus suis, plurima vero subtrahit? Immo illius magis, qui dat ei seipsum cum operibus cunctis.

Nec ideo propria privatur mercede, quia saepe bonum opus cogitur agere. Sicut enim is qui arborem totam commisit praeposito domini sui, ut ex ea fructum colligeret ex quo et domino suo prout eum velle nosset deserviret; ut, inquam, proprium non perdit meritum si ille colligat fructum priusquam maturescat, aut in arbore dimittat e contra donec putrescat, sic monachus qui se totum commisit praelato ut eum custodiret eaque opera tantum ab eo agenda exigeret quae deo placere potius nosset, sic, inquam, propriam non perdet mercedem si quid operis boni agere cogatur antequam velit, vel e contra prohibeatur cum agere velit, donec et ipsam amittat voluntatem agendi. Non igitur omittere debet quidquid boni praelatus ei praecipiat, vel praesumere ut agat a quibuscumque eum prohibeat. Sit enim illius praevidere quid praecipiat quidve prohibeat, huius vero sequi eum in bono per omnia. Sed ut hoc voluntate oboedient, faciat, noverit a simili quot sint voluntatis subditorum genera.

[*Mem.Ans.* pp. 73-4]

. . .

90. Similitudo inter monachum et denarium

Rursus a simili debemus videre, quot in perfecto monacho debeant esse. Tria cuique bono insunt denario, quae cuique bono monacho inesse debent. Denarius quippe bonus puro ex aere, recto pondere, monetaque legitima debet constare. Si enim ex his unum defuerit, venalis esse non poterit. Ut ergo venalis valeat esse, haec tria pariter debet habere.

Haec quoque debet habere et monachus, ut vere monachus esse reputetur. Eius quippe metalli puritas pura est eius oboedientia. Nulla enim inoboedientiae impuritas, sed sola in eo esse debet oboedientia. Rectum vero illius pondus stabilitas est propositi eius. Non enim leviter exsufflari debet ab eo quod accepit, sed usque in finem perseverare stabilis. Illius autem moneta habitus est monachilis atque tonsura, ante et retro, et consimilia. Sicut enim denarius a moneta dinoscitur, cuius regionis sit, sic ab istis monachus, cuius sit ordinis. Is autem monachus, qui adeo est senex ut ante et retro iam nequeat inclinare, denario illi similis est, cuius monetam temporis antiquitas iam delevit. Is vero, qui habitum monachilem non adhuc suscepit et ideo nomen non habet monachi, assimilatur nummo monetam nondum habenti, et ideo nondum venali. At sicut qui thesaurum congregare desiderat, huiusmodi nummum aeque ut habentem monetam amat, sic deus, qui thesauro caelesti nos omnes reponere cupit, huiusmodi hominem aeque ut habitum monachi habentem ibi reponit. Quem autem viderit habitum quidem monachicum habere, sed ex aere impuro, id est inoboedientem esse, hunc thesauro caelesti numquam reponit, sicut nullus denarium falsum suo thesauro reponere quaerit. Quem vero viderit oboedientem esse, etsi aliquando fragilitate peccet humana, non hunc tamen repellit, si statim paeniteat. Ut enim ab invalido denarius falsus, sic a debeli differt monachus falsus. Invalidus quippe denarius minus habet pondus quam debeat, sed illud quod habet, puro ex aere constat. Falsus vero eandem quam bonus monetam praetendit, sed interius latet falsitas aeris. Sic falsus monachus eundem quem bonus habitum habet, sed inoboedientiae falsitas interius latet. Debilis vero sed oboediens, licet non tantam quin cadat quandoque habeat stabilitatem, oboedientiae tamen retinet puritatem. Mox etenim paenitet eum quia deliquit; quod ei praecipitur pura oboedientia facit. Ille ergo ut denarius falsus a caelesti thesauro repellitur, hic vero pro sui modulo vigoris ibi reponitur. Nihil igitur cuiquam prodest habitum monachi exteriorem habere, si non studuerit et interiorem habere.

[*Mem.Ans.*, pp. 76-7]

. . .

2. Omnis denarius haec tria debet habere: monetam, pondus, puritatem. Similiter et omnis professio vitae hominum. Nam denarius vitae monachilis purus et gravis et bene formatus esse debet, et purior et in omnibus perfectior quam clericalis. Similiter et clericalis perfectior in omnibus quam laicalis, differunt enim inter se et moneta, et pondere, et puritate. Nec tamen falsi dicuntur si quisque habet quod et quantum habere debet. Per monetam intellige habitum, religionem, tensuram, cuiuscunque ordinis; per puritatem voluntatem subiectam voluntati dei, quae est purta oboedientia, cui contraria est propria voluntas, quae est inoboedientia.

[*Mem.Ans.*, p. 305]

DATE DUE

FEB 4 '04			
DEC 0 2 2001			